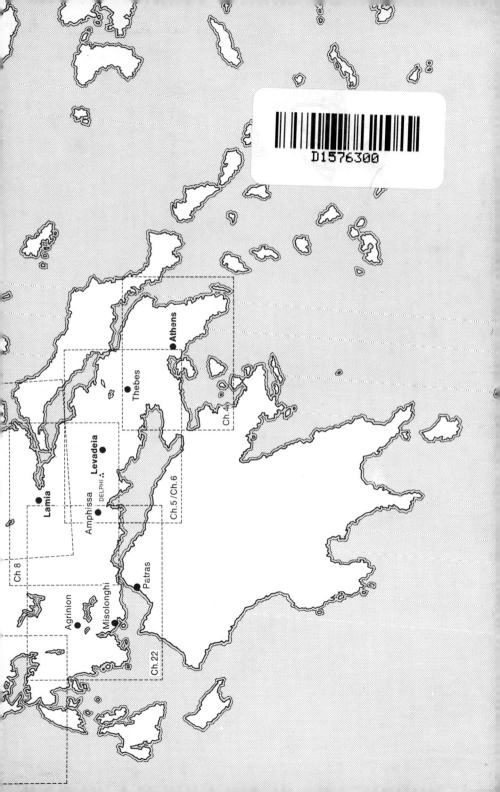

Athens

Thebes

Ch. 4

Levadeia

Amphissa DELPHI ∴

Lamia

Ch.5/Ch.6

Ch 8

Patras

Agrinion

Misolonghi

Ch.22

THE COMPANION GUIDE TO
Mainland Greece

THE COMPANION GUIDES

GENERAL EDITOR: VINCENT CRONIN

*It is the aim of these Guides to provide a Companion
in the person of the author, who knows intimately
the places and people of whom he writes, and is able to
communicate this knowledge and affection to his readers.
It is hoped that the text and pictures will aid them
in their preparations and in their travels, and will
help them to remember on their return.*

SOUTHERN GREECE · MAINLAND GREECE · THE GREEK ISLANDS
THE SOUTH OF FRANCE · SOUTH-WEST FRANCE · BURGUNDY
PARIS · LONDON · ROME · VENICE · FLORENCE
UMBRIA · SOUTHERN ITALY · TUSCANY
THE SOUTH OF SPAIN · MADRID AND CENTRAL SPAIN
JUGOSLAVIA · THE ILE DE FRANCE · THE LOIRE
KENT AND SUSSEX · DEVON AND CORNWALL
IRELAND · EAST ANGLIA · NORTHUMBRIA
NORTH WALES · SOUTH WALES

In preparation
EDINBURGH AND THE BORDER COUNTRY
THE SHAKESPEARE COUNTRY
TURKEY · NORMANDY

THE COMPANION GUIDE TO

Mainland Greece

✦

BRIAN DE JONGH

With a Foreword by
Robert Liddell

COLLINS
ST JAMES'S PLACE, LONDON
1979

William Collins Sons & Co Ltd
London · Glasgow · Sydney · Auckland
Toronto · Johannesburg

First published 1979
© Administrator of the estate of the late Brian de Jongh 1979
Hardback ISBN 0 00 216111 7
Set in Monotype Times Roman
Maps by David Woodruff
Made and Printed in Great Britain by
William Collins Sons & Co Ltd, Glasgow

To
JANE RABNETT

Contents

Illustrations

&

Maps and Plans

Foreword

❧

Brian de Jongh unhappily died on 21 September 1977, too early to see this book published. No one could have been a better companion in Greece than Brian: his wide knowledge of every side of his subject and unflagging enthusiasm were tempered by a critical spirit, gentle but always present. He had wide terms of reference: he was born and spent some of his early life in Smyrna; he had ancestral ties with Holland, Dublin and Andros; he was educated at Lausanne and Oxford. His devoted care of an aged mother kept him in Athens for a large part of his adult life – and as Dr Johnson so beautifully wrote of Pope: 'Life has, among its soothing and quiet comforts, few things better to give than such a son.' It was in Greece that he was happiest. However he was never a *mere* Hellenist; with all his love of Greece he would not exaggerate the claims of every crumbling ruin or of every little frescoed chapel – after all, he had lived in such centres of art as Rome, Cairo and Constantinople.

In this Companion Guide Brian shows himself equally at home in prehistoric and in classical Greece, in the Byzantine world (whose fantastic history had a special appeal for him), and among the Franks and Catalans of the later Middle Ages. More than most Hellenic travellers he shows an interest in the local civilization that survived during the long years of the Turkish occupation; and, of course, modern Greece was his home.

He is therefore an ideal guide to the ruins of Philippi, or to the Byzantine churches of Salonica and Boeotia, as well as to the lesser known (and now, alas, rapidly decaying) painted houses of Castoria or Siatista.

Of contemporary life he writes kindly and amusingly, without condescension, but also without the gush of the romantic philhellene for whom the sourest retsina is nectar and the toughest lump of charred octopus ambrosia, who will talk of the frescoes of Mistra in the same breath as Giotto, or compare bouzouki songs to Bach. Nevertheless Brian appreciated these Greek things, and saw that they had no need to be 'belied by false compare'.

13

For he knew what it is about Greece that is beyond all comparison: the landscape. Travel writers from the time of Dodwell in the early nineteenth century have understood this, but too often guide-books ignore it. Their authors will tell the visitor to go and see a heap of stones interesting only to the professional archaeologist without indicating that the trouble is indeed worthwhile because of the Greek genius for choosing superb sites.

Brian was a patient and brave traveller, an amusing and unselfish companion – and Greek travel even now makes a demand on such virtues. I have travelled over much of the Aegean with him and remember, first and foremost, his rueful but humorous reactions to sea-sickness on that very rough sea – and all the delays and hazards of the journey, and the dreadful food and comfortless lodging that too often awaited the traveller. But he was aware that the very lack of amenities often protected lonely places from being swallowed up by tourism, and rejoiced in the fact that there are still many hidden corners of Greece that can be discovered only at the expense of time and trouble – and of money too, for mules (believe it or not) are about the most expensive means of transport in the world today.

This book begins in Attica and Boeotia, which Brian previously described in *The Companion Guide to Southern Greece*; the first seven chapters are taken from that earlier book, although they have been severely shortened to suit the wider scope of the new volume. The rest of mainland Greece – the country north of Delphi – is an area not covered by Pausanias, the great Greek traveller; it has comparatively few classical associations, and has been much less visited than southern Greece by scholars come to 'look up their familiar quotations'. But the spectacular scenery of the Pindus, the unworldly fascination of Mount Athos, are more exciting than anything the south – or the islands – have to offer.

Brian's descriptions of these places are enhanced by his insight into the character of the Greek people, and his awareness of the effect Greece can have on the visitor. In his Introduction to the guide to southern Greece he wrote:

> Placed at the crossroads of East and West, they are a racially mixed people – in many regions the Slav invasions of the sixth century and the Albanian inroads of the seventeenth have left their mark on the physical traits of the inhabitants. For all their powers of endurance, they sometimes betray symptoms of the lingering malady that afflicted the subject peoples of the Ottoman Empire: the apathy, corruption and nepotism that

14

thwart the smooth working of the modern administrative machine. Periodically, however, the wind of reform sweeps the air, and a backward peasantry is rapidly being replaced by an urban bourgeoisie. Hire-purchase, self-service, parking problems, suburban development, washing machines, television and air-conditioning are becoming increasingly absorbing preoccupations. Nevertheless the Greeks retain a curiously intuitive sense of history (especially their own). Incurably conservative (but not reactionary), they possess a sense of humour – and of the ridiculous – which is very captivating. They can be rowdy, pushing and prodigiously egocentric. As businessmen they are shrewd, even wily – the careers of their hard-headed shipowners have become modern legends. They also have their poets. From Solomos to Seferis it is a notable record. The clarity and brilliance of the light preclude the fostering of false illusions and woolly-mindedness. A Greek, though open-hearted, can be as hard as the light in which he dwells. The landscape, for those who fall in love with it, is a source of imperishable enchantment. The constant interplay between these elements – history, light and landscape – impinge so subtly on the traveller's sensibility that he will suddenly find himself confronted with that ultimate discovery that Lawrence Durrell calls 'the discovery of yourself'. It is very exciting. But make no mistake about it. The edges are sharply outlined, like a Greek limestone mountain or a fifth-century BC frieze. There are no half-tones. The brilliant refractory light hits you in the face – straight between the eyes.

Although Brian's perfectionism and scrupulous accuracy are still evident in this work, he died before completing his final revision. The devotion of several of his friends has helped to make it the book that he intended, so far as this is possible without his presence. The loving care of Jane Rabnett during his lifetime is acknowledged by the author in the dedication, and she has continued to work on the book with his nephew, John Gandon, until its going to press. Peter Megaw has given generous help, particularly over illustrations, and other patient assistance has been given by Bill Barron, Dorothy Lygon, Paul Mylonas and Martin Young.

ROBERT LIDDELL

CHAPTER ONE

Athens: The Acropolis

*Syntagma Square – The Monument of Lysicrates – The Theatre of Dionysus –
The Odeum of Herodes Atticus – The Propylaea – The Temple of Wingless
Victory – The Parthenon – The Museum – The Erectheum – The Areopagus –
The Pnyx*

The centre of Athens is **Syntagma Square**, midway between the
hump of the Acropolis and the taller pinnacled crag of Lycabettus
which overlooks the sprawling ellipse of the modern town. The
square, lined with hotels, travel agencies and air terminals, has a
very up-to-date air. Historically, it is without roots. The names that
spring so easily to the mind, as one approaches Athens and its
Acropolis, ring rather hollow, for there is little here to recall the
past. At night the skyline is bright with illuminated signs. The
Grande Bretagne, with a loggia overlooking the square, is the oldest
and best hotel in Greece, its bar and lounges the rendezvous of high-
powered tycoons and politicians out of office. From Syntagma
Square streets branch out in all directions, their suburban tentacles
encroaching on the foothills of limestone mountains that enclose the
plain on three sides, with the sweep of the Saronic Gulf on the
fourth.

Café tables spread across the pavements of the square. The
kiosks – a focal point in the life of the shopper in Greece – are
festooned with foreign newspapers, magazines and paperbacks, with
just enough room for the salesman to sit perched on a stool, smothered
by stacks of airmail envelopes, films, soap, aspirin, after-shave lotion
and other useful articles. Above the east end of the square, beyond
the orange trees and crowded benches, rises an austere war memorial,
in front of a large bleak nineteenth-century edifice, once the royal
palace, now the Parliament House. Politics are the breath of life to
large sections of the population. Personalities are rated higher than
policies, and loyalty to the man of the moment is sometimes so
fanatical that its only outlet lies in acts of violence. Interim periods
of dictatorship (repressive or otherwise) are accepted as part of the
pattern. To the south the Parliament House is skirted by the National

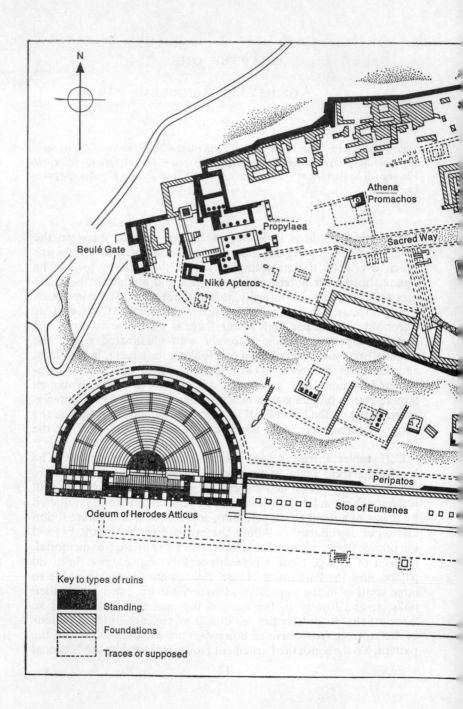

N

Athena
Promachos

Propylaea

Sacred Way

Beulé Gate

Niké Apteros

Peripatos

Stoa of Eumenes

Odeum of Herodes Atticus

Key to types of ruins

Standing.

Foundations

Traces or supposed

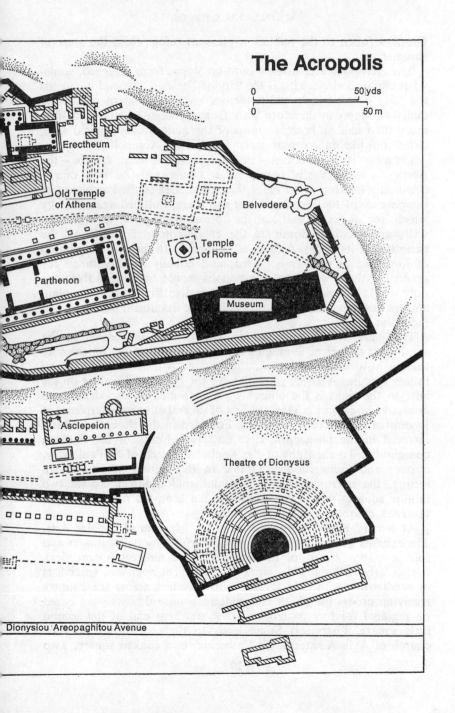

The Acropolis

0   50 yds

0   50 m

Erectheum

Old Temple
of Athena

Belvedere

Temple
of Rome

Parthenon

Museum

Asclepeion

Theatre of Dionysus

Dionysiou Areopaghitou Avenue

Gardens (open to the public), a pleasant refuge from the glare of summer.

The Acropolis area and its built-up slopes form a ragged, somewhat elliptical circle. This is the 'city of Theseus'. Around it extends the 'city of Hadrian', which merges into the modern residential quarters. One can therefore walk from Syntagma Square, in little more than half an hour, to most of the main archaeological sites, strung out like an irregular garland round the Acropolis.

Let alone its associations – mythological, historical, artistic – the Acropolis is physically omnipresent. Consciously or not, one is constantly looking up to see if the colonnades of the Parthenon or the porches of the Erectheum are still there, outlined against a sky which, for weeks on end, can be an astonishingly vivid blue. The walls and bastions dominate the cream-coloured blocks on the periphery of its slopes. A sense of intimacy with this gleaming hump of limestone is quickly acquired; and equally quickly taken for granted. Athens without the Acropolis would be unthinkable; not only would the skyline be different, but also the entire town plan, ancient and modern, would probably have developed otherwise – if indeed at all.

There are several approaches. An obvious one begins at the south-west corner of Syntagma Square. There is much on the way that is historically irrelevant, though not without charm. If you follow Amalias Avenue, you will have the National Gardens on the left; to the right is the church of Ayia Sotira of Lycodemus, an attractive brickwork edifice, the first of several minor masterpieces of Byzantine architecture in Athens. Founded in the eleventh century, restored in the nineteenth, it is now the church of the Russian community. To the right of the Anglican church of St Paul, grey, austere and incongruously Gothic in this urban Mediterranean setting, the narrow passage of Kydathenaion Street crosses two minute squares with wispy shrubbery: a crowded quarter, full of tavernas, churches and dimly lit cafés.

At No. 17 Kydathenaion Street is the **Museum of Popular Arts**. The exhibits include elaborate and colourful national costumes and folk jewellery (mostly of the eighteenth and nineteenth centuries). Particularly striking is the work of the Epirot *terzidhes*, specialists in needlework with gold thread, who travelled across the country receiving orders for lavish embroideries whose designs were based on regional folklore patterns. At the southern end of the second little square, Pharmacis Street leads to the cruciform Byzantine church of Ayia Aikaterini (St Catherine) in a sunken square. Two ancient columns stand in front of a little garden. The building has unfortunately suffered from tasteless restoration.

A few yards away is the **Choragic Monument of Lysicrates** in another minute square surrounded by crumbling houses. The monument is a fantasy: a cylindrical drum of marble on a square stone base, with six Corinthian columns engaged under the architrave. The mutilated frieze of the monument represents the episode of Dionysus's capture by Tyrrhenian pirates and the tricks he played in order to confound them. For the preservation of the monument much is owed to the French Government, which bought it in the seventeenth century. A Franciscan monastery was built around it, and this architectural extravaganza, restored in the nineteenth century, served as the monks' library. Byron lodged here in the winter of 1810–11; he read much in the library, organized boxing matches between Catholic and Orthodox schoolboys and drank with the Mufti of Thebes and the Kaimakam of Athens.

From the Choragic Monument Byron Street leads into Dionysiou Areopaghitou Avenue, which ascends towards the Acropolis. On the right lie scattered marble slabs and truncated columns: fragments of the Sanctuary of Dionysus. A relative hush is perceptible. The tremendous weight of antiquity, which has done so much to fashion the mind and character of modern Greeks, begins to impinge. Two slender unfluted Corinthian columns, once surmounted by votive gifts, stand above a grotto in the south wall of the Acropolis behind the ruined **Theatre of Dionysus**. Hollowed out of the hillside, the auditorium consisted of seventy-eight tiers, whose diameter increased as they ascended, divided into three sectors by diazômas. Originally an earth surface with tiers for distinguished citizens, it was remodelled in the fourth century BC into a stone structure by Lycurgus, an able financier and patron of the arts.

The theatre is a good example of the Greek practice of utilizing a natural declivity for carving out an amphitheatre in some dominant yet central position. Situated at the foot of the citadel, it once commanded a view of the shrubby groves and undulations of the plain. Today nothing but an urban expanse meets the eye. Originally, actors and chorus performed in the circular orchestra, surrounded in Roman times by a water conduit which enabled it to be flooded for the performance of mock naval battles. In the centre was the god's altar on a raised platform, marked by a large diamond-shaped paving stone, around which the chorus revolved in stately measures, chanting dithyrambs to the god. With the development of the art of the theatre, a proscenium, a narrow platform occupying a segment

21

of the orchestra, was added as a stage for the main protagonists. The acoustics were improved by the placing of inverted bronze vessels on pedestals at various points in the auditorium where they received and redistributed the vibrations of sound. Painted scenic props were used and the actors wore large grotesque masks.

The tiers may be less well-preserved than those of other Greek theatres, but the significance of the place is infinitely greater. Here the tragedies of Aeschylus, Sophocles and Euripides were performed for the first time and European drama was born. The throne of the high priest of Dionysus, with its decoration of lions, griffons and, very appropriately, satyrs and a bunch of grapes, is easily identified in the centre of the front row. The concave seats, reserved for archons and priests and once shaded with awnings, are extraordinarily comfortable. The earliest theatrical compositions were accompanied by dancing, mimed scenes and impassioned dialogues. The annual performances, which formed part of the Great Dionysia, were held with much pomp in the spring sunshine, to the accompaniment of flute-playing and the banging of cymbals and drums. The audience did not only seek entertainment; they were genuinely moved by religious exaltation and the desire to honour the licentious young god. During the festival all work in the city ceased, a general moratorium was declared, law courts were shut and prisoners released from jail. Abstinence from wine was considered a mark of disrespect to the god, and bawdy colourful processions wound through the streets.

From the highest tier of the theatre a row of cypress trees leads westward between the ruins of the Asclepeion – a sheltered sanctuary for the sick, dedicated to the god of healing – and the stoa of Eumenes, the work of a philhellenic king of Pergamum in the second century BC, which consisted of a double colonnade and served as a foyer during intervals between the trilogies of plays that lasted all day. From the stoa one regains Dionysiou Areopaghitou Avenue and mounts a broad modern stairway to the **Odeum of Herodes Atticus**, the gift of a wealthy public benefactor of the Antonine era to the people of Athens. The cedar wood roof has vanished and the thirty-two tiers have been restored with marble facings. The stone façade of three storeys is embellished with arches. When floodlit it creates an effect of Roman splendour, the arched openings allowing for an interplay of light and shade, glowing and mysterious, which is absent from the classical simplicity of the monuments on the Acropolis. The contrast is striking – yet the two styles complement each other, as Greek and Roman architecture often does. In front

22

of the semicircular orchestra, a chequer-board of dark blue and white marble, rises the stage and behind it the skene (the stone or marble back-cloth to a stage) consisting of a colonnade with niches for statues, surmounted by a narrow ledge reserved for actors who impersonate the gods. A festival, very different from the Dionysia, is now held every summer (July-September) in the restored theatre. Apart from a cycle of ancient drama, the festival includes performances of the world's leading orchestras, operatic and theatrical companies. Acoustic imperfections are redeemed by the setting: especially the mellow glow of the arched skene and a glimpse of the Parthenon above the massive Cimonian wall. The impression made by the trumpet solo in the Leonora No. 3 overture echoing across the ruins could not be more dramatic.

From the Odeum one ascends to the Acropolis, which has the shape of a polygonal lozenge with a flat top and is five hundred feet high. 'There is but one entry,' says Pausanias. 'It affords no other, being precipitous throughout and having a strong wall.' As one climbs, one is conscious of a feeling of isolation; at the same time, of being at the heart of things, of one's proximity to the city and one's remoteness from it, of an atmosphere that has become unusually rarefied. The perpendicular surface of the other sides is honeycombed with grottoes and defended by strong walls, of which the earliest, below the Temple of Niké Apteros, are called Cyclopean, but are also attributed to the Pelasgi, the first inhabitants of the Attic plain.

As one ascends the stairway, past a platform crowded with touts, guides and motor coaches, a large pedestal of greyish-blue Hymettus marble, once surmounted by a statue of a Roman general in a bronze chariot, stands on the left. In front rises the **Propylaea**, the entrance way to the citadel, one of the masterpieces of classical architecture. Commissioned by Pericles, it was built by Mnesicles, a fashionable fifth-century BC architect. Extending across the west side of the hill, the Propylaea, much of whose complexity of design is due to the asymmetrical slope of the ground, forms an entrance hall to the five gates through which men and horses entered the precinct. The marks of the chariot wheels are still visible. A costly massive edifice of Pentelic marble, it consisted of a central gateway with five openings, on either side of which rise Doric colonnades directly from the stylobate. In the west portico, two rows of three Ionic columns flank the main passage. The ceiling was coffered and embellished with a gilt star in the middle. The huge doors of the gateway, which are not all of the same height, were probably of wood faced with bronze; and the loud grating noise they made when opened is mentioned by Aristophanes. There are two projections: one to the north, leading to the Pinacotheke, where paintings were exhibited on boards; the other, less well preserved, to the south (towards the Temple of Niké Apteros). In the fourteenth century the first Florentine Duke of Athens established his chancery here, adding a second storey, battlements and a tower; in the seventeenth century the Turks, with their customary disregard for historical monuments, turned the marble porticoes into a powder magazine. Struck by a thunderbolt, the ignited gunpowder blew the entablature sky-high and the central part of the building caved in. Much of what we now see standing is the result of laborious restoration by modern archaeologists. A more majestic entrance to a holy precinct can hardly be imagined.

To the right, the **Temple of Wingless Victory** (Niké Apteros) seems minuscule in comparison. Only eighteen by twenty-seven feet, it is a memorial to the Greek victories over the Persians. Pericles entrusted the plans to Callicrates, who so constructed the temple, resting on a stylobate of three steps, that its front pointed in the direction of the Parthenon: an effect probably designed to focus the eye on the more imposing building. This exquisitely proportioned little monument, with its eight Ionic columns composed of mono-lithic shafts instead of the usual series of superimposed drums, was demolished by the Turks and the materials were used for the con-struction of a defence wall. A century and a half later King Otho commissioned the restoration of the temple. The original materials fortunately lay at hand, but the greater part of the frieze is so mutilated that it is difficult to identify the headless figures. The east frieze represented the assembly of the gods; the other three are believed to have depicted scenes from the Persian Wars, contrary to the usual practice of portraying mythical feats on the friezes of temples.

Returning to the Propylaea, one passes out of the east portico into a vast esplanade littered with the debris of centuries. To the left is the Erectheum, to the right the Parthenon on a culminating terrace crowning the entire precinct. There is no vegetation: nothing but rock and marble; and sky overhead. How often one has seen it all before – in reproductions. But there is one thing one had not anticipated, perhaps: the sheer physical dominance of the Parthenon, with its famous honey-coloured patina and splendid almost squat self-assurance. In the second century AD Pausanias described the Sacred Way, which led obliquely up the incline from the Propylaea

24

to the east front of the Parthenon, as a jumble of statues, pedestals, and votive offerings. Today nothing remains but the sun-baked bases, the ruts formed by ancient water-ducts, the sockets from which innumerable columns sprouted. At intervals faint incisions in the rock, intended to prevent horses and sacrificial animals from slipping on the hard smooth surface, are noticeable. Here, as in the sanctuaries at Delphi and Olympia, buildings are seldom parallel to each other. The Greeks sought symmetry, but not parallelism, which they considered monotonous.

The Temple of Athena Polias, tutelary goddess of Athens, or **Parthenon**, as it came to be known, stands on the site of an earlier temple burned by the Persians on the eve of the battle of Salamis. The new temple was the brain-child of Pericles; Ictinus, assisted by Callicrates, was the principal architect; and Phidias, the greatest statuary of the age, was in charge of the sculptural decoration. The plans were the most ambitious and architecturally daring ever attempted. Little wonder that the building, primarily a place of worship, soon came to be regarded as a national treasury, containing bullion, archives and votive gifts of immense value. It is constructed entirely of Pentelic marble, and not one of its forty-six Doric columns is exactly the same height as any other. The slight convexity in the middle of the columns prevents the eye from being automatically carried upwards along the shaft (it moves up and down); the columns thus acquire volume and elasticity and relieve monotony. This all important *entasis*, as it is called, was intended to correct an optical illusion, for a perfectly straight column invariably appears thinner in the middle when seen against a background of bright light. The resultant effect of strength and harmony is particularly evident from either end of the north and south colonnades. Other architectural refinements include the oblique line of the cornices of the pediments and the gradual rise of the stylobate to a point which is highest in the centre. There is, in fact, hardly a straight line in the building. The ultimate effect of all this entasis, almost invisible to the untrained eye, is to create an impression of a perfectly proportioned edifice growing organically out of a natural eminence.

The sculptures, executed by Phidias and his pupils, and originally painted over in brilliant hues of red, blue, green and yellow – the effect, it is thought, may have been rather gaudy – consisted of ninety-two metopes, a frieze five hundred and twenty-four feet long running along the entire circumference of the exterior walls of the cella, and two gigantic pediments, at each corner of which lions' heads projected. The decoration is arranged in three tiers – on, as

25

it were, three different religious levels – embracing the entire cosmos in which the Greeks of the fifth century BC had their being. First came the Phidias frieze, representing the procession of the Great Panathenaea; a masterpiece of animation, with men and animals depicted in actual motion. The Parthenon frieze depicted every section of the population – on foot, on horseback, in chariots – participating in the procession. Parts of the frieze, though much damaged, may be seen on the west front. In the equestrian groups the prancing horses seem to be defying the attempts of the young riders to bridle them. Other plaques are in the Acropolis Museum and the remaining fifty-six in the British Museum. The angle of vision is very awkward, for the frieze towers forty feet above the spectator, who has little room to manoeuvre in the narrow colonnade.

From the human bustle of the frieze we move on to the metopes, which represent the gods and mythological heroes engaged in epic contests with giants, Centaurs and Amazons, symbolic of the victory of mind over matter. These were of inferior quality to the frieze. Thirty-two remain in their original position, between triglyphs, but they are mutilated almost beyond recognition. Other surviving metopes are in the British Museum and the Louvre. There is also one in the Acropolis Museum. Finally, on the highest level, crowning the whole structure, we enter the realm of the divine, the sculptures of the pediments representing two of the most venerable scenes in Athenian mythology: the birth of Athena, when she sprang fully armed from the head of Zeus 'with a mighty shout, while Heaven and Earth trembled before her';[1] and her contest with Poseidon for possession of the city. The most important fragments are in the British Museum. Except for a cement cast of Dionysus and the superb heads of three horses of the chariots of the Sun and Moon at either end of the east front and two headless figures in the west, the Parthenon pediments are now no more than two gaping wounds in a scarred and mutilated structure.

The huge cella of the Parthenon is now open to the sky. The interior arrangement can be traced from any ground plan: first (east to west), the *pronaos*, an outer porch, then the *naos*, the inner shrine housing Phidias's great chryselephantine statue of Athena, over forty feet high and adorned with precious stones – probably as garish as it was awesome in the sombre glow of the sacred chamber; then the Parthenon proper, the chamber of the goddess's virgin priestesses, where the treasure and bullion were kept (a nice juxta-

[1] Pindar, Ol. vii, 35.

position of religion and finance); finally the *opisthodomos*, a back chamber corresponding to the pronaos.

In the fifth century the temple was converted into a Christian basilica consecrated to the Mother of God (traces of painting are discernible on the interior north-west wall) and Phidias's statue of the goddess was removed to Constantinople.

After the Frankish conquest of the Levant in 1204, the Parthenon became a Latin church. Two and a half centuries later, after the fall of Constantinople, Athens was visited by the conqueror, Sultan Mehmet II, who could not resist converting the Parthenon into a mosque, to which a minaret was added. As such it remained until the Morosini explosion, only to suffer further damage during the War of Independence. It was not until 1930 that the restoration of the north colonnade, with the drums, capitals and fragments of architrave left lying about since the seventeenth century, was completed by Greek archaeologists. Thus, in spite of siege, pillage and desecration, the bare bones of Pericles's brain-child, with its honey-coloured columns and the matchless subtlety of its proportions, have survived the vicissitudes of centuries.

The view from the Parthenon embraces the whole Attic plain. It is most spectacular at sunset, when the famous violet light spreads across the bare slopes of Hymettus and for one miraculous moment is reflected in the buildings of the entire city. In summer the Acropolis is open for four successive nights during the full moon period. Figures stumble about between pools of light reflected from marble slabs and fluted drums strewn around the stylobate. Others move stealthily amid the shadows of the colonnades.

From the east front of the Parthenon you descend to the **Acropolis Museum**, a unique showcase of Archaic sculpture of the seventh, sixth and early fifth centuries BC. All the exhibits were found on the Acropolis. In Archaic sculpture the males, generally youths, are nude, whereas the females are fully clothed, for it is not until Hellenistic times that Eastern influences cause Greek modesty with regard to the nude female figure to be swept away in a wave of sensuous opulence. All Archaic statues, male and female, from the earliest to the latest, are, whether pleasing in a conventional sense or not, based on the Greek concept of perfection in shape. The *kouroi*, narrow-waisted youths exulting in their beauty and athletic prowess, stand rigid, left leg slightly forward, head and neck very erect. The oblique eyes protrude, and a faintly mocking smile, hinting at a quiet sophisticated sense of humour, plays about the full sensual lips. In spite of the ritualistic stiffness of the figures,

27

reminiscent of Egyptian models, they are, in the words of Lord Clark, 'alert and confident members of a conquering race'. But the best kouroi are in the National Museum (see p. 55). It is the reed-like maidens, the *korai*, presented as votive offerings to the goddess, that exercise the greatest fascination in the Acropolis Museum. In their main attributes they differ little from the kouroi, except that they are fully and stylishly dressed, and the arrangement of the hair is extremely elaborate. The korai represent fashionable young women of Athenian society in the aristocratic age of the Peisistratae, clad in a skin-tight tunic, the chiton, and a frequently jewelled mantle, the *himation*, which falls in symmetrical pleated folds in front of the breast. In spite of variations in size (most korai are about three-quarters life size), hair style and details of drapery, one is struck by the prevailing conformity.

In the entrance hall a large marble effigy of Athena's owl (No. 1347) establishes the goddess's symbolical authority. To the left, a charming fourth-century BC bas relief (No. 1338) depicts eight nude male figures preparing to perform a Pyrrhic dance. Room I contains part of a seventh-century BC pediment (the earliest extant one in Greece) from a small treasury, subsequently destroyed. Executed in painted tufa (traces of red, green and black), it represents the struggle of Heracles with the Hydra, whose innumerable coils are fashioned like octopus tentacles. In Room II the impact really begins to be felt. Fragments of a large primitive pediment from the original temple of Athena (sixth-century BC) depict Heracles slaying Triton, while a friend of Triton's, a monster with three winged bodies (No. 35), looks on. The composition – what remains of it – is full of vitality, the expression of the three faces one of grotesque whimsicality. The **Moscophorus** or Calf-Bearer (No. 624), representing a man bearing a sacrificial calf to the goddess, is a far more evolved work of art. The best preserved of four exquisitely carved little Archaic horses (**No. 575**) are the two central ones, who turn their heads towards each other, as though engaged – somewhat shyly – in social conversation. Fragments from the early temple of Athena destroyed by the Persians are among the chief exhibits in Room III.

But the greatest enchantments are reserved for Room IV. First comes the **Rider** (No. 590), which formed part of a small equestrian composition, believed to be the work of Phaidimos, greatest of Archaic sculptors. The head is a cast from the original in the Louvre; none the less its charm and liveliness, with the almond-shaped eyes and firm expressive lips set in the familiar teasing smile, make it one of the most attractive in the museum. Particularly decorative are the elaborate bead-like curls across the forehead and the long locks, strung like corals, hanging behind the large ears. But it is the monolithic upward thrust of the torso from the wasp waist that is most impressive; a perfect achievement of grace and naturalness, in spite of the absence of movement. In the same room are the korai, ranged in a circle on pedestals: formal, architectonic in conception, often haughty, always amused. A world of aristocratic ease, poise and serenity, destined to perish forever in the holocaust of the Persian Wars. No. 679, the **Peplos Koré** (so-called because she is wearing a heavy woollen *peplos* over her chiton), her bosom framed between parallel plaits of hair, is a masterpiece of sixth-century BC Attic sculpture, also probably the work of Phaidimos. The body, true, is block-like (in the lower part flat in front and round at the back), but the head is both authoritative and refined, the modelling miraculously rounded, the expression cynical, yet full of a kind of detached felicity.

Room V is dominated by a larger than life-size koré (No. 681), as formidable as her sisters in Room IV are diminutive, and fragments of a pediment from an older temple (No. 631), depicting gods and goddesses victorious over fallen giants in a *gigantomachia*. Passing into Room VI one is suddenly conscious of a change, a break with the past. We are in the fifth century. The mocking smile has vanished, and emotion is reflected in pensive expressions and relaxed attitudes. The change of mood is most striking in the **Kritios Boy** (No. 698), a perfect reproduction of the human body, its weight evenly and naturally distributed. An effortless poise has replaced the taut formality of the strictly frontal position. But in the sweeping away of rigid class distinctions, which followed the fall of the Peisistratae, the Kritios Boy seems to have lost his sense of humour. A small plaque in low relief (No. 695) represents a **Mourning Athena**. Emotion has broken through, and the limbs have grown supple in the process. Again there is the new distribution of weight, the goddess's body being slightly tilted forward, leaning on her spear; only the toes and ball of the left foot touch the ground.

In Room VII there is a well-preserved metope (No. 705) from the Parthenon, portraying a struggle between a Centaur and a Lapith woman (remarkable for the modelling of her body in the round) and two fine heads of horses (No. 882) from the Chariot of Poseidon which formed part of the sculptural decoration of the west pediment of the Parthenon. Room VIII is dominated by **fragments from the Parthenon frieze**, stunning examples (notice how shallow the relief is) of crowds in motion, full of dash, energy and liveliness. **No. 973** (relief from the balustrade of the Temple of Athena Niké Apteros) depicts a maiden removing her sandal. Although her chiton is so thin that the contours of the flesh stand out firm and rounded, deep shadows lurk mysteriously in the folds of the loosely flowing drapery. Finally, in Room IX there is a fourth-century BC head of Alexander the Great (No. 1331), sensuous, full-lipped, conventionally handsome, and a fragment of a relief depicting a serene authoritative Niké crowning Heracles, while Athena looks on.

From the museum one follows the line of the north-east rampart, past a belvedere overhanging a steep incline once cluttered with mean little medieval houses grouped round the blue-domed twelfth-century church of St Nicholas Rhangabes. Westward, below the walls of Themistocles, extend central Athens and the northern periphery. Beside one rises the **Erectheum**: for some, the supreme moment on the Acropolis.

The temple, completed during the last years of the Peloponnesian War, occupied the site of the holiest place on the Acropolis. Its origins go back to the beginnings of Attic religion. This is the spot where Athena brought forth the olive tree in her contest with Poseidon for the possession of the city.

The Erectheum is situated on lower ground than the Parthenon, and its complexity is in sharp contrast to the monolithic grandeur of the larger temple. Built on different levels, on the foundations of the edifice destroyed by the Persians, it had no side colonnades but three porticoes different in size, style and execution. From every angle the spectator obtains a different view: startling, novel, sometimes confusing. The side opposite the Parthenon consists of a blank wall of marble courses, broken at the west by the **Caryatid Portico**; it is the least attractive, for the architect, probably Mnesicles, had to cope with a sloping site and the inclusion of three separate shrines – those of Athena Polias, Poseidon and Erectheus – the Pandroseion, which contained the ancient olive tree planted by the goddess, as well as altars of other semi-deities. The temple served several purposes, all of profound religious significance. Architecturally the whole edifice, it has been suggested, was intended as a counterweight – more modest in dimensions and different in style – to the Parthenon. The heavy drapery of the Caryatids may have been meant to harmonize with the fluting of the columns of the Parthenon, but these six hefty maidens, in spite of their brave self-conscious simper, seem to be crushed by the weight of the ornamental roof they support on their cushioned heads. One is a plaster cast, the original being in the British Museum – one of Lord Elgin's least

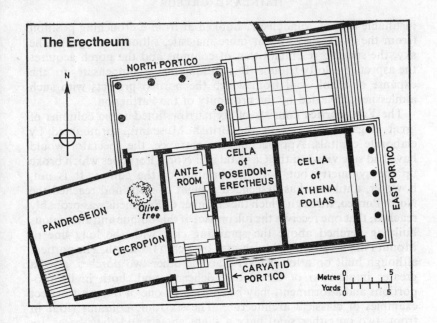

The Erectheum

NORTH PORTICO

N

PANDROSEION

Olive tree

ANTE-ROOM

CELLA of POSEIDON-ERECTHEUS

CELLA of ATHENA POLIAS

EAST PORTICO

CECROPION

CARYATID PORTICO

Metres 0 ___ 5
Yards 0 ___ 5

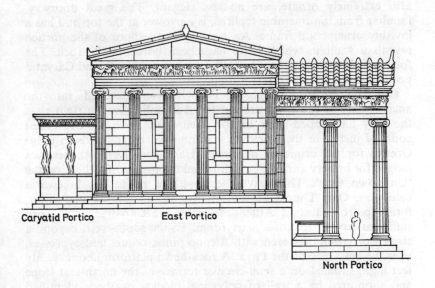

Caryatid Portico   East Portico

North Portico

justifiable acts of 'vandalism'. Looked at from a crouching position (from the east), they appear more majestic, silhouetted against the sky, the spacing resembles that of columns and the porch acquires the aspect of a lofty tribune. But nothing really compensates for the expanse of blank wall from which the portico projects with such aimlessness, dwarfed by the proximity of the Parthenon.

The **East Portico** consists of six narrow fluted Ionic columns of great elegance (one is in the British Museum), surmounted by elaborate capitals. Approaching the entrance, the spectator would have had side views of the Caryatid and North Porticoes which broke up the symmetry but not the harmony of the edifice. It is not, however, until one has descended a flight of steps and reached the **North Portico**, through which the chamber of Erectheus was probably reached, that one receives the full impact of this unique and anomalous building perched above the sprawling city, with the long line of Mount Parnes forming a bluish-grey barrier in the north. The portico, although built on a lower level than the other two porches, gives a greater impression of thrust and delicacy, and, both in its proportions and adornment, may be considered one of the most perfect examples of classical architecture. The six Ionic columns (four in front, two on either side) have a slight entasis and their bases are embellished with plaited decoration. The beautifully carved capitals, also extremely ornate, are no less elegant. The great doorway, familiar from innumerable replicas, is narrower at the top and has a lavishly ornamental frame. An opening in the floor of the portico reveals a vault in which holes have been bored in the rock. The four half-columns on the west wall, between the North and Caryatid porticoes, are a Roman restoration.

One now passes through the Propylaea and descends into the ancient part of the town around the Acropolis. On the right rises the grey flat-topped rock of the **Areopagus**. Here sat the oldest court of justice in the world, first summoned by the gods to judge Orestes for the crime of matricide. Here, too, Demosthenes was judged for bribery and St Paul addressed the people of Athens on the 'Unknown God'. They gave the apostle a polite but lukewarm reception. Only Dionysius the Areopagite, an erudite councillor, future patron saint of Athens, took up the Christian cause with sufficient fervour to suffer martyrdom. To the south-west, beyond a stretch of ground covered with Aleppo pines, cedars and cypresses, rises the eminence of the **Pnyx**. A rock-hewn platform about twenty feet high, situated on a semi-circular terrace of the north-east slope and supported by a wall of polygonal blocks, has been identified as the celebrated *Bema*, the tribune from which generations of orators addressed the assembly of the people of Athens in the shadow of the temples of the Acropolis. Nightly performances of *Son et Lumière* (Greek, English and French versions), with splendid floodlighting effects on the Acropolis, are held on the Pnyx throughout the summer.[2]

The road then skirts the north-west bastion of the Acropolis and plunges into the maze of the Plaka – 'old Athens', once gay and picturesque, now full of tourists and nightclubs. But it is less confusing to explore the Plaka, the adjacent area of the Agora and the other monuments of the 'City of Theseus' by taking a completely different route starting from Syntagma Square.

---

[2] Also in summer, performances of folk-dances by the Dora Stratou Company are given in a new open air theatre below the Acropolis. The performers, from the Aegean Islands and Epirot Mountains, are amateurs and the music and costumes are authentic.

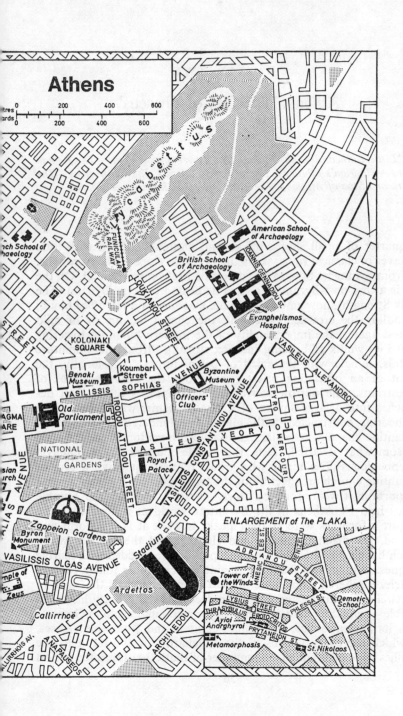

Athens

metres 0 200 400 600
yards 0 200 400 600

Lycabettus

FUNICULAR RAILWAY

nch School of
haeology

French School of
Archaeology

American School
of Archaeology

British School
of Archaeology

IOANNE GENNADIOU ST.

Evanghelismos
Hospital

LOUKIANOU STREET

KOLONAKI
SQUARE

VASILEUS ALEXANDROU

Koumbari
Street

AVENUE

Benaki
Museum

Byzantine
Museum

VASILISSIS

SOPHIAS

VASILEUS

SPYRO

MERCOURI

Officers'
Club

IRODOU ATTIDOU STREET

CONSTANTINOU AVENUE

YEORYIOU

AGMA
ARE

Old
Parliament

VASILEUS

VASILEOS

ssian
urch

NATIONAL

GARDENS

Royal
Palace

LIAS AV.

Zappeion Gardens

Byron
Monument

Stadium

VASILISSIS OLGAS AVENUE

mple of
Zeus

Ardettos

ARCHIMEDOU

ALLIRRHOIS AV.

ANA
PAUSEOS

Callirrhoë

ENLARGEMENT of The PLAKA

ADRIANOU

MNESICLES ST.

DENTELOU
STREET

Tower of
the Winds

LYSIUS STREET

THRASYBULUS

EROTOCRITOS

PHLESSA ST.

Demotic
School

Ayioi
Anarghyroi

PRYTANEION ST.

Metamorphosis

St. Nikolaos

CHAPTER TWO

Athens: 'The City of Theseus'

✤

The 'Little Cathedral' – The Plaka – The Tower of the Winds – The Roman Agora – Hadrian's Library – Monastiraki Square – The Cerameicus – The Agora and Stoa of Attalus – The Theseum – The Kapnikarea Church

A quarter of small shops, offices and churches, dotted with little enclaves of classical ruins, skirts the northern slope of the Acropolis.

From Syntagma Square one descends Metropoleos Street. On the left is a tiny post-Byzantine chapel dedicated to Ayia Dynami (The Holy Strength), now embedded in the masonry of a tall office block; straddling the crowded pavement, the chapel has an air of mild protest against the impersonality of the modern buildings towering above it; whiffs of burning incense, drifting through its miniature portals, mingle with the smell of petrol fumes; occasionally, the chant of an officiating priest rises above the strident voices of pedestrians. The narrow canyon of Metropoleos Street then debouches into a large square of the same name, where the official Cathedral, constructed with materials plundered from seventy Byzantine chapels, raises its ugly nineteenth-century façade. Beside it, somewhat dwarfed, rests the **'Little Cathedral'**, or Panayia Goepoepicoos (The Virgin who grants requests quickly), a gem of Byzantine church architecture of the twelfth century, whose modest proportions (twenty-four by thirty-six feet) indicate the humble status held by Athens in the Byzantine world at a time when the Empire's fortunes were at their peak. In style it is cruciform and domed, the drum is slender and elegant, and the exterior walls, which have a glowing ivory-smooth patina, are studded with marble plaques. On the west front the quaint but charming fourth-century BC frieze, pilfered from some ancient monument, tells the story of the twelve months of the year. The decoration is a dotty historical jumble – something that one encounters again and again in Greece – with its ancient stelae, Corinthian capitals and Byzantine crosses, to which the coats-of-arms of the Villehardouin and de la Roche families have been added – a reminder of that often-forgotten period of Frankish rule, when Athens was governed by the Crusaders and their Latin descendants.

Metropoleos Square is a good place from which to watch the Epitaphios (Good Friday Procession), when the bier of Christ, heaped with flowers, is borne through the streets at night. The procession is led by the Archbishop of Athens and all Greece, followed by church dignitaries in tall cylindrical hats, flanked by acolytes in red and purple shifts tottering under the weight of enormous banners. The procession is followed by a shuffling crowd of worshippers, hands cupped round lighted candles. Everywhere there is a smell of stocks and incense. The Epitaphios has one point in common with the Panathenaic procession – the people are part of the procession, not just spectators.

At the southern end of the square P. Benizelou Street leads into Adrianou Street, the 'aristocratic' quarter of Athens in the eighteenth and early nineteenth centuries, now a maze of drapers' shops, butchers' and undertakers'.

At the Demotic School (neo-classical façade) one turns into Phlessa Street. This is the beginning of the **Plaka** proper, its steep alleys criss-crossing the north slope of the Acropolis. The whole quarter now seems to be earmarked for nocturnal pleasure and the tourist trade. In spite of the garish dolled-up quaintness there are still some enchanting spots. Take the tavernas first. These are a very good Greek institution, and the ones in the Plaka are among the most popular, though by no means the best. Greeks do not go to tavernas only to eat and drink; but to indulge in *kephi*, which means to sing and shout and make a great deal of noise; and they expect other people to do so too. Sometimes there are itinerant guitarists. The most popular drink is *retsina*; to some it is an acquired taste: dry, astringent, with a slight flavour of turpentine. A convivial party is not unlikely to send a brimming carafe (or copper mug) to a table of complete strangers: all the more reason to do so – this is very Greek – if they are foreigners. At all costs the foreigner must be fêted; and in return the Greek flattered. The foreigner must be left in no doubt that Greeks are the finest people in the world; and he is expected to say so – fulsomely.

The food consists of *taramosalata* (a purée of smoked fish-roe), *souvlakia* (pieces of pork or beef grilled on a skewer), *kokkeretsi* (chopped liver and sweetbreads twined in guts, highly seasoned with garlic and roasted on the spit), the ubiquitous *feta* (a white, sometimes flaky, goat's milk cheese) and the inevitable tomato salad (in winter replaced by finely chopped raw cabbage). At the more sophisticated tavernas the food is on more international lines. Among the bottled wines, Carras (red, white and rosé) is the best. Demestica (red and white) is much cheaper. Tavernas, with a few exceptions, are only open at night. The more pretentious ones sometimes have the defects without the qualities of the humbler ones. Some of them have floor-shows and dancing.

At the end of Phlessa Street, past the taverna of Palaia Athena, Erotocritos Street begins. The houses could not be smaller, the alleys narrower. Everything is in miniature. It is like a film set for some Greek island scene. At the top of the rise, Erotocritos Street swerves right and, past the Byzantine chapel of St John the Divine (eleventh- and twelfth-century), one enters a shady little terrace outside the tavernas of Psathas and Attalos. This is an enchanting place – remarkably peaceful in the daytime – which not even the twang of electric guitars and the hum of polyglot voices can wholly desecrate. The houses are painted with washes of ochre, dove grey and Siena red; the shutters are green or blue. The narrow tiled courtyards are filled with pots of fuchsias, hibiscus and geraniums. From the taverna of Erotocritos a path leads up to O Yeros tou Mouria (The Old Man of the Morea), one of the most popular and expensive tavernas in the Plaka. Above towers the floodlit North Portico of the Erectheum.

From this point the steps of Mnesicles Street lead into Prytaneion Street, at the end of which (left) appear the blue domes of the church of Ayios Nikolaos (St Nicholas) Rhangabes: twelfth-century, but so much restored as to retain little of its original antiquity. Above the church more tavernas command a superb view of the 'City of Hadrian' and its monuments, with the floodlit pine-fringed summit of Lycabettus crowning successive layers of apartment blocks.

From Prytaneion Street I like to descend into the sunken garden of the church of Ayioi Anarghyroi (SS Cosmas and Damian), the Arabian twins, patron saints of medicine and surgery, martyred by Diocletian. The whitewashed church, to which a porch with four marble columns has been added, was built at the beginning of the Turkish occupation in the form of a single-aisle basilica.

One then enters Thrasybulus Street, passes the tourist shops and nightclubs, ascends the first stairway on the left and reaches the derelict shell of the Old University, screened by large wild fig trees. The abandoned *magna aula* of this modest institution of higher studies now echoes only with the strains of pop music from neighbouring bars haunted by the more disreputable elements of the Plaka. The alleys become so narrow that no wheeled traffic can manoeuvre. From the Old University it is only a few steps up to the church of the Metamorphosis (Transfiguration), another charming Byzantine chapel of the fourteenth century, situated below the pines and cypresses skirting the 'Long Rocks' of the Acropolis. The tiny altar is made from the capital of an ancient column. From here the road, now wider, leads round the north-west bastion of the Acropolis to the Areopagus.

One retraces one's steps to O Yeros tou Mouria and descends the stairway of Mnesicles Street, past a group of rather bogus tavernas, turns left into Lysius Street and, at the end of it, enters the spacious square of the Tower of the Winds, known as Oi Aeridhes (The Windy Ones). The pink- and ochre-washed houses were once the balustraded mansions of the capital's embryo bourgeoisie. The square is now a crowded car-park. A railing runs round two sides of a complex of ancient ruins. At night, when moonlit, it is one of the most romantic places in Athens.

The **Tower of the Winds**, or Horologium of Andronicus Cyrrhestes, rises beside an umbrageous plane tree in a depression below the square. West of it extends the Roman Agora. The octagonal tower is an architectural fantasy, the creation of a philhellenic Syrian of the first century AD. In 1676 Dr Spon of Lyons, one of the earliest Western scholars to visit Greece, identified it as a hydraulic clock. A bas-relief, portraying the features of the different winds, runs round the eight sides. The roof, an octagonal pyramid, was surmounted by a weather-vane in the form of a Triton. A small round tower against the east front served as a reservoir for the clock, connected by an aqueduct with the spring of Clepsydra on the Acropolis. The passage of Diogenes Street, at the north-east end of the square, leads to a decent unpretentious taverna, the Platanos, situated in a shady court.

In the rectangle of the **Roman Agora** are the ruins of an Ionic peristyle with a double gallery surrounding an interior marble-paved courtyard. Traces of a building with a loggia at the south-east angle have been identified as the Agronomeion, headquarters of the market police. Two arcades run south of the Tower of the Winds. At the west end (Dioscuri Street) stands the Gateway of Athena Archegetes (first-century AD), with four heavy Doric columns surmounted by an unadorned pediment still intact. Within the excavation area there is a square brick building with multiple domes and a colonnaded porch, once the Fetiye Mosque, built in commemoration of Sultan Mehmet's entry into Athens after the fall of Constantinople, now a clearing-house for archaeological finds. Beyond the church of the Taxiarchoi (Archangels) one enters Areos Street.

On the right rises the block of the west colonnade of **Hadrian's Library**. A single fluted Corinthian column, all that remains of the central portico, stands isolated from the smooth blackened shafts of the colonnade. The façade of the main entrance, charred by fire, is in Aiolou Street, where six Corinthian columns (two survive) supported consoles. Built by Hadrian in the second century AD, the library possessed a courtyard surrounded by a hundred columns, a pool and garden.

The most striking feature of adjoining Monastiraki Square, hub of downtown Athens, is a Turkish mosque, the former Pazar Djami (Market Mosque), a square block faced by a loggia and supporting an octagon, which has served as both a prison and museum. At the east end of the square, in the middle of which rises the unusually tall drum of the modernized tenth-century church of the Panayia (The Virgin), begins Pandrossou Street, commonly referred to in English as 'Shoe Lane'. The alley is full of antique shops and is faintly redolent of a Turkish bazaar. Hellenistic coins, Attic figurines, rugs, icons, embroideries are on sale at the more expensive antique shops. There is also a lot of Victoriana (opaline vases, egg-cups, etc.) and filigree silverware from Yannina in the north. Prices are high, and bargaining is the norm.

At the right of Monastiraki railway station, Iphaistiou Street, a humble counterpart of Pandrossou, forms part of the blacksmiths' and coppersmiths' quarter. The shops are full of brass and leather objects. There are also some antique shops. The second turning to the right leads to the flea-market, where tin baths and an amorphous assortment of rusty metal appliances are on sale. From the flea-market one rejoins Ermou Street at its more squalid lower end and proceeds west, with a view of the gas-works in front.

Beyond the little Byzantine church of Ayioi Asomatoi (The Saintly Incorporeal Ones), its exterior brickwork decoration stylishly restored, is the entrance to a vast sunken field of ancient ruins in the form of an irregular rhomboid, dominated by a large coffee-coloured modern church. At the west end lies the **Cerameicus**, a necropolis of funerary altars.

Lying just outside the city walls, the cemetery of the Cerameicus, final resting place of countless public figures, was destroyed in the first century BC when Sulla breached the defences of beleaguered Athens. The level of the ground continued, nevertheless, to be raised by the superimposition of more sepulchres, and the excavation of graves continues to this day to yield funerary offerings. The place is now a jumble of shattered stelae (carved marble grave-stones) on different levels, with fosses, corresponding to the ancient alleys, cleaving through mounds and knolls that look like abandoned earthworks. The surviving stelae – the finest are now in the National Archaeological Museum – line the right bank of the Alley of the Tombs which begins at the Piraeus Street entrance (now closed) and whence it is best to start a tour (west to east) of the site.

First, there is a relief depicting a Roman funeral banquet, attended by the dreaded Charon, purveyor of souls to the Underworld, followed by a representation of a huge Molossian dog, its paunch seamed with protruding veins; next comes the Monument of Dionysius of Cocytus, crowned by a lively well-preserved bull about to charge, and then the Monument of Dexileos with a cast of the original stele now in the adjoining museum. A large well-preserved though artistically inferior stele depicting a girl seated beside her standing mother rises above the bank of a lateral alley. Class distinctions are preserved, and the graves of slaves are marked by truncated columns. *Loutrophoroi*, slender pitchers with two handles, reserved for bachelors' graves, litter the banks of the fosse. Slender marble *lecythoi*, which resemble the loutrophoroi except that they have only one handle, are scattered among the shrubs. A simple and beautiful relief of a maiden bearing a lustral vase crowns the site of the shrine of Hecate above the Alley of the Tombs at the south-western end of the necropolis.

South-east of a large unidentified circular building are vestiges of the city walls raised by Themistocles and restored by Conon. Next (east) are the ruins of the Pompeum, where all the props used in the Panathenaic procession were stored. Six small banqueting halls project from a court surrounded by a colonnade (column bases are preserved), once a favourite haunt of that somewhat bogus philosopher, Diogenes. To the north are the stylobates and frag-ments of walls of the Dipylon Gate, the main commercial entrance way into Athens, which was connected with the Agora by a *dromos* (public way) lined with porticoes filled with statues of poets, phil-osophers and statesmen. The quantity of column bases, the water conduits and the ruts of chariot wheels in the paved ways, give one an idea of the importance and dimensions of this congested 'monu-mental' entrance way.

The little museum of the Cerameicus stands by the gate through which one leaves (or enters) the site. In Room 1 are stelae; among the finest is the fifth-century BC **Monument of Dexileos**, depicting a

41

warrior mounted on a frisky horse in the act of overwhelming his foe; in another a young man, the departed soul, is represented draped in a flowing chlamys; then a grandmother holding her dead grand-child on her lap, the folds of her peplos billowing over her head and following the contours of both her body and the baby's. An earlier period is represented by a perky Archaic sphinx, its head turned at right angles to its body. In Room 2 we go further back: to the funerary offerings of the late Mycenaean, Protogeometric and Geometric periods which include a ninth-century BC bronze bowl of Phoenician workmanship, a figurine of a beast of burden carrying a load of four jars, a round terracotta work-basket (?) with a design of swastikas surmounted by four geometric horses, a water jug in the form of a ship's hull. In Room 3, devoted to black-figured and red-figured vases from the Archaic to the Hellenistic periods, there is a fine sixth-century BC amphora, found in a child's grave, decorated with three black figures advancing across the painted band in a Dionysiac dance processional. Room 4 is a repository of sherds from amphorae which received awards for their outstanding work-manship at the conclusion of the Panathenaic procession.

North-west of the Cerameicus a series of dreary streets leads to the site of Plato's Academy, the southern corner of which is marked by the church of Ayios Triphon (St Triphon). All that remains is an ancient boundary stone – amid the garages and workshops of sub-urban working-class Athens. Nearby are remains of a prehistoric settlement – sections of walls, foundations of an elliptical-shaped edifice and other habitations, a necropolis which has yielded vases and tools in obsidian: proof, if it were needed, that the Attic plain was inhabited in the Heroic Age.

On the way back from the Cerameicus turn right at Monastiraki Square into Areos Street; right again, opposite the west colonnade of Hadrian's Library into Adrianou Street. Crossing the road over the railway, you then enter the **Agora**. It would be a mistake to expect any of the splendour, complexity or visible ruins of the Roman Forum. One's first impression is of a vast bombed site. This ancient market place, once the social, commercial and administrative hub of Athens, where business was transacted, legislation passed and gossip exchanged, lies in a hollow, littered with ruined fortifications, eroded plinths and truncated columns: a legacy of desolation left by the Heruli, a northern tribe associated with the earliest Gothic invasions.

The pathway follows the route of the Panathenaic procession. On the right rise three giant statues of Tritons with elaborate fish-tails on plinths ornamented with olive branches. This Stoa of the

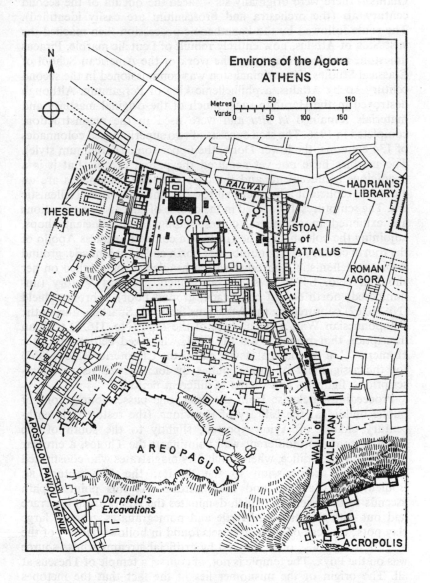

Environs of the Agora
ATHENS

Metres 0 50 100 150
Yards 0 50 100 150

N

RAILWAY

HADRIAN'S
LIBRARY

THESEUM

AGORA

STOA
of
ATTALUS

ROMAN
AGORA

AREOPAGUS

WALL of VALERIAN

APOSTOLOU PAVLOU AVENUE

Dörpfeld's
Excavations

ACROPOLIS

Giants – there were originally six – faced the odeum of the second century AD (the orchestra and proscenium are easily identified). The route followed by the Panathenaic procession then reached the vast **Stoa of Attalus**, now entirely rebuilt of Pentelic marble, Piraeus limestone and local clay tiles: the work of the American School of Classical Studies. The original stoa was commissioned in the second century AD by Attalus, a philhellenic king of Pergamum. Although destroyed in the Herulian sack, much of the original masonry and materials remained *in situ* and were used in the reconstruction, completed in 1956. The stoa consists of two superimposed colonnades of 134 columns, the lower Doric, the upper Ionic (Pergamum style). The marbles have not yet acquired the patina of age, but it is a prodigious achievement, and the cool spacious colonnades are an authentic replica of a market hall towards the end of the Hellenistic era. The sculptures discovered in the course of successive excavations are exhibited in chambers, corresponding to the ancient shops, adjoining the colonnade. They include a colossal headless Apollo of the fourth century BC (unnumbered; north end of colonnade, ground floor), a Hellenistic Aphrodite with a headless Eros perched on her shoulder (No. S473), a small but athletic Winged Victory (unnumbered; north end of colonnade, ground floor), a bronze shield (No. B262) captured by the Athenians from the Spartans during the Peloponnesian War, a statue base of the *Iliad* (No. I1628) with an inscription that begins 'I am the Iliad, who lived before and after Homer . . .', a mechanical device called the Cleroterion (No. I3967) for the assignment of public duties by lot; as well as vases, inscriptions, figurines and sherds of different periods.

Proceeding clockwise from the Stoa, one passes foundations of public buildings: the Library of Pantainus, (the restored eleventh-century church of Ayioi Apostoli, slightly to the south of the Library, contains indifferent wall paintings); the Tholos, a circular fifth-century BC edifice, where dwelt fifty magistrates who constituted a permanent commission to the Senate; the fifth-century BC Bouleuterion (Senate); and the Metroön. At this point a path ascends to the **Theseum**, which dominates the Agora from a terrace laid out with flowerbeds. Myrtle and pomegranates grow in large clay pots; replicas of ancient vessels found in hollows cut out of the neighbouring rock, once watered by artificial streams whose source was on the Pnyx. The temple is not, of course, a temple of Theseus at all. The origin of the misnomer lies in the fact that the metopes depict the exploits of the Attic hero. It was, in all likelihood, a temple of Hephaestus, god of forges, and the whole vicinity was inhabited by blacksmiths. The din of coppersmiths' workshops in Iphaistou Street still echoes across the working-class quarter.

The temple, of the Doric order, the first in Greece to be built entirely of marble, is dated to the mid fifth century BC (just prior to the Parthenon) and was one of the earliest attempts to restore the monuments destroyed during the Persian invasion. Bronze statues of Hephaestus and Athena Hephaistia, patron deities of industrial workers, adorned the cella. It has thirty-eight columns (six instead of the usual eight on either front) with a pronounced convexity in the shaft. Of the remaining eighteen metopes, ten (east front) represent the exploits of Heracles and eight (north and south) those of Theseus. The pronaos frieze, which is very mutilated, depicts a battle (unidentified) watched by six Olympian deities. The vaulted roof of the interior dates from the fifth century AD, when the temple, like so many others, was converted into a Byzantine shrine. Although the best preserved classical temple in Greece, the Theseum is not the most inspiring. The plain Doric style, so supremely effective in Ictinus's monumental plan of the Parthenon, loses much of its vitality in the smaller edifice. Its position, lying in a trough between the Acropolis and the western hills, may also account for its lack of an air of authority. Nevertheless, when seen from the upper gallery of the Stoa of Attalus, framed within surrounding shrubberies, it appears startlingly alive in its exterior completeness.

The clockwise route leads down into the Agora again. On the left lie foundations of a small temple of Apollo Patroös (fourth-century BC), followed by bases of columns and fragments of pediments marking the site of the Stoa of Zeus, in whose shade Socrates lectured to students. On the right is the site of the Altar of the Twelve Gods, the starting-point for the measurement of all distances from Athens, and, beyond it, the main entrance (and exit).

On the way back to Syntagma Square, you may turn left at the corner of Ermou and Aiolou Streets. A pretty flower market extends across the little square of Ayia Irene, beside a church of the same name. Pots of gardenias, oleanders and hibiscus, their scarlet trumpets turned towards the sun, are ranged beside orange trees in wooden tubs and boxes filled with basil; clematis and bougainvillea trail from trellised bamboo sticks.

Halfway up Ermou Street there is a charming view of the little eleventh- and twelfth-century **Church of the Kapnikarea**. One of the best preserved Byzantine churches in the capital, the Kapnikarea is a typical example of the cruciform plan, which was established throughout the Greek mainland in the twelfth century. It is built of stone embellished with brick courses. The little cupola above the additional chapel on the north side is an example of the tendency to increase the number of domes. The outer porch with two small columns leading to the door with beautifully decorated marble jambs and lintels has a very coquettish air. The frescoes in the interior are modern, but good. Between the Kapnikarea and Syntagma Square Ermou Street becomes a crowded shopping quarter. At the corner of Syntagma Square, Papaspyrou and Dionysos, large pavement cafés, get all the morning sun. On summer nights they are the haunt of the chic demi-monde.

CHAPTER THREE

Athens: 'The City of Hadrian'

❧

Hadrian's Gateway – The Temple of Olympian Zeus – The Stadium – The Benaki Museum – The Byzantine Museum – Mount Lycabettus – The Church of the Holy Theodores – The National Archaeological Museum – Colonus

In summer the city gives an impression of dazzling whiteness. The suburbs are blanketed in a metal-coloured haze and there is an almost North African air about the parched plain. A great deal of nineteenth- and early twentieth-century Athens was demolished in the 1950s. For years the city echoed with the crash of the pickaxe and the grind of pneumatic drills. Row upon row of well-appointed white- and cream-coloured apartment blocks, their terraces shaded with bright blue awnings, rose and still go on rising, from the rubble. Here and there skyscrapers tower above them.

It is best to begin at the entrance to the National Gardens and follow Amalias Avenue as far as the statue of Byron in the arms of a lady representing Hellas. At this point, **Hadrian's Gateway** marks the boundary between the two ancient cities. Two inscriptions on the frieze give the directions: to the west, 'This is Athens, in times past the City of Theseus'; to the east 'But this is Hadrian's and no longer the City of Theseus' – a quarter of public gardens and residential streets lined with false-pepper trees.

The gateway, with its Roman arch surmounted by a Greek portico probably intended to symbolize the marriage of the Greek and Roman worlds, is not one of the happiest achievements of the Emperor's architects. The Emperor himself was something of an amateur architect: a fact that may account for its lack of professionalism. Originally, it may have looked more impressive framed between two Corinthian columns on either side (their bases are still visible), but it could never have borne comparison with any of the great triumphal arches of Rome. The marble arch rests on two square Corinthian columns. The Greek portico on the upper level has three bays, the middle one crowned by a pediment. The effect is one of awkwardness, of something which has not quite come off.

Nevertheless, it remains a landmark, an outpost of traffic-choked central Athens.

The gateway leads to the esplanade of the **Temple of Olympian Zeus**, supported on both sides by strong buttresses, of which there were originally a hundred. The history of the temple, one of the most impressive ruins in Athens, is a chequered one. It was begun by the Peisistratae in the sixth century BC on the site of an older temple. Work was interrupted by the fall of the Peisistratae and the Persian Wars, but resumed in the second century BC by a Seleucid king of Syria who would employ none but the best Roman architects. It was finally completed in AD 132 by Hadrian, who placed a majestic effigy of himself and a jewelled snake beside the gold and ivory statue of Zeus in the cella. During the Middle Ages the temple served as a quarry.

Close by the partially restored Propylaea of the temple lie some gigantic column bases of the earlier Archaic edifice; to the west are vestiges of an ancient road and of the ubiquitous walls of Themistocles. Further west are the foundations of a Roman thermal establishment with column bases at the east end and of two fourth-century BC houses among the juniper bushes.

The temple itself is approached from the Propylaea. With two rows of twenty columns at the sides, three of eight at each front, it was one of the largest in the Graeco-Roman world. The Roman architects' attempt to extend the columns, surmounted by magnificent Corinthian capitals, to the greatest possible height without giving them an air of exaggerated attenuation is completely successful. No Greek architect of the classical age would have dreamed of going so far. Of the 124 columns only 15 remain – tall and fluted, their capitals adorned with elaborate acanthus leaf mouldings. Impressive at all times, they seldom look more magical than when floodlit, emerging from the penumbra of darkness of the surrounding gardens.

Left of the entrance to the temple enclosure an acacia-lined alley leads to another field of ruins below the retaining wall of the esplanade. It is a scene of considerable confusion, but archaeologists have recently identified foundations of temples of the Archaic period and of the fifth and second centuries BC. To the south-east is a cliff-face: site of the **Callirhoe Spring** ('the beautifully flowing'), the only source of good drinking water in ancient Athens.

Beyond the Temple of Olympian Zeus Vasilissis Olgas Avenue runs between the Zappeion Gardens on one side and a tennis club, swimming pool and playground on the other. A clearing between the shrubberies of the Zappeion Gardens reveals the neo-classical porch of a large horseshoe-shaped building in which exhibitions are held. It also houses the National Broadcasting Institute. The curve of Vasilissis Olgas Avenue ends in a fork. Vasileos Constantinou Avenue leads to the Hilton, a crescent-shaped palace of marble that might have aroused the envy of Hadrian, and to Vasilissis Sophias Avenue, lined with Embassies and expensive blocks of flats which have replaced the nineteenth-century neo-classical houses of the Old Athenian families. Beside the Hilton is the National Gallery (Ethnike Pinacotheke), filled with Greek nineteenth-century paintings, some Flemish works and four El Grecos, one of which is of considerable distinction: **The Angels' Concert**, an unfinished work, depicting a complex group of swirling figures mantled in draperies that follow the contours of their contorted attitudes. At this point Ioannis Gennadeiou Street leads up the slope of Lycabettus to the fine neo-classical building of the Gennadeion Library, which possesses a collection of rare books on Greece, Byronic relics and Edward Lear water-colours.

South-east of the fork of Vasilissis Olgas and Vasileos Constantinou Avenues lies the **Stadium**, capable of accommodating upwards of sixty thousand spectators, built in a wide ravine of the pine-clad hill of Aedettos in the fourth century BC. Five centuries later its forty-four tiers were faced with marble at the expense of Herodes Atticus, a public-spirited millionaire. An idea of the magnitude of the work is obtained from the fact that as many as a thousand wild beasts took part in the gladiatorial shows and Roman circuses over which Hadrian presided. In the Middle Ages the stadium was reduced to a quarry. Later travellers describe it as overgrown with corn, the crumbling diazômas as grazing-grounds for goats. In 1895 a modern Herodes Atticus, George Averoff, a wealthy cotton merchant, financed the reconstruction and refacing of the tiers with Pentelic marble, and the first revived Olympic Games were held there the following year.

From the highest tier of the Stadium there is a good view of Hadrian's Athens and its twentieth-century expansion. Irodou Atticou Street, a cool shaded way, mounts gradually from the Stadium to the new Palace on the right. Further up, on the left (No. 1 Koumbari Street) is the **Benaki Museum**. Two generations of a family of cotton magnates from Alexandria have dedicated themselves to the assembly of this impressive collection of icons, jewellery, silverware, woodcarving, embroideries and relics of the War of Independence. Wandering through the spacious high-ceilinged rooms of this former private residence, one is constantly being reminded, as one turns from bejewelled weapons to gorgeous chasubles, from religious paintings to lavish textiles, of the proximity of Italy in the west, of Islam in the east.

Room A contains relics of the War of Independence (No. 955 is Byron's portable writing-desk). Large canvasses of battle scenes by Greek nineteenth-century artists recall the swashbuckling manner of Delacroix's imitators. Ecclesiastical objects from various parts of Asia Minor fill Room B. No. 31 is a gorgeously embroidered banner from the Pontus. Room Γ is devoted to Byzantine and post-Byzantine works: an elaborate icon-stand in gilt carved wood; a large sixteenth-century icon of the Transfiguration (No. 123); a **St Anne and the Virgin** (in a scarlet mantle), painted by Emmanuel Tzanes, an important iconographer of the sixteenth-century Cretan School (No. 126); the **Hospitality of Abraham** (No. 64), a fourteenth-century symbolical representation of the Holy Trinity (the relaxed attitudes of the figures are unusual in a Byzantine icon, and the subtle shading of reds and blues is rendered with great sophistication).

In a way the Benaki Museum is a curtain-raiser – the Byzantine Museum another – to the great religious art of Salonica, Mistra and Mount Athos, where late Byzantine art flourished during the fourteenth and fifteenth centuries.

Room E contains objects of Turkish provenance of the sixteenth and seventeenth centuries. The show-piece is a restored **seventeenth-century reception room** from Cairo, with a mosaic floor, fountain and cascade from which water trickles into a small basin. The tiles are Persian, the inscriptions Cufic, the atmosphere cool and redolent of a grand Moslem house. On the walls sixteenth-century velvet fabrics from Brusa, chiefly used as cushions, are decorated with floral designs of brightly coloured tulips and carnations. Upstairs in Room Z there are two sixteenth-century icons of the Nativity (Nos. 516, 518) and the 'Miracles of the Holy Girdle' (No. 1150) with pronounced Venetian influences.

More relics of the War of Independence in Room H include an unusual painting of 'The Battle of Karpenisi' (No. 646). The painter was an illiterate peasant. His aerial view of the set-piece battle is crude and childish, but the detail is full of charm and fantasy. Room K contains two early El Grecos. The first (No. 1542), a much mutilated icon of St Luke painting the Virgin, is of purely historical interest, being the only extant work of Greco's in the style of the Cretan school of iconography; it was painted before he left his native Crete for Venice. The other (No. 1543) is an Adoration of the Magi, an early work, belonging to the period of the artist's apprenticeship in the workshop of the aged Titian, whose guiding hand is discernible in the architectural background, the approach to foreshortening and the balanced grouping of the figures. In Room Δ there is a large seventeenth-century bed, its curtains and pillows embroidered with threads of light green, brick red and Prussian blue. The jewellery in Room N ranges from gold cups of the third millenium BC to French gold snuff-boxes. Case 106 contains a collection of rare Byzantine jewellery.

The Chinese ceramics in Room Ξ (Neolithic, T'ang, Sung, Ming) are displayed against a background of sumptuous carpets from Isphahan and Samarkand. In Room I there is a comprehensive selection of **embroideries** (mostly seventeenth- and eighteenth-century) from the islands and Epirus. The most elaborately worked pieces were usually reserved for household objects, such as pillow-cases, bedspreads and valances. In the basement there is a magnificent collection of national costumes and, in a small room beside the staircase leading to the upper storey, a collection of strange Graeco-Roman bone carvings – crude but fascinating depictions of Dionysus, Aphrodite and marine deities and sea monsters gambolling in the waves, thought to have been used as ornamental adjuncts to pieces of furniture.

Koumbari Street leads into Kolonaki Square (more officially Philikes Hetairias) on the slope of Lycabettus. The little garden in the middle, laid out with flowerbeds and orange trees, is the haunt of foreign nannies and their Greek charges. The centre of a smart residential quarter, the square retains an atmosphere of old-fashioned intimacy trying to come to terms with impersonal modernity. Two sides are lined with confectioners', where Athenians, young and old, sit for hours in the spring and autumn sunshine, interlarding their conversation with Anglo-American slang and outdated French expressions. At Boccola's the speciality is *loukoumadhes*: small fried cakes of dough, served very crisp, drenched in honey and sprinkled with cinnamon. From Kolonaki Square you turn into Neophytou Vamva Street (corner of the British Council) and regain Vasilissis Sophias Avenue. On the left, just beyond the isolated block of the Officers' Club, is the **Byzantine Museum**.

Preceded by a rectangular court with a marble fountain flanked by two cypress trees, the main building is a rectangular block with a double loggia designed in 1840. The Byzantine Museum might well be visited (or revisited) *after* the traveller has been initiated into the iconographic and theological complexities of this thousand-year-old

51

art at the more important sites of Daphni, Hosios Loukas and Mistra – for it is not in Athens that Byzantine art and architecture make their greatest impact. The amorphous objects, many of a liturgical character, displayed in the Byzantine Museum then fall into place more easily and their significance is more quickly grasped.

Room 1 (ground floor) contains early Byzantine sculpture: No. 92, a boy bearing a calf, reminiscent of the Moscophorus in the Acropolis Museum; No. 93, Orpheus, his head crowned by an eagle, playing on his lyre to the animals which form an open-work frame round the figure; No. 95, a crude but charming Nativity, with two Giottoesque papier-mâché trees on either side of the crib. More sculptures (plaques with crosses, Byzantine eagles and effigies of the Virgin) crowd Room 2. Room 3 is in the form of a reconstructed but not altogether convincing Byzantine cruciform church with marble revetments. In Room 4 there is an iconostasis with elaborate woodcarving, twelve panels representing scenes from the life of Christ and a canopy surmounted by a colourful model of a Byzantine church painted with floral designs and scenes from the life of the Virgin. The first room (right) on the upper floor contains illuminated manuscripts and icons. Among the latter: a Crucifixion (No. 157) with a star-studded background; a Virgin and Child framed within a sequence of the twelve feasts of the Orthodox calendar (No. 177); a beautiful fourteenth-century **Crucifixion** (No. 169) with the elongated columnar figures of an anguished Virgin and St John in brown and dark blue garments silhouetted against a background of the houses of Jerusalem depicted in a narrow band along the lowest section of the panel. On the walls of the second room hang fragments of thirteenth-century church frescoes; in the third room are displayed censers, chalices, sprinklers and charming little diptychs and triptychs. The fourth room is full of church vestments, together with the celebrated **epitaphios** from Salonica, an exquisitely embroidered fourteenth-century fabric depicting the Lamentation over the body of Christ. At once a technical *tour de force* and a masterpiece of one of the minor arts, it is composed in three panels, with the outstretched body dominating the middle one; the figures are woven with gold and silver threads, stencilled with blues and greens against a gold background, and the stitches are so varied that they create an impression of constantly changing colour-tones.

On the way out, it is worth looking at the wing on the right which contains more icons, glittering with golds and reds and blues, of all periods: a St Andrew (No. 1545); an austere seventeenth-century

St John the Baptist (No. 1578) with chestnut-coloured wings out-stretched against a background of gold and green; a seventeenth-century Descent into Hell (No. 1210), in which a scarlet-robed Christ is surrounded by prophets and kings; a fourteenth-century Virgin and Child (No. 1582), known as the **Panayia Glycophilousa** (The Sweetly Kissing Virgin), an outstanding relic brought to Greece by refugees from Asia Minor in 1922, which looks like the archetype of all Duccio's madonnas.

Loukianou Street, the first to the left opposite the Byzantine Museum, mounts steeply up **Mount Lycabettus**, past the British Embassy residence – once the home of Eleutherios Venizelos, Greece's greatest twentieth-century statesman, liberator of Crete and architect of the victorious Balkan Wars. At the end of the street a paved path zigzags up to the summit of the pinnacled crag. The funicular railway starts from the corner of Aristippou and Cleo-menous Streets. At Easter a Resurrection service is held in the white-washed chapel of St George which crowns the peak, and soon after midnight a long candlelight procession winds down the hill like a trail of glow-worms. Immediately below the chapel there is an expensive restaurant. The view embraces the whole of the plain and the Saronic Gulf, with the Megarid and the Isthmus in the west, the distant hump of Acro-Corinth at the gateway of the Peloponnese, and, beyond it, on a very clear day, the peak of Cyllene.

The limits of Hadrian's Athens have now been reached. The National Archaeological Museum – a journey back in time, for one starts with Agamemnon, spans a dozen centuries and finishes before Hadrian was born – lies at the other end of the town. The walk from Syntagma Square leads through the main shopping quarter. First Stadiou Street. On the left is the expensive Athenée Palace Hotel; and Kolokotronis Square, with statues of Tricoupis, the nineteenth-century statesman, and an equestrian Kolokotronis, hero of the War of Independence; then Klauthmonos Square. At the north-west end of the square lies the **Church of Ayioi Theodoroi** (The Holy Theodores), eleventh-century Byzantine, built of stone with brick courses and an exterior Cufic frieze. Cruciform in plan, with a tall drum (a feature of the small Byzantine churches in Athens), its proportions are exquisite.

From Klauthmonos Square Korais Street leads into E. Venizelou Avenue, more commonly known by its original name of **Pane-pistimiou** (University) **Street**, which, together with parallel Stadiou Street, forms the main axis of central Athens. Immediately facing one rises an imposing group of neo-classical buildings. From left to right: the National Library, faced with a Doric portico; the University, with a painted colonnade; in front of it, statues of Korais, champion of linguistic reform, and Gladstone, whose government ceded the Ionian Islands to Greece in 1864; finally, the Academy, with a portico and pediment, and statues of Plato and Socrates seated on either side of the entrance. All three edifices were built of Pentelic marble on plans drawn up by nineteenth-century Bavarian architects. The group of buildings is dominated by two tall fluted columns crowned with statues of Apollo playing his lyre and Athena armed with lance and shield. The traffic jams, the creeping line of blue and yellow buses, the impatient pedestrians fulminating against the red lights – all the stridency of a modern Mediterranean street – seem to enhance the incongruity of this splendid display of neo-classical panache with Lycabettus, its fantastic peak rising out of a sea of apartment blocks.

Between the University and Syntagma Square there are several landmarks among the shops of Panepistimiou Street: the Bank of Greece; the Catholic church of St Denis the Areopagite; the neo-classical mansion (now the Supreme Court of Appeal) in which Heinrich Schliemann, excavator of the sites of Troy and Mycenae, lived with his beautiful Greek wife; and two large cafés, called Flocca and Zonar: the heart of cosmopolitan Athens. Parallel to Panepistimiou Street runs Academias Street, with more shops, offices and a modern little opera house, the *Lyriki Skene*, where in 1942 an as yet unknown plump young girl called Maria Callas, with a haunting deep-throated voice, made her debut in *Tosca*. In the opposite direction from the University, Panepistimiou Street descends towards Omonoia Square, the centre of a network of crowded commercial streets and a station on the railway which links the Piraeus and the northern suburbs with the capital. The National Theatre, whose annual season (November-April) often begins with a play by Shakespeare, is round the corner in Ayiou Constantinou Street.

From Omonoia Square Patission Street, a long straight avenue, penetrates into another world: the residential area of Patissia, a dreary urban extension dating from the inter-war years, now the mecca of the new bourgeoisie. The first large building on the right is the marble Polytechnic School. Beyond it a wispy public garden with some tired-looking palm trees forms a frontage to the **National Archaeological Museum**. Here are some, if not most, of the greatest ancient sculptures in the world, monumental and diminutive, Archaic, Classical and Hellenistic, and a collection of painted vases, ranging from huge amphorae to delicate lecythoi, so vast and varied in execution and detail that imagination boggles at the ingenuity of the ancient potter's skill. Smaller objects, daggers, jewels, figurines, death-masks, shields, ornamental boxes, inscriptions, even toys, fill in the gaps, so that one is able to obtain a picture – hazy and confused perhaps, but still whole and in the round – of man's tastes and occupations, of his changing attitudes to religion, sex, death, recreation and athletics from Mycenaean to Roman times. The existing arrangement of the exhibits is not ideal; the rooms are not always numbered (nor are some of the exhibits); and there is as yet no complete catalogue.

Immediately facing the entrance is the Mycenaean room, filled with gold objects excavated from the royal shaft tombs at Mycenae and other prehistoric sites. The quantity of gold objects is breathtaking; equally astonishing is the degree of sophistication achieved by jewellers, potters and goldsmiths of this prehistoric age.

A pedestal, on which the gold death-mask of an Achaean king of the fifteenth century BC is placed, faces the entrance to the Mycenaean room. No. 384 is a **drinking cup** in the form of a bull's head with gold horns and muzzle and a gold sun composed of strap-shaped petals on the brow. The bull-taming scenes on the **Vaphio gold cups** (Nos. 1758, 1759) illustrate the perfection achieved by representational art in the Mycenaean age. In the large **Warrior Vase** (*c.* 1200 BC) heavily armed hoplites march in single file, while a woman standing at the end of the processional bids them farewell. All the robustness and militaristic vigour of the Mycenaean world, as opposed to the more effete charms of palace life in Minoan Crete, seem to be represented here. Two cases, on either side of the entrance, contain precious objects dating from 1500 to 1200 BC. **No. 3908**, a crude but charming statuette, in the right annexe, where most of the exhibits are idols of Cycladic provenance, represents a male figure seated on a throne, playing an unidentified musical instrument, possibly a harp. In conception and execution, it might be an object from a contemporary exhibition of abstract sculpture. Its date is *c.* 2400–2200 BC.

Back in the entrance hall, one proceeds clockwise into the first of six halls devoted to Archaic sculpture. An air of essential masculinity prevails. The powerful-bodied kouroi (young men, often athletes, later soldiers), huge monoliths hewn out of the crystalline rock, represent a monumental image of man. The most striking of the earlier kouroi is No. 2720 (late seventh-century BC), '**The Colossus of Sunium**'. The cast of his features, set and wooden, is distinctly Egyptian, but no Rameses possesses the muscular tension or freedom of pose enjoyed by this giant Greek youth. No. 3686, of a later date, is more evolved. The formal stylization is there, but the excessive stiffness is less evident; the hair is more elaborately arranged and there is a vestige of a smile on the lips which have grown more full and sensual. But it is No. 3851, the **Anavyssos Kouros** (*c*. 520 BC) a strong-limbed youth, marvellously self-assured, a perfect embodiment of human – though not divine – dignity that dominates the scene. Traces of red paint are visible on the coral-shaped locks that fall down his shoulders from the head-band, and the whole surface of Parian marble has a roseate glow. His smile is more radiant than that of any other kouros. The modelling is opulent, the tension less extreme.

In the next two halls we pass into the fifth century. The Archaic smile, iron self-control and taut muscular strain have gone. Realism has been substituted for symbolism and sculpture has begun to describe and idealize. In the **Eleusinian votive relief** (No. 126), Demeter presents an ear of corn to her protégé, the youth Triptolemus, who is commanded to instruct man in the cultivation of the earth, while Koré crowns him. The **young athlete crowning himself** (No. 3344) is another work of Attic perfection. In spite of the low relief the flesh has the resilient quality of youth; the boy's thoughtful expression reflects the solemnity with which victory on the racetrack fills him.

The bronze **Poseidon** (No. 15161), a work of the mid fifth century, drawn up from the sea-bed off Cape Artemesium, represents the god larger than life-size, his left arm outstretched, his right hand holding a trident (which is missing) about to be hurled. Nothing better expresses the Greek concept of a god as a physically perfect man than this springy, superbly healthy Poseidon.

The next six rooms (the first three separated from the others by a rectangular hall) contain the stelae (marble grave-stones carved in relief so high that the figures appear to be sculptured in the round) which lined the alleys of the Cerameicus and other ancient necropolises. The scenes represented are intimate family affairs. The departing soul, which has a remote other-worldly expression, is often depicted in the act of shaking hands with its next-of-kin. Every visitor has, or will have, his own favourites. Among the ones I never like to miss are **No. 717**, an athlete, the so-called 'Salamis youth', who holds a bird in one hand and raises the other in a farewell gesture, his young escort leaning mournfully against a marble plinth; **No. 3790**, a servant girl holding up a baby in order that the departing mother may cast a last look at it; **No. 869**, the so-called

'Illissus stele', a hooded old man taking leave of his son, a hunter, whose dog and little escort crouch at his feet. Every one of the stelae is a variation on the same disturbing theme of man's preoccupation with death, expressed in terms of the artist's sense of perfection of form. In none is this perfection so apparent as in No. 3472, in which a pensive husband, clad in a beautifully draped chlamys, bids farewell to his seated wife.

At the end of the long rectangular hall the famous **Jockey Boy** (No. 15177), a second-century BC bronze, rides a disproportionately large horse (recently and not wholly successfully restored). In the room on the left are terracotta and bronze figurines. No. 16546, Zeus about to hurl a thunderbolt, is almost a replica in miniature of the Poseidon of Artemesium, but perkier, more stocky.

Turning right (and right again), one enters a succession of halls filled with fourth-century BC and Hellenistic sculptures. The **Ephebe of Anticythera** (No. 13396) may be the famous Paris by Euphranor. The striking if hefty young man with somewhat effeminate features is, in fact, holding some round object (the apple?), now missing, in his right hand; but there is a slickness, even an impersonality, about him, as in many fourth-century BC bronzes, that conjures up a vision of an efficient sculptor's workshop where equally polished models are run off the line in a stream. The young man is entirely physical, but unlike the sixth-century kouroi or the fifth-century riders of the Parthenon frieze, he has no interior life.

Less spectacular, but more compelling, are two bronze heads: one of a **bearded philosopher** (No. 13400), with piercing inlaid eyes and a face of remarkable intellectual power, and No. 14612, a man of the first century BC, known as the **Man from Delos** – a meditative creature with weak undecided mouth and anguishing doubts. Then turn to the **Tegean head** (No. 3602), believed to be by Scopas, representing Hygeia, goddess of health. In the complete harmony of its forms, this oval face crowned by soft wavy hair is the personification of serenity, a wholly evolved expression of idealized feminine beauty in Parian marble.

Returning to the central rectangular hall, one passes into the hall of the bronzes (extreme south-east end). First there is a fully clothed matronly Artemis of heroic stature of the third century BC. The fourth-century BC Athena, crowned by her familiar helmet decorated with griffons and owls, possesses a more poised and relaxed air. But the hall is dominated by the so-called **Piraeus Apollo**, probably of the late sixth century BC and certainly the earliest known large-scale hollow-cast Greek bronze statue (it is well preserved, except for a crack down the left thigh). The detail may be of a coarser texture, less finished – especially in the treatment of the hair – than that of later bronze statues. Yet few others convey such a positive impression of achieved symmetry and balance or possess more of the formal dignity associated with Archaic sculpture. This truly hieratic Apollo is as holy, as 'heroic' an image as anything in Greek art, and he takes his place beside the Poseidon of Artemesium and the Charioteer at Delphi among the Greek sculptor's supreme achievements in bronze. The remaining statues suffer by comparison.

The second floor of the museum (staircase in the long rectangular hall) possesses the enormous collection of **painted vases**. The evolution of Greek painting from the earliest times can be traced in these products of the potter's workshop. The exhibits are displayed chronologically, but the absence of a catalogue is a handicap. First there are the vases of the Geometric period (twelfth to seventh centuries), ornamented with superimposed bands; then the Archaic period (seventh to mid sixth centuries), characterized by Orientalizing features, such as lotus flowers, palmettes, sphinxes and other animals. These are followed by Attic vases of the sixth century. The bands have now disappeared and the decoration consists of mythological scenes (figures in black). Luminous figures in red, which acquire corporality as they move from left to right in attitudes associated with Dionysiac processionals, appear in the fifth and fourth centuries. By the fifth century the drawing has become exquisitely fine and pure: especially in the **white-ground lecythoi**, slender funerary vessels with a black base and neck. The figures are painted in very light shades with an extraordinary economy and sureness of touch. Originally placed on stelae, the lecythoi, with their melancholy depictions of sepulchral scenes in which the figures of the deceased seem to have lost all solid substance as they sit or stand wearily in a kind of occult silence – sometimes they are ferried across one of the rivers of the Underworld – are one of the outstanding contributions made by fifth-century BC Attic vase painters.

At the time of writing, a selection of objects recently excavated on the volcanic island of Santorin, the ancient Thera, is displayed in an annexe to the vase rooms. If not Plato's Atlantis, as some believe, the Thera finds at least cast another chink of light on the enigma of the prehistoric Mediterranean world. Geologists and archaeologists agree that, in c. 1500 BC, Thera was destroyed by an earthquake, followed by an eruption of such unprecedented violence that showers of pumice and ashes are thought to have buried the Minoan townships of the Cretan seaboard over a hundred miles to the south. A similar, if not more terrible fate, befell the island capital itself, where a relatively sophisticated civilization flourished contemporaneously with that of Minoan Crete. Patient archaeological research has brought to light a series of astonishing examples of this civilization. Among the **ceramics** are two vessels painted with swallows and ears of barley, nippled ewers used for fertility rites, spouted jars, and a strange utensil, its bottom perforated like a sieve and decorated with white lilies on a reddish-brown ground (Showcase 1); another nippled ewer, like a stork or pelican with a long upturned spout resembling a beak, and a wine jug painted with crocuses are displayed in Showcase 2.

In the **frescoes** there is abundant evidence of the love of nature that inspired artists of the mid second millenium BC. The best preserved is the Spring fresco, which originally covered three walls of a room. On a white ground red lilies sprout in bunches of three from inky-blue rocks, their yellow stems waving in the breeze while pairs of mating swallows fly overhead. In the Boxing Match fresco two bejewelled boys, clad in loin-cloths, with long Minoan hair-style locks, are depicted in the stylized attitudes of boxers about to engage in contest. The male head of a so-called 'African' with full parted lips, wearing a large round earring of the kind usually associated with Nubians, is thought to suggest the existence of commercial and cultural relations between the Minoan-Mycenaean states and the peoples of North Africa. The upper part of a fresco of a young priestess with pouting vermillion lips and blue hair is remarkable for its state of preservation. But most astonishing of all is the large wall-painting depicting a naval expedition executed in the manner of a frieze, with scenes of warships, a coastline with three cities, and a headland, groups of human figures and lions chasing deer.

Among the furnishings – mementos of a way of life obliterated in a cataclysm of more than Pompeiian proportions – are a three-legged table for keeping food warm with charcoal placed on a lower shelf, and a wooden bed just large enough to accommodate a member of the under-sized prehistoric Mediterranean race.

Before leaving the museum, the visitor should not miss the **Hélène Stathatos collection**, displayed in a hall to the right of the Mycenaean. It consists of jewellery and gold decorative objects ranging from the Bronze Age to the Byzantine period. The refinement of execution of these objects of the minor arts of the Hellenistic period – probably used as household ornaments by wealthy Athenian families – provides a clear picture of the high standard of taste prevailing in ancient Athens in its days of political decline.

Finally, the Epigraphical Department has a large collection of historical inscriptions, including Themistocles's decree of 480 BC ordering the evacuation of Athens and proclaiming naval mobilization before the battle of Salamis. The Numismatic Museum contains cameos as well as Greek, Roman and Byzantine coins. Both are situated on the ground floor of the main museum buildings (entrance from Tositsa Street).

From the Museum, one last pilgrimage, Epirou Street, then Neophitou Street, lead westward to the SEK (State Railways) or Larissa Station, the terminal of all trains from Western Europe and the north. The station has an air of Balkan dereliction, with a dimly lit waiting room filled with depressed-looking soldiery bound for remote frontier posts. A little to the south there is another station – the SPAP (Peloponnese Railways) Station. From there Lenorman Street cuts across a sprawling working-class quarter, called Colonos, dominated by a flat rocky mound: the site of the ancient deme of **Colonus**, birthplace of Sophocles, immortalized in his *Oedipus at Colonus*. A marble slab and loutrophorus on the summit mark the graves of two philhellenic German archaeologists. There is no memorial to the greatest dramatist of antiquity.

It is a barren stony place, with a few shrubby pines and dusty cactuses, the box-like houses of suburban Athens spreading for miles around, the Acropolis just visible in the south. The plangent twang of bouzouki records echoes from a little shack: the local taverna. Sophocles was a very old man when he wrote *Oedipus at Colonus*. It was his last play. A deeply religious work, it is full of nostalgia for his beloved birthplace. The story – probably apocryphal – is that he died at the age of ninety, choked by a grape pip, before he could see it performed.

CHAPTER FOUR

Attica

❧

The Piraeus – Phalerum – Sunium – Thoricus – The Mesogeia – The Sanctuary of Brauronian Artemis – The Monastery of Daou-Pendeli – Marathon – Rhamnus – Mount Pentelicus – The Amphiaraion – Acharnae – Phyle – Mount Hymettus – The Daphni Mosaics – Salamis – The Eleusinian Mysteries – Eleutherae – Aegosthena

Attica is in the form of a triangular peninsula, washed on two sides by the Aegean Sea. Its main features are rock and purity of light. The soil is poor, the substrata so solid and imporous that it is less subject to earthquakes than most of the country. Athens stretches across the southern end of the central plain. The coastline is broken by barren promontories and sandy beaches fringed with Aleppo pines. Ruined sanctuaries and whitewashed chapels shelter in the folds of rocky valleys. Sheets of pale grey asphodel, the immortal flower of Elysium, spread across the hillsides, and dusty paths are lined with aloes and wild fig from whose pliable wood theatre seats, garlands and other ornaments were made in antiquity. The streams are mere trickles, dry in summer. Goats, for centuries the peasants' sole source of wealth, browse among parched shrubs. Everywhere there is the pungent scent of thyme and wild marjoram. In spring the boulders are speckled with round apple-green tufts of spurge, and the hard ground is covered by clusters of grape hyacinths and little mirror orchids with yellow-bordered blue petals. In autumn there are deep pink cyclamen, and golden crocus-like sternbergia whose favourite habitat seems to be around country graveyards. The landscape may not be the most beautiful in Greece, but it is seldom without interest.

An anti-clockwise route is the most practical.[1] First comes **the**

[1] Motor coaches go to the obvious places – to the 'sights'; but their itineraries necessarily omit some of the remoter spots. I throw out the following suggestions for whole or half-day trips by car (the former marked with an X), always starting from and returning to Athens: (1) X The Piraeus-Sunium – Thoricus – Brauron – Mesogeia villages (a long day); (2) Daou-Pendeli – Marathon – Rhamnus; (3) Mount Pentelicus – Kephisia – The Amphiaraion; (4) Acharne – Mount Parnes; (5) Deceleia – Oropus; (6) Acharnae – Phyle; (7) Kaisariani – Mount Hymettus; (8) X Daphni – Eleusis – Eleutherae – Aegosthena (a long day).

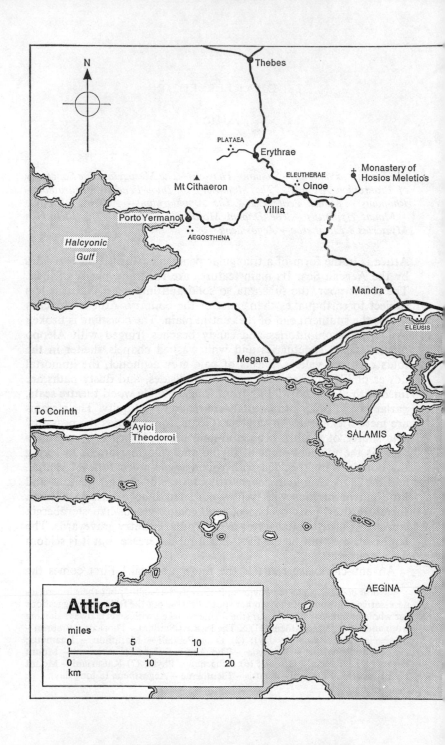

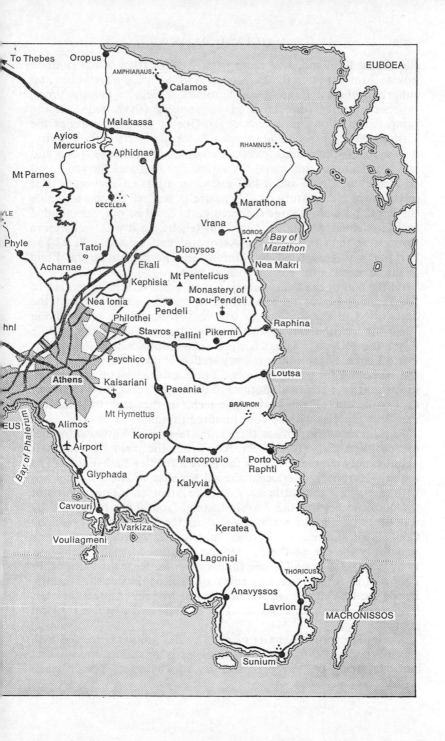

Piraeus: a headland, five miles from Athens, from which nothing now separates it but a flat built-up area of factories, warehouses and suburban houses. It has three harbours, which, in ancient times, possessed nearly four hundred ship-houses (sheds with sloping ramps situated on the water's edge). One of the great ports of the Eastern Mediterranean and the main industrial centre of the country, it is a shabby colourless place: a complex of breweries, soap and spinning factories and metal foundries. For centuries the roadstead of Phalerum, a mile and a half away, served as an anchorage. But in the early fifth century BC, Themistocles realized the use to which the headland and its three sheltered ports could be put. Sea-minded and far-sighted, he built the harbour (encircling it with walls more formidable than those of the Acropolis) and created a fleet. The harbour was completed by Cimon, and Pericles built the Long Walls connecting the capital with its port.

At the end of the Peloponnesian War, when Athens submitted to the superior power of totalitarian Sparta, Lysander ordered the destruction of the Piraeus, as well as the demolition of the Long Walls. It was the end of the imperial dream. During the Middle Ages, the Piraeus was no more than a fishing village, known as Porto Leone. South of the railway station is Karaiskaki Square and the anchorage for island steamers. Twice a day, at noon and sunset, listing and over-crowded, flotillas of these small craft nose their way cautiously out of the harbour, which, in the days of Athenian maritime supremacy, held four hundred triremes.

For dinner at the Piraeus there is the taverna of Vasilaina (corner of Aitolikon and Vitolion Streets). From the main harbour it is about twenty minutes' walk to the more attractive **Pashalimani** (The Pasha's Harbour), a crescent-shaped expanse of calm water lined with cafés, once the battle station of the Athenian triremes. Parts of the corniche beyond the Naval Hospital (south) are buttressed by fragments of ancient walls restored in the fourth century BC by Conon, the distinguished Athenian admiral. North-east (Canaris Square) is the site of the Skeuotheke, a great arsenal which, says Pliny, contained arms for one thousand ships. Near the harbour, in Philhellinon Street, are the ruins of a little Hellenistic theatre. Beside the theatre a small Archaeological Museum possesses stelae, fragments of sculpture excavated at Salamis and two fine classical helmets.

A winding corniche, parts of whose sides are pock-marked with grottoes and niches for votive offerings, leads to the third and smallest harbour facing the sweep of the bay of Phalerum. **Tourcolimano**

(The Turkish Harbour), the ancient Munychia, is composed of tiers of white houses clinging to two sides of a natural amphitheatre, with a bluff, crowned by the Yacht Club, on the third. Yachts, caiques, *trechandiria* (fast-sailing fishing-smacks), motor launches and dinghies crowd the oily waters of the miniature harbour; the waterfront is lined with open-air (indoor in winter) fish restaurants.

From the top of the hill above there are fine views of the three harbours, of Salamis and the Saronic Gulf. All around cheap modern blocks are going up daily; here and there survive traces of neo-classical architectural fantasy: peeling rosette-bordered casements and flaking spiral balustrades – sometimes a ruined Caryatid porch. The corniche winds down to the bay of Phalerum where the sea is now so shallow that ambitious land reclamation schemes are already under way.

Several bouzouki tavernas border the coastal road between the sea and a stretch of low-lying ground, often flooded by the autumn rains. Here orchestras of bouzouki players sit stiffly on a stage and play to an audience of solemn-faced diners. The food is not always good and the uninitiated are inclined to be over-charged. Soon after midnight (this is the best time to go, and order wine and fruit, having dined elsewhere) the local clientèle begins to turn up. As soon as they start to dance the atmosphere undergoes a breath-taking change. All is now zest and enthusiasm, the music louder, the bouzouki soloists more dashing and inventive in their improvizations. The music, Anatolian in origin, brought to mainland Greece by refugees from Asia Minor, is invariably in the minor key. Of all the dances, the *zeibékiko*, a *pas seul* danced by a man, is the one nearest to the Greek heart. Its main features are complicated acrobatics, scything movements of the arms, repeated slapping of the ground and symbolical gestures connected with sex and Mother Earth.

Past the bouzouki tavernas lies the Race Course. At right angles to it, Syngrou Avenue leads back to the centre of Athens. Beyond the Race Course the coastal road passes (left) a spacious cemetery overlooking the sea. The slope is dotted with graves of British Commonwealth soldiers killed in the Greek campaigns of the Second World War and the December 1944 revolution when British troops, a month before greeted as liberators with ringing speeches and garlands of flowers, were reluctantly drawn into a murderous five weeks' battle with Greek Communist-led forces.

After Alimos, the ancient Halimus, birthplace of Thucydides, begin the beaches, uncomfortably overcrowded at the height of summer. At Glyphada there are bungalows, the fashionable Astir *plage*, nightclubs, good (and expensive) fish tavernas; at Cavouri, green with pines, the Cape Zoster of antiquity, smart villas; at **Vouliagmeni**, the most attractive, two pellucid bays fringed with pines and red cliffs. The Astir Hotel is first class, and there is a sheltered anchorage for yachts and a warm fresh-water pool with mineral properties, emerald green in colour, backed by a forbidding slate-grey cliff. On the isthmus between the two bays the foundations of a sixth-century BC temple of Apollo are embedded in the sand, surrounded by flowering shrubs. Varkiza comes next: a strand of fine white sand, with a hinterland of rolling vine country, followed by a fiord-like inlet approached through a tunnel of rock; then more and more seaside villas and Lagonisi, with its beaches, Xenias Hotel and expensive bungalows; and Anavyssos, once the haunt of smugglers, on the edge of a salt marsh, where the great stocky-limbed kouros in the National Museum was discovered in 1936.

After Anavyssos comes **Sunium**, the southernmost promontory of Attica, with its temple, hotels and villas. The hills behind the steep pine-clad coastline are bare except for bushes of sage and juniper, with a new purity of contour that suggests the proximity of the Cyclades – Keos and Kythnos are clearly visible. An isolated rocky headland surrounded by vestiges of an ancient semi-circular wall, is crowned by the fifth-century BC **Temple of Poseidon,** built on massive substructures necessitated by the conical rise of the ground. The work of the architect of the Theseum, its columns – fourteen of the original thirty-eight are standing – are Doric but more slender than usual. They lack entasis and consequently look somewhat fragile, almost like stilts. The flutings, too, are fewer in number, and this also probably detracts from the stolidity associated with the Doric order. The dimensions are almost identical to those of the Theseum, except that here the architect has increased the height of the columns. As nothing remains above the architrave of the south colonnade it is difficult to judge what impression the building as a whole may have made when crowned with metopes, cornice and pediments. In view of the spectacular nature of the position, the increased height should have added something to the upward thrust so singularly lacking in the Theseum. The marble out of which the temple was built came from a local quarry: very white and without the mellow patina that the Pentelic crystalline limestone acquires. Column-bases are disfigured with the scratchings of innumerable signatures, including Byron's. An expanse of sun-dazzled sea extends unbroken towards Crete, and on a clear day Milos, whence came the Venus in the Louvre, is visible.

The inland road back to Athens passes through Lavrion, the ancient Laurium, where zinc and manganese are now mined in place of the silver that contributed so much to the wealth of ancient Athens. By the second century AD the deposits had been exhausted. About one kilometre north of the dusty mining town, surrounded by slag-heaps and melancholy silhouettes of abandoned chimneys, a branch road (right) leads to the extremely ancient **site of Thoricus**, a Cretan naval station during the Minoan age. Later it was fortified by the Athenians and served as an important military outpost guarding the maritime approaches to the silver mines. On the slope of the hill, overlooking the fields and slag-heaps, are the remains of a fourth-century BC **theatre**, unique in shape and construction. Following the declivity of the hillside, the cavea is elliptical instead of semi-circular: a typical example of Greek ingenuity in adapting architectural conventions to the requirements of nature. Originally it must have been little more than a place of entertainment for garrison troops. Beyond the branch to Thoricus, the road climbs a steep pass and descends slowly into the plains of **the Mesogeia**.

The Mesogeia is the loveliest part of Attica, an undulating vine country streaked with olive groves and dotted with sugar-loaf hills, now menaced by increasing suburban and industrial development. In the east, a chain of mountains, snow-capped in winter, infinite in their variety of forms, suggests the approach of another world – the mountains of Euboea. Byzantine shrines are scattered about the countryside. The most interesting are the eleventh-century church of the Taxiarchoi (The Archangels), believed to have been built on the foundations of an Early Christian basilica, Ayios Petros (St Peter's) where the narthex connects with the naos through a triple arcade and fragments of Greek, Roman and Early Christian art have been discovered, and Ayios Georghios (St George's), domeless, in an olive grove, divided into five sections by transverse walls (one of which is in the form of an iconostasis) – all within easy walking distance of the main road.[2] The east coast has a succession of sandy beaches. One of the most attractive is **Porto Raphti**, an almost circular bay, its entrance little more than a mile wide, guarded by a sugar-loaf islet crowned by a Roman statue.[3]

The red soil of the Mesogeia is the richest in Attica, the villages the most prosperous. The present inhabitants are of Albanian

[2] For the Archangels, the traveller should ask the way at the village of Kalyvia ; for St Peter's and St George's at Marcopoulo. Also he should enquire where the keys can be obtained, in case the churches are locked, as they are likely to be.

[3] The branch road to Porto Raphti is at Marcopoulo.

origin, and some still speak a native dialect. Descendants of seventeenth-century immigrants, imported to cultivate a countryside rapidly becoming depopulated under Ottoman maladministration, they continue to dwell in their original settlements, mostly in Attica and the Peloponnese.

At Marcopoulo, famous for its bakeries which produce the best country bread and *paximadia* (crisp rusks flavoured with aniseed) in Attica, there is another fork to the east (besides the one to Porto Raphti). It leads past a Frankish tower of the thirteenth century into a shallow valley, where an orchard of fig trees winds towards a marshland and the sea. The swamp, bordered by low hills, is the **site of ancient Brauron**.

Recent excavations on the marshy site have revealed a large fifth-century BC stoa (parts of the colonnade have been restored) with a marble stylobate. Little remains but foundations of the Doric Temple of Artemis. A series of late **fifth-century BC reliefs** of exquisite perfection, portraying sacrificial rites in honour of the goddess, is displayed in the little museum. Seldom have the billowing folds of women's garments been reproduced with such virtuosity. North-east of the sanctuary, on the side of a hill covered with sheets of pink and white anemones in early spring, are the ruins of an Early Christian basilica and a round building believed to have been a baptistery.

After joining the main road again one reaches **Paeania**, most northerly of Mesogeian villages, where there is a modern church in the main square decorated with frescoes by Kontoglou, a contemporary painter who has turned to Byzantium of the Palaeologue epoch for his models. Every inch of space is covered with frescoes of saints, prophets, warrior angels, Fathers of the Church and all the familiar scenes from the lives of Christ and the Virgin. The great compositions of the Dodecaorton, the Twelve Feasts, with which the traveller will soon become familiar, are as stylized as anything in the great Byzantine churches of Daphni, Hosios Loukas and Mount Athos. The skill in imitation is so remarkable that one is inclined to ignore the technical virtuosity. In terms of pure pastiche, the Paeania church is a *tour de force*.

Close by is the taverna of Kanakis, where in fine weather lunch is served in secluded little boscages surrounded by fields of Paper White Narcissus. In spring the scent of orange blossom and lilac is intoxicating. The food is simple: hors d'oeuvre, souvlakia, honey and nuts; and a resinated rosé wine called *kokkinelli*. Opposite the taverna rises a sugar-loaf hill terraced with vines and kitchen gardens, crowned by stately pines. The immediate background is formed by the screen of Hymettus, steep, bare and desiccated, gashed with rocky ravines: rather cruel-looking. This side of Hymettus has none of the rounded smoothness of the western flanks which often make this extraordinary mountain look like a huge grey elephant sprawling across the plain.

At Stavros, north of Paeania, there is a fork. The west-bound road leads back to Athens, skirting the northern ridge of Hymettus, crowned by the little Byzantine church of St John the Hunter (twelfth-century with seventeeth-century additions), recently divested of its homely whitewash and rather too stylishly restored. A whole circuit of south-east Attica has been completed: a long drive.

*

The eastbound road from Stavros cuts across the northern Mesogeia to the Euboean channel and the field of Marathon. At Pallini a branch road leads to the pine-fringed beach of Loutsa. Beyond Pikermi, where there are good tavernas, the road crosses the gully where a party of distinguished English and Italian travellers, driving back from a visit to the battlefield of Marathon in 1870, was kidnapped by brigands. The incident was not without political repercussions.[4]

At the next fork, one road leads (east) to Raphina, a little port lined with overcrowded fish restaurants whence steamers sail for southern Euboea and Andros, most northerly of the Cyclades; another climbs the foothills of Pentelicus in a north-west direction to the **Monastery of Daou-Pendeli**, concealed in a lonely pine forest. Osbert Lancaster calls the church (twelfth-century, restored in the seventeenth), 'a dotty triumph of provincial art'.[5] It is, indeed, a curiosity, with numerous arches and six domes, the tallest surmounting the narthex which is on a different level from the main hexagonal body of the church. Possibly Armenian and Georgian influences, seldom encountered on the Greek mainland, have been at work here.

The main road continues to dip down towards the sea: a wide bay, the bay of **Marathon**, scimitar-shaped, the waves often flecked with white horses raised by the etesian wind. Opposite rise the mountains of Euboea, denuded of vegetation, without a village in sight. From

[4] Romilly Jenkins, *The Dilessi Murders*, Longman, London, 1961.
[5] Osbert Lancaster, *Classical Landscape with Figures*, John Murray, London, 1947.

the narrow coastal belt, dotted with bungalows, hotels and camping sites, roll the pine-covered hills across which the runner, according to the apocryphal story, raced to Athens to announce the outcome of the battle, only to die of exhaustion on reaching the stadium.

Marathon (490 BC) was the first of the three great battles which the Athenians waged with such extraordinary success against the immensely superior power mobilized by Darius for what historians believe may have been an attempt at a great Asiatic invasion of Europe. The effect of the victory – neither as important nor as decisive as Salamis (for the Persians came again, ten years later, in redoubled strength) – was immense in terms of morale.

The site is now a reclaimed marshland. At the point where the foothills advance closest to the shore, a signposted road leads through groves of mimosa to the Soros, a mound raised over a floor on which archaeologists have found traces of charcoal and human bones: the bones of the Greek dead. Pieces of flint have been identified as fragments of arrowheads used by Persian archers. Although Herodotus says the battle was fought close to a swamp, all round the Soros the land is now arable, with vineyards and lemon groves criss-crossed by ditches filled with clusters of Rose of Sharon narcissus in early spring. On one side rise the wooded spurs of Pentelicus, on the other flow the blue waters of the channel.

Beyond the fork to the Soros – northward extends the lovely crescent-shaped beach of Schina, fringed with tall pines – another side road runs west to the hamlet of **Vrana**. Below a steep hill is another tumulus overgrown with asphodel, believed to be the tomb of the Plataeans, the only Greeks who came to the aid of the hard-pressed Athenians. The Plataean memorial has one advantage over the Soros: one can enter it. Eight graves, each with a skeleton – one of an officer, who is actually named – have been uncovered.

On the outskirts of Vrana there is a large ugly construction roofed with corrugated iron. But it too is worth entering. Two large grave circles, composed of piles of stones, contain skeletons of the under-sized men who inhabited Attica in the Middle Helladic period; also of a horse, equally undersized. At various points of the Marathonian plain vestiges of prehistoric foundations and masonry suggest the extreme antiquity of this part of Attica.

About half a mile before the village of Marathona, a turning-point to the right leads across a bleak stretch of scrubland to the **site of Rhamnus**. The terrace was a sacred enclosure, supported on two sides by a retaining wall composed of blocks of dazzling white marble. The foundations of the larger of two edifices have been identified as those of a temple of Nemesis. Of the Doric order, probably the work of the architect of the Theseum, it contained a colossal statue in Parian marble of the goddess. There is some reason to believe that the temple was never finished, for the three steps of the stylobate have not been smoothed and a number of drums of the columns lying about the site have not been fluted. The small temple, almost contiguous to the larger, may have been an earlier shrine of Nemesis, destroyed by the Persians.

From the sacred enclosure one descends a steep glen to a pebbly shore dominated by a knoll. A massive fourth-century BC stone wall, almost gold in colour, emerges out of the evergreens: the remains of the ancient township of Rhamnus. Within the acropolis, thick with brushwood and tangled vines, there are vestiges of watch-towers, barrack-rooms, cisterns and the cavea of a theatre. Clearly a garrison was stationed at Rhamnus – presumably to guard the entrance to the Euripus. The upland valley, the sacred enclosure, the lonely glen, the crumbling fortifications and deserted shore have an austere quality which few can fail to associate with the goddess of retribution.

Rhamnus is a dead-end. Eastward projects the promontory of Cynosure ('Dog's tail', so-called after its shape), with vestiges of classical walls (best approached from the south shore, beyond the Schina beach). Across the waters of the channel rises Euboea. One may, however, return to Athens by another road (fork at Nea Makri, two kilometres south of the battlefield) which skirts the northern slopes of Pentelicus, scarred by the modern marble quarries, as far as Dionysos and thence, through the pine-woods and villas of Ekali, to Kephisia and Athens.

*

Next comes northern Attica. The residential suburb of Psychico, much favoured by foreign residents, is succeeded by Philothei, equally suburban, less fashionable, named after St Philothei, a well-born nun of the sixteenth century who owned vast lands and founded a convent, a hospital and a workshop for weaving (from the profits of which she bought Greek girls out of Turkish harems). From Philothei one enters the working-class suburb of Nea Ionia, where it is worthwhile looking at the twelfth-century **Omorphi Ecclesia** (The Beautiful Church) which has a pretty octagonal drum. Much of the original structure has been spoilt by later inelegant additions. The interior is decorated with frescoes (possibly fifteenth-

71

or sixteenth-century) which are pleasant rather than remarkable. The windows are attractively adorned with Rhodian plates.

Back on the main road, one turns right at the eighth kilometre from Athens and cuts across a cultivated stretch of the central Attic plain, rapidly becoming urbanized, to **Mount Pentelicus**, a bluish pyramid, scarred with the ravages of two and a half thousand years of marble quarrying. It is one of the loveliest of Attic landmarks, although crowned by an all too conspicuous radar station. At the end of the road, Pendeli, one of the richest monastic establishments in Greece, is surrounded by plane trees. Streams trickle down the sides of the mountain. In summer the whole place, an outpost of suburbia, is a vast holiday camp with tents and wooden shacks on the high ground above the maisonette belt.

The slopes above the monastery are seamed with disused ancient quarries: a lunar landscape of white rubble. Mountain goats browse among tufts of heather and thyme which fail to conceal the centuries-old cicatrices (the modern quarries are situated on the northern slopes of the mountain). One cannot approach Pentelicus without a feeling of veneration. The very stuff of the mountain has furnished the raw material for some of the greatest works of sculpture and architecture in the world. 'Of Pentelic marble' – the label is familiar enough from museum catalogues. Distinguished for its opaque quality, as opposed to the snowy whiteness of Parian, Pentelic marble contains an admixture of iron oxide which accounts for the fact that, when exposed to the inclemencies of the weather, it acquires a warm honey-coloured patina.

A track (at present passable in a car with a high clearance) mounts from the monastery along fragments of ancient paved ways between the abandoned quarries of the classical age to two contiguous thirteenth-century Byzantine chapels at the entrance to a cave: once the refuge of eremitical monks who chose to worship in this remote wind-blown place high above the Attic plain. In the south chapel a fragmentary fresco of the Virgin and Child spreads across the little apse. The Annunciation is visible on the east wall. The painted decoration also includes a representation of Michael Choniates, an unusually enlightened bishop of Athens of the late twelfth century. The decoration of crosses, eagles and inscriptions carved on the rock suggests that the chapel is of a much earlier date than the frescoes: in fact, of the pre-Iconoclastic period. The style of the best preserved frescoes in the north chapel, which was used for burials, is of a cruder, more provincial character.

To the north-west lies **Kephisia**, where some old Athenian families still spend the summer in villas set amid shady gardens where nightingales sing. There are also plenty of hotels and new blocks of flats. At No. 1 Metaxas Street, just off the main square, there is a famous confectioner's where an astonishing variety of exotic home-made jams are sold.

North of Kephisia extends a hilly countryside below the wooded spurs of Parnes, with terraced vineyards and olive trees on the slopes of rolling hills and cornfields and vegetable plots in the cup-shaped valleys. To the right there is a glimpse of an artificial lake, one of the main water supplies of the capital. The dam of Pentelic marble, completed by American engineers in 1926, prevents the streams that flow down the mountainsides in winter from escaping through the numerous gullies into the Marathonian plain.

To the west of the road is the ancient village-stronghold of Aphidnae. Beyond the village the pine-woods become thicker, more luxuriant. There are entrancing views of the Euboean channel which begins to contract as it nears the Euripus. A few kilometres beyond the village of Calamos is the **Sanctuary of Amphiaraus**, the Argive seer. The sanctuary is situated in a secluded gully shaded by pine and plane trees. The wind rustling the pine branches is laden with the scent of resin; the only other sound is that of a stream, its banks overgrown with maidenhair, trickling down to the sea.

The ruins are easily identified; on the right, the substructure of a large altar; behind it, the foundations of a fourth-century BC Doric temple, with the base of the cult statue in the middle of the cella; next, the opening of a spring, sacred to the seer, from which he re-appeared from the Underworld, and into which pilgrims threw coins as a thanksgiving. Numerous bases of statues litter the terrace above the altar. Beyond them a marble bench, supported by marble feet, where consultants sat while waiting to be allocated sleeping quarters, bordered one side of a long and impressive fourth-century BC stoa, which had a façade of forty-one Doric columns and was separated into two galleries by a row of seventeen Ionic columns. Here the consultants slept and were visited with oracular dreams. In a pine-clad declivity behind the stoa is the most charming ruin of all: a miniature **theatre**, famous for its acoustics. The proscenium, judiciously restored, is embellished with eight Doric half columns of grey Hymettus marble. Five seats for high priests, admirably preserved, are ranged in a semi-circle round the orchestra.

*

Another road from Athens to the north runs across the plain to the village of **Acharnae**, where ivy, the symbol of the god Dionysus, grew for the first time. Acharnae is now almost wholly inhabited by descendants of seventeenth-century Albanian settlers, and in the cafés it is not uncommon to hear the older generation chatting in the harsh Albanian dialect of the original seventeenth-century *Skipetars*. Beyond Acharnae the road ascends Mount Parnes, the highest though least beautiful of the mountains enclosing the Attic plain on three sides. About two-thirds of the way up the firs begin. Just below the summit, where there are ski-runs, there is an agglomeration of sanatoria, roadhouses, and chalets among the dark conifers. It is all rather Swiss. There is also a modern luxury hotel with a swimming pool, situated on a ledge commanding a spectacular view of central Attica.

A branch road from Acharnae follows a westerly course to the village of **Phyle**. Beyond the well-tended Convent of the Panayia ton Kleiston (The Virgin of the Closed Defiles), probably of late Byzantine origin, perched above a ravine pock-marked with hermits' caves, the road climbs the lonely defile. In front extend escarpments, contorted rock formations and deep crevices; behind there are views of Athens and the plain against the backcloth of Hymettus. The pass of Phyle (over two thousand feet high) is dominated by an impressive free-standing plateau surrounded by a ring of fourth-century BC fortifications, with remains of ramparts and towers commanding the point of intersection of numerous gorges. These fortifications, which replaced an earlier fortress on a neighbouring peak, guarded the shortest route into Attica from Boeotia. In winter there are treacherous snowdrifts and many mountaineers and shepherds have lost their lives in the unsuspected chasms. The quadrangular masonry of the walls, nearly ten feet thick, is well preserved, particularly on the east side. An interesting feature of the two entrances (south and east) is that they were built in such a way as to expose the attackers' right shoulders, unprotected by shields, to the defenders within. The final ascent to the fortress is precipitous.

Yet another north-bound road leads to the thickly wooded area of **Tatoi** on the foothills of Mount Parnes. The taverna of Leonidas is one of the coolest spots in Attica, crowded on August nights with Athenians escaping from the stifling air and burning pavements of the city. The Greek royal family, when not in exile, have a summer palace here and a graveyard for their kings amid the most luxuriant pines in Attica. Beyond the palace, on the spine of the mountain, there are vestiges (twenty minutes' hard climb from a little taverna surrounded by plane trees) of the famous Spartan stronghold of Deceleia. After the pass of Ayios Mercurios the road descends in loops to Malakassa, where it joins the national highway and whence a branch road leads to Oropus on the Euboean channel. By this time the outline of Euboea, which extends from the promontory of Sunium in the south to the Pagasitic Gulf in the north, has become increasingly familiar. There is a comfortable feeling of omnipresence about Euboea. Its peaks are nearly always visible behind the mainland ranges, and the blue streak of the channel is encountered again and again along the coasts of Attica, Boeotia and Phtiotis. From Oropus a ferry-boat crosses the channel to the opposite shore and site of Eretria.

*

Before leaving Athens, it would be a mistake, I think, not to take one last look at **Hymettus**, smooth and elephantine, most homely and familiar of Attic mountains. The road from the centre of Athens cuts across the working-class suburb of Kaisariani and enters a verdant little valley in a fold of the mountain: an oasis of cypresses, olive and plane trees. At the head of the valley, under a large plane tree, a spring gushes forth: a fertility spring, according to superstition. Above the spring is the **Monastery of Kaisariani**, with its church, dedicated to the Presentation of the Virgin, built in alternating courses of brick and stone. An eleventh-century foundation, for long inhabited by monks who kept beehives, it has undergone considerable restoration. The wall paintings in the narthex, apse and pendentives are of the post-Byzantine period. Around the well-kept court are the monastic bakeries, a mill and bath-house, once also used as an olive-press. Kaisariani is not important in the history of Byzantine church architecture, but its elegant little drum and cupola, its warm red-brick roofs, even its somewhat incongruous seventeenth-century campanile, all shaded by pine branches, compose into a charming spectacle of rusticity on the fringe of the suburban belt.

Above Kaisariani the steep mountainside is covered with stunted shrubs: cistus, juniper and terebinth; and the aromatic sage, thyme and lavender, which, together with the grape hyacinth and purple crocus of spring, feed the famous Hymettus bees. Hymettus honey is now produced throughout Attica; but the Greeks believed that the first bees in the world came from Hymettus. Beyond the monastery the road climbs past the pretty little Byzantine church of Asteri to a bleak summit in the form of a plateau, which commands an immense panoramic view of the whole of Attica and the islands of the Saronic Gulf.

*

The road to the west, to Corinth and the Peloponnese, crosses a ridge of hills from which there is an incomparable view, best seen at sunset, of the city spreading round its rocky hills under the 'violet crown' of Hymettus. The road now joins the Sacred Way to Eleusis, once bordered with tombs of illustrious citizens. Today there are petrol stations and suburban residences. On the left the red tiled dome of the church at **Daphni** and the tops of three cypress trees appear above the high walls with which the Crusaders encircled the monastery; within it they established a Cistercian community in the thirteenth century. Dedicated to the Dormition of the Virgin, Daphni is one of the most important Byzantine monuments in the country. The church is of the middle eleventh century, a golden age in Byzantine art – the age of the Comnene dynasty, which held the stage for a century.

The interior of the church is a classic example of eleventh-century church architecture: a wide squat dome and drum, supported by four pendentives, the four arms of the Greek Cross plan meeting in the central square, with the sanctuary in the apse behind the iconostasis, the narthex in the west front. The mosaics have suffered from neglect and desecration; some have been restored; but enough survive to illustrate the perfection achieved by Byzantine mosaicists of the best period.

On entering the church, one's first impression is of a large expanse of whitewashed walls. There seems to be little of the Byzantine 'gorgeousness' that the Benaki and Byzantine Museums promised. But each of the extant compositions merits careful examination; each is a work of art. The iconographic disposition is not haphazard, but strictly liturgical and symbolical, for the Church is a visual image of Heaven, and the iconographer the servant of the theologian. It therefore helps to have an idea of the iconographic arrangement (mosaics or fresco) of a typical Byzantine church interior in one's mind. The dome is Heaven, where Christ reigns in glory. He is surrounded by guardian Archangels, fully armed. Below them are the apostles or prophets who announced His coming. In the central apse, behind the iconostasis, the Virgin holds the Child. She, too, is flanked by Archangels. We now descend from Heaven to Earth.

76

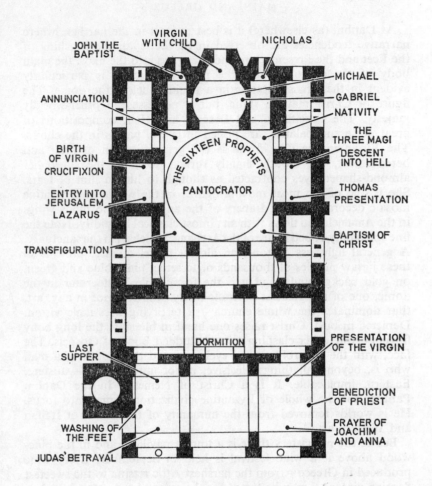

The Church, Daphni

The walls are covered with portraits of saints, monks, ascetics and Fathers of the Church. Above them, on high panels, and in the squinches below the pendentives, unfold the great scenes from the lives of Christ and the Virgin, the *Dodecaorton* (The Twelve Feasts). Particular prominence is given to the Crucifixion and Descent into Hell, which reveal the mystery of the Resurrection. Other scenes from the Gospels are often added, generally in the narthex.

At Daphni (as elsewhere) it is best to start in the narthex, where narrative tendencies are observed in the Betrayal, the Washing of the Feet and the Presentation, and then pass into the naos, the main body of the church, where the new 'humanism' is particularly evident in the **Transfiguration** in a squinch below the dome. The figure of Christ may be static, but it possesses an other-worldly majesty. The **Crucifixion** and **Descent into Hell,** compositions of great poise and balance, are placed in lateral panels in the choirs. The Virgin in the Crucifixion is the personification of grief and bereavement, her mouth slightly turned down at the sides, her almond-shaped eyes contracted as though to hide a film of tears. She is one of the most moving figures in the whole of Byzantine mosaic decoration. The drapery of the angel with enormous wings in the **Annunciation** flows with an almost classical limpidity. Note the fine splendidly-robed figure of the **Archangel Michael** in the sanctuary. A general lightness of tone, an almost pastel quality, prevails in these jigsaw puzzles of thousands of tesserae, pink, blue and green, on gold backgrounds. But it is the formidable **Pantocrator** in the dome, one of the greatest portraits in Byzantine, if not in any, art, that dominates the whole church – a terrifying Messianic vision. Depicted in bust, Christ raises one hand in blessing, the long bony fingers of the other clasping a jewel-studded Book of Gospels. The face, with the superbly arched eyebrows and the mouth of a man who is, beyond all things, decisive, if not unforgiving, is austere, Eastern, implacable. It is a Christ of Nemesis. In the Daphni Pantocrator the whole of Byzantine civilization comes into focus. He is worlds removed from the humanity of the Christ of Italian and Western art.

Beside the monastery there is a tourist pavilion, and in the pine-wood above it a wine festival is held in September. Every wine produced in Greece – from the harshest Attic retsina to the sweetest Samian vintage – may be tasted for the price of the entrance ticket. The red brick dome and roofs, the stone courses and arched windows of the floodlit church provide an impressive background.

Beyond Daphni the road descends towards the landlocked bay of Eleusis. On the right are the foundations of a temple of Aphrodite and a piece of rock hollowed out into niches for votive offerings. Fragments of white marble chiselled in the form of doves, the goddess's sacred birds, were found at the foot of the rocky hillside. The crescent-shaped bay is sealed off from the open sea by the pine-clad island of Salamis. The battle, culminating point of the second Persian invasion (480 BC) was fought in the narrow strait between the eastern tip of the island and the mainland, where Mount Aegaleos tapers off into the sea.

We continue on the **Sacred Way** taken by Athenian pilgrims bound for the celebration of the Eleusinian Mysteries, once lined with statues, shrines and votive monuments, now a traffic-congested highway running across the Thriasian plain, bordered by factories, foundries and refineries. To the right, a few yards from the sea, is a natural reservoir of salt springs, the Rheiti, fringed with reeds, the haunt of wild fowl since time immemorial: an incongruous site in this agglomeration of industrial installations. Just before we enter the shabby little town of **Eleusis**, birthplace of Aeschylus, a road to the left leads to the ruins of the sanctuary: least inspiring of ancient Greek sites, yet second only to Delphi in religious significance. The ground is flat and featureless; Parnes in the background does not present its most impressive aspect; and smoke trails from factory chimneys in the vicinity.

Below the rocky ledge, close to the sea, extend the ruins of the principal seat of worship of Demeter and Koré, in whose honour the Eleusinia, most sacred of Greek mysteries, were celebrated every September and attended by thousands of pilgrims from all over Greece. The holy edifices, whose jumbled foundations we now see, were built, rebuilt and refashioned by the Peisistratae, by Cimon and Pericles (after the Persians had destroyed the sanctuary), by Lycurgus in the fourth century BC and by the Antonine emperors in the second century AD. Literally nothing remains standing, for Alaric and his Goths seem to have gone about their usual work of destruction with unprecedented thoroughness. Moreover, the successive reconstructions and restorations on different levels over a period of eight hundred years make it very difficult to identify the foundations.

The sanctuary, hemmed in by a nightmare complex of industrialization, lies between the low ridge of an acropolis and the sea. Left of the Great Propylaea, an Antonine reconstruction, is the opening of a well, once the fountain around which the Eleusinian women performed ritual dances. Next comes the Lesser Propylaea, also a Roman construction, which had an astonishingly opulent decoration. On the cliff to the right two caves are preceded by a little walled-in terrace. This is part of the Sanctuary of Hades. The caves represent the entrance to the Underworld and the exit from which Koré emerged every spring to bring light and fertility into the world again. The outline of the god's temple is discernible in front of the larger cave. Returning to the Sacred Way, one reaches the platform of the Telesterion, where the Mysteries were performed. Bases of columns

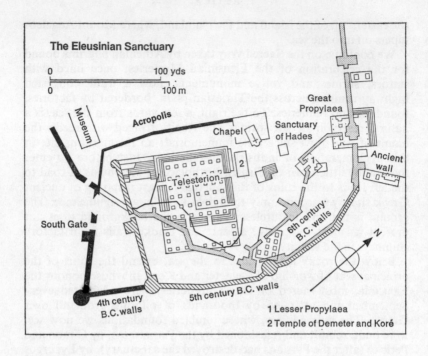

The Eleusinian Sanctuary

0   100 yds
0   100 m

Museum

Acropolis

Chapel

Great Propylaea

Sanctuary of Hades

Ancient wall

2

Telesterion

1

South Gate

6th century B.C. walls

N

4th century B.C. walls

5th century B.C. walls

1 Lesser Propylaea
2 Temple of Demeter and Koré

are easily identified. The fifth-century BC interior consisted of six rows of seven columns, believed to have been Ionic, surrounded by tiers (those on the west side are well preserved), on which as many as three thousand people could stand. It had an upper storey, where the *hiera*, the holy objects connected with the ceremony of initiation, were kept, crowned by a wooden roof. The ruins of this extraordinary building are now no more than a mass of shattered blocks of masonry from successive restorations. Were the site less constricted by urban development and had the landscape one bit of the grandeur of Delphi or serenity of Olympia, it might be easier to visualize the almost barbaric spectacle and to speculate on the religious exaltation experienced by the initiates, or *mystae*, as they proceeded in torchlight procession to the Hall of the Mysteries.

North of Eleusis the road winds across a rugged countryside. In March the *Anemone blanda*, with its sky-blue strap-shaped petals, grows profusely in the scrubland of the valleys below Mount

Cithaeron, an austere, even grim-looking mountain. Its contours are not elegant, but the steep slate-grey slopes, sprinkled with silver firs, and the lonely brushwood country at their foot, were reputed to be the haunt of Pan, god of shepherds. Here lions, bears and wild boar had their lairs, and stags roamed the forests. As one descends into a deep sunken valley, the remains of a stone tower rise immediately on the right. It was probably part of a system of ancient watch-towers along the frontier between Attica and Boeotia. At the village of Oinoe a side road ascends to the **Monastery of Hosios Meletios**, a Byzantine foundation, considerably restored, situated on a little mountain ledge among plane and poplar trees.

Beyond Oinoe the entrance to a narrow pass is screened by a steep eminence crowned by ruined fourth-century BC ramparts: the fortress of **Eleutherae**, which guarded Attica and the Megarid from invasion from the north. It failed to do so in 1941, when British Commonwealth forces retreated through the defile after a vain attempt to hold up the German panzers. The fortifications are well preserved, particularly the north wall (eight feet thick and built in regular courses), dotted with square towers provided with two gates in the lower storey and loopholes in the upper. The best view of the enceinte is the backward one, from the north, as one climbs the defile which ends in a bleak plateau, whence the road descends in hairpin bends into the Boeotian plain.

Just before Eleutherae a road to the left climbs to the mountain village of Villia and descends in a series of wide loops between pine forests to the little harbour of Porto Yermano on an inlet of the Halcyonic Gulf. There are enchanting views of the calm expanse of water, with the Boeotian mountains forming a screen to the north, marred only by a far too conspicuously sited modern hotel. At the end of the descent, the remains of the fortified **acropolis of Aegosthena** are scattered among the pine-woods. To the left of the road rise admirably preserved fourth-century BC ramparts in the form of a rectangle and the ruins of fifteen square towers, larger than those at Eleutherae, complete with gates, posterns and windows. The most impressive section, with four large square admirably preserved towers crowning the east wall, is on the landward side, although the fortress must originally have been built as a defensive post against invaders from the sea. Many of the towers, especially those erected towards the end of the fifth century BC, were designed to carry a wooden catapult from which stones were hurled and arrows slung at attacking forces. Two abandoned late Byzantine chapels add an incongruous note to the ancient military site. On lower ground are the foundations of an Early Christian basilica. Along the placid pebbly shore there are some modest tavernas. In summer the fields and olive groves, littered with blocks of ancient masonry, are crowded with campers, the beach infested with horseflies. The sun shimmers on the pellucid sea and a haze screens the wooded spurs of Helicon that ascend abruptly from a barren deserted coastline.

CHAPTER FIVE

Boeotia

Thebes – Plataea – Leuctra – The Sanctuary of the Cabeiroi – Thespiae – Ascra – Thisbe – Domvraina – Haliartus – The Copaic Basin – The Sanctuary of Apollo at Ptoion – The Lakes – The Monastery of Sagmata – Gla – Orchomenus – Skripou: The Church of the Dormition – Levadeia – Chaeroneia – Daulis

Back in Athens, the traveller looks to the north-west: towards Delphi. The approach, through what are virtually the southern confines of central Greece, is very rewarding. The landscape, particularly in the mountains, is superb; there are fragmentary ancient sites and Byzantine churches and the name of one famous battlefield succeeds another.

Beginning at Athens, road and rail follow a roughly parallel course along the east coast. After making a wide loop round a wooded spur of Parnes, they descend into the first and least interesting of the Boeotian plains, watered by the Asopus, the only local stream to flow straight into the sea without first forcing a way through an underground channel. A round trip is not practicable in Boeotia, which is virtually a large hollow isthmus enclosed between coastal ranges. Most travellers cross it in a day, with deviations to the more important sites – Plataea, Orchomenus, Ptoion. Two, or even three, days would allow time for a more roundabout and extensive itinerary.[1]

Beyond the watershed between Attica and Boeotia the landscape becomes more continental, less Mediterranean. The vegetation is no longer confined to the olive, cypress and oleander. Maize, cotton and tobacco take over. Flat agricultural plains succeed one another, flanked by barren foothills – austere grey on a cloudy day, fierce ochre at the height of summer – with hazy spruce-covered mountains in the distance, Parnassus towering above them all. The marshes, now drained and forming large tracts of wheat fields, once abounded

---

[1] In order to explore Boeotia thoroughly one can stay at Thebes, or Levadeia, where there is only a limited choice of hotels. At Delphi, on the other hand, there is every kind of accommodation, from luxury hotels to rooms in village houses. The distance between Delphi and Levadeia is only fifty kilometres.

in wild fowl. Lying on the main invasion route from the north, Boeotia has witnessed the passage of many conquerors – Dorian, Persian, Macedonian, Roman, Frankish, Norman, Spanish, Turkish and German. Today the inhabitants are mainly devoted to agriculture.

The road runs westward across the Asopian plain. There are tantalizing glimpses of the vivid blue streak of the Euripus, now approaching its narrowest point. Between the road and the sea lies the field of Delium, where the Athenians, after committing the sacrilege of converting a temple of Apollo, sacred to the Boeotians, into a fort, suffered their first major defeat in the Peloponnesian War in 424 BC.

Facing the channel is the bay of Aulis, where Agamemnon's fleet was becalmed and Iphigenia sacrificed. The ruins of the Temple of Artemis are too negligible to justify a visit. Tanagra, once famous for its painted terracotta figurines, has little to offer but a military airport. Beyond the airport there is a fork. The highway continues westward. Another road turns east: to the Euripus and Euboea. The third goes to **Thebes**, and 'no city in Greece', we read in the Dictionary of Greek and Roman Geography, 'possessed such continued celebrity'. The celebrity is not always to its credit.

Theban mythology is among the richest in Greece; Theban history, if less distinguished, is full of incident. Recalling its famous past, travellers are drawn to the City of the Seven Gates, only to find themselves in a dreary provincial town with little to recommend it except a good lightly resinated wine (rosé), scattered vestiges of ancient ruins, a fine museum and some dilapidated Turkish houses spreading across a chain of low hills overlooking the Cadmeian plain. But it is as difficult to avoid Thebes geographically as it is to ignore the fascination of its history and renown. Most of the main streets are evocatively named after the great figures of Theban mythology and history.

The centre of the town is on the highest hill, site of the ancient acropolis, the Cadmeia. Cadmus came from Phoenicia; he founded Thebes, colonized Boeotia and introduced letters into Greece. The record of Thebes during the Persian Wars, when its army joined that of Mardonius in fighting the united Greeks, was beyond contempt. The slow-witted Thebans, obsessively jealous of the more lively Athenians, proved to be even more vindictive than the Spartans. After the Peloponnesian War, in which they sided with Sparta, they tried to persuade Lysander to raze Athens to the ground and sell the population into slavery. The Spartan leader, to his credit, refused.

In the second half of the fourth century BC, under the statesmanlike leadership of Epaminondas and Pelopidas, oligarchical Thebes appears in a more sympathetic light. But with the death of Epaminondas decline set in. After the Macedonian conquest, a revolt, instigated by the Athenian Demosthenes, called down upon Thebes the fury of Alexander the Great. The future world-conqueror ordered his scarlet-coated soldiers not only to level the city to the ground, but also to slay six thousand Thebans and take thirty thousand prisoners.

After Alexander's sack, the city sank into oblivion until the Middle Ages, when Benjamin of Tudela found it large and prosperous, full of Jewish silk-workers, whose lavish creations adorned Byzantine emperors and their consorts. The silk trade even survived the twelfth-century invasion of the Normans, who carried off numbers of Theban weavers to Palermo. The trade is dead now, but mulberry trees still grow around the town. With the arrival of the Frankish barons, Estives, as it was then called, became the seat of the de la Roches, who styled themselves 'Dukes of the Athenians and Thebans'. The plight of thirteenth-century Athens must indeed have been tragic for them to choose this dreary, humid place instead of the Attic city of light for their official residence.

Of the ancient walls there are only some rudimentary fragments. Alexander's sack was very thorough. East and west the town was bounded, as the centre of the modern one still is, by the streams of Dirce and Ismene. Theban monuments, which gave the city its forbidding aspect, have never been described as beautiful.

The archaeological enthusiast should start at the south-eastern end of Amphion Street (where it meets Polyneices Street), opposite a cypress-clad hill. Here a few courses of massive primitively wrought limestone blocks form two round bases on either side of the street: the foundations of two flanking towers of the prehistoric Electran Gate, named after the sister of Cadmus. Crossing the centre of the town in a roughly south-north direction, one sees the foundations of what are believed to be a section of the palace archives and a palace bathroom (corner of Epaminondas and Gheorghiou Streets). Turning right (east) into Antigone Street, one encounters some impressive ancient masonry on superimposed levels. The rubble of a palace of the Mycenaean period in which Laius, Oedipus and Creon probably held court lies nearby (left) in Pindar Street. Tablets found here are inscribed with Linear B dated to the thirteenth century BC.

At this point it is best to continue in a northerly direction along Pindar Street to the site of one of the seven gates, from which the great ancient road led to the north. The site of the Homoloid Gate is now occupied by the museum. The courtyard, filled with inscriptions of a late date, severed limbs of statues and Moslem tombstones, formed part of the enceinte of the Frankish castle overlooking the plain. To the right (east) stands the fine squat tower, called Santameri (corruption of St Omer), the only surviving section of the thirteenth-century fortress built by St Omer, part-lord of Thebes, an arrogant Flemish baron who spent a great part of his generous dowry in raising fortifications throughout his scattered domains in the Peloponnese and mainland Greece.

Even the most hurried traveller in Boeotia, unlikely to be impressed by the prehistoric rubble of ancient Thebes, should not, in my opinion, miss the museum, which is small and well arranged. From the entrance hall you pass into the Tanagra room in which are displayed the larnaces, cinerary urns or coffins of baked clay dated to c. 1400–1200 BC, excavated at nearby Tanagra. Unique in Greece, these singular and beautiful urns, rectangular in shape and of varying sizes, stand on four squat legs. They contained, as some still do, the bones of distinguished Tanagran citizens who died over three thousand years ago. Stylized processionals of priests and animals with human faces are painted in black and orange – sometimes red – on the exterior surfaces. In a showcase on the left are prehistoric funerary gifts in the form of miniature pieces of furniture of exquisite workmanship. Once more we have an example of the veneration in which death was held by the Greeks of all periods. These enchanting little terracottas do not, admittedly, possess the lavish quality of the Mycenaean grave gifts wrought in gold and precious stones. But the motive, the underlying idea, remains the same: the dead are immortalized in the minds of the living by the quality of the works of art beside which they rest in eternity.

The two halls to the left contain prehistoric pottery, fourteenth-century BC cylinder seals of lapis lazuli, whose Anatolian origin suggests the existence of trade relations between Thebes and Phoenicia, and ceramics of the finest quality of the Geometric, Archaic and classical periods. The unusual stelae of black stone, carved with the finest of incisions, depicting Boeotian warriors in combat at the battle of Delium, are best seen from an oblique angle. Among the exhibits of the sixth and fifth centuries BC displayed in the last hall is a male torso in the finest fifth-century BC sculptural tradition (unfortunately the statue is headless, armless and legless). The showpiece is the sixth-century BC Ptoion Kouros which came from the Sanctuary of Apollo at Ptoion (see p. 92). As usual, geometrically conceived – in terms of idealized shape – the youth's smile is no less enigmatic, his posture no less heroic than those of the Attic kouroi; only the stylized coral-shaped locks which fall down the back of the neck are much less finely modelled.

The normal axis of travel in Boeotia is east-west or vice-versa, with deviations into the foothills of the ranges flanking the plains. The first is to the south, along the old Athens-Thebes road through undulating fields, home of the *Tulipa boeotica*, a lovely bell-shaped tulip with a black centre in the form of a star. The village of Tachi, where some classical masonry is built into the springs, may well be the site of Potniae, a shrine sacred to Dionysius.

At the village of Erythrae, a third of the way up the ascent of Cithaeron, a turning to the right (west) leads to the **site of Plataea**. Boeotia has always been the scene of violent armed clashes. None does more credit to Greek arms than the third and decisive battle in the Persian Wars.

A circuit of walls, about two and a half miles in circumference, can be traced round the cornfields sloping down towards the stream of the Asopus. There are no vestiges of the ancient township. On a terrace near the north-west wall there are foundations of a temple, possibly of Hera. There is no sign of the sanctuary of Demeter around which there was fierce fighting, but on whose holy ground no Persian corpse was found. Herodotus suggests that the goddess, remembering the barbarians' desecration of her most sacred shrine at Eleusis, prevented them from setting foot in her Boeotian temple.

Plataea has a noble record of fidelity to the Athenian alliance, dating from the sixth century BC. At Marathon it was the only state to send a contingent to assist the hard-pressed Athenians. During the Peloponnesian War the Plataeans never wavered and withstood a famous siege for two years. When the depleted garrison was forced to surrender, the Thebans did not leave a single Plataean alive and they destroyed all the buildings. Plataea thus paid heavily for her loyalty to Athens. Philip of Macedon restored the city and Alexander the Great built the ramparts, which are now very ruined (best preserved on the west side); but one can walk for quite long stretches along a line of low walls overlooking the level meadows where so many Persian men, hopes and ambitions perished.

The next battlefield on the westward route represents a historical milestone of a very different character. Of the victory of Thebes over Sparta in 371 BC at Leuctra, Pausanias says it was 'the most famous ever won by Greeks over Greeks'. It is the familiar story of Greek tearing Greek to pieces.

Just before one re-enters Thebes from Plataea, a dirt road to the left (south-west) crosses a stretch of treeless but well-watered country to the hamlet of **Leuctra** on a low hill overlooking the battlefield. The site is marked by a modern plinth adorned with some ancient marble slabs. The battle was fought north of a tumulus easily identified near the commemorative plinth. The tumulus we now see is probably the Spartan sepulchre. There is little else. I asked a peasant if there were any *archaia* (ancient things) nearby. He led me across a field, scrabbled among the corn and pointed to a stone slab, which might have formed part of a stele and was inscribed with the name *MYPON*, projecting out of the muddy soil. The inscription could not have referred to the sculptor, who, although a native of neighbouring Eleutherae, died about a hundred years before the battle. The slab, the man said, was recently ploughed up by a tractor.

Following the main Thebes-Levadeia road, we soon reach a track (signposted) which leads southwards to the so-called **Sanctuary of the Cabeiroi** (reputedly the sons of Hephaestus) lying in a fold of rolling green hills criss-crossed with hedgerow-bordered paths. The Cabeiria were mysteries or fertility rites, possibly orgies, celebrated chiefly in Samothrace and Lemnos, but also in Boeotia. The ruins are fairly extensive but infinitely perplexing, covering a considerable chronological span. The apparent east end of a temple of different periods now forms the skene of a theatre (parts of which are well preserved), remarkable for the shallow arc of the semi-circle, and focused on an altar: the scene no doubt of some orgiastic rite. On the outskirts of the sanctuary an open square is formed by what were once three chambers. Masonry as late as that of the Roman period is evident. The absence of historical data and the confusion arising from the superimposition of successive levels of foundations, all of different periods, does little, however, to detract from the pastoral quality of the scene, with wild flowers growing in the shade of luxuriant shrubs and sheep browsing on the hillsides which enclose the curiously concave site.

Returning to the main road, one can make another southward deviation, longer and more rewarding, across an extension of the same hilly region to **Thespiae**, which, with Plataea, shares the distinction of being one of the two Boeotian cities that remained unrelentingly hostile to Thebes.[2]

Thespiae, like its pretty twin village Leondari, from which it is

[2] A rough country road joins Leuctra with Thespiae. The traveller need not return to Thebes if he wishes to visit both sites.

separated by a shallow ravine, spreads across a shelf overlooking the plain to the south, where the barely identifiable ruins of the ancient site (notably the foundations of a temple of the Muses) are scattered. The finds from the so far perfunctory excavations are at present stacked in a village house called *to mouseio* (the museum) into which it is not always easy to gain admission. The god worshipped here was Eros, a primeval deity, symbolizing sexual vigour, armed with flaming torches which he aimed at gods and mortals alike. It is not until Hellenistic times that Eros is sentimentalized by poets and artists, becomes the son of Aphrodite and finally the plump little Cupid rendered so popular by Roman artists. The original Greek Eros was a more virile deity. A festival in his honour, known as the *Erotidia*, was held every four years, and the cult statue consisted of an erect monolith to which every bride offered a tress of her hair representing her youth and a girdle symbolizing her virginity.

Near here too flowed the reed-fringed stream into which the youth Narcissus gazed so long and intently that he fell in love with his own image. Pausanias finds the story 'absolutely stupid': Sir George Wheler, travelling in Thespian territory in the seventeenth century, was nevertheless pleased to find the narcissus growing everywhere in profusion.

From Thespiae a dirt road to the west climbs the rocky cone-shaped foothills of Mount Helicon. You pass an eminence: possibly the natural stronghold to which the Thebans fled when their country was overrun by northern tribes at about the time of the Trojan War. On it stand the ruins of a medieval watch-tower like a skeleton in stone, commanding a view of a desolate pyramidal peak crowned by a ruined Hellenic tower: all that remains of **Ascra**, birthplace of Hesiod, founder of the first school of poetry on the Greek mainland after Homer. Today it seems a remote and grandiose place, from which there is a wide prospect of the Valley of the Muses, now, alas, deforested. To visit the valley one must leave the car and walk for about an hour in order to scrabble amid the stony ground for traces of an altar and an unexcavated cavea of a third-century BC theatre. Of the supposedly idyllic beauty of the haunt of the Muses little remains but its evocative associations, some almond trees and the fir-covered heights of Helicon above.

Back in Thespiae, one can make an agreeable detour to **Thisbe** and the southern coast of Boeotia. The road runs west through a narrow plain, between the foothills of Helicon and Cithaeron. It is pastoral country and in late spring the road is bordered by banks of pale bluish-mauve *Iris xiphium* (Spanish Iris). To the south, on a clear day, one can see the peaks of Peloponnesian mountains: a spectacular backcloth to the foreground of barren Boeotian coastal hills.

The red-roofed village of Thisbe lies at the foot of an outcrop of rock: a sleepy undefiled place, without a sign of a tourist, motor coach or plastic chair. Only a taverna, where I have had the best country bread in Greece. A plateau, east of the village, seemingly ringed round by vicious stinging-nettles, is littered with remains of extensive walls and squat square towers dated to the period of Alexander the Great, when the place must have served as a military outpost against invaders from the Corinthian Gulf. The circuit, which follows the crests of hills on different levels, is about a mile in circumference. The masonry is regular and polygonal and the joining of the blocks reveals fine workmanship. Foundations of walls shelve down in terraces to a fertile bowl-like valley, where flights of pigeons wheel overhead in the sky. At the foot of the plateau the rock is honeycombed with caves, thought to have served as ancient sepulchres.

Southward the road cuts across the hollow basin, following the course of an ancient causeway built in order to prevent the whole plain from being flooded when the autumn rains set in. It must have been a curious sight: one half a lake or at least a marsh; the other cultivated land. A bleak mountain stretch follows. One descends in hairpin bends to the rugged bay of **Domvraina**, broken with numerous coves and minute fiords. The road ends at the inlet of Ayios Ioannis. It is barely a hamlet: a ramshackle house or two, a brightly painted caique rocking at its moorings, some peasants turning over the soil on ledges planted with fennel, artichokes and onions. Bare headlands stretch eastward. The great bay, with its islets and numerous anchorages, has always been noted for violent squalls, as the winds funnel down the stony valleys from the mountain-tops of Helicon and Cithaeron.

At Tipha, which forms the east arm of the bay and is at present inaccessible by road (it can only be approached by caique or yacht), there are substantial fifth-century BC walls, towers with polygonal masonry, doorways with pediments, as well as visible underwater masonry. Whether a squall is blowing or the sea is blue and pellucid, the bay of Domvraina remains, in its remoteness and intricate configuration, one of the most impressive land-seascapes on the southern mainland.

Beyond the southward fork to Thespiae and Thisbe the main Thebes-Levadeia road leaves the melancholy plain. The ground rises, then dips down into the basin of the former Lake Copais: a shimmering expanse of cotton fields, surrounded by cliffs and mountains which, in early antiquity, rose sheer from the shallow water's edge. Once the haunt of cranes, now of migratory storks, the lake or swamp – today the main cotton-growing region of Greece – was reclaimed by French and British engineers at the end of the nineteenth century. Strabo's assertion that the whole basin had in fact been drained by the inhabitants of ancient Orchomenus is borne out by the discovery of a primitive but intricate system of dykes encircling the entire Copaic 'lake', whereby the various streams were channelled by an ingenious network of canals into *katavothra* which disgorged their waters into the sea. Archaeologists have located long low mounds, the remains of ancient dykes, stretching across considerable tracts of the plain, either in unbroken lines or with gaps at intervals. Here, as indeed throughout most of Boeotia, one is constantly aware of geology: of subterranean channels coursing through limestone ranges; of curious hump-shaped mounds of slate-grey rock emerging out of a mirage of sun-drenched arable land; of lakes descending on different levels like stepping stones towards the Euboean channel.

At the south-east end of the basin, beyond Mount Sphingion, a grim pyramidal rock, lies Homer's 'grassy Haliartus', still surrounded by 'well-watered meadows'.

At **Haliartus** the traveller has the choice of two routes. One leads direct to Levadeia, skirting the base of Helicon, whose constantly changing outlines dominate much of the Boeotian landscape. Neither as grand as Taygetus nor as beautiful as Parnassus – and not nearly as high as either – it is often well-wooded, rugged but never forbidding.

If one opts for this route, it would be a mistake, I think, to omit visiting the site of yet another ancient battlefield and penetrating a more pastoral area of the Helicon country. West of Haliartus the range recedes in the form of a wide arc of flat cultivated land. A side road runs south through cornfields and olive groves between hedgerows of broom and wild pear. To the right a ruined Catalan tower crowns an isolated hill, site of ancient **Coroneia**, where the Panboeotia, a great religious festival 'common to all the Boeotians', was held in the temple of Athena Itonica. The temple stood in the plain in front of the hill.

It was on the level ground around the ancient town that the Boeotians inflicted a major defeat on the Athenians under the impetuous Tolmides in 447 BC. The victory had such a tonic effect on the morale of the Boeotians that they were able to throw the Athenians out of the whole of their country. The ruins of Coroneia are virtually obliterated. Below the Catalan tower I have in vain tried to identify the theatre, temple foundations and walls – all of considerably later periods than the fifth century BC – said to lie below and around the Catalan tower. Leaving the acropolis hill to the left, the road climbs the mountainside, forming the east arm of a great bite into the Helicon range whose peaks compose into a perfectly-shaped crescent around the olive groves and cotton fields. The road ends at the modern village of Coroneia, perched high above the fruitful plain. Hollyhocks grow in profusion in back gardens and the scarlet of geraniums is splayed across the whitewashed walls of village houses.

The second route, of greater interest, follows a rough arc round the plain, reaching Levadeia via Ptoion, Gla and Orchomenus. From Haliartus a road cuts across the cotton fields to the north and reaches the main Athens-Salonica highway below a line of hills, whose rocky sides rise abruptly from the reclaimed swamp.

A miniature canyon cuts through the wall of cliff, opening out into a rugged little valley entirely enclosed by beige-coloured hills. Above the village of Acraephnion, where the Thebans took refuge after the destruction of their city by Alexander the Great, a track climbs the western slope of Mount Ptoion, which has a triple peak and was named after a son of Apollo. It is not easy to locate the ruins. A whitewashed chapel, shaded by a large holm-oak, is the landmark to look for. Behind it rise the terraces of the **Sanctuary of Apollo**, an oracular seat. On the first terrace are the base of a tholos building and a rectangular cistern where consultants purified themselves before ascending to the second terrace, across which lie traces of stoas buttressed by a few courses of the retaining wall, and finally to the third, marked by foundations of a Doric temple of Apollo. Above the temple a spring called Perdiko Vrysi (The Partridge Spring) that gushes out of the rock has been identified as the site of the oracle. The waters of the spring connect with the cistern below. Climbing from one terrace to another, one tends to sink ankle-deep into a soft mossy deposit seamed with trickles of water. It is as though the whole mountain, through which some of the main katavothra carve their way to the sea, had a subsoil of underground rivulets. From a ledge slightly south-east of the ruins there is a fine view of the winding inlets of Lake Hylice below.

The lake itself, main water supply of Athens, is skirted by the Athens-Salonica highway. Obviously once a crater, on a lower level than the Copaic basin, its configuration is of fascinating complexity – a series of figures of eight of different dimensions. Barren rocky banks rise from a succession of fiords of crystal-clear water. At times the conical summits and contorted volcanic shapes overlooking the winding shore give the impression of a lunar landscape; at others of Japanese prints. A katavothron connects Hylice with the smaller lake of Paralimni, which lies in an even deeper depression, and can be approached by a track off the highway which passes through the village of Mourikion and descends into a narrow shut-in basin, where the shallow water lies motionless in an elliptical expanse against a screen of slate-grey cliff. It is an astonishing sight: unexpected, desolate, bizarre.

On the way back from Paralimni one passes through the village of Hypaton. From here a rough dirt road climbs the steep side of Mount Hypatos (Mount Highest) in a series of terrifying hairpin bends. On the higher slopes the track winds through tall *Arbutus andrachne* trees, among whose leathery grey-green leaves grow clusters of creamy-white flowers, and whose wood was used for making looms in antiquity. The summit, a wind-blown plateau, carpeted in spring with the grape hyacinth and yellow iris, is crowned by the buildings of the **Monastery of Sagmata**.[3] Ruined chapels below the summit suggest the monastery's one-time importance. To them probably flocked the inhabitants of the plain, fleeing from the endless succession of invading armies.

The church of the Transfiguration, built on the site of the hermitage of a holy man, is a twelfth-century foundation of the 'golden age' of Byzantine architecture. Rising diagonally from an irregular rectangle bordered by cells (largely of the post-Byzantine period) and monastic outhouses, the church has an exo-narthex and a narthex added in the fifteenth (or sixteenth) century. The plan is cruciform and tri-apsidal, with a dome (which collapsed in 1914 and was replaced by an unimpressive wooden one) supported by four slender columns of blue-veined white marble. The original marble screen of the sanctuary has been replaced by a wooden iconostasis, but some of the original sculptural embellishment is embedded in the wall above the south door of the narthex. The **mosaic floor** (its dimensions are 100 square metres) in the naos is a fine example of the floor mosaicist's art of the twelfth century, lavishly decorated with eight circular designs within a circle and a geometric border.

[3] At the time of writing the monastery is inhabited by a single monk. The traveller should enquire at the village of Hypaton whether the monk is in residence. The monastery is connected by telephone with the village post office.

Rejoining the highway and following a north-west course, one reaches the village of Castro. A road to the right, less than a mile long, runs across the fields to the so-called **Isle of Gla**, one of the strangest prehistoric sites in Greece. The 'isle' – it obviously was one once, washed by the shallow waters of the Copaic lake – is a natural curiosity: a low triangular eminence with a ramp on the north, flanked by two defensive buttresses, and a two-mile circumference of Cyclopean walls without towers that follow the contours of the cliff. Dominating the north-east basin below Mount Ptoion, it may have been a principality of the Minyans (a pre-Hellenic people who descended from Thessaly into Boeotia), which formed part of a system of fortifications guarding the shores of the lake. The cliffs, never higher than two hundred feet, are pitted with caves and katavothra. On the inner side of the gate to which the ramp leads there was a small courtyard. Below the north-east redoubt is another double gate. Moving north-north-west you reach the central redoubt; north of it are foundations of a palace with two wings (L-shaped), built of sun-dried bricks (the base is of stone), on the highest point of the eminence. All round, the countryside is dotted with rocky humps, like huge grey animals squatting on the cornfields of the drained marshland. There is not a house, not a tree, not a browsing goat. Only the bees, the sage and the fennel.

North-east of Gla lies the ugly mining village of Ayios Ioannis. At the base of the hillside, immediately below a chapel of the same name, there is an enormous arc-shaped cave with a double entrance which marks the site of the Great Katavothron where the Melas, one of the main Boeotian streams, is drained underground and, after flowing through the limestone barrier, pours into the Euboean channel.

The road continues across bleak mountain country; as it descends towards the coast, past the restored Byzantine church of Ayios Nikolaos, wisps of foul-smelling smoke drift up from a straggling village at the head of a deep narrow inlet ringed round by nickel mining installations. Site of **ancient Larymna**, whose name has been inherited by the modern village, it is believed to have been the chief port of the Minyans. In Hellenistic times Larymna, main emporium of Boeotia and a harbour of some strategic value, was defended on the landward side by a semi-circular enceinte of strong walls, strengthened with towers, substantial remains of which are identifiable – the masonry is both rectangular and polygonal, the hewn stones being of a white and sometimes unusual tawny colour. In the choking polluted atmosphere one may search along the shore for fragments of fourth-century BC port installations – including piers used for closing the harbour in time of war – some of which are submerged, though still visible, and gaze through watering eyes at the grandiose scree-rent cliffs of Euboea rising sheer across the water.

Back at Castro one follows a dirt road running beside canals to the village of Orchomenus. The stream of the Melas, now called the Mavropotamos (the black river), issues out of a katavothron at the north base of Mount Acontium (the Javelin), a barren forbidding chain of hills guarding the approaches to this region of fens through which streams course sluggishly between banks of waving canes. Between the road and Mount Acontium extend traces of one of the oldest prehistoric sites in Greece. Indeed, so great was the antiquity of **Orchomenus**, capital of the Minyans, that its golden age was little more than a memory in classical times.[4]

The most impressive surviving edifice of Minyan civilization is the **Treasury of Minyas**, claimed by Pausanias to be the first treasury ever built, and 'a wonder second to none either in Greece or elsewhere'.[5] Situated just off the main road, this beehive tomb was excavated by Schliemann. It is approached by a *dromos* cut through the hillside, leading to a tapering doorway with a formidable lintel of blue schist. The diameter of the vaulted rotunda, now roofless, is about forty-five feet. Holes for bronze rosettes are discernible on the walls, of which eight courses survive. The fact that the circular chamber is open to the sky enables the spectator to get a better impression of the concavity of the structure than is possible in the Treasury of Atreus at Mycenae. On the other hand, there is a total absence of that atmosphere of centuries-old putrefaction which contributes so much to the macabre quality of the Mycenaean sepulchre. A corridor connects the rotunda with a small square funerary chamber, with palmettes and rosettes carved in low relief on the ceiling, where the original Minyas were supposed to have been buried.

From the Treasury the way up to the citadel is steep and stony. One passes traces of buildings of the Neolithic, third millenium BC and pre-Archaic periods. The upper terraces were reconstructed by Philip and Alexander. On the final jagged outgrowth of rock are the remains of a square tower. The ramparts, best preserved on the

[4] The Boeotian Orchomenus should not be confused with the ancient city of the same name in Arcadia.
[5] One should ask at the Church of the Koimesis at Skripou (the modern hamlet) for the guardian who has the key of the Treasury.

south side, are of the fourth century BC. Although by this time the greatness and wealth of Orchomenus were no more than a memory, Mount Acontium still possessed strategic value, dominating the bottleneck between the plains.

The end of Orchomenus came in 364 BC, as a result of the endemic feud with Thebes. Three hundred Orchomenian horsemen, aided by Theban traitors, prepared an attack on Thebes. The plot was betrayed and Orchomenus totally destroyed, its male population slaughtered and the women and children sold into slavery. This barbarous sack aroused the revulsion of neighbouring states and confirmed the reputation for cruelty earned by the Thebans.

The temple of the Charities is thought to have been situated east of the road, opposite the Treasury and a theatre of the Hellenistic period with well-preserved tiers and a ruined proscenium. The site is now surrounded by cotton fields, canals and mud-flats, and the temple replaced by the Byzantine **Church of the Koimesis** (Dormition of the Virgin) of Skripou, the oldest cross-inscribed edifice in Greece. An inscription dates it to 874. It is constructed out of large blocks of stone of unequal size, clearly of ancient origin (such as the drums of columns built into the interior west wall); and the general effect, while one of spaciousness and sturdiness, is heavy and awkward. The architect, while employing the Greek Cross plan, retained certain features of the basilica: the three aisles, for instance, and the triple windows of the narthex, each with two colonnettes. More attractive are the courses of carved reliefs – a form of church decoration soon to disappear from Byzantine art – separating the three zones of the interior. Children play in the forecourt and old women sit in the sun, while hens peck desultorily among truncated pillars and fragments of the cornice and closure panels of the original marble screen.

Close to Orchomenus lies **Levadeia**, chief town of Boeotia, its houses with red-tiled roofs spreading fanwise across the foothills of Helicon on either side of a narrow gorge. A clock tower, presented by Lord Elgin, is a conspicuous landmark. Behind the town rises a screen of spruce-covered heights. Westward towers Parnassus, misty blue in colour, its summit snow-capped from November to May, often wreathed in cloud. In its elevation, in the symmetry and harmony of its forms, in its dramatic upward surge from the plain, no other Greek mountain, except Taygetus in the Peloponnese, is more impressive. Levadeia, with a local trade in blanket-making, has an animated air. Scarlet, green and magenta blankets hang out to dry from wooden balconies, ramshackle dwellings spread across the

'The Upper City' – walls, temples and gateways, crowned by the Parthenon.

Prancing horses on the west frieze of the Parthenon.

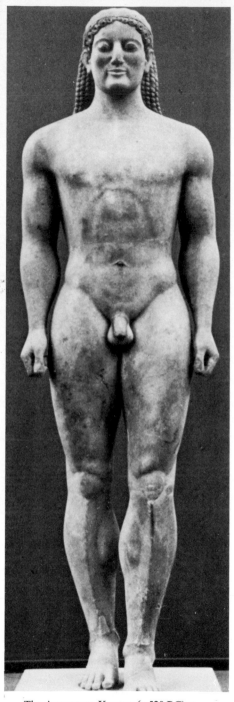

The Anavyssos Kouros (c.520 BC): a strong-limbed youth, marvellously self assured, a perfect embodiment of human dignity.

The Koré (No 685 in the Acropolis Museum) a representative of the world of aristocratic ease, poise and serenity which perished in the holocaust of the Persian Wars.

slope of a rocky eminence crowned by a medieval castle, and streams cascade down the hill.

At the foot of the castle hill the Hercyna issues out of a sunless canyon. Plane trees form arbours over the ice-cold stream, which is spanned by a little arched Turkish bridge. The springs on the east bank flow into two pools: Lethe (Oblivion) and Mnemosyne (Remembrance). On the west bank niches for votive offerings have been carved out of the cliff-side. The largest of these forms a kind of stone chamber with rock-hewn seats, the favourite refuge of Turkish governors who came here to smoke their *narghiles* or doze through long soporific summer afternoons. Everywhere there is water: oozing, trickling, gurgling. Below the rocky precipices, among the shady planes, there are open-air cafés and tavernas, and a modern swimming pool where divers plunge into water drained from the pool of Lethe.

Nearby was the Oracle of Trophonius. The oracular chamber was in an underground chasm in a sacred grove containing a temple with a statue of Trophonius, a Minyan semi-deity, by Praxiteles. Leake, most reliable of nineteenth-century topographers, placed the grove on the east bank of the Hercyna, but not as far as the upland plateau associated with the hunting-grounds of Persephone, to which the gorge ultimately leads.

To the right (west) of the gorge a high crag is crowned by the castle, the earliest Catalan monument in Greece. The ruined towers, walls and archways of the keep are reminders of a strange period of Spanish rule in Greece. In the winter of 1311 a band of Catalan soldiers of fortune, originally hired by the Duke of Athens to fight the Greeks and who were owed extensive arrears of pay, descended into Boeotia, accompanied by an immense train of women, children and baggage, resolved to settle accounts with their Frankish debtors by force of arms.

The Catalans, though outnumbered, had laid their plans with cunning and foresight. Flooding the fields between Skripou and Levadeia by digging canals into which the waters of the Cephisus flowed, they were defended by a quagmire covered with a carpet of scum that looked like grass. The Duke of Athens, waving his banner of a golden lion on an azure field sown with stars, personally led the attack, followed by his golden-spurred knights in coats of mail. Plunging their horses into the morass, they were unable to move forward or back, and men and beasts became sitting targets for the bolts and arrows of the Spaniards who bore down on them, yelling 'Aragon!' The massacre of the French was appalling. The battle was decisive. Frankish power in central Greece was broken in a few hours. Henceforth Attica and Boeotia became the domain of Spanish (and later Florentine) overlords.

West of the Cephisian battleground lie Chaeroneia and Daulis. Both can be visited from Levadeia in a half-day. **Chaeroneia**, where Plutarch was born and died (AD 46–120) and wrote most of his works, lies in the narrow plain between Mounts Acontium and Thurium. Astride the main invasion route from the north, it was a position of great strategic importance. In ancient times it was a flowery place, the Grasse of the Hellenic world, famous for the manufacture of therapeutic unguents distilled from lilies, roses and narcissus.

The antiquities are visible from the road. The cavea of a little theatre, without the usual supporting walls at the side, is well preserved (the skene, however, has gone). Behind it fragments of ruined towers and walls, which enclosed the ancient city, ascend the hill. The marble **Lion of Chaeroneia** stands in a cypress grove a few minutes' walk from the centre of the village. Its artistic merit, if any, is overshadowed by its historical associations, for it surmounts the collective grave of the Theban Sacred Band, wiped out in a murderous combat with the young Alexander's phalanx at the battle of Chaeroneia. In the War of Independence Odysseus Androutsos, most predatory of revolutionary leaders, hacked it to pieces in the hope of finding it full of treasure. Subsequent excavation of the tumulus on which it lay revealed over two hundred skeletons – presumably of the Theban Sacred Band. The Lion, put together at the beginning of the present century, now rests on its haunches, open-mouthed, staring fatuously from its marble plinth, against an imposing background of Parnassus. In the adjacent museum are displayed prehistoric armour, weapons and terracottas from the tumulus of the Macedonians who fell in the battle.

Chaeroneia was a decisive battle. By the summer of 338 BC Philip of Macedon was ready to force the gateway into Boeotia and subjugate all continental Greece. On a blazing August day, the Macedonian army, well trained, admirably equipped and expertly commanded, faced an army of disunited Greeks, held together only by the exhortations of Demosthenes. Road and rail follow a parallel course across a stretch of level ground between the Cephisus and the village where the battle was fought. After the engagement Philip is accused of indulging in unseemly mirth, of getting drunk on the field of battle and jesting in the most ribald manner as he inspected the corpses of his foes piled up in the blood-soaked streams. But he is said to have wept at the sight of the Theban dead, privileged members of the Sacred Band. They had borne the brunt of Alexander's onslaught and fought with courage and self-sacrifice. They died to a man, all with chest wounds. In time the battle acquired a kind of romantic aura, its outcome being identified by succeeding generations as the end of the democratic Greek city state.

In 87 BC another decisive battle, equally disastrous to Greek arms, was fought on the field of Chaeroneia. The Hellenistic world of Alexander the Great's successors was crumbling before the irresistible tide of Roman conquest. An army of Mithridates, King of Pontus, around whom Hellenism had rallied, put up a last stand in the Chaeroneian bottleneck. The forces of Mithridates were so totally annihilated that Sulla himself claimed Boeotia to be impassable for the piles of corpses.

West of Chaeroneia the foothills of Parnassus alternately advance and recede into the plain, forming a fascinating sequence of different perspectives. The first turning to the left (south) leads to the village of Ayios Vlasis and the acropolis of Panopeus, native city of Epeius, who built the Trojan Horse with the aid of Athena. There are remains of two well-preserved gateways and six towers of the fourth century BC.

Another spur is crowned by **Daulis** (south-west of the main road) which is worth visiting, if only for its striking position. From the village one climbs a cultivated slope, dotted with water mills, to the acropolis. There are remains of a gate over ten feet wide between two towers – the one on the right is medieval. The square towers of the ramparts, covered in holly-oak, overhang a torrent-bed strewn with huge boulders. The whitewashed Convent of Jerusalem, surrounded by cypresses, is perched on a ledge of Parnassus above the acropolis, just below the belt of firs. To the south-west a track leads across desolate contorted hills to the Cleft Way and thence to Delphi. The course of history has flowed past in the plain below, the never-ending armies from the north hardly ever pausing to desecrate this elegiac fennel-covered place. Only Philip of Macedon halted long enough to destroy the town, where the men, though few in number, were renowned for their height and strength. The fortress was rebuilt, we know, because Livy refers to the town's impregnable situation on its 'lofty hills'.

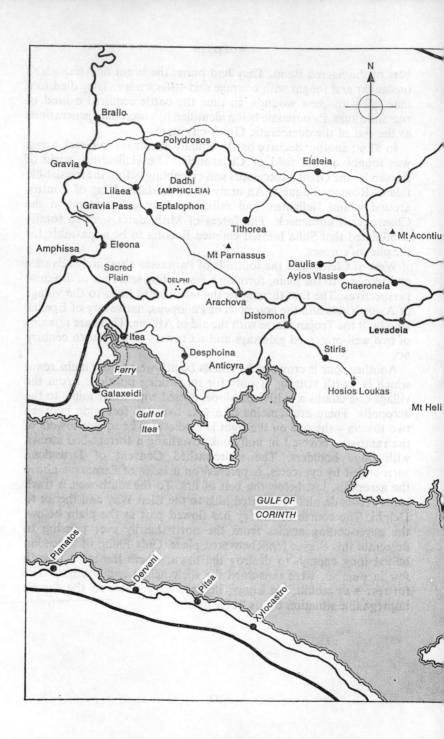

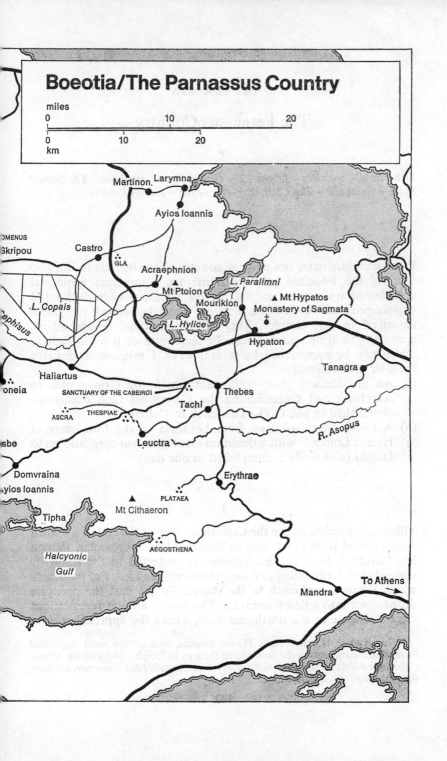

Boeotia/The Parnassus Country

miles
0 ————— 10 ————— 20
0 ————— 10 ————— 20
km

OMENUS
Skripou

Martinon. Larymna

Ayios Ioannis

Castro

GLA

Acraephnion

Mt Ptoion

L. Paralimni

Mourikion

Mt Hypatos
Monastery of Sagmata

L. Hylice

.L. Copais

ephisus

Hypaton

Haliartus

Tanagra

oneia

SANCTUARY OF THE CABEIROI

Thebes

Tachi

ASCRA

THESPIAE

R. Asopus

sbe

Leuctra

Domvraina

Erythrae

yios Ioannis

Tipha

PLATAEA
Mt Cithaeron

AEGOSTHENA

Halcyonic
Gulf

To Athens

Mandra

CHAPTER SIX

The Parnassus Country

❧

*Tithorea – Amphicleia – Lilaea – The Gravia Pass – Amphissa – The Sacred
Plain – Galaxeidi – The Cleft Way – Anticyra – Hosios Loukas*

Parnassus dominates not only the country of the Boeotians, but also
that of the Phocians and Locrians: an amorphous geological
complex of spurs and foothills, narrow plains, sombre defiles and
cup-shaped valleys. Few travellers are likely to visit all the places
described in this chapter. They will pass some, ignore others,
according to their chosen route. In the centre of it all is Delphi,
which can be approached by several ways. I propose to describe
these in two sections:

(i) An arc running from Tithorea through the Gravia pass to
Amphissa and Galaxeidi on the Corinthian Gulf (easily accomplished in one day) – then back to Delphi.

(ii) A rough westward loop from Levadeia to the Monastery of
Hosios Loukas,[1] with a deviation (south) to Anticyra, and on to
Delphi (also easily accomplished in one day).

I

Tithorea is perched above the Cephisian valley at the end of a branch
road parallel to the dirt road to Daulis. More spectacular, though
less beautiful, than Daulis, Tithorea is protected to the south by
vertical cliffs terminating in a huge three-cornered ledge of Parnassus
which forms a backcloth to the village. To the east the precipice
drops sheer into a desolate ravine. The town's ancient fortifications
were strongest to the north and west, where the approaches were

---

[1] The average traveller visits Hosios Loukas, one of the most important
Byzantine monuments in the country, on the way to Delphi. The journey Athens
– Hosios Loukas – Delphi (or vice versa) is a comfortable day's journey, allowing
for stops and minor deviations.

undefended by nature. Fragments of fourth- to third-century BC walls of regular ashlar masonry, with low towers covered with moss and ivy, are scattered about the vegetable plots, forming an arc round the more exposed slopes.

Huddled round the base of the cliff, the village is picturesque and salubrious, with narrow streets interspersed with outcrops of ancient ivy-mantled masonry. The eastern end overhangs the ravine through which flows the Kakorevma (The Evil Torrent). The gorge winds inland, into the heart of Parnassus. On the right, just beyond the last houses, is a cave where the Tithoreans took refuge during Xerxes's invasion.

East of the Tithorea fork a track to the north crosses the Cephisus and leads to **Elateia**, once the most important place in Phocis after Delphi. Its capture by Philip in 339 BC, followed by the victory of Chaeroneia, laid all central Greece at the mercy of the Macedonian king. The ruins are vestigial. Three kilometres to the north-east are the more impressive standing walls of a **Sanctuary of Athena Cranaea** on a hill now called Castro Lazou.

The main east-west road continues to skirt the base of Parnassus. After passing the entrance to another great gorge, one reaches the undistinguished village of Dadhi, site of **ancient Amphicleia**, where orgies, which Pausanias found 'well worth seeing', were held in honour of Dionysus. West of the village, remains of Hellenic masonry are embedded in what must have been the retaining wall of the ancient acropolis, crowned by a ruined Venetian tower commanding a view of corn, tobacco and cotton fields, with formidable mountains closing round on all sides as the plains contract into a narrow enclave.

Leaving the shady village of Polydrosos behind, the road skirts the precipitous slopes of Parnassus, slashed by more gorges. About a kilometre before one reaches **Lilaea** vestiges of an ancient tower appear on the bleak ridge of a steep hill. Ancient Lilaea was razed to the ground by Philip of Macedon during the Third Sacred War. It now marks the beginning of a mountain road which climbs to the beautiful village of Eptalophon, sprawling across seven hills on different levels amid streams and boscages of poplars against a background of rugged cliffs remarkable for the perfection and symmetry of their forms. After reaching the watershed the road enters a silent world of fir forests, crosses a desolate plateau and winds down to Arachova (see p. 111) and the navel-shaped valley of the Pleistus, with Delphi perched on its bastion in the west. In summer, driving or walking along one of the numerous tracks that wind through cool dark forests, one catches occasional glimpses of the scorching Phocian lowlands thousands of feet below.

Back in the plain, one can make a minor deviation from Lilaea to a British military cemetery. Rows of well-tended graves contain the bones of British and Russian sappers killed in the Macedonian campaigns of the First World War. Around them extends the shadeless level ground, like an immense crater, surrounded by the razor-sharp crests of the mountain rim. To the south a slender nodular peak guards the entrance to the **Gravia pass**, which we now enter in order to complete the circuitous route to Delphi. The road from here, originally built by the Anglo-French army in 1917 so as to shorten their lines of communication with the Macedonian front, runs between the torrent-rent buttresses of Parnassus and Ghiona. Forests of ilex and fir spread across the higher slopes. Beyond the watershed, which connects Parnassus with the Locrian massif of Ghiona, there are glimpses of a vast sea of olive groves curling round the bases of rocky foothills and flat-topped mountain ledges. No village could be more idyllically situated than Eleona, amid a jungle of olive trees, with water cascading from one vine-covered terrace to another.

The descent ends at **Amphissa**, built around a tapering crag planted with cypresses and littered with the ruins of a medieval castle, in the shadow of a crescent of jagged heights formed by Parnassus and Ghiona. By the nature of its commanding position at the head of the Crissaean plain, ancient Amphissa was the chief city of Ozolian Locris.

In the thirteenth century the d'Autremencourts of Picardy built a strong castle on the site of the classical fortress, whose impregnability is mentioned by Livy and of which there are vestiges of quadrangular and polygonal walls, and called it Salona; later Catalan conquerors renamed it La Sol and made it their most important fief in the country. The castle had three enceintes, whose ruined ramparts are now fringed with tall umbrella pines. The climb is steep, the medieval ruins exiguous. A fine monolithic lintel, probably of ancient origin, surmounts the entrance gate. A circular tower crowns the keep. There are also remnants of two churches – Byzantine and Frankish (or Catalan) and, at the foot of the hill (south), a charming Turkish fountain with arcades. The castle, which guarded the southern exit of the Gravia pass, formed one of the bulwarks of central Greece.

In 1821, when the War of Independence broke out, Amphissa was the first citadel in mainland Greece to be captured by the Greeks. Turkish troops and inhabitants, rounded up on the castle slope, were massacred to a man on the orders of the Greek chieftain Panourias. No more than a brigand turned patriot, this unsavoury man devoted his period of rule in Amphissa to the sole cause of personal gain, and the long-suffering Amphissans, having exchanged a 'foreign tyrant' for a 'national hero', were compelled to maintain his retinue of cretinous robbers at their own expense. The case of Panourias is an object-lesson.

It is no distance from Amphissa to the twelfth-century Byzantine **Church of Ayios Sotiros** (Holy Saviour), but the key must be obtained from the church of Ayios Nikolaos on the west slope of the town. A track winds up an escarpment, past a gipsy encampment, to a ledge on the mountain side overlooking the northern end of the plain, where the olive groves contract between rocky foothills.

The church is a classic example of twelfth-century architecture. The exterior apse, in front of which a plane tree provides shade, is interesting in that the central window, divided by a colonnette, is placed within an arched frame, whereas the side ones are contained within square surrounds. The contrapuntal effect thus created is both harmonious and pleasing. Three parallel brick inlays decorate the window surrounds, and there is considerable evidence of the tile decoration much favoured by twelfth-century architects who wished to embellish church exteriors with geometric designs. In the interior the two columns supporting the dome are crowned by elaborately carved capitals. Some fine sculptured fragments from the original marble screen are ranged along the north wall of the naos.

South of Amphissa the road crosses the **Sacred Plain**, which is surrounded on all sides by lofty mountains. Peaks, ridges, slopes seem to develop organically out of the primeval convulsion. The density of the olive trees is legendary, the gnarled trunks being among the most ancient in Greece.

The road ends at **Itea**, the port of Delphi, at the head of a muddy gulf where cruise ships anchor. The place has a wasteland air, and its drab 'modernity', in such close proximity to the sacred landscape, strikes one as a profanity. But there are good hotels which are useful when there is no accommodation at Delphi. There is also a ferry-boat service to Aeghion on the Peloponnesian coast. A new road runs along the barren western shore of the gulf, now rendered hideous by extensive mining installations. It leads to **Galaxeidi.**

Often called the future St Tropez of Greece, Galaxeidi is built on a headland flanked by a bay and a pine-fringed creek which provide excellent anchorages for yachts. There is a fine view across the inland sea towards Delphi and the escarpments of Parnassus. The houses, inhabited by caique-builders, are picturesque but without architectural distinction or historical associations. Skeletons of broad-beamed caiques litter the waterfront. The bathing is not good, for the rocks are spiky, the sea soupy; and at the height of summer there are swarms of flies.

Galaxeidi, however, has a thirteenth-century Byzantine church.[2] Above the town the road ascends into the olive belt, circling a bluff overlooking the sea. Across the Corinthian Gulf rise the Peloponnesian ranges, slashed by great gorges. The **Church of Ayios Sotiros** (Holy Saviour) nestles in a cypress grove surrounded by olive trees. A transverse barrel vault at the south end gives the impression of a dome (seen from the interior) which has been added to the basilica. The wall paintings are too poorly preserved to merit attention. Reliefs in the exterior apse, probably from the screen of an earlier church, are decorated with stylized pine cones and cypress branches in the angles of the crosses.

A caique service connects Galaxeidi with Itea. It is a short but memorable journey. The oily waters of the gulf, dotted with barren islets, like petrified porpoises, are ruffled only by the caique's wash. A silver haze hangs over the groves of the Sacred Plain, within the amphitheatre of tremendous mountains.

From Itea a road climbs one of the final seaward bulwarks of Parnassus, providing an admirable view of the complexities of coastline, plain and mountain, to a concave upland plateau in which the large village of Desphoina lies. The road descends through shadeless valleys to the deep, hidden bay of Anticyra and thence to Hosios Loukas.

II

There is only one way from Levadeia to Hosios Loukas – the road to Delphi. It begins by winding round a series of rolling eroded hills in a wide trough between Helicon and Parnassus. From no other point I know is the perfection of form of Parnassus seen to greater advantage – a well ordered mass of soaring limestone, its buttresses and escarpments, square, rectangular, curvilinear, rent by deep ravines running in parallel vertical courses. It is lonely country. There is only a Vlach hamlet, some sheep-folds, a *khani*, or resting place, shaded by great plane trees. Goats scrabble among prickly shrubs

---

[2] The traveller should ask at the police station where to get the key of the church, which is usually locked.

on the precipitous slopes – a landscape, one feels, specially designed to guard the approaches to Delphi. On every side mountains soar above the **Cleft Way**, the ancient junction of the three roads from Delphi, Daulis and Thebes.

Soon there is a fork. The turning to the left (south) leads to Distomon, a centre of guerrilla activity in the last war. Here there is another fork. The road to the south descends abruptly to the bay of Anticyra, on the Corinthian Gulf. The rocky broken coastline is dotted with mining installations. A corniche runs eastward, and the shell of a little Byzantine church of Ayios Panteleimon lies at the mouth of a stony valley. Fragmentary remains of the ancient walls of Anticyra are scattered across a bluff.

The other road from Distomon (to the east) passes through Stiris, famous for its sheep's milk yoghurt of the richest quality, and runs along a ridge of windswept hills to the **Monastery of Hosios Loukas**. The church and its dependencies overlook a bowl-like valley with cultivated strips laid out in chequer-board fashion, enclosed on all sides by steep slate-grey spurs of Helicon.

The original chapel, dedicated to St Barbara, was built by the disciples of a holy man from neighbouring Stiris. He was called Luke – 'Hosios' being the Orthodox equivalent of a 'blessed man' in the Western Church – and his fame soon spread beyond his native mountains. He died in the middle of the tenth century, his humble shrine became a place of pilgrimage, and a monastery was founded. In Constantinople, Theophano, daughter of a cabaret-owner and wife of three successive emperors, heard of it and thought of embellishing it. Her son, the Emperor Basil II the Bulgar-Slayer, is believed to have added impetus to the enterprise in the course of his triumphant tour of Greece at the beginning of the eleventh century. Throughout the Empire there was a surge of creative activity. It was the beginning of the Byzantine Golden Age. Hosios Loukas remains a typical example of the Byzantine tradition of imperial patronage of remote monastic establishments.

The almond orchards and patchwork fields in the cup-shaped valley, owned by the once flourishing community of monks, now reduced to a handful of white-bearded old men, have been expropriated by the government. Until recently dilapidated outhouses spread across the rectangular terrace. Now there is a tourist shop and a bar. But by sundown the last motor coach has gone, the echo of the last transistor died away. The foothills of Helicon form a dark screen round the empty valley. In spring the air is heavy with the scents of broom, honeysuckle and lemon blossom.

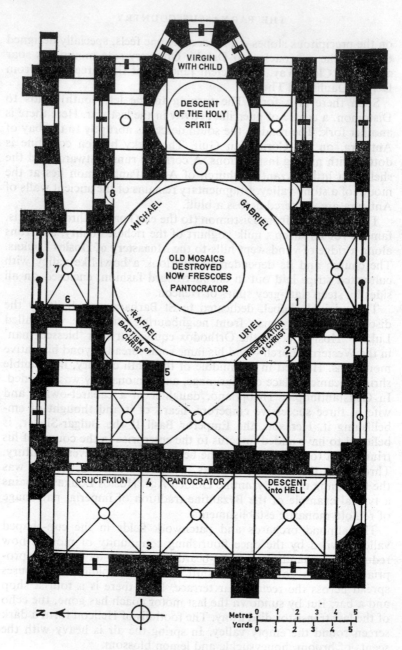

VIRGIN
WITH CHILD

DESCENT
OF THE HOLY
SPIRIT

8

MICHAEL

GABRIEL

OLD MOSAICS
DESTROYED
NOW FRESCOES
PANTOCRATOR

7

6

RAFAEL
BAPTISM of
CHRIST

URIEL

PRESENTATION
of CHRIST

1

2

5

CRUCIFIXION   4   PANTOCRATOR   DESCENT
into HELL

3

N

Metres 0 1 2 3 4 5
Yards 0 1 2 3 4 5

Hosios Loukas

The main church (eleventh-century) is a tall cross-inscribed edifice, with lavish brickwork exterior decoration, surrounded by monastic cells and a refectory. The windows, which possess sculptural embellishments, are divided into three sections by columns of different coloured marbles. The interior is one of the finest extant examples of the Byzantine effort to create a harmonious unity out of colours, cubes, bricks, paste, stone and marble. Bands of white sculptured marble divide the sumptuous multi-coloured revetments into two levels, the floor is of jasper and porphyry, the marble screen elaborately carved and every inch of wall space in the narthex, dome, apses and transepts glows with mosaics against gold backgrounds. There are also some less important frescoes of a later date.

The narthex comes first. A subtle and basic unity underlying the disposition of the figures of the apostles on the various arches is achieved through their attitudes – quarter-views or turning movements, so that they all ultimately point to the Pantocrator, whose image once filled the space above the door leading into the naos. Two of the most striking portraits are those of **St Peter** (east wall) and **St Andrew** (west wall) with lively expressions and disproportionately large heads. Among the scenes from the life of Christ the most impressive are the **Crucifixion** (left) and **Descent into Hell** (right) in shallow lunettes. The bulky figure with heavy tubular legs on the Cross is, in spite of its monolithic columnar quality, contorted with physical pain.

In the main body of the church and in the side chapels the iconographic arrangement adheres strictly to the established programme. In the first zone (vaults and chapels), saints intermingle with ascetics, prophets, bishops and provincial holy men in a gallery of portraits which, at first, tend to overshadow the narrative scenes on the upper register. There are few concessions to grace, none to sentimentality. Among the portraits those of St Demetrius (south transept), St Basil (lunette in north-east transept), Mercurios, the soldier-saint, with sheathed sword (north-west arch, left on entering) and a lively St Nicholas (lunette in south-west corner) are worth noticing. In the north transept there is a bust of the **Blessed Luke** himself, severe and monkish, his hands raised in worship. In numerous arches and vaults the Archangels and military saints act as guards of honour. The busts within medallions, unlike those of the apostles in the narthex, are portrayed frontally.

High up above the world of holy men extends the sphere of divine beings, at the summit of which Christ Pantocrator (in this instance missing) dominates the universe. In the apse the Virgin and Child are represented seated on a cushioned throne decorated with elaborate inlay, against a concave gold background which creates an effect of immense spaciousness. In the dome of the sanctuary the twelve apostles are seated round the symbol of the Trinity. Below the central cupola are the spandrels in which scenes from the Dodecaorton are depicted: a beautiful **Nativity**, in which the figure of Joseph with enormous black eyes and the animals leaning over the crib lend an extraordinary homely quality to the scene; a **Baptism,** in which Christ stands shoulder-high in the waters of the Jordan while two angels advance towards him bearing elaborately designed towels.

As there is little differentiation in colour tones, the austere mosaicist of the eleventh century at Hosios Loukas tends to over-emphasize the modelling of his figures. The mosaics at Daphni are certainly more evolved and sophisticated in technique and execution, but Hosios Loukas, in its completeness, in the power and intensity of the figures crowding its walls, in its elaborate decorative detail and majestic proportions, remains a more imposing and convincing example of an eleventh-century Byzantine church.

Below the church is the crypt of St Barbara, containing the tomb of the Blessed Luke, painted with crude frescoes of the peasant school of Cappadocia. Adjoining the main church is the chapel of the Virgin, chronologically slightly earlier than the main church, entered through a tenth-century exo-narthex with a triple portico crowned by a loggia. The dome above the cruciform naos is supported by four granite columns. The lavish Opus Alexandrinum pavement has a curious slant.

CHAPTER SEVEN

Delphi

᭟

'The shrine that is the centre of the loudly echoing earth.'
PINDAR, *Odes*, P. vi.

Arachova – The Oracle – The Sanctuary of Apollo: The Treasuries; The Stoa of the Athenians; The Temple of Apollo; The Theatre – The Stadium – Marmaria: The Tholos; The Temple of Athena Pronaea – Sybaris – The Corycian Cave – The Museum

Isolated by a ring of mountains, Delphi has always been subject to violent climatic and geological pressures. Earthquakes and landslides are common. Shadows of clouds that dissolve and re-form drift across the olive groves. Torrential showers blot out the landscape, and thunder echoes in the hollows of the valley. In summer the heat is trapped within the arena of refractory limestone, and the cliffs, pitted with primeval fissures, reflect a peculiar radiance which seems to derive its glow from the interior of the rock.

Several ways of approaching the sanctuary have been described in Chapter 6; but the direct route from Athens through Levadeia is the one most travellers take. After the fork to Distomon the road climbs between jagged peaks. Fir trees spread across the higher slopes. Every outline acquires a razor-edge sharpness, the atmosphere a rarefied quality, the blue of the sky a new intensity. One has a sensation of approaching a place of immense significance in the affairs of men. At the top of the pass the curtain is raised with a tremendous flourish. The gorge lies below, the mountains crowding round to complete the famous umbilical effect. In the distance a buttress of cliffs, concealing the sanctuary, juts out to meet another wall of rock; beyond it there is a tantalizing glimpse of the olive groves of the Sacred Plain.

In the immediate foreground a double-peaked bastion of Parnassus, over three thousand feet high, is crowned by the grey stone houses of **Arachova**, its clock tower perched on the summit of a crag overhanging cultivated strips which descend in terraces to the bottom of the gorge.

A large modern hotel, in sharp contrast to the rustic atmosphere of this mountain eyrie, commands a fine prospect of the gorge. Tourist shops display local handicrafts: woollen bags, carpets, blankets. The colours are crude and gaudy, but some of the bedspreads and tablecloths embroidered with old regional designs, and fleecy rugs called *flocatas* are attractive. The red wine of Arachova is good, if rather heady. The local cheese, made from goat's milk, its wax rind moulded in the design of a wickerwork basket, is more of a curiosity than a delicacy. Arachova is the starting-point for the ascent of Parnassus (a local guide is indispensable), for the visit to the Corycian Cave (see p. 120) by car, and for the drive across Parnassus to Gravia (described in reverse on p. 104).

Beyond Arachova the road descends, between shelving ledges planted with almond trees, into the vine belt. Ominous signs of rock blasting in the valleys below portend new irrigation schemes. The gorge continues to narrow. The ruins of an ancient necropolis herald the approach. The road loops round a huge projecting bluff and enters the inner amphitheatre of rock. The ruins of the sanctuary – broken columns, polygonal walls, grey stone tiers, red-brick Roman rubble – are splayed across the steep hillside. Unfortunately, the most prominent architectural feature is the modern building of the museum, with sheet glass windows, surrounded by shrubs and flowerbeds. A wall of cliff rises sheer from the ultimate ledge of the sanctuary, and hawks and vultures hover overhead. In the valley below olive trees of immense antiquity mantle the precipitous banks.

Hotels and tourist shops line the main street of the village of Delphi, which clings to another great projection of rock. The original hamlet, built over the sanctuary, was removed stone by stone to its present position when the excavations began at the end of the last century. Most of the hotels have magnificent views. One lunches and dines on terraces, shaded with awnings, overlooking the gorge. Shopping is much the same as at Arachova, a bit more expensive, with a lot more junk thrown in. On Sundays and feast days shepherds with complexions tanned by sun and wind to a rich golden hue come down from mountain sheep folds to drink coffee and listen to the news in the cafés. Sometimes, in the evening, flushed with ouzo or wine, they perform a lively *tsamiko*, to the accompaniment of a wailing clarinet. The antiquities are confined to two areas: the Sanctuary of Apollo above the main road, and the Marmaria, in an olive grove below the Castalian Spring. These (and the museum) can be rushed through in one long exhausting day. A longer stay is unlikely to be regretted.

The Tower of the Winds or Horologium of Andronicos Cyrrhestus – an architectural fantasy created by a philhellenic Syrian of the first century AD.

Kapnikarea Church, one of the best-preserved Byzantine churches in the capital, is a typical example of the cruciform plan.

Eleusis: jumbled foundations of the holy edifices.

Marble stele from the Cerameicus: a
mother bids farewell to her child.
(National Archaeological Museum).

The powerful head of the bronze
Poseidon, also in the Museum.

It is only five minutes' walk to the Sanctuary of Apollo. The earliest references to it are purely mythical. They tell of roving shepherds being suddenly seized by an uncontrollable frenzy as potent exhalations issued from a fissure in a rocky ledge and pouring forth garbled prophecies in the name of Apollo. In time a temple was raised to the god above the sacred pit. Symbol of youth, light and beauty, Apollo is the most consistently Greek of Olympian deities. Although vain, uxorious and narcissistic, he has many attractive qualities: an affection for flocks, an interest in medicine and astronomy, a love of music and poetry.

The Apolline cult developed rapidly and a priestess, the Pythia, was installed in the temple, where she chanted the ambiguous riddles that exercised such a powerful influence over men's actions for ten centuries. As a panhellenic sanctuary, Delphi possessed a far more profound religious significance than Olympia, and four Sacred Wars were fought for its preservation. From the beginning, the sanctuary's purpose was wholly oracular, existing solely for communicating the counsels of the gods to mortals. Strabo believes 'the position of the place added something. For it is almost in the centre of Greece . . . and people called it the navel of the earth.'

The oracle was administered by five elected priests who claimed descent from Deucalion. They had complete control of administration, were responsible for the Pythia's political brief and were represented in Athens and elsewhere by agents. The fame of the prophecies was established as early as the eighth century BC; by the sixth, votive gifts were pouring in from every part of the civilized world. Croesus alone presented the shrine with a gold statue of a lion, a gold mixing-bowl that weighed a quarter of a ton and a silver wine vessel that held five thousand gallons. As an instrument of policy, the oracle's influence was by no means negligible. In the Persian Wars it tended to be defeatist, in the Peloponnesian War it showed a pro-Spartan bias. It was consulted among others by Oedipus, Agamemnon, Cleomenes, Philip of Macedon and Alexander the Great. To the latter the priestess cried, 'My son, none can resist thee!'

The oracles were generally extremely equivocal. Can one blame Croesus, when told he would destroy a mighty empire if he crossed the Halus, for failing to realize that the empire in question was his own? Little is known of the relations between priests and politicians, but there can be little doubt that string-pulling went on behind the scenes. Most of the problems, upon which the consultants sought the god's arbitration, related to cultivation of crops, love affairs,

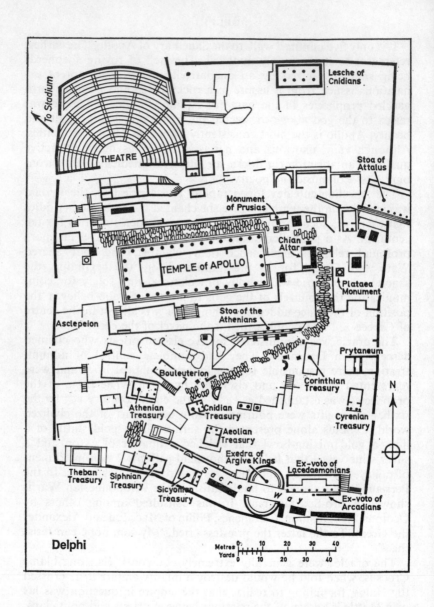

Delphi

Metres 0 10 20 30 40
Yards 0 10 20 30 40

intended marriages, journeys, loans, the sale of slaves. They had to pay a fee and sacrifice a goat, sheep or ox.

At an early stage Delphi was admitted into the Amphictyonic League, one of whose main responsibilities was to safeguard the sanctuary's interests and treasure. But the inhabitants of neighbouring Crissa grew increasingly envious and rapacious; they exacted heavy tolls from consultants approaching the oracle, and their assaults on female pilgrims scandalized the Delphians. The first Sacred War (c. 590 BC) broke out and Crissa was razed to the ground. In the second Sacred War Athens and Sparta sparred over the ownership of the sanctuary. In the mid fourth century, the Phocians, out for loot, seized the sanctuary, thus provoking the third Sacred War. In the last Sacred War the aggressors were the Locrians of Amphissa, who wanted to cultivate their lands, until then undefiled by spade or ploughshare, which the League considered sacred to Apollo. In the end Philip of Macedon had to be called in to put an end to Locrian profanity.

In the third century BC bands of Gauls descended on the sanctuary. The invaders had the elements ranged against them: not only frost and snow, but also earthquakes followed by landslides. Scrambling down the precipices of Parnassus, the Greeks attacked them in the rear. Panic broke out and, in their frenzy, the Gauls slaughtered each other by the hundreds. It was left to Sulla, two centuries later, to plunder the shrine with his usual appalling thoroughness. After him the insatiable Nero carried off five hundred bronze statues to Rome. The philhellenic Hadrian and the Antonines did what they could to restore Delphi to its former splendour, but it was too late. The god's utterances no longer carried conviction. Acceptance of bribes by priests was rife and consultants became sceptical. In the fourth century Constantine the Great removed many works of art to Constantinople. The sanctuary was closed down by the Emperor Theodosius the Great in his famous edict of 393.

In time a hamlet grew up on the ancient deposits. In the seventeenth century Wheler observed traces of marble tiers on the terrace of the stadium and identified niches for statues beside the Castalian Spring. Between 1892 and 1903 the French School of Archaeology at Athens excavated the sanctuary and the Marmaria.

The sanctuary is screened by a semi-circle of cliffs, the rose-coloured Phaedriades, mottled with tufts of evergreens. Stunted pedestals and foundations of treasuries spread across a hillside covered with vetch, mullein and cistus. The bronze and marble statues have long since vanished: looted by Roman and Byzantine emperors or hacked to pieces by Goths and Visigoths. To the east the Castalian stream issues out of a rocky cleft and flows into the hollow valley, enclosed within a ring of mountains that no human hand could have fashioned with a more perfect sense of symmetry. Across the gorge a zigzag mule track climbs the arid wall of Mount Cirphis like some crude graffito scratched by the hand of a giant. Hundreds of feet below the Pleistos trickles sinuously between olive groves towards the Sacred Plain.

The **Sacred Way**, a steep narrow ramp in the form of a double hairpin, begins at the lowest (east) end of the enclosure, beside the brickwork remains of a small square-shaped Roman agora, identified by two unfluted Ionic columns. The paved ramp climbs between bases of statues and treasuries which once jostled against each other on the steep incline. It is all very congested and confusing. The fact that the sanctuary is built on a succession of narrow ledges further complicates the layout. In summer the sun is scorching and cicadas drone relentlessly among parched shrubs.

On the right lie the foundations of the rectangular **ex-voto of the Lacedaemonians**, with traces of a parapet, once adorned with statues of Spartan admirals, against the interior wall. On the west side an imposing exedra, embellished with statues of Argive kings (the bases have been restored), was raised to commemorate the foundation of independent Messene. Next come the treasuries which contained the archives and national treasure of the various states. On the left are the foundations of the **Treasury of Sicyon**, followed by the substructure of the **Treasury of Siphnos**, with slabs carved with egg and dart moulding scattered around it. The visible remains are negligible, but there is a partial restoration in the museum. Other treasuries are scattered about the hillside. To the unprofessional eye they are no more than a mass of rubble, wholly incomprehensible.

At the apex of the first loop, the restored **Treasury of the Athenians** stands on a prominent ledge, one of the landmarks of the sanctuary. Only thirty-three by twenty feet, it was the first Doric edifice to be built entirely of marble. The walls grow thinner as they ascend in order to convey the illusion of height, and the effect of squatness made by the low roof was probably relieved by an acroterium of an Amazon on horseback surmounting the gable. It is not one of the masterpieces of classical architecture.

The Sacred Way now slants obliquely up the hill between foundations of votive edifices. On the left are the remains of the **Bouleuterion**, or Senate House, where the committee of five transacted business and formulated policy. Beyond it is the rock, reinforced by modern masonry, from which the Sibyl Herophile, who alternately called herself wife, daughter and sister of Apollo, chanted the first oracles. A natural fissure in the ground nearby is said to be the entrance to the lair where the serpent Python dwelt. Three steps lead up to the **Stoa of the Athenians**, in which the spoils captured from the Spartans in the Peloponnesian War were displayed. Three of the original eight miniature Ionic columns which supported a wooden roof are ranged against the massive stone-dressing of a great polygonal wall. The interlocking irregular-shaped stones have a smooth honey-coloured surface and were designed to reinforce the god's temple, which was situated directly above the wall, in the event of earth-quakes. Opposite is the open space of the *halos*, or threshing-floor, where Apollo's victory over Python was celebrated every seven years.

At the apex of the second loop a sharp ascending turn to the left (north) leads to the round pedestal of the votive offering set up by all the states who fought at Plataea. Facing it is the **altar of the Chians,** also commemorating the Greek victory over the Persians, composed of rectangular slabs of grey-blue marble – a conspicuous but un-inspiring monument, twice restored during the present century at the expense of wealthy Chian shipowners. Beyond it is a rectangular plinth with a garlanded frieze once crowned by an equestrian statue of Prusias II.

Vertical cliffs rise above the high-lying terrace. A modern ramp climbs the east entrance of the stylobate of the **Temple of Apollo,** which commands a prospect of the whole precinct and the stupendous circular panorama. The perspective is enhanced by the restoration of three massive Doric limestone columns which reflect the changing light – grey, brown or gold – according to the time of day, their huge calcified drums conveying an impression of the scale of the building which was almost as large as the Parthenon.

Of the historical origins little is known, except that the Archaic temple was gutted by fire. In the late sixth century BC it was replaced by a splendid edifice raised by the Amphictyons, restored in the fourth century after an earthquake. The existing foundations and stylobate belong to the later construction. But it is the sixth-century Amphictyonic temple that acquired such fame. A panhellenic subscription was raised to obtain the necessary funds. A massive peripteral temple of the Doric order on a three-tiered stylobate of bluish marble, its front was adorned with marble columns, several drums of which still survive.

Little remains of the sculptures of the temple – only some truncated

117

limbs from the pediment, now in the museum. Among the most famous was the gold effigy of Apollo, behind an altar of eternal fire fed by piles of fir-wood. The seat of the oracle was in the adytum, a chamber penetrated only by priests. The fissure from which the exhalations emanated has not been identified. The priestess was a young virgin, until, on one occasion, she was raped by an impious lecher. After that only older and less attractive women were employed. The Pythia sat on a gold tripod above the fissure, which had a narrow mouth. In a state of frenzied exaltation, munching laurel leaves, she then recited the equivocal conundrums which the bewildered consultants interpreted with the aid of qualified advisers. Sometimes the effect of the exhalations on the priestess was so great that she would leap dementedly from her tripod, suffer from convulsions and die within a few days.

Above the temple a Roman stairway mounts to the **theatre** (originally fourth-century BC, of white marble, restored in grey limestone by the Romans). The cavea has only thirty-three tiers, divided by a paved diazôma, but they are well preserved: so is the orchestra, which is composed of irregular slabs and surrounded by the usual water-conduit. No Greek theatre is a more perfect expression of an architectural creation in relation to its setting, the sweeping forms of the stone tiers repeated in the rocky hemicycle of the Phaedriades. The highest tier is the loveliest viewpoint. In the late afternoon the glow of the Phaedriades is reflected on the slopes of the encircling mountains which turn pink, mauve and finally a deep cobalt blue. The valley fills with obscure shadows. For all its grandeur, it is an intensely serene landscape.

To the right of the theatre, beyond the dried-up stream of Cassiotis, which watered the sacred groves of laurel and myrtle and flowed through a secret channel into the adytum of the temple, where the Pythia drank from its waters before prophesying, a path leads to the site of the **Lesche of the Cnidians**. Its walls were of unburnt brick, and the interior was in the form of a rectangular atrium. Four stone socles for wooden columns which supported the wooden roof are all that remain of this famous rest-house, where pilgrims sought shade and shelter.

From the theatre another path climbs (left) between bushes of arbutus and blackberry to the **stadium**, culminating point of the ancient city. The best preserved of Greek stadia, it once seated seventeen thousand spectators. Built in the mid fifth century BC, it probably did not possess stone accommodation until the fourth. Most of the existing tiers are of the Antonine period. Of the Roman triumphal arch there remain four pillars. On the north bank, against the cliff-side, are twelve well-preserved tiers divided into as many sections by stairways; on the west and south, where there is a sharp declivity buttressed by a polygonal wall supporting the mountain shelf, only six. A slight concavity in the centre was intended to prevent the spectator's view from being obstructed by his neighbours.

Like the Olympic Games, the Pythian festival, also a panhellenic celebration, was held every four years. The athletic programme was the same as at Olympia, with the addition of a long race for boys and, last and most spectacular of all, a race in bronze armour. Victors were crowned with wreaths of laurel. There was no other reward except the adulation so dear to the Greek heart. The honour of a victory at the Pythian Games was second only to that of an Olympic award. Music played an important part. There were singing and flute solo compositions, and later lyre-playing.

From the stadium there is a short cut to the centre of the village. It is more rewarding, however, to zigzag down through the sanctuary, regain the main road and, walking east, reach the **Castalian Spring**. Although now a parking place for motor coaches, this remains an idyllic spot. Large plane trees shade the stream issuing out of a ravine which cleaves the Phaedriades in two. The source, whose water is ice-cold and extraordinarily clear, is the site of an ancient cult-worship. Above the spring is the niche of an old shrine. Consultants and athletes purified themselves by washing their hair in Castalia's lustral water before proceeding to the temple and the stadium. A path leads a short way into the gloomy ravine between the Phaedriades, strewn with huge boulders, pitted with unsuspected crevices. Rocks occasionally crash down from above.

Beyond the café below the road a path winds down past the ruins of the fourth-century BC **gymnasium**, with Roman additions, distributed on different levels and buttressed by supporting walls. This was the practice-ground for athletes entered for the Pythian Games, with a covered race-track in the form of a colonnade running parallel to the open-air one. Among the weeds and thistles lies a stone slab with a groove and socket, believed to have been equipped with a husplex, a mechanical device that made a loud noise as it fell, thus giving the signal for the start.

Beyond the gymnasium the path continues down the hill under shady olive branches to the **Marmaria**, the Sanctuary of Athena Pronaea – less spectacular than Apollo's, but no less beautiful. Carpeted in spring with grape hyacinths and bee-orchids, it extends across a rectangular shelf below the eastern projection of the Phaedriades. Chameleons slither along ruts and cracks in the hacked masonry; bees swarm in the sweet-smelling bay trees. First comes the stylobate of an austere fourth-century BC **Temple of Athena**, guardian of the precinct. Foundations of other temples and buildings, slabs of bluish limestone and fragments of broken drums litter the terraced olive grove. But the pride of the sanctuary is the **Tholos**, a circular fourth-century BC edifice on a three-stepped platform. A work of extreme elegance, it had an outer ring of twenty Doric and an interior one of ten Corinthian columns and was crowned by a conical roof. The gutter of the entablature had a rich ornamentation, including lion-head spouts, one of which is preserved above a restored metope. Three stout yet graceful Doric columns, surmounted by a lintel and fragments of metopes, rise from the stylobate. What purpose the temple served is not known. The setting, with the valley contracting to its narrowest point, is peaceful and bucolic. There is none of the overcrowding that creates such a jigsaw puzzle effect in the Sanctuary of Apollo.

Beyond the Tholos are the substructures of two **treasuries**: the first, that of Marseilles, is thought to have been an elegant little building in the Ionic style, contemporary with the Treasury of Siphnos. Next comes the debris of the early fifth-century BC **Temple of Athena Pronaea**, built of tufa on the site of a much earlier edifice. Three thick Doric columns still survive at the north-west corner and two enormous boulders, lying across the stylobate, provide evidence of the repeated landslides. Beyond the Marmaria lies the necropolis of the ancient city.

Several paths descend through terraces of olive groves to the bed of the Pleistos. Vestiges of the polygonal masonry of supporting walls are visible. In autumn donkeys carrying huge panniers filled with olives clamber up the stony tracks. There are few dwellings: only an occasional chapel, ruined or abandoned. At the bottom of the gorge the feeling of isolation is complete. The stream of the Pappadia trickles down from the Castalian Spring, and there is a grotto, surrounded by contorted boulders, said to be the ancient Sybaris, where the Lamia, a sphinx-like monster that ravaged the countryside, dwelt in a subterranean lair. The walk takes about two hours.

A longer walk or ride (about six hours there and back) is to a more famous grotto, the **Corycian Cave**. The path climbs the southern wall of the Phaedriades behind the village to a highland plateau of stones and stunted pines dominated by the summit of Parnassus. The cave, to which the track ultimately leads (it is essential to have a guide), is at the north-west end of the plateau below the fir belt. I confess I cannot share the enthusiasm of Pausanias, who found it, of all the caves he had ever seen, the finest. Euripides extols its 'mountain-chambers', of which there are said to be forty, their damp walls shining with pink and green reflections. The light of a candle reveals stalactites and stalagmites. The cave was named after the nymph Corycia, beloved of Apollo, and was sacred to the nymphs and Pan. The final ascent to the cave (twenty minutes' hard climbing) can also be reached by car along a rough road from Arachova.

The museum, its barrack-like façade somewhat incongruous in this most classical of landscapes, is situated halfway between the Sanctuary of Apollo and the village. Before entering it is worth looking at two fourth-century AD **floor mosaics** (right of entrance). The decoration is largely composed of birds. The larger one, however, has a wider zoological range, and the mosaicist has reproduced a number of stylized animals.

The interior of the **museum** is spacious and well lit, but few of the precious fragments are numbered. At the top of the flight of stairs stands an ovoid stone object, a copy of the original sacred stone, the omphalos or so-called navel of the earth, with its interlocking marble fillets symbolizing the continuity of life, which was placed in the adytum of the Temple of Apollo. From here on the arrangement is more or less chronological.

Room 2 is full of interest. The **Naxian Sphinx**, a heraldic work of the mid sixth century BC, towers up on a marble plinth crowned by an Ionic capital. Seated on her hind paws, with scythe-shaped wings and a bosom ornamented with stylized feathers, she gazes imperiously into space.

Fascinating fragments of the **frieze of the Treasury of Siphnos** are ranged along the walls. Dated to the sixth century BC, the figures are without the least trace of crudity. The sculptures, though battered, quickly come to life. In the battle of the gods against the giants (north side) a tornado of agitation galvanizes the figures into action. Apollo and an exultant Artemis aim arrows. A stocky-limbed Ares, smirking with self-confidence, takes on a couple of giants over the prostrate body of a third. The east side depicts seated gods debating the issue of the Trojan War. The detail of the frieze is fascinating. Both the pliability of the stylized drapery and the difference in texture between the naked flesh and the long ringlets of the head-dresses point to the chisel of a master sculptor. Particularly beautiful are the filleted manes and tails of the horses in the south frieze. The reliefs ran round the entire building, framed between decorative fillets. In its entirety, with its crowd of agitated figures and prancing horses, the frieze must have been a masterpiece.

Room 3 is dominated by two crude and impressive early sixth-century BC figures of **Cleobis and Biton**, the Argive boys who, in the absence of oxen, harnessed themselves to a chariot and bore their mother across the plain to the Temple of Hera, where she was chief priestess. For their pains, the goddess rewarded the youths with eternal sleep. Cleobis (right), who is better preserved than his brother, possesses all the 'inner mobility' associated with later, more polished Archaic kouroi. Tough, stocky, with short muscular arms, he is endowed with remarkable tension, ready to spring forward and harness himself to his mother's chariot.

Rooms 4–8 contain fragments of metopes from the Athenian Treasury; figures (with uncompleted backs) from the Temple of Apollo; metopes and coffers from the ceiling of the Tholos. In Room 7, beside two bronze kalpis (elegantly shaped ewers with three handles), there is a fine stele of an athlete extending his arms to the right, while a bereaved child, no doubt his servant, gazes up from the right-hand corner.

In Room 9 the **Column of the Dancing Girls**, an unusual monument of the Hellenistic period, soars towards the ceiling. The shaft, about thirty feet high, was so carved as to resemble a gigantic acanthus stalk, the foot of each drum being surrounded by luxuriant foliage. Grouped round the highest tier of leaves are the three girls performing a hieratic dance. In spite of the fundamental awkwardness of the composition, the girls' drapery is loose and flowing and they possess much of the life and grace which the more solemn Caryatids of the Erectheum lack. The nude athlete, the **Thessalian Agas**, winner of fourteen awards at panhellenic festivals, is a good late fourth-century BC marble copy of a bronze work by Lysippus.

The bronze **Charioteer** stands alone in Room 10, against a pale grey background. He could not be more effectively exhibited. The life-size figure, made up of seven separately cast parts, belonged to a quadriga placed on the terrace of the temple, the gift of a Sicilian tyrant in the first half of the fifth century BC. Only the shaft and yoke of the chariot survive. The heavy tubular drapery of the tunic, perfect in its symmetry and rhythm, creates a columnar effect that distinguishes this work from all other Greek statues. From all angles, the figure remains stately, if disproportionate, for the sculptor was endeavouring to correct the distortion which is inevitable when life-size figures are viewed from below.

Room 11, although not without interest, is an anti-climax. Passing out of this last hall one is suddenly confronted with a staggering view of the Phaedriades framed within sheet-glass windows. Russet-coloured, they tower up on either side of the ravine that slashes them into two separate but complementary volumes; on the periphery, the olive groves, watered by rivulets of the Castalian Spring, shelve down into the valley, and purple shadows shift across the outer ring of mountains. The spirit of harmony that must have existed between the creative genius of the Greeks and the external visible world in which they dwelt is not now beyond the bounds of comprehension. What is more difficult to understand is how that colossal hoax, the Delphic oracle, could have taken in so many people for so long.

CHAPTER EIGHT

Eastern Roumeli

Mount Oeta: Heracles's funeral pyre – The Valley of the Spercheus – Lamia – Thermopylae – The Castle of Boudonitsa – Hypati – Karpenisi – The Monastery of Proussos

Turning north from Delphi, the traveller has to find a way across a confused mountain region of northern Greece known as eastern Roumeli (from the Turkish Roum, i.e. Latin Romania), inhabited by a sturdy people, proud of their warrior traditions and reputation for probity. Homer called them 'great-hearted'.

The obvious thing to do is to retrace one's steps through Amphissa and the Gravia pass and drive up to the hamlet of Brallo overlooking the western apex of the Phocian plain. Just beyond the hamlet there is a fork. The road to the west leads into a massif of great splendour. At all points of the compass rise the peaks and escarpments of Mount Oeta, and in the further distance, to the south and east, those of Ghiona and Parnassus. Winding up into the complex of ranges, the road passes through the alpine villages of Oiti and Pavliani, ablaze with hollyhocks in summer, often snowbound in winter. Then the chestnut forests begin: dark tracts covered with bracken. The altitude increases and one enters the conifer belt.

At the signpost *'Pros Kataphygion'* ('to the refuge') a dirt road mounts fir tree-covered slopes to a barren upland. Another signpost marks the site of the **funeral pyre of Heracles**, where an ancient shrine, among the loneliest in the country, was raised to commemorate the hero's metamorphosis into a full-fledged deity.

Here, according to tradition, Heracles, his tormented body corroded by the 'garment of damnation', implored his son to

> . . . cut down a pile of branches
> of firm-set oak and robust wild olive,
> Then lay my body on the pyre and kindle it
> With a flaming torch of pine. Do this in silence –
> I will have no weeping there, no lamentations – [1]

---

[1] Sophocles, *The Women of Trachis*. The 'garment of damnation' is the magic robe, stained with the poisoned blood of the Centaur Nessus, unwittingly

His colossal limbs racked with pain, the 'sacker of cities', the symbol of incomparable masculine strength, ended his career on this lonely seven thousand foot high mountain-top with more dignity than he had showed in his relations with men and monsters. It remained for Sophocles to immortalize his ascent, amid peals of thunder and flashes of lightning, to the marble halls of Olympus, where his father granted him immortality and a charming wife.

The site, which includes the outlines of a megaron and stoa, is littered with limestone slabs, fluted drums and fragments of triglyphs. Unexcavated, these stones have weathered time and the elements for over two millenia. In this rarefied atmosphere, the contours of the central mainland massif assume the aspect of a map. Geography is omnipresent, the emphasis on symmetry pronounced. The vertical spine of the Pindus, dividing the country in two, meets the horizontal chain of Callidromion, Oeta and Panaetolikon. Parallel to it, the Ghiona-Parnassus-Helicon range shuts off all central Greece from the south. It is like a reversed Cross of Lorraine, with the valleys and cultivated plains filling in the interstices between the lateral arms.

Back at the fork beyond Brallo, one follows the road that climbs a lower ridge of Oeta and descends in the dizziest hairpin bends in Greece into the shut-in **valley of the Spercheus**. Eastward, hundreds of feet below, the streams of the Asopus and Gorgopotamos trickle through gorges, and katavothra force their way underground to pour their efflux of silt and sludge into the Spercheus and thence into the Malian Gulf. East of the road, the Athens-Salonica railway line – a remarkable piece of French nineteenth-century engineering – winds through a silent wooded country. A long viaduct spans the Gorgopotamos torrent: scene of a much publicized exploit during the Second World War, when Greek guerrillas, aided by British parachutists, blew up the bridge cutting one of the main supply routes to the Libyan front in 1942. The railway line passes through seventeen tunnels and, clinging to successive ledges, descends the rocky Trachinian precipices which fall sheer, as Sophocles says, from 'Oeta's virgin fields' to the lowlands of 'summer pleasure'.

At the base of the range the road runs across a flat cereal- and tobacco-growing strip, watered by the streams of the Spercheus, to Lamia. Plato calls it 'the pleasant land of Phtiotis'. Frogs croak on muddy banks. On moonless nights myriads of fireflies flit among

---

presented to Heracles by his wife Deianeira, a Calydonian princess whom the demi-god had rescued from a gruesome Acarnanian river god.

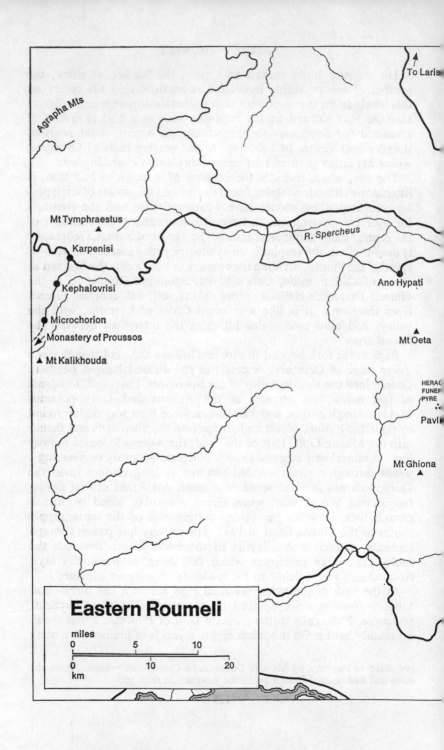

To Laris[...]

Agrapha Mts

Mt Tymphraestus ▲

R. Spercheus

Karpenisi

Kephalovrisi

Ano Hypati

Microchorion

Monastery of Proussos

Mt Oeta ▲

Mt Kalikhouda ▲

HERAC
FUNER
PYRE

Pavl[...]

Mt Ghiona ▲

Eastern Roumeli

miles

| 0 | 5 | 10 |

| 0 | 10 | 20 |

km

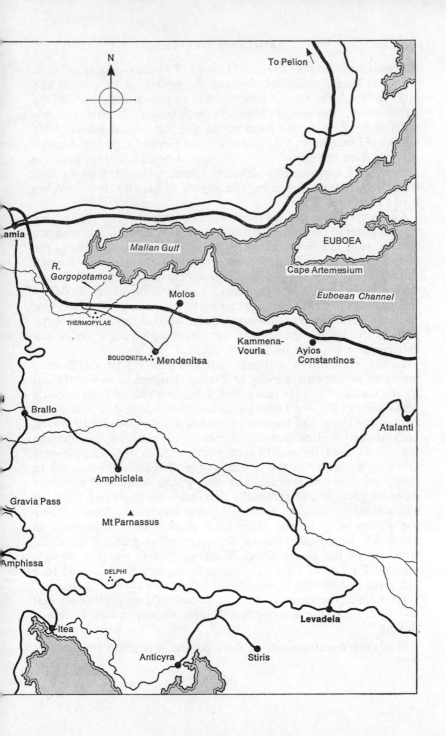

the reeds bordering the stream in honour of whose river god Achilles, who was born hereabouts, fostered the growth of his golden hair and, in Pindar's words, became the 'bronze-armed host of the Myrmidons', the descendants of Eurymedusa, a local princess seduced by Zeus in the form of an ant: an animal subsequently considered sacrosanct throughout central Greece. Here too Achilles trained, from the age of six, to dispose of bears and lions in single combat and consequently developed such physical strength that when passionately embracing the objects of his affections he often broke their ribs.

Lamia sprawls across the foothills of the Othrys range. Although a pivotal point in the lines of communication running north to south, east to west, it offers nothing in the way of sightseeing except the ruined walls of a Catalan castle, built on classical and Roman foundations, scattered among military barracks on a hill spiked with cypress trees above the town. The battlements are Turkish.[2] It is pleasant to sit in the shade of a plane tree, where *kourambiédhes*, buttery shortbreads coated with powdered sugar (a Lamian speciality), popular throughout the country, are served with Turkish coffee in a café beside a fountain in Laou Square.

Lamia remained a military centre. Here Walter de Brienne mustered an impressive array of knights destined to be slaughtered by the Catalans in 1311 (see p. 97). When the War of Independence broke out in 1821, the Turks assembled twenty thousand men in and around the town, and the cobbled streets were crowded with horses, pack-animals and ammunition dumps, while greedy-eyed Albanian soldiers ravaged the neighbouring farms. After the war, Thomas Gordon, an officer in the service of the Greeks, commissioned to stamp out local brigandage, was dining with friends off a dish of excellent game he had personally shot, when his house in Lamia was surrounded by bandits. Gordon's party escaped by jumping over the garden wall, leaving some tasty morsels for the brigands to finish off. Brigandage was so far accepted as part of the social structure of the young Greek kingdom that it was not thought unusual for one of Gordon's would-be captors to be invited to a ball given in Athens in honour of King Otho and Queen Amalia.

At Lamia, the traveller has the choice of two diversions: east and west. I take the east one first. It is the shorter: a long half-day's driving.

---

[2] Entry into the castle area is not always possible. A brigade is often stationed there.

*

A few kilometres beyond the town the **Alamanna bridge** spans a
tributary of the Spercheus: scene of a much romanticized episode
in the opening round of the War of Independence. A large Turkish
force, moving out of Lamia, was met at the bridge – across which the
main Athens-Salonica traffic now streams – by a small band of
determined Greeks under Athanasios Diakos, a deacon who had
abandoned a religious vocation for a military career in the ranks of
the *armatoloi*, a local militia whose members, although officially in
the service of the Sultan, worked for the cause of independence
with a courage and sense of responsibility rarely encountered among
the distracted Greek patriots. At this early stage the Greek uprising
shone like a beacon to the oppressed peoples of the Empire. The
personal ambitions of rival leaders had not yet vitiated the noble
effort. Diakos was youthful and lion-hearted. But an overwhelming
superiority in numbers enabled the Turks to cross the stream. Diakos
was captured and roasted alive. His death remains enshrined in
story-book and folk-song. 'Upright' and 'smiling', surrounded by
Turkish soldiers, he stood on the spit and 'insulted their faith and
called them filth . . .'[3] In Lamia, an undistinguished statue of the
hero adorns the square (named after him) where he was roasted.

As the valley opens out towards the once marshy shore of the
Malian Gulf, the mountain wall rises abruptly from the plain.
North of the road a modern bronze statue of Leonidas marks the
site of Thermopylae. No other major ancient site is more disappoint-
ing. The deposits thrown up by the 'Hot Springs' have created new
alluvial soil and there is no sign of the pass where five thousand
Greeks made their heroic stand in August 480 BC against Xerxes's
army – according to Herodotus's doubtless vastly exaggerated
estimate – of five million men. After the failure of their 'reconnaissance in force' at Marathon, the Persians were taking no chances
and the army they had assembled for the invasion of Europe was
undoubtedly a prodigious one by contemporary standards. In the
fifth century BC the swamp advanced so close to Mount Callidromion
that it left only the narrowest passage for men and chariots. Even
five centuries later Strabo found that the constantly changing configuration of the marshland, fed by streams trickling through under-

[3] From an anonymous song quoted by C. M. Woodhouse, *The Greek War of
Independence*, Hutchinson's University Library, London, 1952.

ground channels, made the countryside extremely complicated. Today the bog is replaced by cultivated fields.

A tumulus opposite the statue of Leonidas is supposed to cover the bones of the Spartan dead. Standing on this mound, one can try to work out the different moves in the battle (probably no more than a holding operation intended to give the Greek states time to deploy their armies). But it is all very baffling. Where was it that the Great King encamped, while he waited in rage and bewilderment at the temerity of this handful of Greeks? In the plain? But it was then an unbridgeable morass. Where was he stationed, when, after launching the attack, he watched the battle 'and three times in terror for his army . . . leaped to his feet'?

Herodotus is the most colourful guide. Throughout two whole days Xerxes beheld his best troops decimated by the skilled archers of the little Greek force. Disheartened by such tenacity, he accepted the offer of a Malian traitor, Ephialtes, to lead part of the Persian army along a secret track, the hidden Anopaea, into the heart of the mountain, whence it could wheel round and attack the Greeks in the rear. The Immortals, guided by this abominable man, marched all night, says Herodotus, 'concealed by oak-woods'. At dawn they looked down on the Phocian encampment. Forewarned of the Persians' approach, for 'the marching feet made a loud swishing and rustling in the fallen leaves', the Phocians tried to cut off the tip of the scythe threatening to envelop the whole Greek position. But the Persians by-passed them, descending by the mountain path on the main body of the Greeks, whose soothsayer had already foretold their doom.

Leonidas, the Spartan king, who claimed descent from Heracles, dismissed most of his allies, insisting with typical Lacedaemonian pride that the honour of making the last-ditch stand should belong to Spartans only (the suggestion that the Peloponnesian allies, aware of the hopelessness of their situation, actually abandoned Leonidas cannot be ruled out). In the morning, continues Herodotus, Xerxes 'poured a libation to the rising sun', and attacked 'the three hundred': all warriors of mature age, personally picked by Leonidas. Caught in the pincers, the Spartans performed prodigies of valour. After Leonidas was killed, they retreated into the narrowest part of the pass, where they fought with daggers, bare hands and even their mouths, until each one fell. After it was all over, Xerxes ordered the head of Leonidas, 'against whom he felt fiercer anger than against any other man', to be cut off and 'fixed on a stake'. Later, a column was raised where the Spartans fell – there is, alas, no vestige of it.

On it was inscribed the famous epitaph:

> Tell them at Lacedaemon, passer-by,
> That here obedient to their laws we lie –

For centuries the 'Hot Gates' remained the only pass through which an invading army could enter southern Greece. In 279 BC it was defended by the Greeks against two hundred thousand Gauls; in 207 BC by the Aetolians, allied to the Romans, against the Macedonians; in 181 BC by Antiochus, King of Syria, against the Romans. In April 1941 officers and men of the British Expeditionary Force bathed in the sulphur springs – where the Persian reconnaissance rider had seen the Spartans combing their hair as they stripped for exercise. At night, with the RAF driven from the skies, the Australian and New Zealand brigades, encamped below the ridges of Callidromion, watched German armoured forces, their searchlights probing the clefts and gorges, assemble unmolested in the plain. Like the Persian archers, the German tanks suffered heavy casualties. But a repetition of the fatal turning movement – this time on an infinitely wider scale – caused the Expeditionary Force to abandon the position. It is curious how each time the defenders of Thermopylae have lost the battle.

Five kilometres south-east of Thermopylae a side road climbs between hedgerows of arbutus and agnus castus. At the village of Anadra, the pine belt is reached; eastward, where Callidromion tapers off into a series of jagged peaks towards the Euboean channel, there is a sudden view of the **castle of Boudonitsa** crowning a beige-coloured hill, around which the hamlet of Mendenitsa nestles among walnut trees and vegetable plots. Boudonitsa, site of ancient Tarphae, which derives its name from the thickly wooded country, was one of the Crusaders' main bulwarks guarding central Greece from invasion from the north. Any hostile force attempting to round the Callidromion range could not fail to be spotted by sentinels stationed on the battlements.

Most impressive is the north-west polygonal wall of the counterscarp rising sheer from a sloping ledge of stubble. It is five minutes' climb from the modern war memorial to the keep, entered through a postern crowned by a massive lintel. Above it rises a squat tower. Ancient slabs, believed to come from a temple of Hera who was worshipped here, are embedded in the masonry among huge thistles with purple flowers. Ruined ramparts overlook cornfields shelving down to the coast. Here, for over two centuries, ruled the Pallavicini of Parma, then the Venetian Zorsi, who brought something of the splendour of their native cities to this wooded wilderness. Boudonitsa was an Italian, never a French, fief, and the fame and prestige of its Marquis was comparable to the strength of his castle and the elegance of his court. It is not among the largest medieval castles in Greece, but in the grandeur and beauty of its position it is comparable to any. In 1414 the last Italian Marquis, inspired perhaps by the proximity of Thermopylae, defended it against the Turks with a bravery and tenacity that would have done credit to Leonidas. With the fall of Boudonitsa, the whole of central Greece passed into Ottoman hands. The Turkish conquerors destroyed the walls and sold the inhabitants, Italian and Greek, into slavery.

The enclosure is pitted with hollows: once vaulted chambers, overgrown with wild fig trees which exude the sun-baked bitter-sweet fragrance of the milky sap secreted in their stalks. A Gothic arch surmounts one side of the pits, probably part of a chapel, beside the north rampart. The wall-walk is too ruined to serve as a promenade, but village boys, who like to act as guides, scramble to the summit of the square tower, where, silhouetted against a background of fir-covered peaks, they pass the time aiming stones at elusive grass snakes rustling among the thistles.

East of the Boudonitsa fork the highway skirts the coast of Opuntian Locris, winding in and out of shingly coves. Across the water Euboea approaches its northern extremity at Cape Artemesium. In the middle of the landlocked bay lies a wooded islet crowned by a lighthouse, one of a group of three which Strabo calls the **Lichadai**, after Lichas, the herald whom Heracles sent from Euboea to announce his arrival to his wife Deianeira at Trachis. The configuration of land and sea becomes so intricate that at times it is difficult to distinguish the Malian Gulf from the Trikkeri or Euboean channels. The entire maritime strip was once studded with ancient townships: for the most part unexcavated, unidentified or razed to the ground by earthquakes. Along the marshy ground between the road and the sea, east of the village of Molos, Colonel Leake identified the site of **Scarphe** (or Scarpheia), through which Flaminius's legions marched in the late second century BC during the final throes of the mortal struggle between the Roman republic and the Macedonian Empire. The city was later submerged when the waters of the Malian Gulf poured over it after a disastrous earthquake.

The hotels, restaurants and tavernas of **Kammena-Vourla**, a fashionable spa, are strung out along the seashore, at the foot of abrupt slopes sliced by wooded gullies filled with evergreens and coursed by rivulets bordered with maidenhair. New villas spring up almost daily – it is under three hours' drive from Athens – but most of the beaches are narrow, sometimes littered with seaweed, and the water of the Euboean Channel lacks the sparkling quality associated with the Aegean.

Nothing, however, could be more attractive than the inlet of **Ayios Constantinos**, filled with caiques and skiffs, against a screen of hills wooded with umbrella pines. There is a motel and it is pleasant to dine at a modest fish taverna in the sheltered anchorage.

The highway then enters a triangular little plain of well-watered orchards, at the apex of which lies the village of **Atalanti**, whence a road climbs over a shoulder of Mount Chlomon to join the old Athens-Salonica road in the Boeotian plain. Leake placed Opus, capital of Opuntian Locris and birthplace of the Homeric hero Patroclus 'of the lovely eyes', south-east of Atalanti. Here, according to the story recounted by the ghost of Patroclus to Achilles before the funerary games celebrated in his honour below the walls of Troy, the infant hero killed a boy in a quarrel 'over a game of bone knuckles', after which he was taken into the palace of Peleus and taught to behave less irresponsibly.[4] The islet in the bay of Atalanti was fortified by the Athenians during the Peloponnesian War as a deterrent to Opuntian privateers who harassed Athenian trade. After skirting the shallow bay, broken up by little spits of land, the highway climbs a saddle of Mount Chlomon and descends into the Boeotian plain at Castro.

*

West of Lamia, the spa of **Hypati** shelters under the wall of Mount Oeta. Over it all – cafés, restaurants and hotel lounges, crowded with patients suffering from skin diseases – hangs the fetid smell of sulphur. More attractive is the village of **Ano-Hypati**, ancient Hypata, on a high ledge above the spa. In Roman times the local women were famous for the practice of black magic and, according to Apuleius, for their participation in a 'solemn festival in honour of Laughter', celebrated annually with practical jokes. Here Apuleius lays the scene of *The Golden Ass*, in which the lusty Lucius, after rubbing himself with an ointment prepared by the witch Pamphile, is transformed into a dumb and docile donkey, with 'sagging lower-lip' and 'large watery eyes'.[5] The story of Lucius's

---

[4] Homer, the *Iliad*.

[5] Apuleius, *The Golden Ass*, translated by Robert Graves, Penguin, Harmondsworth, 1950.

metamorphosis into a beast of burden acquired immense notoriety and even St Augustine (admittedly before his conversion) was completely taken in by it.

Leo the Mathematician, the fame of whose learning was so great that he was offered a thousand gold pounds and eternal peace to promote education at the Caliph of Baghdad's court, was born here in the early ninth century; in the thirteenth the stronghold, now called Neopatras, was ruled by John Ducas the Bastard, a turbulent rebel of imperial lineage, who escaped, when besieged by a 'loyalist' army, by disguising himself as a servant and rushing through the enemy lines, holding a bridle and shouting for a horse. When this was provided by his guileless opponents, he fled to Athens and enlisted foreign (in this case Frankish) aid to recover his domains from his compatriots – an occurrence not without precedent in medieval Greek history. A century later, the Catalan Fadrique, after ravaging the coasts of Greece, made Neopatras his second capital, styling himself 'Vicar-General of the Duchies of Athens and Neopatras'.

It is a painful climb from the village square to the site of the Catalan **castle** (it is essential to ask the way). During part of the near-vertical ascent, the path is shaded by plane trees and thick brambles which form an arbour over a trickle of water from a mountain stream. Winding round a rocky eminence, one perceives a lone crag crowned by a circular tower and fragments of ramparts. The Catalans could not have chosen a more inaccessible site on which to perch a castle whence they could detect hostile armies threading their way through the western and northern defiles of the mountain arena. But ruined watch-towers are not the sole legacy of the Catalan conquerors. The impact made by this strange Spanish interlude on the local inhabitants was considerable and, strangely, lasting. Regarded as one of the perennial scourges the Greeks had learnt to accept as a law of nature, the rough soldiers of fortune of the Catalan Grand Company picked wives for themselves from among the Frankish aristocracy they had defeated at the battle of the Cephisus – 'noble ladies', adds Finlay, 'for whom the day before . . . they would have counted it an honour to be allowed to hold their wash-basin' – and soon earned a terrible reputation for cruelty. For centuries the epithet 'Catalani' remained synonymous with murderers, rapists and torturers. In a peasant ditty a ravished Greek girl, after confessing her shame, implores the Almighty to deliver her seducer into the hands of Catalans – no more awful fate could have been wished on him.

Another more important road west of Lamia follows the course of the Spercheus until the tobacco and cotton fields peter out below the foothills of Mount Tymphraestus (7695 feet), linchpin of the Oeta and Othrys offshoots of the Pindus. Its elegant tapering peak is a landmark throughout much of central Greece. The road ascends between silver firs, affording backward views of the ribbon-like valley, streaked with alleys of poplars, skirts a village amid cherry orchards named after the mountain and enters a shut-in alpine valley through which flows the torrent of the Karpenisiotis. At the end of it is **Karpenisi**, a humble summer resort with some hotels and restaurants. An expensive new hotel – all sheet-glass windows – crowns a more distant bluff. After dark, on summer nights, glow-worms flash signals to their mates in the shrubberies bordering the road leading up to it. Largely rebuilt after its destruction by both Germans and Communist rebels during and after the Second World War, Karpenisi has nothing to offer in the way of sightseeing. But the air is crystalline. It is also one of the two starting-points (the other is Agrinion in western Roumeli) for a visit to a famous place of pilgrimage: the Monastery of Proussos. The road is in a deplorable condition, but the experience more than rewards the endurance test undergone by the driver in getting his car through the narrow defiles and up and down the dizzy hairpin bends overhanging terrible precipices.

A short descent from Karpenisi ends in a well-watered valley of maize fields, cherry and apple orchards. Here **Kephalovrisi** marks the site of a notable engagement during the War of Independence. A Turkish force of four thousand men was surprised one summer night in 1823 by Marco Botsaris, one of the ablest champions of Greek independence, and three hundred and fifty Suliots, a warrior tribe of Albanian descent. The Turkish commander's tent was pitched in a low-walled enclosure protecting the beehives which still spread across the hillside. But although the Turks were taken unawares, some of their veterans were, in Finlay's words, 'on the watch when the head of Botsaris rose above the wall and showed itself marked on the grey sky, and a ball immediately pierced his brain'. The gloom cast over the Suliots by the death of their leader did not prevent them from indulging in an orgy of plunder. For years they were to disport themselves with the ornamented yataghans and silver-mounted pistols they acquired in an engagement which, though by no means decisive, was rendered popular by historians and versifiers of the more romantic episodes of the war.

The road passes through the plane tree-shaded village of Microchorion – site of the Suliot encampment – at the foot of Mount Chelidonia (Mount Nightingales); another peak, that of Mount Kalikhouda, towers immediately to the east of Gavros. One crosses the Karpenisiotis, bordered by ilex and plane, and enters a gorge rent with screes whose higher levels of rock reflect a bright purple light when just touched by the sun's rays. The gorge narrows to a point where it is no more than forty yards wide, with the road imprisoned between walls of granite, alternatively brick-red, brown and purple. The chapel of Ayios Sostis (St Saviour) clings to a ledge of cliff above.

Beside the torrent of ice-cold water, I stopped at a *khan*, called the '*Spiti tou potamou*' (the house of the river), where an old peasant and his incongruously stylishly dressed grandson (on holiday from Athens) offered me welcome refreshment. From here, in the gloomy shade, I looked up at the sunny face of the cliff and saw a hatchet-shaped aperture in the rock; beyond it blue sky. Through this *perasma* (passage) the venerable wonder-working icon of Proussos is said to have once flown in its quest for a final resting place. The stratification of the winding gorge becomes more curious, the rock seamed with vertical zigzags and squiggles like music notes. Climbing above the bed of another ice-green torrent, the Krikelliotis, abounding in trout, which swirls round a vertical bluff, one sees the distant peak of Panaetolicon, the ubiquitous 'Arab's Head', which dominates the Aetolian massif. As the road ascends one looks down on ranks of nodular outcrops of rock, overgrown with tufts of ilex, rising like ninepins out of the gorge. On the opposite bank of the torrent extend forest tracts. As the gorge opens out between fir-clad heights, one catches a glimpse of the houses of **Proussos** scattered across a cultivated slope above an irregular bowl, out of which more rocky cones, sometimes with spherical or bulbous summits, rise in terrible disarray. Winding among these awesome precipitous bluffs, the road descends towards the bowl, making for a needle of rock crowned by a clock tower.

In the shade of plane trees, beside a chapel, lie the ruins of a Greek secret school, founded during the Turkish occupation by Cosmas the Aetolian who tried to instruct his uncouth fellow-mountaineers in the virtues of their Hellenic heritage. Nearby is the church of the **Monastery of Proussos**, thought to be the site of a sanctuary of Athena and later a Christian shrine which became the refuge of an anchorite. The monastery is an unattractive modern building raised on the charred foundations of several earlier monastic establishments. The church, an ordinary cruciform domed little edifice, is strikingly situated in a deep concavity of vertical rock; it has thus been protected for centuries from the boulders that hurtle down in the course of landslides. The painted decoration of the interior is undistinguished.

In the courtyard pilgrims, holding long tapers, drag themselves penitentially on hands and knees to a side chapel which contains the flying **icon of the Virgin Proussiotissa**, famous for its healing powers. Solemn-faced worshippers queue in single file, their pained expressions suggesting the ordeal they have endured while crawling across the paving stones. They enter the dimly-lit interior and kiss the holy image. Only the brown faces of the Virgin and a Semitic-looking Child are visible, the rest of the ancient icon being elaborately silver-plated. Like so many other thaumaturgical icons in the country, it is apocryphally attributed to the hand of St Luke and particularly revered because it is said to have been brought to Greece by an aristocratic Byzantine youth from Broussa in Bithynia. Directed by the Virgin herself in a dream, he rescued it from the impious hands of imperial agents during the second Iconoclast period (ninth century). Unfortunately the icon seems to have given him the slip in the course of the journey. At Hypata peasants informed him they had seen it flying in the direction of the Eurytanian mountains. In another vision, the Virgin informed the young nobleman that she had finally selected the abode for her icon and directed him to the cave of Proussos (named after Broussa), where he founded the first church of the Proussiotissa. To this day, in spite of its inaccessibility, the icon has not ceased to be venerated by streams of pilgrims during a whole week in August.

The library and museum of the monastery contain little of interest: post-Byzantine Books of Gospels, filigree work, reliquaries and crosses.[6]

Beyond Karpenisi a fine west-bound road winds through the highlands of the southern Pindus, overhanging rugged gorges which run parallel in a north-south axis. To the north rise the pyramidal peaks of the Agrapha mountains, so remote and wild as to have remained 'agrapha' (unwritten) in the Turkish tax-collector's rolls. For pure form and structure there is little in Greece to compare with them. Hereabouts a British military mission had its nomadic headquarters during the Second World War, supplying Greek resistance forces with arms and gold pounds. Its efforts to prevent the rival Right and Left wing factions from fighting each other instead

[6] The west-bound traveller may make use of a rough road which links Proussos with Agrinion via Thermon (see p. 346).

of the enemy were not always crowned with success. The road descends in loops through wooded country into the Megdova basin, a large artificial lake, at the bottom of which lies a submerged Byzantine church of the ninth century: one of the many once tucked away in this secluded mountain area where the faithful could worship their beloved icons without fear of molestation by the provincial agents of Iconoclast emperors. On two sides of the lake, north and east, mountains rise sheer, ranged one behind the other like screens, escarpment upon escarpment, wooded on the higher levels, with the Megdova flowing swiftly between scrub-covered hills towards the Acarnanian plains in the west.

CHAPTER NINE

Thessaly: The Plain

Domokos – Pharsala – Larisa – Crannon – Tyrnavos – Elasson: The Church of the Olympiotissa – Mount Olympus

The northbound traveller who may not wish, nor have the time, to visit the Volos area and the Pelion villages can drive straight across the Thessalian plain.[1] His goal would be Larisa. There he can choose between two routes: across the foothills of Olympus or through the Vale of Tempe. Both lead directly into Macedonia.[2]

North of Lamia road and rail climb the Othrys mountains, a lateral offshoot of the Pindus range, once associated with the legend of the flood of Deucalion, the Noah of Greek mythology. When Zeus, incensed by the degeneracy of mankind, caused a flood to wipe out the human race, Deucalion, the Phthian king, hastily built a ship in which he placed his wife and abundant provisions. When the swollen waters retreated, the vessel landed on one of the summits of Mount Othrys (some mythographers alternatively suggest Parnassus, Athos or Etna). Zeus then instructed Deucalion to throw stones behind his back as he went to offer sacrifice at the sanctuary of Themis, a primeval personification of law, order and equity. From these stones sprang a race of men more to the liking of the father of the gods.

The puce-coloured slopes, also associated with the seat of Hellen, founder of the Hellenic race, are featureless and unwooded, but

[1] The Pelion villages and beaches (together with the Volos periphery), most conveniently reached from the national road along the east coast, are described in Chapter 10. The Meteora monasteries, at the north-west apex of the Thessalian plain, deserve a chapter to themselves (see Chapter 11).

[2] The traveller wishing to follow the route described in the present chapter, without making the far more interesting diversions to the Pelion villages and Meteora monasteries, will not find it a very long one. But it would mean reaching Servia or Katerini (both in Macedonia), neither of which offers any attractions or amenities, late in the evening. To drive on to Salonica in the dark would be exhausting. A wiser alternative, I think, would be to break the journey for the night at Larisa, the Thessalian capital. A visit to Crannon could thus be included in the itinerary.

there are fine backward views of the receding backcloth of Mount
Oeta. The monotony of the descent into the lowlands is relieved by
the ruined walls of a medieval castle on a rocky eminence above
Domokos, the ancient Thaumakoi (the Wonder City), so-called
because of the immense prospect it commands of the flat chequer-
board of central Thessaly. Here an enthusiastic but undisciplined
Greek army suffered a humiliating defeat in 1897, when only the
diplomatic intervention of the Protecting Powers prevented Sultan
Abdul Hamid's German-trained divisions from advancing on the
capital.[3]

The plain of Thessaly, the most spacious in Greece – Herodotus,
supported by modern geologists, says it was originally a lake – is
sealed in by mountains: in the west by the serrated spine of the
Pindus, in the north by Olympus and the desolate Cambunians,
in the north-east by Pelion and Ossa, with Othrys bolting the door
in the south. When Xerxes entered the plain and the guides pointed
out how thoroughly shut in by mountains it was, the Great King
decided that should the Thessalians not submit to him, he would
block the only exit, the vale of Tempe, and flood the whole country.
The climate is one of extremes, and in summer a metal-coloured haze
hangs tantalizingly over the legendary mountains. So heavily
blanketed in cloud is Olympus – no epithet of Homer's is more
apt than that of 'cloud-gathering Olympus' – that even its foothills
are seldom visible from the plain. In remotest antiquity the Aeolians
dwelt here, and Endymion, beloved of the Moon, was a native of
the country. Then, like Lacedaemon, it was inhabited by the Hera-
clidae, descendants of Heracles. Afterwards the Thesprotians
crossed the Pindus mountains and reduced the Thessalians to serf-
dom. The plain soon became highly populated; oligarchical governments flourished; and the landed gentry led a life of opulence and
ease. The horses of Thessaly, which still graze in the cornlands, were
famous throughout Greece, and the Thessalian cavalry was an
important factor in every war. Philip of Macedon found the country
hard to conquer; when he did, it was useful to him in grain, horses
and manpower.

Why Strabo should call this featureless landscape, pock-marked
with little oases of stunted trees, 'a country most blessed', remains a
mystery. Deep cart-tracks furrow the cornfields around dust-caked –
in winter mud-encrusted – villages, and in spring storks perch with
an air of impervious elegance on the domes of red-brick churches.

---

[3] 'The Thirty Days' War' between Greece and Turkey.

Huge sows wallow beside filthy troughs, like the swine sacrificed to Aphrodite who was worshipped in the ancient cities of the plain. But most of the Thessalian lowlands defy description. How right Sterne was when he said there is 'nothing more terrible to travel-writers than a large rich plain if it is without great rivers or bridges, and presents nothing but one unvaried picture of plenty'.

The road passes through the villages of **Neon Monastiron** (the well preserved walls of ancient Proerna, a minor Thessalian township, spread across the hillside to the right) and **Pharsala**, the ancient Pharsalia, scene of Caesar's masterly set-piece battle: first of the three engagements fought on Greek soil or in Greek waters – Pharsalia, Philippi, Actium – that decided the fate of the Roman world. Low rocky hills overlook the fields through which the stream of the Enipeus flows, and where the 'flower and strength of Rome', says Plutarch, met 'in collision with itself'. The level ground was admirably suited to the advance of Caesar's brilliantly-led battle-trained legions against the amorphous force assembled by Pompey whose morale was already shaken by a series of alarms and omens, culminating in the sight of a ball of fire issuing above Caesar's tent and landing in the middle of his own camp. In a few hours, Plutarch continues, 'the plains of Pharsalia were covered with men, horses and armour', and the great Pompey, famous for his majestic countenance and 'languishing eyes', was fleeing towards the sea, his army routed, his tents and pavilions decorated with embroidered carpets and garlands of myrtle, abandoned to Caesar's cohorts. Today Pharsala is remarkable only for its earthquakes and *halva*, a popular sickly-sweet preparation made from sesame seeds.

Beyond the stream of the Enipeus, which hardly lives up to Ovid's description of '*Enipeus irreqietus*' and whose river god sparred with Poseidon for the love of the beautiful princess Tyro, a chain of barren hills crosses the plain in an east-west direction. On their shadeless slopes were fought the two battles of Cynoscephalae (The Dogs' Heads), so-called after their ugly mis-shapen forms. In the first engagement (346 BC) Pelopidas, the friend of Epaminondas, was killed by the forces of a powerful Thessalian tyrant who was disputing Theban supremacy; in the second (197 BC), Philip V of Macedon, commanding an exhausted army largely composed of old men and boys, was routed by the legions and elephants of Flaminius.

The road continues across the plain. Occasionally there are settlements of Vlachs, descendants of the medieval Wallachians, who dwell in alpine villages in the Pindus, but in winter descend into the lowlands, with their sheep, women and prickly sense of personal pride. In the Middle Ages Thessaly was overrun by these nomads whom Benjamin of Tudela likened to mountain goats leaping from stone to stone, plundering and ravaging as they went, but 'invincible in battle and not to be tamed by any King'. After them came the Serbs, pouring over the Macedonian border in the fourteenth century, flushed with the victories of Stephen Dušan who dreamt of establishing a great Slavonic empire and very nearly did. The chaos created by a civil war in Constantinople gave the upstart Dušan the opportunity to crown himself 'Emperor of the Greeks and the Serbs'. On his Serbian governor of Thessaly the new 'Emperor' conferred the presumptuous title of 'Caesar'. But by the end of the fourteenth century the rivalries of Serbs, Greeks and Wallachians were swept away in the Ottoman conquest. The Turks repopulated Thessaly with peasants from Asia Minor, and leisure-loving pashas carved large estates out of the lands abandoned by the frightened Greeks. Consequently Thessaly was one of the few provinces in the country in which villages grew up with mixed Greek and Turkish populations. This triple influx – Wallachian, Serb and Turkish – left a Balkan stamp on the province.

Larisa, the provincial capital, through which the vanquished Pompey fled to the sea, lies at the north-eastern end of the plain. A garrison town and important centre of communications, with plenty of hotels and a motel on the Athens-Salonica highway, it is a useful halt for the traveller. More than one military plot has been hatched in the local barracks and officers' messes, and the success of any attempt at a military take-over of the country is said to depend largely on the role played by the army corps stationed here.

In antiquity the city was ruled by the Aleudae, whose mythical founder, a golden-haired cowherd, was courted by a dragon – dragons, according to Aelian, in one of his zoological treatises, being 'excellent judges of beauty'. In the classical age we know that Gorgias, the glamorous Sicilian Sophist, was greatly honoured as a teacher of rhetoric at the court of the Aleudae who, somewhat boorish people themselves, liked to be surrounded by scholars. Pindar too was a much venerated guest, and Hippocrates died here at the age of over a hundred – a fitting life-span for the 'father of medicine'. The acropolis, which overlooks a loop of the Peneius, the chief river of Thessaly, is now crowned by a modern cathedral reached by a winding stairway with bizarre stone dressing. On the south side of the cathedral a fluted column, an Ionic capital and some broken marble plaques mark the site of a temple of Aphrodite. East of the cathedral rises a squat block of masonry; formerly a

Turkish fort with blind arches and a substructure which preserves features of the architectural style of the original market town, to which all the produce of Thessaly was once carried by beasts of burden. Here Edward Brown, a seventeenth-century English traveller, observed 'five thousand camels for the service of the Grand Seignor'. Two hundred years later another generation of dromedaries was sketched by Edward Lear, as the animals loped, in single file, with their stupid supercilious expressions across the plain.

The local archaeological museum is housed in a former mosque (Ayios Vessarionos Square). It contains fossilized remains of pre-historic monsters dated to the Inter-Glacial and Last Ice Ages, discovered in the sandbanks of the Peneius, Neolithic tools and weapons from neighbouring sites, roughly carved fourth-century BC stelae excavated on the acropolis and reliefs with figures of mounted horsemen depicted riding towards a symbolic tree.

From the southern periphery of the town a dirt road runs south-west to the site of ancient **Crannon**. The custodian, without whom it is too difficult to find the way, is generally in the café in the hamlet of the same name. The acropolis once spread across a low treeless eminence, nearly a mile in circumference. Now littered with sherds, it commands an immense prospect of corn and maize fields, the former grazing grounds of the flocks of the ancient Scopadae, a Thessalian royal family proverbial for their power and wealth. In summer the site is best visited in the late afternoon when the rolling fields of stubble turn pale yellow and the outlines of mountains – Pindus, Olympus, Ossa ranged in a horseshoe round the northern end of the plain – emerge out of the heat haze. One of Crannon's most distinguished visitors was Simonides, the lyric poet and rival of Pindar, who honoured the Scopadae in verses celebrating the victories of their swift-footed mares in races held in the shadeless prairies. But the Scopadae, like most Thessalian rulers, were uncouth and mean; they refused to pay Simonides for his services as a court versifier. So they met with retribution, relates the poet in one of his elegies, when the roof of the building in which they were feasting collapsed over their heads. Fortunately, Simonides had just been ordered to interview two suspicious-looking youths lurking outside the palace gate. The young men turned out to be the Dioscuri, protectors of the laws of hospitality who flew about the country disguised as sparrows. They promptly paid the poet half the arrears owed to him.

The only extant remains of Scopadic power are three extremely well preserved **fifth-century** BC **tholos** tombs: mausoleums with beehive conical roofs – a survival of the first Mycenaean-type royal sepulchre on a smaller scale. The first tomb I visited was circular, the second (further south) square with a square doorway supported by three half-engaged pieces of masonry resembling colonnettes, the third (still further south), possibly the resting place of some Scopadic king, had traces of painting on the wall. The masonry of the three tombs is in the best fifth-century BC tradition. Numerous mounds of earth scattered about the acropolis area are thought to be more tombs awaiting the attention of archaeologists. There is a spaciousness about the scene, untouched as yet by any visible human habitation; the swallows' nests in the tholos tombs alone suggest the neglect to which this evocative site has been relegated.

It was in the open plain here, in the summer of 322 BC, that Antipater, strengthened by Craterus's contingents from Asia, mustered a strong force of infantry, cavalry, archers and slingers to deal a death-blow to the brave but insubordinate remnants of the insurgent democratic states, led by Athens, which had hoped to throw off the Macedonian yoke after the death of Alexander the Great.

To the east of the tholos tombs, walking eastward across more humps and undulations, past the post-Byzantine church of Zoodochos Pighi (The Source of Life) one comes to a large, well preserved Roman kiln for firing pots. All this part of Thessaly was strongly contested by the armies of the Roman Republic in their wars with the Macedonian Empire, and after the final Macedonian defeat it became a flourishing Roman province.

North-west of Larisa the first place of any importance is **Tyrnavos**, a hot dusty little town below a spur of Olympus. Allegedly the best ouzo in Greece is made here, and the cafés in the large public square are well stocked with it. On the first day of Lent an unusual procession, originating in some primitive Orphic rite, winds through the streets. The participants, men only, carry large earthenware objects shaped like phalluses. They call themselves 'phallus-bearers' and take the proceedings very seriously, turning a deaf ear to the ribald remarks of the youthful spectators.

After Tyrnavos the road penetrates deep into the Cambunian range, past the ruins of a second-century BC watch-tower perched on a conical hill at the entrance of a spacious valley streaked by Homer's 'delectable Titaresius', a fast-flowing tributary of the Peneius which curls round beige-coloured hills between thickets of poplars and whose waters, adds the poet, did not mingle with those of the main stream but floated 'along the top of them like oil'. A gradual ascent ends in a little plain, with **Elasson**, a market town, spreading on either side of a stream spanned by an old Byzantine bridge and surrounded by hills of white clay soil. Homer calls it 'white Olosson'.

The ancient citadel stood on a hill above a ravine, now crowned by the somewhat over-restored Byzantine **Church of the Olympiotissa** (The Olympian Virgin), whose senior prelate, the Bishop of Elasson, was among the delegates who travelled to Russia in 1589 to found the Patriarchate of Moscow. Commissioned by that indefatigable church-builder, the Emperor Andronicus Palaeologus II (1282–1328), the Olympiotissa is architecturally similar to many churches in Salonica (see the Holy Apostles, St Catherine's). The juxtaposition of a low narthex and tall naos is striking. Elegance is not lacking in the architect's conception. But the harmony of volumes and interrelation of planes of the earlier cruciform church are markedly absent. The elongated drum, which we see again and again in Macedonia, at first excites, then palls. In the end, one realizes that it vitiates the sturdy structural unity for which earlier Byzantine church-builders were justly famous. The interior frescoes of the late Byzantine period are poor in artistic quality, narrative in style, conventional in execution. More striking are a fine marble column in the entrance door between the narthex and the nave and the carved wooden two-leafed door (west) dated c.1300. Islamic influences are evident in the ivory inlay of the panels, each of which is carved with different designs of meshes forming circles, crosses, triangles.

Beyond Elasson the country becomes less domesticated. Olympus draws nearer, the huge massif buttressed by chalky foothills. There are some formidable views of deep crevices, filled with snow all the year round, of the 'Needle', the highest peak in Greece (9750 feet), and of the dolomite of the Throne of Zeus soaring skywards. It was because of this physical dominance over all other structurally more beautiful mountains that the ancient Greeks presumably chose its summit, which represented Heaven itself, as the residence of the gods.

After crossing a bleak windswept saddle of the Cambunians, the road descends towards Servia in western Macedonia.

An alternative route over the Olympus country into Macedonia begins at a fork beyond Elasson. The north-east-bound road climbs to a region of bare uplands at a very considerable altitude. In summer the cold can be penetrating. Crossing the watershed, the road, which has now completed a full semi-circle of Olympus, winds through forests. Immediately to the south the 'Needle', now seen from a new angle, projects above a mass of naked rock; chasms fall vertically down to wooded foothills.[4] The villages of Kallithea and Ayios Demetrios afford a welcome sign of domesticity. The east Macedonian coastal strip comes into view and the road, after rounding bluffs and scarps, ends at the town of Katerini in the plain.

[4] For the most impressive view of Olympus, see p. 178.

CHAPTER TEN

Thessaly: The Pelion Villages

❧

Phthiotic Thebes – Volos – Demetrias – Pagasae – Mount Pelion: Miliés;
Tsangaradhes; Kissos; Zagora; Macrinitsa; Ano-Volos – Pherae

From Lamia to Volos, starting-point for a visit to the Pelion villages, is easy: a couple of hours' drive along the national road. From Stylis, which lies on the Malian Gulf, the Callidromion range is seen to peter out, not without some spectacular flourishes, into the Euboean Channel. The shallow waters of the gulf, whose ancient inhabitants, says Aristotle, established a 'democratic' military regime by admitting every serving or ex-hoplite to a share in government, form one of those deep inroads which the Aegean is constantly making into the land mass.

Skirting the southern foothills of the Othrys range, one has some tantalizing glimpses of the Oreos Channel between Euboea and the mainland, with great cliffs alternately advancing and receding across the water. The road then enters the dreary seaward end of the Thessalian plain, with Almyros, a dusty shanty town, in the middle of it, and poplars fringing the pebbly shore of a mud-coloured inland sea. Beyond a branch road to Volos rises a range of low hills, once crowned by the acropolis of ancient Pyrasus. To the left, between the ridge and the box-like houses of maritime Nea Anchialos, extends a field of impressive ruins in a fenced-in enclosure. This is the Early Christian **site of Phthiotic Thebes** (not to be confused with the more illustrious Boeotian Thebes). In antiquity Pyrasus was the chief maritime centre of Thessaly, and in the Hellenistic era it endured a frightful siege by Philip V, a martial king of Macedonia and unbridled alcoholic, who ostentatiously renamed it Philippopolis. The ruins are mostly of the Early Christian period and Procopius records that Justinian considered the city, the senior bishopric of Thessaly, of sufficient importance to strengthen its walls.

Fragments of towers and ancient fortifications are discernible along a circuit of over two miles. The Early Christian site, not yet exhaustively excavated, is a muddle, and ground plans are jealously guarded by archaeologists still working on the site. It is best to

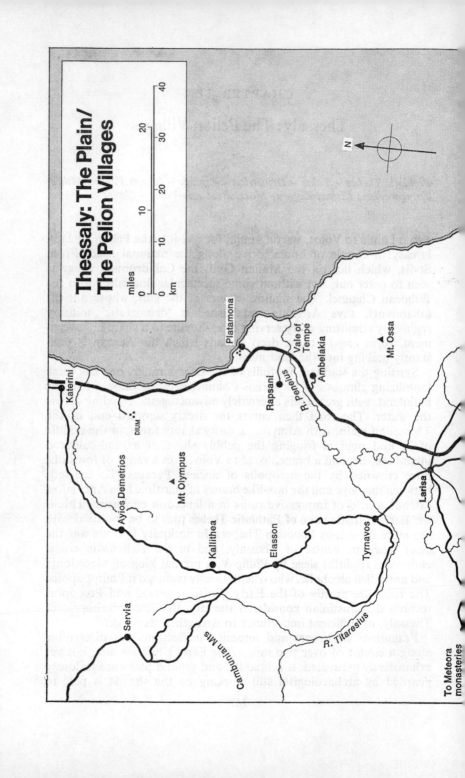

Thessaly: The Plain/
The Pelion Villages

miles

km

10   20   30   40

N

Katerini

DIUM

Platamona

Mt Olympus

Ayios Demetrios

Kallithea

Elasson

Tyrnavos

Rapsani

R. Peneius

Vale of Tempe

Ambelakia

Mt. Ossa

Larisa

Servia

Cambunian Mts

R. Titaresius

To Meteora
monasteries

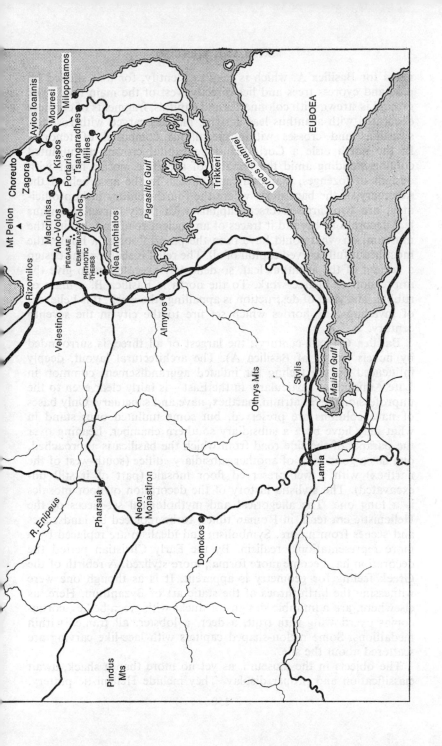

make for **Basilica A**, which is easy to identify, for it is shaded by pine and cypress trees and lies directly west of the main road. The ground is strewn with colonnettes and capitals, fragments of cornices decorated with acanthus leaf designs, plaques carved with rosettes, swastikas and crosses within medallions composed of tendrils. In the north aisle a Corinthian-type capital crowns an unfluted column standing amid the remains of a pebble mosaic floor with designs of lozenges, diamonds and circles. In the apse behind the sanctuary of the baptistery, where the fourth-century bishop officiated, are two large reversed capitals with finely carved acanthus leaf decoration: beyond it traces of an ancient road and, behind the museum, on what could have been the paved floor of a house, the most beautifully carved capital of all. The relief is shallow, the design a variant of the acanthus leaf, so delicately executed as to give the impression of filigree work. To the north is Basilica B, a mass of rubble. The vista of destruction is appalling: the work, it is believed, of invading Slav hordes which set fire to the city in the seventh century.

Basilica C (sixth-century), the largest of all three, is surrounded by hovels (south of Basilica A). The architectural layout, deeply influenced by the feeling for inflated aggrandisement common in Late Antiquity – particularly in the East – is fairly clear even to the unprofessional eye: atrium, narthex, nave and sanctuary. Only bases of nave columns are preserved, but some unfluted ones stand in what may have been a subsidiary southern chamber. Leaning over the parapet of the side road from which the basilica is approached, one has a good view of another subsidiary edifice (south-west of the narthex) with a well-preserved floor mosaic (part of it still unexcavated). The stylistic history of the decoration of floor mosaics is a long one. The allegorical and mythological set-pieces of the Hellenistic era tend, in Roman times, to be replaced by landscapes and scenes from nature. Symbolism and idealism are replaced by a more representational realism. By the Early Christian period the decoration has become more formal, more stylized. A rebirth of the Greek feeling for geometry is apparent. It is as though one were witnessing the birth-throes of the static art of Byzantium. Here, as elsewhere, are admirable designs of ducks with green bellies, cornucopias overflowing with fruit, a deer, a lobster, all framed within medallions. Some melon-shaped capitals with lace-like carving are scattered about the site.

The objects in the museum, as yet no more than a shack, await classification and proper display. They include Hellenistic pottery,

Roman glass, ornate Early Christian capitals, some Christian stelae, among which is a crude but evocative one of a departing soul riding a horse towards an effigy of Death. Beyond Nea Anchialos, the road reaches the Volos-Larisa highway. One turns east to reach the former, which lies at the head of the Pagasitic Gulf, at the foot of Mount Pelion. In antiquity this fertile mountain bastion of eastern Thessaly was known as Magnesia; it was always richer in legend than history. Destroyed by an earthquake in 1955, **Volos** has a somewhat raffish air, in spite of its prosperous bourgeois provincialism. But it has a fine port, and the holds of ships anchored in it are filled with some of the best fruit in Greece – apples, peaches, pears – grown on the Pelion foothills. Until recently a little toy train clattered along a narrow-gauge line down the length of E. Venezilou Avenue and thence through a lush countryside to Miliés. The Xenias Hotel is spacious, well planned and has a private beach. Less expensive hotels line the wide waterfront.

The **site of ancient Iolchus,** home of Jason, has been excavated at the west end of the town. Turning right, off the main road to Larisa, into Papapyriazi Street (and then left), one reaches the hillock of Ayioi Theodori overlooking a brick factory. The acropolis obviously commanded the entrance to the head of the gulf. Only a cluster of hovels and remains of a medieval wall now replace the 'well-made streets', described by Apollonius of Rhodes, where Jason dwelt in a house filled with 'many servants, men and women', and costly ornaments. Strabo believes the town was destroyed from the earliest times. It is not an evocative site. The only identifiable feature is the dry river-bed of the Anaurus, which Jason happened to be fording on a rainy day when he saw an old woman in distress amid the swollen waters. He promptly carried her on his back across the stream, whereupon she revealed herself to be Hera and promised him her patronage.

The **museum,** in Athanasaki Street, possesses a fine collection of painted stelae from Demetrias. Among the most striking are those of an austere headless warrior (No. 235), of Choirele (No. 55) and of three elegantly disposed figures (No. 355). The unpainted stelae include two fascinating examples of the late Roman period: one male and two female figures surmounted by bunches of grapes and the snake of Asclepius (No. 388); and a child flanked by two female figures (No. 422). Crude, rough, yet forceful, these reliefs have a distinct stylistic relation to works of the so-called 'expressionist' school of Early Christian sculpture, in which the Hellenic ideals of grace and charm are replaced by the desire to express a more profound inner emotion. There is also a lovely little torso of Aphrodite (No. Δ715). Among the prehistoric objects are Palaeolithic and Neolithic tools from the neighbouring sites of immense antiquity.

The coastal road south of Volos leads to the **site of Demetrias**, which once enjoyed some fame as a flashy and ostentatious city founded by Demetrius Poliorcetes, one of the most brilliant personalities of the Hellenistic world, whose military career was spent in far-flung campaigns against the Diadochi (successors of Alexander the Great). His private life was scandalous. In Athens he indulged in outrageous debaucheries, even polluting the sacred precincts of the Parthenon. So great was his passion for the elderly prostitute Lamia that he consecrated a temple to her. On another occasion he was enamoured of an Athenian youth, who, loth to respond to the King's advances, was driven into a bathroom where he dived into a cauldron of boiling water, thus seeking, says Plutarch, 'a death untimely and unmerited, but worthy of the country and of the beauty that occasioned it'. On contemporary coins Demetrius is represented with horns, in emulation of Dionysus, his favourite deity. But despite his 'luxury and voluptuousness', continues Plutarch, he was fertile in resource, prompt in the execution of his plans, and had a 'heroic look and air of kingly greatness'.

To the right (west) of the road an ancient theatre is scooped out of a conch-like fold in the hill. The lower tiers are still faced with stone seats and the orchestra, more than a half-circle, is unusually large: probably designed to suit the tastes of its flamboyant founder. Towers rise from the lozenge-shaped enceinte of ruined walls that extend across the hillside.

Beyond the theatre the road bears east. The first turning to the right leads to the **acropolis of Pagasae**, more ancient and venerated than upstart Demetrias, but with even less to offer in the way of visible ruins: only some fragments of ancient walls. The low hill, crowned by a whitewashed chapel, overlooks a salt pan. To the north, the spurs of Pelion rise abruptly from the inland sea which took its name, the Pagasitic Gulf, from this prehistoric site, once the port of Iolchus, and later of Pherae. On the beach below, now dotted with modest tavernas, was built the Argo, on which Jason and the Argonauts embarked, while their friends waved to them from the shore. According to the Delphic oracle, the land of Iolchus would know neither peace nor prosperity until the fleece of the golden ram, on whose back Phryxus fled to Colchis in order to avoid being sacrificed, was brought back on a ship navigated by heroes. They were certainly a famous crew – Tiphys the pilot and Nauplius the navigator, Meleager of Calydon and Polydeuces, twin brother of Castor, Amphiaraus the seer, Butes the bee-master and Idmon, versed in bird-lore, beside Heracles, whose weight, says Apollodorus, was so great that the ship itself 'declared with human voices' that it could not bear it. At the helm sat Orpheus plucking the strings of his lyre.[1]

At Volos begins the circular tour of the **Pelion villages**, where a striking style of peasant architecture, isolated from all outside influences, flourished amid chestnut forests during the Turkish occupation. Tall white houses, timber-framed, with projecting upper storeys and slate roofs and rustic churches with folklore-style frescoes are scattered among the woods. A tour of the 'star' villages takes two days. I am accustomed to following an anti-clockwise route (the reverse is equally feasible), in which case it is best to spend the night at Tsangaradhes. There are daily buses to all the main villages.

The road to the east skirts the seashore. Coastal and inland hamlets spread across olive groves and gardens filled with roses, from whose petals a fragrant oil is distilled, giant dahlias and Canna lilies; in early summer pink and blue hydrangeas, large as cabbages, speckle the silvery groves. A branch road at the twelfth kilometre ascends to **Miliés**. During the Turkish occupation it possessed one of the most important libraries in Greece and a school where geography, chemistry and natural sciences were taught in the early nineteenth century. Greek literary tradition was kept alive throughout the Ottoman period by patriot-scholars in the Pelion villages, whose inhabitants were never tamed by the conquerors. It was at Miliés that the Thessalian standard of revolt against the Turks was raised in 1821.

The road winds along ridges of heather-covered hills, alternately overlooking the Pagasitic Gulf to the south, and the open sea to the north, where two of the loveliest Aegean islands, Skiathos and Skopelos, lie hundreds of feet below. The soil is an unusual purplish-red hue.

Soon there is a fork. One road descends towards the scythe-shaped headland of **Trikkeri**, inhabited by caique-builders, whose ancestors owned broad-beamed vessels which traded with all the ports of the Levant. In the distance Euboea tapers away into Cape Artemesium, off which Xerxes's cumbersome armada, strung out in

[1] Boats leave Volos for Demetrias and Pegasae in summer. The journey takes 10–15 minutes.

153

eight parallel lines, fought the first major engagement of the war with the more nimble Greek triremes in 480 BC.

The other road, crossing the mountain ridge, affords a sudden breathtaking view of Mount Athos, a mirage-like peak thrusting skyward through a pale sea-haze. The heather is succeeded by evergreens. There are interminable windings around vertical clefts as far as **Tsangaradhes**, a straggling settlement of farmhouses in a forest of oak and chestnut trees, at an altitude of 1500 feet. The Xenias Hotel overlooks wooded gorges descending abruptly to the sea. The ferns and brambles are luxuriant; in autumn mushrooms carpet the undergrowth; in winter the rainfall is the highest on the Greek mainland. Everywhere there is the sound of running water – that wonderful crystalline water, served for drinking in thick-rimmed tumblers. Greeks do not drink water only because the body needs a certain amount of liquid. They savour it, like connoisseurs, and make comparisons between the waters of different springs. A civilized approach – Homeric in origin. Below Tsangaradhes, at a distance of less than five miles, lies **Milopotamos,** the first of the tree-fringed sandy beaches along the north coast.

The road continues westward, at a considerable altitude, through **Mouresi** (Mulberry village), where hollyhocks and hydrangeas blaze in shady arbours, to **Kissos**, its esplanade overlooking green hills with the sea beyond. The village is lively, less straggling than Tsangaradhes. The air is cool in summer, fragrant with sun-drenched grass and ripe fruit. The focal point is the **Church of Ayia Marina**. St Marina was a Bithynian holy lady who dwelt in a monastery disguised as a boy and was consequently maliciously accused of fathering the local innkeeper's daughter. The church is a low three-aisled basilica, with a belfry pierced by arches on successive levels. The walls of the interior are covered with post-Byzantine frescoes by Paghonis, a local peasant artist, responsible for the painted decoration of many Pelion churches. His work, though devoid of 'whims', is nevertheless rustic in conception and rendering, engaging in its unpretentious folklore inspiration. Here are no solemn liturgical cycles. The strict undeviating rules of Byzantine iconography are ignored. The iconographer tells simple 'folksy' stories. Superstition rides roughshod over the dogmas of religious painting. From the capitals demons rudely stick out deformed tongues. Although the bright gilding of the iconostasis creates a somewhat gaudy effect, the carving is inventive in detail: a meshwork of carved blooms, tendrils, pert little stags and stylized lions. Right of the iconostasis is a strange fresco of a church perched on a tenuous rock pillar. One wonders if the iconographer had ever visited the rock monasteries of Meteora.

Beyond Kissos the road winds through chestnut forests and round an impressive gorge in the most precipitous part of the mountain. Occasional clearings in the forest provide fretwork frames for vistas of unbroken expanses of sea. A branch road to the north descends to **Ayios Ioannis**, a sandy pine-bordered beach dotted with tavernas, the summer haunt of Voliot trippers, where there are caiques for hire which chug along the coastline. The main road continues towards Zagora. This is the country associated with the Centaurs, the progeny, half-man half-horse, of the impious Ixion, who had the audacity to try to seduce the Queen of the Heavens and was promptly bound to a wheel of flame doomed to revolve eternally in the Underworld. The deserted glades are carpeted with feathery fronds. Nothing stirs in the shade of the interlacing boughs. Imagination alone can recapture the sound of stampeding hoofs, as the squealing creatures, maddened with lust by the charms of the Lapith women, broke up the bucolic ceremonies held in honour of King Perithoös's marriage to the Lapith Hippodameia. This famous mythological conflict, a favourite theme of Greek sculptors, probably symbolized the border raids carried out by warring tribesmen.

Mount Pelion figures in the earliest myths, from the time when the giants piled Ossa on top of it in a bold attempt to besiege the gods on Olympus. It was on Pelion that Apollo, in one of his amorous escapades – he almost rivals his father, Zeus, in concupiscence – surprised the huntress Cyrene, while she wrestled single-handed with a lion, and carried her off to that part of the North African shore that still bears her name. Another famous wedding, that of Peleus and Thetis, the parents of Achilles, was celebrated here. Peleus was the commander of the Myrmidons, an army of ants transformed into warriors, Thetis a Nereid who lived under the sea. But she was also a temperamental, snobbish, sometimes puritanical creature who had a habit of boiling her children in order to test their immortality. The nastiest traits in her character emerged during the period of her courtship with Peleus. Coyly determined to resist his initial advances, she transformed herself into fire, water and a succession of wild beasts and finally into a cuttlefish that rudely squirted ink into her suitor's face. In the end, of course, she gave in, but even after their marriage she continued to sulk – Sophocles calls her 'voiceless' – and when Peleus succeeded in preventing their seventh child, Achilles, from being boiled, she left him in a huff. Homer portrays her in a more sympathetic light, and Pindar describes her as seductive. She is, in fact, a typical example of the often wildly contradictory opinions maintained by Greek poets about the personal characteristics of their deities. In modern folklore, the fearsome Nereids, who transform themselves into bestial shapes in order to torment innocent men, possess all the attributes of the ancient Thetis. The continuity of Greek religion in Christian folklore is nowhere more apparent than on Mount Pelion.

A more attractive mythological Pelion character is the wise old Centaur, Cheiron – doctor, prophet and scholar – who dwelt in a cave below the summit, where medicinal plants grew in profusion, and who was the fashionable tutor of the period, entrusted with the education of such distinguished young men as Asclepius, Achilles and Jason. He paid great attention to physical fitness and character training, feeding Achilles on fawn marrow to make him run fast and lions' entrails to imbue him with courage. For his services to education, Zeus rewarded him with a place in the heavens as the star Centaur.

Zagora is the showpiece of the Pelion. Like Tsangaradhes, it is filled with the sound of streams running between banks of maidenhair. Its orchards produce peaches, pears and plums much prized in the Athenian market. Its wild strawberries unfortunately do not travel so well. Like Miliés, it was a centre of learning, enjoying local self-government under Turkish rule. Although religious fanaticism could provoke the Turks into committing the most appalling atrocities, they were often quite mild oppressors. This mildness did not stem from any political conviction; it merely reflected their innate propensity for indolence.

The older houses of Zagora present a blank wall of two storeys to potential enemies, the projecting third one being surmounted by a roof of irregular slate tiles. Under the Turks folklore art, generally quaint, often charming, remained unaffected by the main currents of artistic fashion. Two eighteenth-century churches are typical. At Ayia Kyriaki (St Sunday), a typical Pelion-style basilica type, faience plates and moulded tulips (here the Turkish influence is clear) are embedded in the apsidal wall. The **Church of Ayios Georghios**, also a three-aisled basilica, situated in a paved square, has the added attraction of an exo-narthex in the form of a wooden colonnade roofed with slate tiles running round the west front and part of the north and south sides (another characteristic feature of Pelion church architecture). The exterior apses are embellished with three rows of half-columns with capitals crowned by trefoils alternating with marble plaques with geometric patterns, rosettes, spirals and spherical designs studded with crosses carved in low relief. The interior possesses an elaborate gilt iconostasis, also of the eighteenth century, which gives the impression of filigree work, and the pulpit is one of the largest and most ornamental I have seen in a village church. On the south wall hangs an *epitaphios*, a fine piece of seventeenth-century embroidery depicting the body of Christ on the bier.

A narrow road descends from the village in hairpin bends to the beach, part sand, part shingle, of **Choreuto** (The Dancing One), famous for its shell-fish, fringed by olive groves and orchards of pear and apple. There are a few old abandoned houses and a taverna. Eastward the mountain rises sheer: a backcloth of shimmering woodland.

Above Zagora the road climbs through plantations of walnut trees. Across the chasm streams cascade from successive ledges. Beyond the beech forests of the saddle, below the radar-crowned summit of Pelion and the winter ski-fields, where Cheiron was supposed to have had his cave, the road begins a winding descent to the Pagasitic Gulf. **Portaria** is a summer resort with a Xenias Hotel, a church with murky sixteenth-century frescoes and an ugly rash of modern villas. From here a branch road follows the contours of a precipitous ravine to **Macrinitsa**: a distance of two kilometres. Tall houses, with more slate roofs than elsewhere on Mount Pelion, compose into a series of built-up terraces so steep that the main entrance to the old timber-framed mansions, once the homes of a flourishing agricultural society, is often on the top storey. Unlike other Pelion villages, Macrinitsa is centred round a terrace with café tables which forms a belvedere overlooking the ravine, shaded by plane trees and flanked by the **chapel of Ayios Ioannis**, whose exterior apse is divided into sections by marble columns alternating with plaques carved with crudely executed but fanciful designs – an ornate cross, a Sun and Moon, a cypress tree, a crouching figure and foliate decoration. The church bell hangs from the branch of a plane tree. From a marble fountain decorated with carved plaques water gushes out of a brass gargoyle.

The **Church of the Panayia** (the Virgin), restored after a recent earthquake, is situated on a higher level, its courtyard flanked by a cypress and chestnut tree. Above the marble-framed south doorway an exterior eighteenth-century fresco depicts the Virgin, holding the Child, seated on an elaborate baroque throne. The three apses are decorated with sculptured plaques, the most striking of which depicts a lion hunt, with a chariot drawn by four horses and a lone

157

bird lurking in the right corner. Within the church there is a fine thirteenth-century marble relief of the Virgin Orans. During the Turkish occupation secret classes in history and theology were held in two adjoining chapels on superimposed levels. At Macrinitsa teachers and priests went about their clandestine activities, propagating Hellenic culture – or what they believed it to be – and the Orthodox faith, within sight of the Crescent flying from the fortress of Volos.

The descent continues. **Ano-Volos** spreads across the southern foothills. Mushroom-like roofs crown tower houses among orchards. The upper storey of the **Condos house**,[2] in a farmyard setting below Macrinitsa's great cliff, contains sixty square metres of frescoes by the eccentric peasant painter, Theophilos, a late nineteenth-century 'primitive' who peddled his way across eastern Greece, singing while he painted, asking for no payment other than the cost of his materials, wearing a fez, pleated skirt, skin-tight woollen stockings and *tsarouchia*. He also liked to dress up as Alexander the Great, who plays an important part in folklore, assumes the attributes of St George and rids the country of the local dragon. Although his frescoes, some of which are no more than brilliantly executed oleographs, are devoid of scale and perspective, Theophilos often conveys an impression of verisimilitude to place and period, and his decorative detail, for all its 'folksiness', has roots in a precise, almost classical, perception of objects. In his work, which has obtained some international recognition, Greek folklore art reaches its apotheosis. His subjects generally derive from episodes from the War of Independence (there are some splendidly bedecked military gentlemen, armed to the teeth, with frozen expressions and ferocious moustaches). Notice the heroic young deacon, Athanasios Diacos, carried off by beturbaned Turks to be roasted alive, and the lavish accoutrements of the camp of Marcos Botsaris near Karpenisi. Whimsical treatment and bold use of colour combine to make the hackneyed stylized scenes come to life. Mythological subjects are not ignored. Hermes in a blue mantle departs on one of his divine errands against a background of a little Greek temple; a peasant-faced Aphrodite with great fat feet holds a trident as she rises from the foam (*pace* Botticelli). One of the most attractive features of the frescoes is the decorative detail: a giraffe munching palm leaves; a blue peacock with emerald-green plumage beside an

[2] To find the Condos house, now a 'Theophilos museum', one asks the way at Anakasia, which lies on the periphery of Ano-Volos. With the help of a friendly lounger in the local café, it is easy to find.

ornamental bowl out of which roses sprout, a frieze of ducks and fish in a stream shaded by blue and yellow flowers. The large view of Macrinitsa, with its terraced houses reduced to boxes, is full of light and freshness. Although Theophilos had no 'inspiration' to draw on other than post-Byzantine religious painting, there seems to be an unconscious debt to Le Douannier Rousseau in a fine panel depicting Mr Condos, a local archon, stiff and self-conscious, wearing a black suit with a high collar, mounted on a richly caparisoned horse in front of his house.

From Volos one drives across the plain to Larisa. Just beyond the point of the crossing with the northbound highway a side road to the south leads in no time to **Velestino**, a village among apple orchards: the site of ancient Pherae, ruled by a succession of blood-thirsty tyrants who were the scourge of central Greece in the fourth century BC and raised Thessaly to the status of a great power. The first of these was Jason (not to be confused with the mythical leader of the Argonauts) whom Xenophon describes as 'the greatest man of his times', capable of taking on 'the rest of the world'. By nature he was violent and ostentatious. At Delphi, on one occasion, he sacrificed a thousand cattle and more than two thousand other animals. Like him, his successors were assassinated. Of these none surpassed in cruelty his lawless and foul-mouthed nephew, Alexander, whose sole religious exercise was the worship of the spear with which he slew his uncle. His own end was plotted by his wife and her three brothers, and his corpse, says Plutarch 'was abused, thrown out and trodden underfoot by the Pheraeans'. With his assassination, the power of the Thessalian despots declined, and the country was soon subjected by Philip of Macedon.

Next to the miniature public garden is a shallow pond with a tiled basin, its surface mantled with sedge: the scene painted by Edward Dodwell in one of his most charming 'Views of Greece'. But in the nineteenth century the pond was fringed with minarets and trees, including a palm, with a broken column in the foreground. Assuming that Dodwell did not invent the column, one is justified in associating the site with the fountain of Hypereia, situated in the centre of the ancient city, and even with the palace of Admetus, 'near the sweet-streaming current . . . that from the lake of Boeobia flows'.[3] Here Apollo, punished for killing one of the Cyclops, was condemned for a year to tend the royal flocks and spend his leisure hours playing such beautiful tunes on his lyre that lions, lured from their lairs on 'Othrys' rugged brow', descended into the plain and

[3] Euripides, the *Alcestis*.

tamely watched 'the dappled hinds in sportive measures bound'.[4] A close friendship sprang up between the king and the god, and the land prospered because Apollo caused all the cows to bear twins, which were not only considered lucky but also to have fertilizing powers (the god himself was a twin).

Within the palace, however, amid the flurry of organizing the ceremonies connected with his marriage to Alcestis, Admetus forgot to sacrifice to Artemis, Apollo's twin sister. The goddess lost no time in expressing her displeasure. When Admetus, anointed and garlanded, entered the bridal chamber, he found that 'no lovely naked bride awaited him on the marriage couch, but a tangled knot of hissing serpents'.[5] Ignoring the omen, he dwelt happily with Alcestis, until the Moerae (the Fates), prompted by Artemis who, like all Greek deities, resented nothing more than a slight, decided the time had come for him to pay for his fatal omission. But Apollo, loyal to his friend, plied the three old arbiters of the thread of life with such copious draughts of wine that they agreed to grant Admetus a reprieve – on one condition. His place in the kingdom of Hades must be taken by another mortal. The young and attractive Alcestis immediately volunteered. Admetus accepted her noble gesture without a qualm – a typical example of the traditional inequality between the sexes that prevails, in more ways than one, in Greek society to this day. But Alcestis was rewarded for her self-sacrifice when Heracles, her husband's friend, rescued her from the very arms of Death. H. J. Rose has an interesting comment to make in this context. The Fates, he says, can get drunk, and Death itself be overcome in physical combat.[6] Few other myths illustrate more clearly the anthropomorphic nature of the Greek gods, the concept of religious worship in terms of physical entities.

Of antiquity all that remains today are some vestiges of a temple of Heracles and of the Larisa Gate on the site of an acropolis, north of the town.

In the eighteenth century Rhigas Pheraeos, a fiery literary-minded patriot, was born here. He set up a printing press for the publication of seditious literature in Vienna, and his martial songs, especially his War Hymn, a quasi-national anthem, have endeared his memory to subsequent generations of Greeks. Betrayed by one of his countrymen, he was captured by the Turks and drowned in the Danube at Belgrade.

[4] Euripides, op. cit.
[5] Robert Graves, *The Greek Myths*, Penguin, Harmondsworth, 1957.
[6] H. J. Rose, *A Handbook of Greek Mythology*, Methuen, London, 1960.

The remainder of the run to Larisa is without interest – across the flat Thessalian plain. It is wise to rejoin the national road at the point marked Rizomilos. To the north extends the shallow lake of Boeobeis, at the foot of Mount Ossa. Propertius refers to its *'sanctae . . . undae'* because Hesiod believed Athena once washed her feet in its waters.

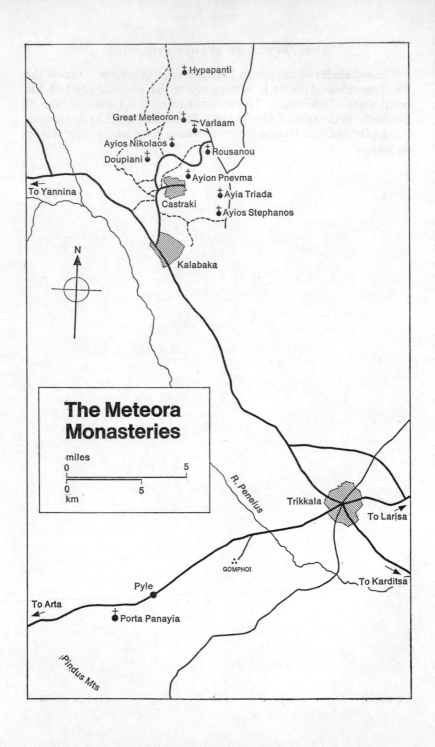

CHAPTER ELEVEN

Thessaly: The Meteora Monasteries

❧

Trikkala – The Church of Porta Panayia – Kalabaka: The Church of the Dormition – The Valley of Rock Pillars – The Broad Rock – The Great Meteoron – Barlaam – Rousanou – The Monastery of the Holy Trinity – The Monastery of St Stephen

The way from Larisa to the Meteora monasteries is across a flat, typically Thessalian stretch of country, watered by rush-bordered streams. Broods of geese waddle around stagnant pools: occasionally alleys of poplars form arbours of shade over a road running more or less parallel to the Peneius, whose banks were inhabited at a time one can only think of in terms of palaeontology. The Palaeolithic fossils and tools excavated along this stretch of the river have been dated to a period between 100,000 and 40,000 BC. To the south extend the stud-farms. Hereabouts were bred the famous mares that took part in contests with Asiatic horses organized by Xerxes, as the Persian host marched southward in 480 BC. The barrier of the Pindus ridge, bluish in colour, gashed by chasms, draws nearer.

A sluggish tributary of the Peneius flows through **Trikkala**, seat of the Slav 'Caesar' in the fourteenth century. Originally called Trikke, noted for its horses, which Phidias used as models for the equestrian statues of the Parthenon frieze, Trikkala is now a lively market town, with a ruined mosque, castellated clock tower and a stone bridge spanning the poplar-lined stream.[1] In summer a furnace of heat, it is dominated by the crumbling walls of a Byzantine fort, site of the ancient acropolis, from whose highest tower the Turkish governor used to hurl his enemies against the city walls. Projecting hooks caught the bodies as they fell; there they were left, dangling in gruesome postures – a warning to all who passed below.

A road from Trikkala to the west passes close by Gomphoi, where village houses are built on foundations of military establishments raised by Philip of Macedon to guard the plain against incursions from the west. Beyond the village of Pyle, lying at the base of the

[1] Trikkala's hotels offer an alternative to those of Kalabaka, as a base for a visit to the Meteora monasteries.

Pindus range, a track crosses a bridge, originally of Byzantine construction, spanning the torrent of the Portaikos which issues out of a cleft in the mountain wall. In the middle of this natural gateway lies the **Church of Porta Panayia** (The Virgin of the Gates). Lofty crags, their higher levels speckled with deciduous trees, frame the gorge. In the evening the dark mysterious tunnel is filled with shifting shadows. Mulberry, plane and cypress surround the monastic walls.

The church was founded in 1283 by John Dučas, the rebellious illegitimate son of an Epirot Despot, who ruled over Neopatras, allied himself with the Vlach nomads and fought both the Franks and the Byzantine Emperor Michael VIII. He married a Vlach, eventually became a monk and was buried in the church at Porta Panayia four years after its completion. Whether its foundation was a bid for salvation in the form of an act of contrition on his part must remain a matter of conjecture. Few Byzantines, however unprincipled in worldly affairs, were without a deep mystical faith in the Orthodox Church. Byzantium produced few agnostics, and no atheists.

The brickwork decoration of the exterior walls of the church consists of rosettes, squares, overlapping arches, and rows of elongated Z-shaped forms: a kind of embellishment repeated more lavishly in a number of churches at Salonica and Arta.[2] A spacious narthex of a later date is crowned by a broad drum pierced by narrow elliptical windows. The frescoes, of a late period, are very damaged. The naos – the walls are now whitewashed – is in the form of a three-aisled basilica, the height of which is increased at the east end by a transverse vault instead of a dome. In spite of this curious juxtaposition of vaulted nave and domed narthex, an air of uniformity prevails. At the west end of the south wall there is a portrait of the founder in the act of being introduced by an angel to the Virgin and Child. The Holy Door of the marble screen, embellished with finely wrought fluted colonnettes, knotted in the centre and crowned with capitals, is flanked by two surviving **mosaics** of superior quality: late thirteenth-century figures, noble and austere, of the Virgin and Child (right) and Christ (left) – a deviation from the strict code of Byzantine iconography in which Christ is normally depicted on the right. Both panels are set in marble frames composed of slender double knotted columns with capitals and surmounted by arches.

[2] The key of the church, which is generally shut, is obtained from a peasant who lives in a nearby hut in a vegetable plot.

Beyond the church the defile contracts. A new road is under construction across the pass whence the Despots of Epirus rode from their capital at Arta to conquer the Thessalian Lowlands. I have walked a couple of miles along it. A torrent is spanned by the elegant arch of a Turkish stone bridge, under a canopy of plane trees where nightingales sing. The bridge, like all those built by the Turks in remote parts of the country, is narrow, stepped and crescent-shaped, intended for the passage of a single man or beast. There is neither a parapet nor balustrade, and one needs to be immune to vertigo to cross the slender arch without mishap. In late spring, trucks, crammed with Vlachs, surrounded by their chattels, sheep and dour unsmiling women, returning from their winter quarters in the plain to remote Alpine villages in the Pindus, grind up the mountainside to the accompaniment of bouzouki music echoing from the migrants' recently purchased transistors.

From Trikkala another road cuts south-east across the plain to **Karditsa**, a market town of Turkish origin, served by a narrow gauge railway running from Volos to Trikkala. Storks' nests crown the roofs of ramshackle houses. General Plastiras, an ambitious cavalry officer with a fierce black moustache, who always rode a black charger and became one of the most controversial political personalities of the twentieth century, plotting military revolutions and brooding in exile when out of office, was born here. Beyond Karditsa the road joins the Larisa-Athens road south of Pharsala.

The traveller who chooses the north-west road from Trikkala is rewarded with one of the most extraordinary sights in Greece. The village of **Kalabaka**, the medieval Stagi (corruption of *stous ayios*, the place of the saints), spreads fan-wise round a projection of huge dark grey rock which, after breaking away from the apex of the Pindus and Cambunian ranges, thrusts forward into the plain in a mass of contorted gneiss, syenite and mica-slate. Behind it extends the labyrinth of rock pillars crowned by the Meteora monasteries, whose eremitical origins and subsequent prosperity form part of the history of Byzantine monasticism. One monastery alone, St Stephen, is visible from the village: perched on the ridge of a lofty wall of rock with a smooth polished surface, slit and rutted at intervals by horizontal seams like gigantic cicatrices and honeycombed with caves and eyries. Over six hundred years ago a young monk named Athanasius, hearing of this wild place, crossed the mountains in search of the refuge it offered him. He had long sought a life of unremitting prayer for the salvation of men's souls, undisturbed by their physical presence. His quest was at an end; and although hermits had preceded him he was the founder of the first 'monastery in mid-air'.

The screen of dolomites is omnipresent at Kalabaka; it seems to cast its reflection across meadows and vineyards bordering the shingly bed of the Peneius, like some sombre radiation from the interior bed of the rock itself. The village has few amenities, other than hotels, petrol stations and a main square crowded with tourist motor coaches.[3] But it possesses a venerable Byzantine **Church of the Koimesis** (Dormition of the Virgin). A three-aisled basilica, it was built in the twelfth century on the foundations of an earlier place of worship. The stone canopy of the ciborium above the altar, carved with intricate foliate designs, has clearly been remade from more ancient materials; so has the imposing marble **ambo**, with its panels sculptured with double crosses, its two stairways and hexagonal pulpit resting on two columns, of porphyry and verd-antique, crowned with a baldacchino in the shape of an extinguisher. The quality of the carving and opulence of the monument, which has been compared to the great ambo at San Clemente in Rome, suggests the prestige attached to the cathedral of Stagi in the Byzantine ecclesiastical world. Among the icons there is a fine double-sided Crucifixion and Dormition (in the latter Christ is depicted in a green glory composed of angels' heads). The frescoes, the work of sixteenth-century painters of the Cretan School, are blackened almost beyond recognition. The text of the chrysobull of the Emperor Andronicus III (1328–41), determining the rights and boundaries of the diocese of Stagi, is painted on the north wall of the narthex.

Only five of the original thirteen **Meteora Monasteries** are still inhabited by a handful of monks (or nuns). They can be leisurely visited in a single day.[4] All the paraphernalia of an increasing tourist trade – polyglot guides, pedlars of ice-creams, postcards and imitation Greek vases, strategically placed below monastery gates – has not yet succeeded in wholly effacing the image of the strange life once led by the Byzantine solitaries and visionaries of Meteora nor in diminishing the grotesque splendour of the scene.

From Kalabaka the road curves round the so-called Black Rock to

[3] Westbound travellers can take a fine mountain road which crosses the Pindus, via Metsovo, to Yannina and thence descends to Igoumenitsa, a port of embarkation (or disembarkation, as the case may be), on the Epirot coast.

[4] The inhabited monasteries, when I last visited them, were open to the public from 8 to 12 and from 3 to 5.

the village of **Castraki** sheltering among vineyards in the shade of a forest of towering pinnacles. On the lower levels the gaps between the rocks are covered with mulberries, oaks, cypresses and evergreen shrubs, while shadows expand and contract across the smooth surface of the pillars and pyramids. Dr Holland, an early nineteenth-century traveller, staggered by the scene that confronted him, believed the original mountain must have been 'cleft and divided in this wonderful manner . . . perhaps by the conjoint operation of earthquakes and of that decay and *detruitus*, which proceed so perpetually over the face of the globe'.[5] Curzon, writing a few decades later, says '. . . the end of a range of rocky hills seems to have been broken off by some earthquake or washed away by the Deluge, leaving only a series of twenty or thirty tall, thin, needle-like rocks, many hundred feet in height; some like giant tusks, some shaped like pudding-loaves, and some like vast stalagmites'.[6] A peculiar aspect of the rock formations, whose height varies between six and nine hundred feet, is the way in which their surface is slit by both vertical and horizontal seams. The former have clearly been caused by the endless trickle of rain water, the latter, it is suggested, by the lapping of waves when the waters of the Thessalian lake beat against the cliffs.

North-west of Castraki rises the round-topped **rock of Doupiani**, studded with eyries, once scaled with ladders by the earliest eremites. Up there, far from the affairs of men, they communed with God and mortified their bodies. Deeming the flesh to be rank pollution, one monk left instructions that his mortal remains should be cast to birds of prey. Soon after his death, another hermit was horrified to see a raven pecking at the dead man's thumbs. Once a week the monks descended from their caves to worship communally in what is now a whitewashed chapel at the base of the cliff.

Above the village looms another huge pudding-shaped mass of conglomerate, known as **Ayion Pnevma** (The Holy Ghost), crowned by two iron crosses. A chapel clinging to a crevice in the rock is dedicated to St George of the Ayion Mandilion – a kerchief stamped, like St Veronica's, with the image of Christ wearing a crown of thorns. Village boys still run races up the side of the cliff, waving coloured handkerchiefs which they hang on a line outside the chapel. Donald M. Nicol suggests this was probably the pinnacle on which the young Athanasius first settled, remaining 'in silent

[5] Henry Holland, *Travels in the Ionian Islands, Albania, Thessaly, Macedonia, etc. during the years 1812 and 1813*, London, 1815.
[6] The Hon. Robert Curzon, *Visits to Monasteries in the Levant*, London, 1849.

prayer and meditation . . . weaving wool, singing as he worked . . .'[7] But when demons were seen circling round his cave, he was persuaded to move to another rock, so lofty that even the forces of evil hesitated to scale it. Bit by bit, Athanasius climbed the formidable **Broad Rock** with the aid of ladders clamped one above the other. A devout hesychast,[8] he chose a cave – halfway up the modern zigzag stairway – as his first abode. The remains of a ladder still dangle from a wooden doorway overhanging the abyss. The sanctity of his life attracted so many disciples that he was finally persuaded to establish a community on the Broad Rock. A monastery thus grew up and came to be known as the Great Meteoron. No woman was allowed near it. Once, when the widow of the Serb 'Caesar' of Thessaly asked for Athanasius's blessing, he not only refused to approach her, but abused her roundly for being a woman and prophesied her imminent death. Three months later she died. His successor Joasaph – the former Joseph Uroš, 'Emperor of the Greeks and Serbs', deposed and blinded by a rival aspirant – enlarged the church, and the monastery enjoyed a period of prosperity, which owed much to the munificence of Joasaph's sister, the engaging Maria Angelina, who married Thomas Preljubovič, the Serb tyrant of Yannina, at the age of ten.

One enters the **Monastery of the Great Meteoron** by a steep rock-hewn stairway. A dilapidated wooden shed projects over the precipice. Here are the ropes, 124 feet long, and windlass, by which men and provisions were originally hauled up. Describing his descent, Curzon says the monks 'arranged themselves in order at the bars, the net was spread upon the floor and having sat down upon it cross-legged, the four corners were gathered over my head, and attached to the hook at the end of the rope. All being ready, the monks at the capstan took a few steps round, the effect of which was to lift me off the floor and launch me out of the door right into the sky, with an impetus which kept me swinging backwards and forwards at a fearful rate; when the oscillation had in some measure ceased the abbot and another monk, leaning out of the door, steadied me with their hands, and I was let down slowly and gently to the ground.'[9] It is said that the last person to have ascended the rock in this

---

[7] Donald M. Nicol, *Meteora, The Rock Monasteries of Thessaly*, London, 1963: an exhaustive history of the monasteries, with a general account of Byzantine monasticism.

[8] For the hesychasts, see p. 202.

[9] The Hon. Robert Curzon, op. cit.

frightening contraption was the late Queen Marie of Romania – presumably between the two World Wars.

The interior of the cruciform **Church of the Metamorphosis** is spacious and unusually high. Maria Angelina's prodigality is evident. The candelabra, pulpits and iconostasis, crowned by a large Crucifixion in an ornamental cross-shaped gilt frame, heighten the atmosphere of brilliance created by the recently restored frescoes, the work of late fifteenth-century Athonite artists. There is little subtlety in colour tones, and although the figures sometimes strike agile, even acrobatic, attitudes, they remain basically static. As straightforward narrative illustrations to the liturgy, they fulfil their function. The large narthex, supported by four columns, is somewhat darker. The frescoes, fussy and full of stylistic mannerisms, are of a later date – the usual blood-curdling Last Judgement, and full-length portraits of Athanasius, founder of the monastery, and Joasaph, his successor, holding a model of the church: gaunt figures with long black beards. In the martyrdom scenes, heavily armed Roman soldiers tweak haloed saints by the ear as they plunge swords into their breasts or set fire to barrels in which rigid martyrs wait stoically to be consumed by the flames.

The **icons** in the treasury are more interesting than the frescoes. After the fall of Constantinople Byzantine fresco-painters seem to have been incapable of inspiration on the grand scale. No great churches were built during the post-Byzantine period; consequently the demand for the painting of large surfaces of wall virtually ceased to exist. But the icon-painter, working in a less expensive medium, preserved, developed and revitalized the best elements in the old tradition. Western influences crept in and enriched narrative iconography. Not all post-1453 icons should be dismissed as mere 'late stuff'. Many of them are genuine works of art. At the Great Meteoron there are several outstanding examples, ranging from the fourteenth to the sixteenth centuries, including an Incredulity of Thomas, with a perky Maria Angelina, wearing royal robes, mingling among the apostles, who gaze at Thomas or chatter among themselves; a boyish St Demetrius, his shield blown by the wind, thrusting his javelin into the leader of a Bulgar host investing Salonica, for which patriotic act two angels crown him and the Hand of God blesses him; a Baptism with a picturesque personification of the river in the form of a naked child and Christ immersed in the waters of the Jordan, while St John baptizes him and angels bear him towels; a diptych of the Virgin (left panel) and a bust of Christ (right panel), his head inclined to the right, his eyes shut; a Virgin holding the Child, receiving an icon from Maria Angelina who, as a mere mortal, is rendered on a smaller scale, bordered by fourteen saints, with niches intended for their relics below each bust (dismembered remains of saints' bodies were believed not only to possess healing powers but to constitute a physical connection between God and man). Equally attractive are the five Menologion icons, with calendars of saints' feasts painted on gold backgrounds: typical examples of sixteenth-century painting in miniature.

The refectory, separated from the church by a courtyard with cypress trees, has a vaulted roof supported by five elegant columns. Below it were stored the enormous wine barrels drawn up by windlass. Water was supplied from cisterns hewn out of the rock.

The view from the Great Meteoron is astonishing. Twisted spectral forms, scarred and rutted, noduled or tapering into pinpoint cones, insulate the winding chasm, strewn with gigantic boulders embedded in lichen and evergreens, from the outside world. Occasional gaps between the rocks afford glimpses of the plain beyond and its welcome cultivated domesticity.

By the fifteenth century the number of monastic settlements had increased, and during the death agony of Byzantium the 'monasteries in mid-air' became asylums of Hellenism and Orthodoxy, where monks could commune with God and invoke his blessing on Greek arms, undisturbed by Ottoman armies advancing across the plain below. After the Turkish conquest there was a marked deterioration in monastic morals. At the Monastery of the Pantocrator a cross-eyed monk had the effrontery to introduce two women, dressed as monks, to serve as his 'companions'. For a time the Great Meteoron was ruled by a contemptible abbot in the pay of the Turks, and for his sin of treachery to the Hellenic cause, always synonymous with that of Christian Orthodoxy, he was anathematized and sent into exile. When he died, his body remained uncorrupted – a sign of God's displeasure. From the seventeenth century onwards, loot, sale and fraud robbed the churches of much treasure.

All that remains of the monastery of the Hypselotera (The Highest One), which crowns an offshoot of the Broad Rock, are an image of two saints painted on the rock and traces of a wooden ladder hanging from a narrow projection just below the summit. On another offshoot is the monastery of Ayios Nikolaos (St Nicholas), with a basilica painted with sixteenth-century frescoes. The ruins of the little monastery of Ayios Ioannis Prodromos (St John the Baptist), uninhabited for over two hundred years, are scattered across the ridge of a vertically slit hump. More spectacular is a completely detached monolith soaring skyward, capped by nothing but a debris of wood and stone, once the monastery of Ayia Moni.

North of the Broad Rock a path leads between mis-shapen tusks and perpendicular cliffs, seamed like organ pipes, to the **rock of the Hypapanti** (Presentation in the Temple). The monastery, long abandoned but recently restored, is situated in a cave halfway up the cliff, reached by a stone stairway. The tiny domeless church is decorated with frescoes of the late thirteenth to mid fifteenth centuries. Icons adorn the elaborately carved iconostasis of gilded wood.

A terrible abyss separates the Broad Rock from a magnificent obelisk, on which the **Monastery of Varlaam** (Barlaam) is perched, soaring out of a mass of bulbous rocks that recall the lunar landscape of El Greco's vision of Mount Sinai. The retreat of a fourteenth-century anchorite, who gave his name to the monastery, it later housed such venerable relics as a finger of St John and the shoulder-blade of St Andrew. The church was founded by two brothers, Theophanes and Nectarios. The monks of the Great Meteoron lent them mules to carry stones to the base of the rock; but records of how the materials for the original windlass were hauled up are tantalizingly withheld. The two brothers imposed a strict discipline on their disciples, partaking once a day of bread, beans and water, and praying half the night. Theophanes, avid of mortification, wore an iron chain tight round his waist, next to the skin. Shortly before he died – it was the hour of sunset and the day of the church's completion – he stretched himself on a couch, carefully arranging his limbs in the shape of a cross. As the breath passed out of his body, an unaccustomed star shone brightly over the monastery and was suddenly extinguished. His sixteenth-century biographer says the air was immediately filled with 'a sweet and ineffable fragrance', and the face of the dead man looked 'like a scented meadow bright with many varied flowers'.[10]

Varlaam, when I last visited it, was more animated than the other monasteries. An elderly monk, his long grey hair arranged in a plaited bun below his cylindrical hat, acted as guide, sold postcards, offered ouzo and accepted a gratuity. Other monks went about their devotions and chores. Although the monastery buildings are in utter disorder, the walls, eaves and roofs, capped by a church with two tiled domes resting on octagonal drums, seem to grow organically out of the bluish-grey rock. A labyrinth of rotting floor-boards and

[10] Quoted by Donald M. Nicol, op. cit.

worn paving-stones leads to deserted cells. One storeroom contains a barrel nearly twenty feet high with a diameter of over six feet, which must have sorely taxed the strength of the monks at the capstan when it was originally hauled up. The disused shed where the contraption was kept, buttressed by stone masonry, projects like some abandoned crumbling belvedere above the ravine.

In the **Church of Ayion Panton** (All Saints) the sixteenth-century **frescoes,** restored in the eighteenth century and again recently, depict the familiar scenes from the Dodecaorton. Everywhere there are swirling draperies, huddled buildings, martyrs, hermits, soldiers, the gold of haloes, the flash of swords, the reds and purples of ecclesiastical vestments. On a lower level, around the portraits of the founders – notice the pinched white-bearded face of the ascetic Theophanes (left) – extends the gallery of humbler saints, including a hirsute Makarios clothed in nothing but his own abundant tresses. In the narthex the mourners in the Dormition of Ephraim the Syrian are ranged round the saint's body like crude prototypes of El Greco's grandees at the funeral of Don Orgaz (painted a quarter of a century later). In the museum there is a small Book of Gospels, once the property of the Emperor Constantine VII Porphyrogenitus (913–59), and a fine **icon of the Virgin and Child** surrounded by angels and apostles in robes of pale mauve, dark green and indigo blue, by Tzanes, the sixteenth-century iconographer. In another icon SS George and Demetrius are depicted in medieval dress, their headgear like inflated berets (Western fashions in dress were imported by the Franks), separated from each other by a column and surmounted by a gold canopy.

Beyond Varlaam the road winds past **Rousanou**: a small monolith crowned by three storeys of seemingly inaccessible masonry. Never one of the more flourishing monasteries, Rousanou, when visited by Curzon in 1834, was inhabited by two half-mad crones who refused to let the rope ladder down to the English traveller, preferring to jabber frenziedly at each other and shriek curses. The modern traveller is assured of a more courteous welcome from the few nuns who still inhabit the convent. Scenes of martyrdom of unparalleled cruelty decorate the walls of the narthex of the church, dedicated to St Barbara, whose emblem is – very aptly in this case – a tower. More impressive than Rousanou is the **Monastery of Ayia Triada** (The Holy Trinity), its balconies and arcades projecting above a rock shaped like a rolling-pin, which, according to local rumour, shifted some distance from the hillside in a recent earthquake. A cave, pitted in the rock halfway up the stone stairway, contains a little chapel decorated with crude paintings of ascetic saints. The exterior of the church, spoilt by a large ill-proportioned narthex, is ornamented with brickwork designs. But the cypresses and shrubs growing around it create a pleasant rustic effect.

The road then emerges from the valley and runs along the ridge of an escarpment to the **Monastery of Ayios Stephanos**, separated from the main rock formation by a narrow chasm spanned by a bridge. The change of scene is remarkable. Nothing towers overhead any more. The horizon is clear. The monastic buildings are as usual crowned by the one rotund and two slender drums of the church, which, in its present eighteenth-century form, has little, architecturally, to recommend it. In relation to their commanding position on this great bastion overlooking the plain, the toy cupolas and untidy outhouses seem insignificant. After the fall of Constantinople, the monastery enjoyed the benefaction of Romanian hospodars and voivodes, who continued the old tradition, maintained by Byzantine princes, of bestowing wealth on remote monastic communities. The church still possesses two treasures: a silver reliquary containing the head of St Charalambos, whose healing powers are said to have staved off many pestilences, and an **iconostasis and bishop's throne** of lavishly carved woodwork with designs of flowers, cranes pecking at vipers and little creatures swinging censers, all meticulously executed in the fussy high relief typical of Epirot woodcarving of the late eighteenth century. A small chapel, hewn out of the rock, with an apse suspended on the brink, is reached through an abandoned refectory. Near the doorway is a portrait of a white-bearded monk holding a scroll: the fifteenth-century founder of the monastery, a certain Antonios, of the imperial family of Cantacuzenus.

Today St Stephen's chief glory is the view from the terrace. The monastery is at the point where the arms of the angle formed by the Pindus and the Cambunians are about to meet. Hundreds of feet below the box-like houses of Kalabaka skirt the base of the cliff. Southward the plain extends in a soporific haze.

There is only one way back to Kalabaka – the way one came.

In his account of the Meteora monasteries, Curzon says Greek monks seem to be obsessed by 'everything hideous and horrible'. His choice of adjectives is open to question. But one does see what he means. The violence of the geological upheaval seems to be reflected in those 'hideous' mortifications of the flesh which Byzantine ascetics considered necessary stepping-stones to salvation. It is also interesting to note that there is not a single reference to the valley of the Meteora in classical literature. The ancient anthropomorphic Greeks were not impressed by wonders of nature – not unless they could relate them to some visible or symbolic association with a human entity or agency.

CHAPTER TWELVE

The Approach to Macedonia

❧

Ambelakia – The Vale of Tempe – Platamona – Dium – Pydna

No traveller in northern Greece can – or should – avoid Macedonia, the largest and richest province in the country. Salonica, the capital, is usually approached from Larisa along the northbound national road. Notwithstanding stops and two worthwhile deviations to Ambelakia and Dium, the distance is easily covered in less than a day (see map of Thessaly on p. 148).

The Peneius, now joined by the muddy Titaresius, meanders in S-shaped loops across the north-eastern apex of the plain studded with brown cone-shaped hills. To the east rises Mount Ossa, whose quarries once supplied verd-antique and serpentine to the workshops of Roman architects and statuaries. At a point just before the plane-fringed river is about to force its way through the mountain barrier stands a derelict Turkish mosque named Baba. In spring storks perch on the crumbling dome. Here the Porte's envoys, after passing through the Vale of Tempe, would pause to worship before entering the plain to impose new taxes on their Greek subjects.

At the toll gate a branch road to the east climbs to the village of **Ambelakia**, named after Ambelon, a companion of Dionysus who died when young and was turned by Zeus into the plant named after him: *ambelos*, i.e. vine. But despite its name, Ambelakia was less famous for its vines than for its madder and walnut bark used in the eighteenth century for dying yarn that acquired fame throughout central and eastern Europe. On the last turn but one before entering the village there is a fine backward view of the pyramid-shaped hills vanishing into the haze. The immediate foreground is filled by an abrupt spur of Olympus, across which extends the village of Rapsani, famous for its red wine.

In the late eighteenth century Ambelakia was the site of the first co-operative in Greece, founded by local weavers and dyers – who used the madder grown on Mount Ossa for dying their yarn a particularly attractive shade of red. The chemical composition of the

175

abundant waters of Ambelakia added a glossy hue to the finished product which was exported to the markets of Europe. In the early nineteenth century strings of camels crossed the mountain passes from the Dalmatian ports loaded with bales of cloth which were dyed at Ambelakia and then carried back to ships sailing for Trieste in order to provide the Austrian army with uniforms. With the ascendancy of the Manchester cotton industry and the discovery of aniline dyes, the importance of Ambelakia and its co-operative declined.

It is now rather a ramshackle place, open to the mountain breezes: so near, yet off, the beaten track. One is seldom out of earshot of running water. From the main square it is no distance to the eighteenth-century **Schwarz house**, once the property of a Hellenized Viennese family, now a virtual folklore museum. Bays project from the ground and first-floor walls. The constant menace of brigandage and the fear of punitive forays by Turkish soldiers account for the heavy wrought-iron grilles protecting the few windows. The ground floor, formerly used for commercial transactions, with the accountant sitting in an enclosure shut off by a wooden balustrade, consists of a wide vaulted room with alcoves. The walls are painted with decorative designs which create an optical illusion of fluted columns. The wall paintings of the living quarters on the T-shaped first floor include an array of cornucopias filled with carnations and a fanciful evocation of the Bosphorus executed in a sober blend of pale blues, greens and browns.

The high-ceilinged top floor, also T-shaped, is virtually one vast reception room with alcoves, in which the distinguished dyers and weavers of Ambelakia were entertained in style. At the edges of the bays are holes in the floor for pouring molten lead down on dangerous nocturnal marauders. Numerous wooden pillars crowned by carved capitals conjure up an image of colonnades receding into a succession of subsidiary chambers, with framed views of bleak mountainsides and a snow-capped ridge of Olympus. On the walls are painted panels of flowers and the foliate patterns of twigs and drooping branches commonly encountered in popular art. There are also imaginary landscapes: some in medallions. Everywhere the Turkish genius for creating a feeling of spaciousness by the judicious breaking up of space itself is reflected in this work of Greek architects schooled in Islamic lay architecture. One chamber, the so-called 'Eagle room', has an elaborately painted ceiling reminiscent of the chinoiserie popular in western Europe in the eighteenth century and an ornate rococo fireplace crowned by the double-headed eagle

Vouliagmeni: two pellucid bays separated by an isthmus where the foundations of a temple of Apollo are embedded in the sand.

The Sanctuary of Artemis at Brauron.

Daphni: the church.

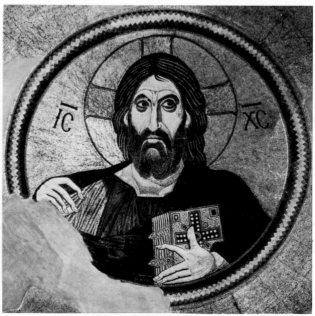

The Pantocrator, one of the greatest
portraits in Byzantine art, dominates the
whole church at Daphni.

of Byzantium. The stained-glass windows are of Viennese provenance. The entire house, with its finely wrought woodwork of turned railings and corniced pillars, is a triumph of architectural and decorative folklore styles: an amalgam of the minor arts of post-Byzantium and Islam, with a touch of early nineteenth-century middle-class Vienna thrown in. To the uninitiated traveller, it serves as a curtain-raiser to the more impressive, if less well-preserved, eighteenth-century houses of western Macedonia.

Back at the toll gate one enters the **Vale of Tempe**. This narrow five-mile gorge separating Olympus from Ossa was believed by the ancient Greeks to have been cut by Poseidon's trident. The Thessalian streams, united in the Peneius, poured through the defile into the sea to join Oceanus, who fathered all the rivers of the world on Tethys, a primeval Aphrodite whose emblems were doves and sparrows noted for their lechery. Birthplace of the laurel, Tempe was associated with the worship of Apollo and visited every nine years by a delegation of aristocratic youths who marched through the vale in procession accompanied by a flute-player, and plucked the sacred laurel destined for the god's oracular seat at Delphi. The gorge has always been much praised for its bucolic qualities by poets, few of whom have been there. Spenser refers to its 'pleasant shore scattered with Flowres', Keats to its 'leaf-fringed legends', Tennyson to 'the long divine Peneian pass'.

Some rather dolled-up belvederes overlook the stream. Along these banks, bordered with lentisk and terebinth, Apollo pursued Daphne, daughter of the local river god. Unwilling to submit to the god's embrace, she was changed by her father into a laurel, leaving her frustrated admirer with nothing to caress but her hair turned into bay leaves. The mountainsides are steep, almost vertical, covered with dark evergreens; a mass of gnarled plane trees border Homer's 'sylvan eddies', which have become rather muddy with the passage of time. But for all its poetic associations, Tempe does not compare with any of the great gorges of Greece, and Polybius and Livy, unlike the poets, rightly described it as rugged rather than pastoral. Its importance, linking the Balkans through Macedonia with the Thessalian enclave and thence the whole of central and southern Greece, was appreciated by the Romans, who built a military highway, roughly followed by the present rail and motor roads.

At the eastern outlet the change of scene is striking. Northward extends a cultivated strip, an unbroken coastline and the pale blue expanse of the Thermaic Gulf, into which two large rivers pour their mud and silt. This is Macedonia. A new climate. After Tempe the air is never so crystalline again, the outlines of the mountains so sharp and dramatic, the sea and sky so vivid a blue. There is no lack of historical sites and associations. But it is Philip, Alexander and their successors who dominate the scene; and after the collapse of the Macedonian Empire, Roman generals and Early Christian martyrs take over, followed by Byzantine emperors and quibbling theologians, by Crusaders and Western adventurers. It remains for Turkish pashas and Greek patriots, merchants and brigands to fill in the tailpiece.

On a bluff to the right rise the ruins of the Crusader **castle of Platamona**, guarding the approaches to the gulf and Salonica, which the Lombards lost to the Epirot Despot, Theodore Angelus, in 1218, when, after a brief but violent siege, they fell from the castle walls, writes a contemporary ecclesiastic, 'like birds from their nests'. The well-preserved walls of the triangular enceinte, dominated by a fine octagonal tower, are outlined against the wooded hills sloping down to the village of Ayios Panteleimon skirted by a sandy beach with tavernas. From now on the backward views of **Mount Olympus** are superb. For the first time one is able to associate the celebrated mountain with the home of the gods. But its contours are more awesome than beautiful. Forests of oak, chestnut and beech spread across the middle slopes. In the afternoon shafts of sunlight fill the ravines, creating new perspectives, and great precipices fall from dizzy altitudes to the plain below. Through one towering glen there is a glimpse of the **Throne of Zeus**, thrusting its peak into the vault of heaven itself. But as often as not the traveller will see none of this. The gods still like to conceal their celestial abode in a blanket of cloud. Soon there is a signpost and a branch road to Litochoron, whence the ascent to the Throne of Zeus begins. The Greek Alpine Club here provides information regarding guides, mules, etc.

Hellenistic Macedonia, over which the figure of Alexander the Great looms so large, begins at a signpost pointing west, to **Dium**, the huge military camp where Philip of Macedon and his infant prodigy son trained their troops. The road is rough and confusing, winding through scrub country to a small village of the same name. The early Macedonian kings considered the place a strategic outpost guarding their southern border from attack through the Tempe defile. They also inaugurated a festival, dedicated to the Muses. Livy and Pausanias refer to the number of statues that embellished the paved ways. They give us no clue as to their artistic merit. But we know that after the battle of the Granicus, Alexander commissioned statues of twenty-five of his favourite Companions who fell in the engagement to be set up at Dium.

In the fourth century Philip was in the habit of celebrating his victories here with games and contests. And all the time the drilling went on relentlessly, the great open spaces of the camp echoing with the thud of plodding feet and the din created by the marching phalanx, each of whose members was armed with a long spear and short sword, a shield large enough to protect the whole body, as well as a helmet, coat of mail and greaves. No foreign army had as yet faced such a solid impenetrable front. When going into action it was said to resemble a giant porcupine unfolding its erectile spines. Later the camp was the scene of Alexander's sacrifices before he crossed into Asia. In the course of the accompanying athletic and musical contests he entertained a hundred of the Companions in a magnificent marquee which accommodated a hundred couches. Dium was a place inhabited solely by men, over which Alexander presided both as generalissimo and patron of the arts and sciences. The Romans continued the tradition and maintained Dium as a military encampment whence they could easily deploy their legions across the northern plains. In the Early Christian era it was a bishop's see, and the chants of pious choristers echoed through great basilicas raised on the ruins of officers' messes which had once witnessed the drunken orgies of the young king and his friends. Then came Alaric's visitation, and Dium ceased to exist.

The remains are largely Roman, but the military installations probably followed (with additions) the original Hellenistic ground plan. The maquis-covered ground is studded with clusters of poplars in the shade of which Greek conscripts, based on nearby encampments, may now be seen taking shelter from the midday sun. It is best to begin at the village, whence the north wall, which formed one side of the square, runs west to east. Tower bases are discernible. At the extreme west end there is a mass of undistinguishable ancient masonry. Next come the fenced-in foundations of an Early Christian basilica with a large mosaic pavement bordered by a red, black and white geometrical design. In another fenced-in enclosure is a section of a well-preserved paved way: possibly one of those reserved for military reviews. It is pleasant to rest here amid the shaded bracken, where the Macedonian cavalry, largely composed of upper-class Thessalian young men renowned for their horsemanship, also probably rested after training. It was somewhere near here too that Philip, while celebrating his presumptuously named 'Olympian' Games, bought a prize horse from a Thessalian horse-breeder for the fabulous sum of one hundred talents (enough to enable a man of the fourth century BC to live on an adequate wage for a hundred years). But the black pedigree stallion, its forehead streaked with a lock of white hair and branded with an ox-head, plunged, reared and proved totally intractable to the cajolings of the most experienced horsemen. Plutarch tells the story – whether or not based on historical documentation is not clear – how Philip glanced, half-smilingly, half-mockingly, at the eight-year-old Alexander who was staring intently at the prancing steed. Approaching it unhesitatingly and realizing that it was only frightened of its own shadow, the boy turned it directly towards the sun and, after gently stroking the sleek black flanks, with 'one nimble leap securely mounted him . . . and let him go at full speed'. There was no mishap. Philip, squinting out of his one eye, cried: 'O my son, look thee out for a kingdom equal to and worthy of thyself, for Macedonia is too little to hold thee.' The boy named the horse Bucephalus (Ox-head), and it accompanied him throughout his campaigns, had to have a city in the upper Indus valley named after it, and, when it died of old age, was accorded a state funeral. Fidelity to his loved ones was one of Alexander's more attractive traits.

South of the enceinte, amid the long grass, is the theatre in a fair state of preservation: a garrison theatre for troops, whether Macedonian or Roman, who had little else to distract them from the monotony of military routine.

From the Dium signpost, the national road runs along the flat coastline: site of numerous camping sites. From Katerini I think it is preferable to take what is called the 'old road' – it takes a little longer to reach Salonica – but it is less monotonous, rising and dipping between the hummocks of a rolling green countryside dotted with prosperous villages.

At Kitros a turning to the right (east) leads to a region of salt-pans, **site of ancient Pydna**, where the passionate Olympias, Alexander's mother, was stabbed to death by order of Cassander during the fratricidal wars between her son's successors. Here too the forces of Perseus, last king of Macedonia, were routed by Aemilius Paulus in a battle begun after an eclipse of the moon predicted by an officer, expert in astronomy, to the Roman legions. But in the hearts of the black-frocked Thracians, mercenaries of the Macedonian king, the natural phenomenon struck such terror that they ran about dementedly, wailing loudly and beating their burnished shields. In this famous engagement, the scarlet-coated Macedonian phalanx collapsed under a formidable charge of Roman elephants, and the poltroon Perseus fled from the battleground on the pretext of sacrificing to Heracles – a deity, says Plutarch sarcastically, who was 'not wont to regard the faint offerings of cowards'. Livy has left an account of the way in which the Romans transported the terrified elephants down the precipices of Olympus, lowering them by means of a succession of broad planks supported by wooden posts used like drawbridges on different levels. Once they reached low ground the great lumbering beasts felt more at home, and the thunder of their stampede across the plain, already alive, Plutarch says, 'with the flashing of steel and the glistening of brass', was decisive. The battle of Pydna (168 BC) turned the scales. In a matter of hours, Aemilius Paulus, the Roman patrician, was master of the moribund European empire of Alexander the Great. Of visible remains there is little. Only two tumuli on the slope above the shore are thought to be sepulchral mounds erected over the Macedonian dead: sole memorial of a Greek defeat that opened the way to the East for Roman arms.

After Kitros there is **Methone,** where Philip lost an eye while besieging the Athenians in their last colonial stronghold in northern Greece (354–3 BC). He allowed the inhabitants to leave the city with no more than one garment on their backs and distributed their lands among his Macedonian henchmen. The road continues north, then east, serving the little townships and villages of the seaward end of the Emathian plain. A bridge spans the Haliacmon river, where a British Commonwealth expeditionary force made an unsuccessful attempt to stem the Nazi onrush in 1941; another crosses the Vardar. Real waterways, rising in the Balkan highlands, now replace the oleander-bordered streams consecrated to ancient river gods. The traffic increases. The flat monotony of rice and tobacco fields is unrelieved. One is soon among the tanneries and factories of the outskirts of Salonica.

CHAPTER THIRTEEN

Salonica: The Second City

❧

Via Egnatia – The White Tower – The Archaeological Museum – The Arch of Galerius – The Rotunda of St George – The Basilicas: 'Acheiropoietos'; St Demetrius; St Sophia – The Panayia Chalkeon – The Roman Agora – The Ramparts – The Chapel of Hosios David – The Latin Churches: Prophet Elijah; St Catherine's; The Holy Apostles; The Church of St Nicholas Orphanos

In Roman times travellers passed through the Golden Gate into what is now **Vardari** (alternatively Axios) **Square**, just beyond the railway station.[1] From here **Egnatia Street** crosses the city west to east, roughly following the ancient Via Egnatia, which began on the Adriatic and ended on the Hellespont, marked throughout with milestones commemorating the names of deified emperors. Triumphal arches spanned the highway; under them marched the legions, bearers of Roman law and order in exchange for Oriental riches. Here in Turkish times Edward Lear watched peasants bringing goods for sale 'in carts drawn by white-eyed buffali'. Fruit- and vegetable-bearing trucks have replaced the wild oxen of the Macedonian plains, and instead of a mob of blackamoors and Jewesses, 'their hair tied in long caterpillar-like green silk bags, three feet in length',[2] office and factory workers now thread their way through the congested traffic. In the First World War an Allied Expeditionary Force marched along Egnatia Street and camped on the waste-ground around Vardari Square; close to the bazaars and brothels gutted by the great fire that swept the city in 1917 – caused, ironically, by the carelessness of a French soldier.

For almost two thousand years Salonica has held the rank of second city of the Greek world: second after Constantinople in the

[1] It is through Vardari Square and along Egnatia Street that the traveller enters Salonica if he has followed the road described in Chapter 12. The national road follows a more or less parallel route into the town, closer to the sea.

[2] Edward Lear, *Journal of a Landscape Painter in Albania, Illyria, etc.*, London, 1851.

Byzantine period, after Athens in modern times.[3] Founded in the late fourth century BC on the site of ancient Therma, where Xerxes stayed in the summer of 480 BC while his fleet cruised in the gulf, it later served as a refuge for the exiled Cicero; and St Paul had an affection for the inhabitants 'from whom sounded out the word of the Lord', in spite of the frivolity of the women, of whose Roman finery he strongly disapproved, exhorting them to 'adorn themselves . . . with shamefacedness and sobriety . . .' For a time it was to Thessaloniki, strategically situated at the outlet of the Balkan trade routes, that Constantine the Great contemplated transferring the capital of the Empire, and when his choice fell on Byzantium, the chagrin of the inhabitants was equal only to their indignation that such a prize should go to an upstart colony on the Bosporus. But by the end of the fourth century, with the triumph of Christianity assured, the city's course was fixed. Scene of countless sieges and hair-splitting theological disputes, it was destined, under the protection of its patron saint, Demetrius, to play a role in Byzantine affairs – eventful, often heroic – second only to that of Constantinople.

The modern city, liberated from the Turks only in 1913, at the conclusion of the First Balkan War, is strung out along a grid of parallel and intersecting streets between the hills and the sea. Uniquely well-preserved basilicas and domed Byzantine churches, among the most important in the country, provide an air of mellowness to an otherwise wholly urban prospect. Parallel to Egnatia Street runs **Tsimiski** (alternatively Megalou Alexandrou) **Street**, the main shopping quarter, its pavements bordered with Syrian hibiscus. The food is better than elsewhere in the country, and the confectioners are crowded with Thessalonian ladies devouring cream cakes and Oriental pastries – *cadaif* (shredded wheat soaked in syrup and stuffed with chopped almonds) is a great favourite. There are hotels for every purse, and the Mediterranean Palace, on the waterfront, easily distinguished by its pseudo-Moorish architecture, is, in its flashy way, first class. The climate is one of extremes. In winter icy winds funnel through the Balkan valleys; fog is not unknown. In summer a pall of torrid humidity hangs over the tall new blocks stretching round the bay towards the suburb of **Karaburnaki**, where there are good fish tavernas beside the pale listless sea.

[3] Today the Greeks call the city Thessaloniki. I refer to it as Salonica, as it is commonly known by English-speaking peoples, and as Thessaloniki only in Early Christian and medieval contexts. The inhabitants are referred to as Thessalonians.

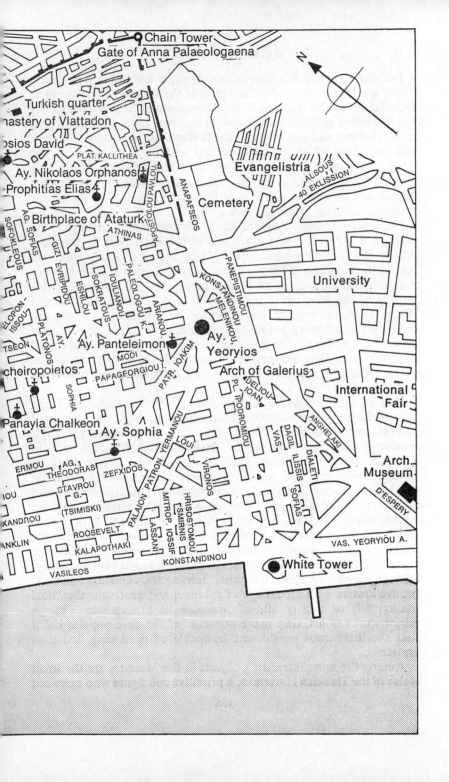

For the sightseer Salonica is, above all, a Byzantine pilgrimage. There are two obvious alternatives: (for the traveller in a hurry) to look briefly at the mosaics of the Rotunda and St Demetrius; (for the Byzantine enthusiast) to book rooms at a hotel for three nights (two full days) and leisurely visit the twelve most important churches. The evolution of styles, architectural and decorative, covers the whole span of Byzantine history, and the itinerary is roughly chronological. Roman ruins, Byzantine monuments and old Turkish houses are all enclosed within a horseshoe enceinte of Byzantine ramparts with Turkish additions.

For the Hellenistic, Roman, Early Christian and Early Byzantine periods, it is best to begin at the end of the waterfront, by the cafés among the shrubberies below the **White Tower**, the only surviving fort of the maritime defences, within whose circular walls a body of mutinous Janissaries, grown from a praetorian guard into a power-hungry rabble, were put to the sword in 1826, when Sultan Mahmud II the Reformer carried out a wholesale liquidation of this increasingly reactionary corps. On the landward side of the 'Bloody Tower', as it came to be known, extends a public garden speckled with the peony-like flowers of Syrian hibiscus, their large curled petals creating a spangled effect against the dark green bushes on moonlit nights.

East of the gardens lie the grounds of the International Trade Fair (held every September), whose origins go back to a medieval market organized on St Demetrius's day to promote the city's handicrafts. Facing them is the **Archaeological Museum**, a well-designed modern building. The wide range of exhibits, both as regards style and provenance, suggests the proximity of those northern lands which have done so much to shape the history and character of Salonica: of those once mysterious trans-Danubian wastes where Targitaus, son of Zeus by a daughter of a river god, was born, and whose son Leipoxais was singled out to become the founder of the wild and prolific Scythian race. Moving anti-clockwise round the atrium one observes (as in most museums in the country) ancient vases, greaves, weapons, terracottas, animal figurines, bronze kraters with mouldings of sphinxes and grotesque theatrical masks; all, or mostly all, of Macedonian provenance. Though minor works of art, they make nonsense of the once popular belief that the 'barbarous north' was incapable of producing first-class craftsmen.

Among the more interesting objects in the Museum are the small **stelae of the Thracian Horseman**, a primitive cult figure who exercised a profound influence on the national consciousness. The horse was the emblem of the Scythians, and Scythia bordered on Thrace. Consequently, the religious cults of both peoples possessed many points in common. In the early carvings (they were funerary or votive offerings), roughly modelled in shallow relief, the enigmatic Horseman is represented as a hunter, holding a spear and galloping towards a tree, around which a snake is coiled. Later the heroic hunter assumes a sacerdotal or semi-divine character and is depicted crowned with a wreath. In Roman times he wears military dress. In the Early Christian period his memory helped to mould the popular image of St Demetrius. He is still mounted, but now proceeds in stately fashion towards an altar crowned by a pine cone in front of the serpent-entwined tree. A composite character, probably some father-figure of the Thracian race, he is also part Asclepius, god of healing, whose emblem was a snake that possessed curative properties, part Rhesus, leader of the Thracian contingent in the Trojan War, famous for its swift-running horses.

The last hall (or first on left of entrance), a treasure house of **Hellenistic objects** of the most intricate workmanship found in Macedonian tombs, provides an exciting climax. Gold and silver trinkets studded with pearls and enamelled panels alternate with bronze kraters, perforated drinking bowls on hoofed stands (in which aromatic leaves were dipped to add a fragrant flavour to the wine) and skilfully wrought **jewellery** of the second century BC, which includes an exquisite pair of ear-rings ornamented with precious stones and pendant Erotes. At the far end of the hall, above all these priceless *objets d'art*, towers a huge urn, known as the **Derveni krater**,[4] its bronze surface covered with appliqué silver gilt figures in a crowded bacchanial procession. Prowling animals intermingle with human forms striking ecstatic attitudes, vine tendrils terminate in ornate leaves and maidens and youths recline gracefully below the lip. One moves round the glittering object with increasing fascination. Attributed to Lysippus, one of the great Peloponnesian sculptors and a contemporary of Alexander the Great, the Derveni krater possesses all the natural ebullience of Hellenistic art before the elegance and discipline inherited from the Classical age was tarnished by over-sumptuousness and florid ostentation. The free articulate figures have not yet become contorted, nor the fluid expressive gestures theatrical.

From the museum it is about five minutes' walk to the junction of

[4] Derveni is a village north of Salonica, where the krater was found in a tomb.

Anghelaki and Egnatia Streets, with the Aristotelian University buildings on the right (east). All this area once formed part of a vast imperial compound – palace, circus and mausoleum – now a commercial-cum-residential quarter, dominated by the triple **Arch of Galerius**, the Dacian shepherd who became a Roman Emperor – and not a very attractive one. The south arch has gone, but the middle piers are carved with stone reliefs of puny figures devoid of grace and individuality. An unimpressive replica of the great triumphal arches of Rome, it was probably considered good enough for a provincial capital. The sculptures tell the story of the success of Roman arms against the Parthians in the early fourth century. The women behind the altar symbolize the universe conquered by Galerius, who offers sacrifice (right), while his father-in-law, Diocletian (left), watches approvingly. Neither lions, elephants nor prisoners who beg the victor for mercy come to life.

South-east of the arch extended the circus, scene of a horrible massacre in the year 390. The most popular charioteer of the day courted the favours of a boy slave of Botheric, the hated Gothic commander of the local garrison. Shocked by the laxity of Mediterranean morals, Botheric imprisoned the charioteer, whose outraged followers promptly murdered the commander and his officers. Their bodies were dragged through the streets amid scenes of great acclamation. The prudish but choleric Emperor Theodosius I the Great, who relied on his Gothic commanders for discipline in the army, ordered a swift and savage retaliation organized, says Gibbon, 'with the dark and perfiduous artifice of an illegal conspiracy'. The people of Salonica were summoned to the circus to applaud their released idol. The exits were barred and Theodosius's troops fell on the unsuspecting crowd with drawn swords. According to Gibbon, the carnage lasted three hours; at a conservative estimate seven thousand Thessalonians were slaughtered. But the Church, of which Theodosius was such a militant champion, found it difficult to condone this bloody reprisal. The Emperor was temporarily excommunicated and forbidden to wear the imperial regalia during his period of atonement.

A colonnaded avenue connected the Arch of Galerius with a circular edifice, raised as a mausoleum for this 'notorious and faithful servant of the demons', as a medieval monk described the bull-necked, pale-faced Caesar, arch-persecutor of Christians. But destiny played a trick on Galerius. In the mid fifth century his mausoleum was converted into a Christian place of worship, later dedicated to St George, most popular of Eastern warrior-martyrs; now a museum of Early Christian art, it is known as the **Rotunda of St George**.

Architecturally it owes much to the circular buildings which Galerius probably saw when campaigning in the East. The basic plan is simple and grand: a towering cylinder with eight bays supporting a wide dome. Its Eastern character remains unaffected by the transformation of the arched recess opposite the entrance into an apsidal altar-space. Fragments of sculpture, Roman, Early Christian and Byzantine, ranged along the walls of the other bays, include a fine tenth-century **plaque of a Virgin Orans** (the Virgin with arms outstretched in an attitude of prayer) spreading frontally (her head unfortunately is missing), her left leg slightly flexed. The symmetrical yet gentle pliability of the folds of the mantle recall the drapery of classical Greek sculpture. Equally impressive is another tenth-century **plaque representing the Hosios David**, a holy man in the act of prayer, the pleats of whose hood are rendered by means of simple incisions.

Mosaics surviving from the original Christian decoration include Alexandrian motifs of birds and fruit within the octagonal medallions which decorate the soffits of several bays. But it is the huge **mosaic panels**, originally made up of some thirty-six million tesserae, in the circular band round the shallow dome that provide the mystical quality peculiar to this extraordinary building. Only seven panels survive. In each, two martyr saints, ritualistic figures with arms outstretched in the *orans* gesture, stand against crowded architectural backgrounds of immeasurable fantasy. Examination of detail is unfortunately ruled out by the height of the dome; reproductions alone reveal the refined modelling of the martyrs' heads, the vivacity of their expressions, the classical folds of their chitons. The variety of personalities, ranging from the boyish Porphyrius to the hoary Philip, constitutes the earliest of the portrait galleries of these holy men whose figures decorate the walls of aisles, barrel vaults and side chapels throughout the country.

Behind the patrician-like saints, suspended within ornamental arches, extend the architectural background: vistas of glittering gold crowded with rich plumage and looped curtains. A limited sense of depth is contrived by an incorrect but complex use of different perspectives which enables the onlooker to view the figures and buildings on a vaulted surface far above the normal trajectory of vision without undue disproportion. These architectural fantasies, which were to exercise a powerful influence on later book illumination, are full of Eastern motifs: knotted columns crowned with Corinthian capitals, arches, friezes and cupolas. In each panel pavilions frame the centre-piece, generally an apse or exedra. The mood is elegiac. Peacocks strut across parapets and swans float above ornamental cornices; candelabra hang from bejewelled canopies and turquoise curtains are drawn back to disclose pendant lamps or lighted candlesticks on either side of a ciborium with a loggia behind. There is little hint of Byzantine austerity. The Hellenistic-Syrian influences are still too strong. All the ecstasy of Eastern Christendom is symbolized in this opulent image of the Church Eternal. To the earliest worshippers, brought up in the Hellenistic tradition of Eastern luxury, this was identifiable as Paradise.

During the Turkish occupation the church was converted into a mosque and a minaret raised beside it. Today the vast echoing interior is empty but for the sculptural fragments in the bays, a person selling postcards, and pigeons fluttering about in the dome among these celestial fantasies of masterly mosaicists.

West of the Rotunda, out of a secluded court, where the local inhabitants assemble on hot summer evenings to gossip, rises a shapely brick-domed drum crowning the twelfth-century **Church of Ayios Panteleimon,** once a dependency of an Athonite monastery (the frescoes in the interior have not yet been cleaned). Regaining Egnatia Street and turning right up Ayia Sophia Street, one reaches the fifth-century **Basilica of the Mother of God,** restored in 1910, squatting in a sunken square. Its exterior architectural severity reflects the dignity implicit in its polysyllabic name – the *Acheiropoietos* (Not made by Human Hands) – so-called because in it once hung a miraculous icon of the Virgin that no human hand had fashioned. Passing from an atmosphere of Early Christian ecstasy, we now enter the arena of teleological polemics. This austere basilica commemorates the Alexandrian-sponsored decision of the Council of Ephesus (431) which established that the Virgin was indeed the Mother of God, the Theotokos, thus triumphing over Nestorius, Patriarch of Constantinople, whose championship of the rival 'Mother of Christ' formula provoked a succession of theological storms that came near to wrecking the unity of the new Church. The Thessalonians entered with zest into the controversy. Politics and nationalism played their part and the rival doctrines frequently reflected the antagonisms and jealousies of the different sees. The consecration of the 'Acheiropoietos' to the Mother of God, following the defeat of the Nestorians at Ephesus, was a deliberate slap in the face of Constantinople, whose claim to the exalted status of 'New Rome' still ruffled Thessalonian feelings.

The interior of the church has, in spite of a certain bleakness, an imposing overall architectural unity. The windows, divided by short columns, are disposed symmetrically in two rows, thus relieving the general design of both monotony and clumsiness. Tribunes, where the women congregated, form loggias whose east-west axial lines are repeated in the colonnades of the nave. Columns of greyish-white marble are crowned by magnificent **Theodosian capitals**, an elaborate version of the Corinthian, with spiky acanthus leaves turned back on themselves as though by the wind, which was evolved in the fifth century and has been named after the Emperor Theodosius II. The fashion spread, but it was in Salonica and Constantinople that this sumptuous marble embellishment achieved its most sophisticated form.

Many images were probably removed during the Iconoclast periods of the eighth and ninth centuries, when the reproduction of the human form in religious art was proscribed by the puritanical emperors of the Isaurian dynasty; consequently, only a few **mosaics** – decorative work of a high order – survive in the soffits of the arches. The lyrical exuberance of the Rotunda mosaics is replaced by a more formal conception of nature, but the colours are unusually lavish. Lilies, poppies, sunflowers, nasturtiums and fruit-bearing branches sprout from ornate vases; foliate wreaths wind round crosses and sacred books; octagons enclose fruit and birds. Gold backgrounds swarm with fish and plump blue pheasants. But for all its harmony, the 'Acheiropoietos' remains somewhat cold and unevocative.

Ayia Sophia Street mounts directly from the 'Acheiropoietos' to Ayiou Demetriou Street and thence (turning left) to the holiest spot in Salonica: the site of St Demetrius's martyrdom. A spacious church with sloping roofs and rows of arched windows spreads across a narrow esplanade. The unweathered brick indicates a modern construction, but the amplitude of the proportions suggests an ancient design. It is, in fact, a faithful replica – the result of years of patient archaeological research and reconstruction – of the **Basilica of Ayios Demetrios**, twice destroyed by fire. On feast days the ringing of multiple church bells echoes across the roofs of hotels and office blocks shelving down a slope once crowded with medieval mansions, hospices and public baths. The whole history of Salonica is bound up with this church. It is at once the spiritual centre and common meeting-ground of the inhabitants in a way that no other Christian place of worship in Greece has ever been.

With the transition from paganism to Christianity, the popular image of the martyr inherited some of the Thracian Horseman's

191

attributes. Like him he is a heroic warrior, and his mystical relationship with the Virgin has affinities with the Horseman's association with Bendis, a Thracian deity who symbolized rebirth after death. Of Demetrius himself we know little except that he was an upperclass young man whose military prowess won for him the patronage of Galerius. But his conversion to Christianity infuriated the Caesar, who promptly imprisoned him in a bathing establishment. To make matters worse, Nestor, an athlete friend of Demetrius's, also a Christian, challenged and killed the champion gladiator, the imperial favourite of the moment. This was too much for the irascible Galerius. Nestor was summarily executed and Demetrius, suspected of instigating the gladiator's downfall, speared to death in the public baths (now the crypt of the church), where he was afterwards buried by Christian friends. From this contemptible exhibition of human vindictiveness an obscure martyrdom derived its venerable character and a great cult centre acquired its popularity.

The church has been rebuilt on the fifth-century plan. Original materials, such as chancel portico arches, Theodosian capitals and column shafts of green and dark red marble, were re-used in the modern construction. But the frescoes, porphyry revetments and the mosaics which adorned the north aisle were lost forever in the 1917 conflagration.

It is curious that the Iconoclasts of the eighth and ninth centuries removed neither those north aisle mosaics nor the few panels which are preserved elsewhere in the church in their original positions. They may have feared a public outcry. Healer of the sick, protector of children, Demetrius was also guardian of the city. He *is* the city. The faith of its inhabitants in his ability to protect them was unlimited. They say he would be seen sallying forth in shining armour to rally the defenders against the barbarians: in the sixth century against the Slavs, whose invasion fleet he scattered by invoking a sudden storm; in the eleventh against the Petcheneg hordes from the Danube; in the twelfth against Tancred and his Normans whose atrocities, according to a contemporary historian, created a 'bottomless gulf of enmity' between Greeks and Latins. In the thirteenth, he drove out the Lombards, not without military assistance from Theodore Angelus, the ambitious Despot of Epirus, who forthwith crowned himself emperor in the city of St Demetrius and compelled the Latin barons to make obeisance to him as '*altissimo imperator graecorum*'. Believing they had at last inherited the coveted imperial mantle, the Thessalonians were enraptured. But John III Vatatzes, the other émigré emperor, whose seat was at Nicaea, marched on Salonica

Mount Parnes: the Monastery of Kleiston clings to the cliff side.

The tall eleventh-century church of Hosios Loukas, whose interior is one of the finest examples of Byzantine art.

Hosios Loukas: Mosaics of the Virgin and Child in the apse, and the twelve
apostles seated round the symbol of the Trinity in the dome of the sanctuary.

and quickly disposed of the upstart 'empire'. This time St Demetrius did not intervene. It was a matter of internal politics, between Greek and Greek.

Even in 1430, when Salonica fell to the Turks, St Demetrius's intercession with the Ottoman governor was not unsuccessful, for his shrine was spared desecration. All other churches were converted into mosques and the inhabitants put to the sword. The fall of Salonica, which preceded that of Constantinople by twenty-three years, was the penultimate warning to the pusillanimous leaders of the West, who stood by, as though bemused, watching the downfall of an empire which, for all its cruelty and corruption, was still the heir of Athens and Rome and the repository of every human value they cherished. Within a century the Ottoman armies had entered Budapest and were besieging Vienna.

The layout of the reconstructed basilica is simple: narthex, nave and two aisles separated by colonnades, transept and tribunes on three sides. At the west end of the south aisle colonnade, a Theodosian capital of great fantasy surmounts an ancient pilaster. Stone images of birds nestle among bunches of grapes, and fat peacocks with rippling feathers drink out of a cantharus. Other fifth- and sixth-century capitals crown dark green columns in various parts of the nave, with strange effigies, minutely carved, of winged animals and rams and lions' heads peeping over frilled edges of acanthus plants. The serrated lace-like leaves, carved in deep relief and curled backwards, create astonishing light and shade effects.

The surviving **mosaics**, probably of the early seventh century, are half-hidden among the aisles and piers. The technique of mosaic work was even more highly developed in Salonica than in Italy. In the grading and setting of tesserae (the average measurement in the St Demetrius panels is four millimetres), in the blending of colours and creation of shading effects, Salonica was in advance of Rome. Even at times of acute military crisis the mosaic workshops hummed with activity. The panels, which are not disposed in any apparent order, were votive offerings to the thaumaturgical saint. The holy persons are represented frontally; great attention is paid to symmetry, and, in spite of their wooden attitudes, they emerge as figures of great nobility depicted in a state of contemplative ecstacy.

In a clockwise tour of the basilica the first panel, high up on the west wall of the north aisle behind a fifteenth-century sarcophagus of Florentine workmanship, is a fragment depicting St Demetrius and the Angels. In spite of poor lighting, the only surviving angel, which has a gentle protective expression, blowing a trumpet as it emerges out of stylized clouds, is easily distinguished. The two panels on the north-east pier of the nave, placed like icons in front of the sanctuary, are far more impressive. The first is of **St Demetrius and the Children**. The young saint has thick wavy hair, and the expression of his large black eyes is compassionate yet penetrating. The right hand is raised in a gesture of salvation and his physical beauty not without an air of celestial serenity. An earth-bound figure, with an extra-terrestrial nature. The round-eyed faces of the two children over whom the slender saint towers protectively are so life-like that little seems to distinguish them from the small boys playing hide-and-seek among the marble columns, to the accompaniment of their mothers' unabashed chatter in the side aisles. In the other panel, the **Virgin and St Theodore**, on the north-east pier, the colouring is more sober, but the dark puce of the Virgin's mantle is very effective against the pale greenish-blue background. A slim elegant figure, holding a scroll, she is represented in semi-profile, in the act of intercession on behalf of mankind. St Theodore, a military gentleman, black-haired and black-bearded, hands outstretched, possesses all the weight and volume which the ethereal Virgin lacks. There seems to be no relation between the two figures, as though their juxtaposition were a matter of pure accident.

The three panels on the south-east pier are probably the best known. The faces are ,clearly portraits, the style monumental, and there is no attempt at symbolism. In the central panel we see **St Sergius**, a young Roman officer martyred in Syria, where the desert nomads revered him as their patron saint: a tall youth with curly hair, a gold circlet round his neck, wearing a chlamys decorated with alternating trefoils and rayed circles. There is an unmistakable similarity between the modelling of the saint's face and that of St Demetrius in the panel with the children. Perhaps both mosaics were the work of the same artist. Both are equally moving. The flanking panel, according to the inscription, depicts **St Demetrius between the founders** of 'this famous house'. The figure of the young martyr, just perceptibly levitated so as to suggest his saintly status, is grand and noble, his ornate chlamys spangled with diamond-shaped cubes. The ascetic face is unusually small and somewhat pinched, and although it lacks the spiritual quality of the beautiful head towering above the children, the eyes retain the same penetrating expression. The founders, by contrast, are robust stocky officials with slab-like beards, their feet firmly planted on the ground. The figure on the right, believed to be the treasurer, holds a purse full of money; the one on the left represents a bishop with a distinguished career in the defence of the city during the Slav invasions. Their rectangular nimbuses indicate they were living when the work was executed. The third panel represents **St Demetrius and a deacon** who was so distressed by the church's destruction by fire that the saint took pity on him, visited him in a dream and prophesied its imminent restoration. A report of the dream reached the ears of a senior cleric, and shortly afterwards some wealthy patrons were persuaded to commission the rebuilding of the church (the seventh-century edifice). The saint's right hand is placed affectionately on the shoulder of the deacon, a stolid wooden figure, who reverently touches his protector's chlamys: a gesture indicating that he had been visited in a dream by a celestial being.

A stairway to the right descends through brickwork chambers to the **crypt**. Adjoining a marble-paved cloister, lighted by windows on the street level, is an apsidal chamber, the centre of the cult, connected with the sanctuary by two stairways, which incorporates part of the original structure of the Roman baths where Demetrius was murdered. A shrine built over the martyr's grave possessed healing powers and thousands of pilgrims flocked to it to be cured. In the fifth century Leontius, a prefect of Illyricum, was so impressed by the relief he obtained from a paralytic condition, diagnosed as incurable by his physicians, that he commissioned the construction of a magnificent church (the original edifice destroyed in the seventh century) in honour of this new Asclepius. A round basin between an arc of piers and a marble ciborium with six slender unfluted columns crowned with Theodosian capitals was originally connected by a pipe with the source of perfumed therapeutic water, described by a thirteenth-century ecclesiastic as the ocean that girdled the world.

Proceeding down the south aisle, past remains of wall paintings of a later period, one reaches the last major mosaic, depicting **St Demetrius and a woman and child**, on the west wall of the south aisle. It is fragmentary but beautiful. The saint, wearing a gold chlamys, his large gold hands out of proportion with his small head, stands in front of a ciborium. His pale face, lit by almond-shaped eyes, is more mature than in the other panels. On the right a mother and child, bending forward in attitudes of humility, approach through a garden in which a stylized tree grows behind a pilaster surmounted by a vase. The contrast between the Eastern-style background and the Hellenic symmetry of the draperies is characteristic of Thessalonian ambivalence towards artistic influences during the Early Byzantine period.

One returns to the nave. At the end of the south aisle is the **Chapel**

of St Euthymius, a miniature three-aisled basilica, donated by an official in the Byzantine administration. The work of a single painter, its early fourteenth-century frescoes provide evidence of the more attractive characteristics of Late Byzantine painting: light fresh colours, a predilection for free brushwork, statuesque figures given to dramatic attitudes and a tendency towards narrative. The episode from the Communion of the Apostles in the sanctuary is an outstanding example.

Descending from St Demetrius along Ayia Sophia Street, past the 'Acheiropoietos', one crosses Egnatia Street into a small square with palm trees. At its east end lies the domed **Basilica of Ayia Sophia** of the eighth century. The exterior is plain, with an ugly ochre wash above the brick course of the façade; but the interior, in spite of architectural imperfections – unduly small pendentives, clumsily executed arches – is impressive. The aisle columns are crowned with massive capitals in the form of reversed cones and the whole of the square naos is filled with a pale gold light spreading downwards from a shallow dome, decorated with well-preserved mosaics depicting the Ascension, probably of the tenth century. Only the Christ Pantocrator in a medallion supported by two angels, a puny figure with a distorted head and grotesque expression, is an earlier work, possibly of the late eighth century, according to a monogram of the Empress Irene, a fanatical Athenian-born lady of great beauty who not only reversed Byzantine policy in the cause of the restoration of the icon cult but deposed her own son and had his eyes gouged out. Below the Pantocrator an insipid Virgin in a violet mantle supplicates Christ as he ascends to heaven. She is flanked by two rather pert Archangels and **twelve apostles** somewhat clumsily levitated like Rhine maidens, separated from each other by stylized trees resembling Egyptian feather fans that sprout from conch-shaped rocks. The strict frontality of the figures in the St Demetrius panels is replaced by a marked, if awkwardly executed, attempt to express emotion through gestures and movement. Some of the apostles are in deep meditation, others stare raptly at the glory of the Ascension, while the inscription below runs: 'Ye men of Galilee, why stand ye gazing up into heaven?' As yet a kind of stilted mime seems to be the only medium of expression, but within the grand spherical design, the figures, tragic and fatalistic, resemble some Byzantine version of Sophocles's Elders of Colonus chanting antistrophes filled with presages of doom or a group of peasants seated round a table in a village café: sad, wise, well versed in calamity. Much of the effect of immense solitude created by the vast gold background in the earlier (probably eighth-century) apse mosaic of the Virgin and Child is vitiated by the ungainly matronly figure of the Virgin, on whose lap sits a diminutive Child with an expressive face. A great deal of the disproportion evident in the mosaic decoration of the church, which for all its defects reflects Constantinopolitan trends, stems from the Byzantine artist's attempt to present a seated figure within a curved surface to the onlooker below. As yet he knew little about perspective correction.

Chronologically (and topographically) the next church is the **Panayia Chalkeon** in Egnatia Street: so-called, 'The Virgin of the Coppersmiths', because it once served as the mosque of the Turkish coppersmiths in whose noisy quarter it lay. The din of hammers crashing on anvils has been replaced by the cries of fruit-sellers from a neighbouring market. Founded in 1028 and heavily restored in 1934, the church is small in comparison with the spacious basilicas. The transitional style of the domed basilica, as represented at St Sophia, is now succeeded by that of the cruciform church. The triangular pediments and the vaulting on the arms of the Greek Cross of the Panayia Chalkeon, as well as the exterior brickwork decoration (a faithful replica of the original), are forerunners of the inventiveness of later architects. The interior of the church is noteworthy for the faded remains of its original fresco decoration.

On either side of the church are two charming relics of Turkish times: (east) a little brickwork hammam with multiple shallow domes, still in use, called **Loutra Paradeisos** (The Baths of Paradise) resting on the foundations of the Roman agora, a section of which is discernible from the street; and (west) an octagonal mosque converted into an amusement hall called the Alcazar, where boys play billiards and older men drink ouzo. Salonica is full of these little Turkish 'islands', but it is a pity the minarets have gone – for the most part demolished in an orgy of nationalism unleashed by the assassination of King George I, founder of an ill-fated Glucksburg dynasty, shot, while taking a walk in Salonica one spring afternoon in 1913, by a lunatic whose only grudge against the sovereign was that he had once begged money of him and allegedly been refused.

Behind the Panayia Chalkeon and the Baths of Paradise extends the wasteland of Aristotelous Square, where the excavation of the **Roman Agora,** once the commercial hub of the ancient town, is now in progress. Hotels and blocks of flats border three sides of a large quadrilateral of confusing ruins. The custodian may prove a useful guide. At the north-east corner (left of entrance) are the remains of a marble stoa running in a north-south axis. An unfluted

197

column crowned by a Corinthian capital provides perspective. Close by is the Odeum, its entrance way paved with fragments of mosaic (pebbles set in geometric designs), its proscenium embellished with six arched recesses in which musicians played in the instrumental contests popular with the Romans. So pampered were the singers that they would lie for hours on their backs with leaden plates on their chests, purging themselves with emetics and cathartics to keep fit.

At the south-east end of the stoa, rubble conceals what may have been an Early Christian chapel – catacomb-like, safe from the prying eyes of Galerius's spies – with a fragment of wall painting, Roman in style, in which two saints are represented against a background of pale blue sea. Fragments of ancient wells choked with nettles and an intricate system of waterworks, including stone bath-tubs, have been identified along the east-west axis of the quadrilateral. Below ground extend vaulted galleries roofed with shallow domes. A flight of steps leads down to a chamber, penetrated by opaque shafts of light from arched windows, in which a stone pedestal is preserved. On it stood the auctioneer, ringing his bell, amid the swarm of Jews, to whom St Paul, remembering their 'Work of faith, and labour in love', addressed his Letters.

*

Eleutheria Square, near the harbour in which cargo boats load the much-prized tobacco of the Macedonian hinterland, is a convenient starting-point for a tour of the ramparts and churches of the Late Byzantine period. In the tenth century the arms of a mole, originally constructed by Constantine the Great, enclosed the inner port in which the largest vessels sought protection from Saracen pirates. One day in 904 sentinels observed the Arab line of battle, consisting of fifty-four galleys, nosing its way round Cape Ayia Triada. As the high-pitched yells of Arabs and Ethiopian mercenaries drew nearer, the Thessalonians gave themselves up to loud lamentations. Fire belched forth from the enemy's long copper tubes, and cages, filled with half-naked negroes waving scimitars, were swung from raised yards above the seawall. Arrows, stones and fiery missiles rained down on the dazed defenders, who were rapidly overwhelmed. The massacre that followed was total and indiscriminate. But in spite of their success, the conquerors, glutted with loot, slaughter and slaves, sailed away after two days. The pattern of Arab aggression was set for years to come.

From Eleutheria Square one may drive (there is a diesel bus route) or climb to the **Monastery of Vlattadon,** last surviving monastic establishment of the twenty that once flourished in this most Orthodox of Greek cities. Situated on a ledge below the land ramparts, overlooking the city and the gulf, the fifteenth-century church, largely rebuilt in the nineteenth, is of little interest. The garden is pretty. Behind the monastery extends a line of **watch-towers,** forming part of the defensive circuit of the medieval city. The gateway opposite the monastery leads into a wasteland – now marked out for building plots – enclosed on all sides by ruined ramparts. Bleak downs, where children fly kites in spring and jackals howl at night, roll north towards the Yugoslav border. From here many famous sallies were launched against besieging armies, and the giant Viking, Harold Hardrada, brother of St Olaf of Norway, counter-attacked the invading Bulgars in 1040. Hardrada, who was over seven feet tall, had travelled through Russia to Constantinople, where he was made commander of the Varangian Guard, composed of Norsemen and Englishmen specially assigned to ensure the sovereign's protection. The Empress Zoe, who both lost her virginity and succeeded to the purple at the age of fifty, and whose senile amours scandalized the Byzantine court for twenty years, is said to have been greatly attracted by the colossal Norseman. But he soon tired of the Empress's charms and fled to Russia and an early love. Thence, through Norway, he went to England and was killed at the battle of Stamford Bridge.

Behind the monastery the line of towers runs eastward. The fourteenth-century **Gate of Anna Palaeologaena** (named after the wife of the Emperor Andronicus III) leads through working-class villas to the ruins of the **Heptapyrgion,** which consisted of seven strong towers, whence the Sultan's troops poured into the city in 1430, killing every Christian they encountered. The central tower, the most formidable, now a prison, was raised by the Turks a year after they captured the city. At the apex of the angle formed by the arms of the north and east walls rises the Chain Tower (the Turkish Gingirli Koulé), a fine circular keep, girdled by a string course. From here the ramparts descend to the sea in a magnificent horseshoe sweep. The east walls include the well-preserved Tower of Hormidas (perhaps the Sassanian prince who held office under the Emperor Theodosius the Great) who, according to an inscription on the upper part of the bastion, 'completely fortified the city by indestructible walls'.

The descent from the Monastery of Vlattadon leads through the

199

heart of the former **Turkish quarter**, an area of winding precipitous alleys, crossed by open drains and bordered by vine-trellised yards littered with the refuse of decades; some rotting wooden solars supported by corbels shaped like consoles still project from derelict houses. If you are fortunate enough to come across one of these little oases, you may then see priests in pill-box hats panting up stepped paths and hear doves cooing in walled gardens, while children with huge black eyes stare at you from under stunted acacias and flea-ridden donkeys loaded with panniers of fruit stumble across the cobblestones. The smell of dust and dung and over-ripe vegetables is mixed with that of syringa and jasmine.

At this point the clock has to be turned back – over a thousand years. An intricate system of alleys (it is wise to keep asking the way) leads to the fifth-century **Chapel of Hosios David**, once part of a large monastery, in a little garden filled with pots of basil and fuchsias. Last time I was there the key of the chapel was kept by an old woman who lived next door. Originally a square edifice, subsequently truncated, it contains, within its apse, a damaged but very beautiful mosaic, primitive but profound in religious feeling, untarnished by the more sophisticated techniques of later centuries. The crowded composition depicts the **Vision of Ezekiel**, who raises his hands in fear, an almost elfin expression on his face, as he averts his gaze from 'the likeness of a throne, as the appearance of a sapphire stone'.[5] Opposite him Habbakuk, more meditative, records the miracle in an open book. Above the prophets a young and beardless Christ (fashionable at the time) sits on a rainbow within a large circular glory, shafts of light radiating from the figure like spokes from the hub of a wheel. His face, more Early Christian than Byzantine in feeling, emanates sanctity, compassion, authority. At his feet flow the four rivers of paradise, in whose waters two fish and a frightened river god symbolizing paganism take flight. The heads of the apocalyptic beasts emerging from under the rim of the glory are awkwardly executed, but they have a very human quality – particularly the lion of St Mark with its large baleful eyes. The colour scheme is a subtle blend of orange, pale yellow and different shades of green.

From Hosios David you descend to the **Church of Prophitis Elias** (Prophet Elijah). Probably of eleventh-century origin, built on the site of a Byzantine palace overlooking the city, this bulky edifice, frequently reconstructed, is architecturally very complex, with additional north and south apses creating a trefoil effect and an

[5] Ezekiel, I, 26.

elongated apse projecting clumsily from a box-like cruciform structure crowned by a high polygonal drum decorated with blind arches.

To the west, nestling among a cluster of dilapidated houses is the more attractive **Church of Ayia Aikaterini**, in the purest architectural style of the fourteenth century. Airy little cupolas crown tall polygonal drums and a portico surrounds three sides. The exterior brickwork decoration is elaborate. The fragmentary frescoes, depicting Christ's miracles, were badly damaged when the church was converted into a mosque, but the artist's endeavour to create an illusion of architectural depth by means of successive planes and to model the rounder somewhat fleshy faces in a freer, more painterly manner is evident. Although lacking the sturdiness of Early Byzantine architecture, St Catherine's possesses all the elements that make up the typical small church of the Palaeologue period:[6] warm-coloured brickwork decoration, multiple domes, arched windows, arcades with glass frontages, a clearly outlined Greek Cross plan.

The westerly route continues downhill. Traces of the west rampart, supported by blind arches, emerge out of banks of garbage. It is best to head for Ayiou Demetriou Street – either from Hephaistionou Street (the direct route from St Catherine's) or Stournara Street, which skirts the west rampart – cross it and enter a little square, undisturbed by motor traffic, where the walls, apses and domes of the early fourteenth-century **Church of Ayioi Apostoli**, girdled with multiple bands of brick inlay, rise out of a sunken enclosure. On summer evenings, when the sun goes down, women drop in for vespers and a priest waters the orange trees and flowerbeds in the court, where children play with a rubber ball.

One of the most attractive churches in Salonica, architecturally it differs little from St Catherine's (except that it is larger), with a lofty central drum and four subsidiary ones at the angles of the square. The narthex façade is embellished by four pilasters with Theodosian capitals supporting arches filled with brick inlay. The whole exterior is a masterpiece of lavish and ingenious interplay of stone, mortar and brick. The fashion certainly had earlier origins, but it is not until the fourteenth century that Byzantine architects achieve an extraordinary virtuosity in the creation of unlimited geometrical permutations with bricks of different colour, size and shape which they handle with the skill of a mosaicist. This art, a

[6] The so-called Palaeologue period corresponds to the two centuries (mid thirteenth to mid fifteenth) when the Byzantine throne was occupied by a single dynasty, that of the Palaeologoi. The founder was, as usual, a usurper.

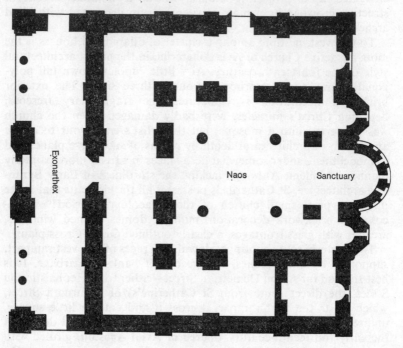

Church of the Holy Apostles, Salonica

Exonarthex

Naos

Sanctuary

minor yet characteristically Byzantine one, is nowhere better illustrated than at the Holy Apostles.[7] The zigzag cornices, rosettes, crosses and colonnettes, the string courses and step-patterns, especially those of the three apses, are integrated with the harmony and brilliance of design of a Persian carpet, and with as much feeling for poetry as for geometry. An element of frivolity, almost of skittishness, is sometimes apparent in the garlands of hieroglyphics. For all its riotous charm, the extravagance of this embellishment carries the seeds of its own decay.

This last phase of artistic creation in Salonica, of which the Holy Apostles is the highlight, corresponds with the development of the Hesychast movement which set priest against priest and split their flocks into hostile factions. Bricklayers and mosaicists were adding their final touches to the Holy Apostles when the storm of the

[7] There are other outstanding examples of this form of exterior church decoration at Arta and of an earlier variety at Castoria.

Hesychast dispute swept Salonica. The word is derived from *hesychia*, the Greek for quiet, and the Hesychasts, like Hindu exponents of Yoga, with eyes staring at their hearts, their limbs arranged in specially prescribed postures, devoted themselves to prayer and meditation by means of physical aids to spiritual concentration. Gregory Palamas, Archbishop of Salonica, a progressive theologian and champion of Hesychasm, later canonized, insisted that when Christ assumed the form of the human body at the Incarnation, he 'made the *flesh* an inexhaustible source of sanctification'. This was too much for the conservative opposition, and Barlaam, a bigoted monk from Calabria, descended on Salonica to rally the forces of reaction and defend God's 'impenetrability'. The battle raged throughout the fourteenth century. At the Holy Apostles, gorgeously robed prelates, Palamites and Barlaamites, hurled anathemas at each other. The unity of the Church was threatened and families were split in two in the best traditions of Greek party politics. In the sphere of art, the static liturgical canons of Byzantine iconography, so tenaciously preserved for nearly ten centuries, were not unaffected. The greater stress on physical movement, strictly denied to the monumental figures of an earlier age, may owe something to the Hesychast contention that the body in itself is not evil, as well as to the fact that Byzantine artists, now visiting Italy in increasing numbers, were unlikely, on returning home, to have wholly forgotten the lessons they learnt in the West.

The naos of the Holy Apostles is a perfect Greek Cross, with four marble columns, crowned by Theodosian capitals supporting the central drum; behind the sanctuary are three elliptical apses. The smell of incense is strong. An old woman in black lights a candle in front of the holy images; another sits in a pew staring into space. The greater part of the walls is washed a dirty pink. Turkish graffiti pock-mark the damaged frescoes of the first zone.

The surviving **mosaics**, stylistically typical of the so-called Palaeologue 'renaissance' in religious art, are clearly the work of first-class Constantinopolitan artists. The emphasis is on movement and tension. In the **Entry into Jerusalem** (west vault of north side) the elders rush forward to meet the procession against a background of towers, roofs and domes; the children spreading their clothes in the path of the ass and the little boys cutting branches on the tree strike acrobatic attitudes like medieval buffoons turning somersaults at the head of a royal procession. A beautiful design of concentric bands of foliate and geometric patterns separates the Entry from the **Transfiguration**, in which the oblique shafts of light radiating from the figure of Christ seem to reflect the Hesychast doctrine that the outward physical appearance of all divine activities resides in Uncreated Light. In the north vault (east side) the **Descent into Hell** is treated in a very dramatic fashion. A dour purposeful Christ with heavy-lidded eyes, the corners of his mouth turned down, his mantle blown back by the wind, raises the aged Adam from Limbo, while Eve, her hands outstretched, awaits her turn in front of a crowd led by Abel and a prophet. The garments are of different shades of green, brown and gold, softened by luminous patches of pearl grey. The balance and symmetry of the central interlocking figures of Christ and Adam are apparent in every line, whether of limbs or drapery.

In the **Nativity** (south vault of east side) the crouching Joseph and the shepherds who bear the tidings are simple rustic creatures. The faces of the mourning apostles in the **Dormition of the Virgin** above the main doorway are treated as portraits with individual expressions. The cruel bony hand of the Pantocrator in the dome hints at the familiar representation of a militant uncompromising Christ, a saviour of souls on his own terms. Below him are ranged prophets holding scrolls. Of the four Evangelists in the pendentives, the contemplative Matthew is the best preserved. Occasionally, a hint of preciousness is evident in the facial expressions. In his desire to dramatize, to stress human individuality, the fourteenth-century artist no longer appears to be filled with the same deep religious fervour that inspired the great static monumental figures of the St Demetrius panels. Only in the frescoes, which are in a much poorer state of preservation, one observes a more monumental character reminiscent of slightly earlier models.

There remains one last Byzantine pilgrimage. On the way, however, the sightseer must project himself for a moment into the closing years of the Ottoman Empire. From the Holy Apostles Ayiou Demetriou Street follows a west-east direction. Towards the end of it Apostolou Pavlou Street winds up the hill through the fringe of the former Turkish quarter. A plaque on a crimson-painted house, beside the Turkish Consulate, identifies it as the **birthplace of Mustafa Kemal**. The son of a local customs official and a fair-skinned Macedonian lady of Moslem faith, the future Ataturk, 'father of the Turks', grew up here, in the late nineteenth-century squalor of the decaying Levantine port, where shadows of minarets lay across potholed streets littered with dung and dimly-lit cafés echoed with the screeches of pig-tailed Jewesses weaving through groups of soldiers bristling with sabres, daggers and pistols, their close-cropped Tartar-shaped heads crowned with furry black fezes. At the army cadet school, Kemal galvanized the Salonica branch of the 'Young Turk' movement and plotted the overthrow of the corrupt regime of Sultan Abdul Hamid II: the first step in a programme of national regeneration which was to culminate in the expulsion of the Greeks from Asia Minor, the foundation of the Turkish republic and the doom of the *Megali Idhea* (the Great Idea) of a revived Byzantine Empire romantically fostered by Greek nineteenth- and twentieth-century politicians.

Beyond Ataturk's house a labyrinth of narrow streets (a taxi saves a lot of time and frustration) leads to Kallithea Square and the small but important **Church of Ayios Nikolaos Orphanos** (St Nicholas the Orphan), which once formed part of a fourteenth-century convent. There are three things to bear in mind about St Nicholas: (i) the key, at the time of writing, has to be obtained from the Archaeological Museum; (ii) although in the form of a tiny three-naved basilica with a narthex in the unusual shape of a Greek letter π, it is chronologically the last of the surviving Byzantine churches of Salonica; (iii) good lighting and the church's diminutive proportions enable one to devote all the attention to detail which the lofty ill-lit interiors of earlier churches preclude.

The **frescoes** are not among the masterpieces of late Byzantine art. Illustrative, picturesque, even fussy, they nevertheless possess a quality of ingenuousness which is wholly disarming. Take the narthex first. Across the east wall extend two bands of small compositions depicting the miracles of St Nicholas, the Lycian bishop who was patron of sailors, merchants and pawnbrokers. The cycle is full of story-book detail. In one episode the saint, standing in a boat propelled by five rowers, gazes up at a billowing crescent-shaped sail as he prepares to cast a phial of soothing magic oil on the turbulent waters. The south wall is devoted to **scenes from the miracles of Christ**. In the Wedding at Cana the bridal couple, crowned and wearing jewel-studded robes, are seated at an ornate table loaded with food, while the Virgin whispers in Christ's ear: 'They have no wine.' The Woman of Samaria, with almond-shaped eyes and a Semitic olive-skinned face, lowers a golden pitcher into the decorated well-head, as she asks Christ: 'How is it that thou, being a Jew, asketh drink of me . . .?' On the north wall St Catherine and St Irene stand frontally, bejewelled and resplendent in royal robes; and a beautiful Christ, depicted as a beardless boy with haunting eyes, is seated on a throne surrounded by priests and choristers. The inscriptions above the roofs and canopies of the background is taken from the great canticle of the *Akathistos Ymnos* (The Hymn Sung Standing Up), first chanted at a thanksgiving service in Constantinople after the city's deliverance from the Avar menace in 626.

In the apse the **Virgin Orans** stands on a golden dais, flanked by two adoring angels: a figure of authority, her eyes fixed in an oblique glance to the left, her gold-fringed robe draped in symmetrical zigzag folds. Her gentle expression, however, has much of the flaccidity of Palaeologue painting. The same 'sweetness' is apparent in the faces of the Archangels. The cycle of Twelve Feasts spreads across the nave, with the Transfiguration flanked by the Entry into Jerusalem and Crucifixion, crowned by the Ascension. In the Nativity, subsidiary episodes full of homely detail are grouped round the conch-shaped manger: Joseph meditating; the rustic shepherds, inhabitants of a biblical Forest of Arden, hear the news; the bathing of the Child in an ornamental basin into which an attendant pours water from a gold ewer while another dips her hand in to test the temperature. At the east end of the south aisle Christ holds an open Book of Gospels. The austerity of previous centuries has been tempered. His beneficent expression is identical throughout the church – an indication that a single artist employed the same model for all the portraits of Christ.

Everything is on the minutest scale; but colour, opulent as a peacock's plumage, is used unsparingly to match, blend and contrast. Lime greens vie with sealing-wax reds, sombre purples fade into amethyst shades, and the brown, maroon, puce or copper tones of gold-fringed robes glow against inky-blue backgrounds. No longer are the heavenly beings the austere symbols of an extraterrestrial majesty or expressions of a mystic revelation. Beautiful, pert, cunning, playful, contemplative – they are all somehow identifiable: the plump, lavishly bedecked page attending the horses in the Adoration, the aquiline-faced apostles in the Washing of the Feet, the forbidding Caiphas giving counsel to the Jews, the bored indifferent Pilate washing his hands, the compassionate Christ who appears before the myrrh-bearers in the garden, the prophets and saints in the lower register. One sees their faces in Salonica every day.

CHAPTER FOURTEEN

Western Macedonia:
The Lowlands

٭

*Pella – Edessa – The Macedonian Tombs – Mieza: Aristotle's Academy –
Verroia – Vergina*

West of Salonica extend the lowlands of the large province of
Macedonia. The Hellenistic sites, including Pella, birthplace of
Alexander the Great, and three beautifully situated towns on the
mountain periphery, overlooking the Emathian plain, can be visited
in one long day.

Twenty-seven kilometres west of Salonica is a fork in the road.
The northern prong leads to the Jugoslav border (past Polycastron,
where there is a British military cemetery – reminder of the long
frustrating campaigns on the 'forgotten front' of the First World
War), the western crosses the Vardar, passes another fork (to
Larisa and the south) and enters the reclaimed marshland of
Emathia, a former miasma of malarial mosquitoes. In the middle of
it lies **Pella**, where the conquest of Asia was conceived in the royal
residence of Philip of Macedon, where Agathon recited his flowery
verses and the *Bacchae* of Euripides was first performed. Herds of
water buffaloes graze in the flat treeless cornlands. In the south
Olympus looms in the haze, in the west the Vermion range forms a
barrier, thickly wooded, skirted by orchards. Foundations of
Hellenistic houses paved with floor mosaics spread across the fields.
Buses and lorries roar past. It is not an evocative site. The low
acropolis to the north has still to be excavated; also the palace
where Alexander was born – at the very hour, according to a
Magnesian writer quoted by Plutarch, when the Temple of Diana
at Ephesus was destroyed by fire and panic-stricken soothsayers
ran through the city, prophesying that 'this day had brought forth
something that would prove fatal and destructive to all Asia'.

In antiquity Pella was surrounded by navigable marshes extending
from the acropolis to the Thermaic Gulf. It is, for most of the year, a
damp torrid place, and it may have been the climate that effected

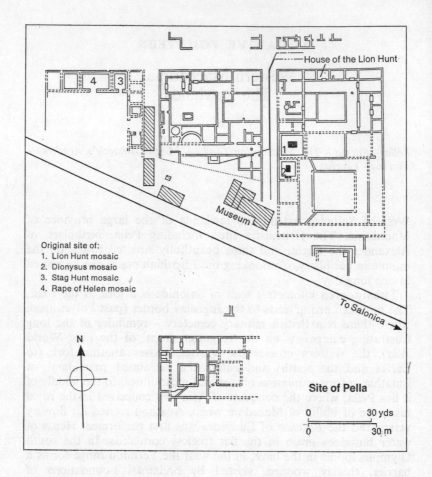

House of the Lion Hunt

Museum

To Salonica

Original site of:
1. Lion Hunt mosaic
2. Dionysus mosaic
3. Stag Hunt mosaic
4. Rape of Helen mosaic

N

Site of Pella

0   30 yds
0   30 m

what Plutarch calls Alexander's 'hot constitution'. There is no sign now of the muddy waters in which the much-prized *chromis*, a large fat fish, spawned its young. Livy says the citadel rose 'like an island from the part of the marsh nearest to the city, being built upon an immense embankment which defies all injury from the waters'. He also mentions 'a wet ditch' spanned by a single bridge 'so that no access whatever is afforded to an enemy . . .'

Right of the road are foundations of what must have been a complex of spacious habitations, at a short distance from Philip's palace, where his wife Olympias practised 'those fanatical operations', says Plutarch, in which serpents glided 'out of the ivy in mystic fans, sometimes winding themselves about sacred spears, and the women's chaplets', thus providing a spectacle that no man could witness without terror. It was with one of these reptiles that Philip discovered her lying in such a compromising position that he presumed her to be having intercourse with a god in disguise. God or serpent – it was exactly nine months later that this extraordinary woman gave birth to Alexander.

Entering the site (north of the road), the visitor faces a temporary storehouse; here are displayed two of the great **floor mosaics** composed of large pebbles of different colours. In Hellenistic times the subjects of this lavish form of house decoration were generally confined to historical and mythological events. Later, throughout the Roman world, the mosaicist's art became a flourishing trade, the artist himself an interior decorator with wealthy patrons. The Pella mosaics are among the earliest and grandest extant examples. The first is the **Lion Hunt**, in which two male figures, brandishing swords, attack a lion with a dark mane and erect tail. The attitudes of both men and beast, with the agitated backward sweep of the hunters' mantles, form a perfectly balanced composition. Clearly outlined shading effects, achieved by the use of grey pebbles, mark the sinews of naked limbs and folds of drapery. The suggestion that the hunter wearing a triangular head-dress represents Alexander in the act of being rescued by Craterus during a lion hunt at Susa is based on pure hypothesis. There is nothing to suggest the physical traits of the young world conqueror, generally depicted by the painter Apelles with a rather melting expression, his head inclined to one side. The second mosaic represents **Dionysus riding a panther**. The god is depicted as a flabby young man holding a thyrsis, and his soft effeminate body provides a striking contrast to the powerful lithe panther. The surface is flat and there are none of the three-dimensional shading effects observed in the Lion Hunt. The composition, which is devoid of detail, achieves an impressive economy.

To the right of the mosaic pavements a temporary museum houses architectural fragments, jewellery and specimens of Hellenistic paintings. Among the sculptures are a fifth-century BC life-size dog couchant, relaxed yet alert, full of a kind of dormant agility, and a small male torso crowned by a Hellenistic head with a voluptuous expression thought to resemble Alexander's. The bronze figurines include a supple little panther devouring a stag: a masterpiece of anatomical observation.

North of the museum are foundations of four palatial houses with fragments of pebble mosaic floors (decorative designs without figures); to the east (right) lies the clearly outlined structure of the late fourth-century BC **House of the Lion Hunt** (so-called after the mosaic pavement found here), which consists of a succession of chambers with a peristyle court surrounded by broken fluted Ionic columns (six have been restored), bordered on the east by an ancient street, where clay water pipes lead through the rock. The ruined house lends scale and perspective to the whole site. Fragments of plaster work, of bronze doorways and ornamental blocks suggest that it was an important official residence. There is little evidence, however, of the elegance of an ancient Greek palace or citadel, which generally grows organically out of a natural rocky base. In some such colonnaded court it is possible to imagine Philip, one-eyed and lecherous, surrounded by his under-age concubines, indulging in nightly debauches. On one of these occasions, relates Plutarch, he so infuriated Alexander that the young prince seized a wine-cup and hurled it at his father. Philip, in an alcoholic daze, slipped and rolled on the floor, whereupon Alexander cried: 'See there, the man who makes preparations to pass out of Europe into Asia, overturned in passing from one seat to another.' There was little family unity at Pella, and soon after this incident Alexander retired to Illyricum, leaving his morbidly possessive mother in her native Epirus.

West of the House of the Lion Hunt, across more foundations, is the magnificent mosaic of the **Stag Hunt,** which adorned a floor of another residence. Two stags are hunted by two naked youths armed respectively with a sword and double axe. Anatomical details – muscles and joints – are subtly emphasized by shading effects, fingernails and toenails outlined in black pebbles, and the hunters' wavy hair is reproduced by the juxtaposition of alternate dark and light coloured stones. The composition is triangular, and the apex is formed by the elbow of one hunter and the cloak ends, blown back by the wind, of the other. In the centre is the larger of the two stags. In spite of the formal framework the figures remain intensely alive, and their predatory expressions reflect the excitement of the kill. In contrast, the border, a formal flower pattern, is pastoral and tranquil in tone: crocuses, lilies and honeysuckle, tendrils and acanthus leaves are seen from an oblique angle and drawn by an artist with a professional knowledge of botany.

South of the main road a modern building is filled with fragments of pebble pavements from the House of the Stag Hunt. Huge pieces of a series representing the **Rape of Helen** (a charioteer, horses and flowing garments of a handmaiden are the best preserved) indicate the extent of floor space originally covered. In a field to the south-west are foundations of a large circular building, whose purpose has not yet been identified, with four round annexes symmetrically disposed and surrounded by an open gallery and circular wall.

Much excavation remains to be done at Pella before we know more about the actual physical surroundings in which Alexander spent his childhood among the savage Thracian women whom Olympias brought from the heights of Mount Haemus to fill the palace with their ululations. After Philip had been assassinated and Alexander embarked on the conquest of Asia, Antipater kept his official residence at Pella. In the late fourth century Cassander, after assuming Alexander's mantle in Europe, established a new capital in the Chalcidice, and the city declined in importance. In Roman times it was crossed by the Via Egnatia. Today it is no more than a bus stop and filling station.

Beyond Pella the plain is dotted with pine-clad mounds. Patches of swampy ground among the wheat fields recall the marshes described by Livy. After **Yannitsa**, once a holy Moslem place, in whose dilapidated mosque descendants of the Ottoman conquerors of Macedonia are buried, the plain contracts, and avenues of trees relieve the monotony: not the cypress and olive of the south, but aspens and Lombardy poplars, limes and birches. Cows graze in meadows. At **Skydra**, a fruit-canning centre through which the Voda flows sluggishly, there is a fork. One road mounts to Edessa, the other runs parallel to the railway as far as Verroia. The approach to **Edessa** and its waterfalls (a short deviation) is through cherry orchards. The little town is strung out across the ridge of a wooded escarpment of Mount Vermion. Factory chimneys have now re-placed the minarets that once thrust their pointed turrets out of shady groves: a scene which Edward Lear found 'difficult to match in beauty'. The ascent, streaked by cascading streams, ends in the main square, where an open-air café spreads under an arbour of plane trees in whose branches nightingales sing. A juke-box booming out the latest Western pop music drowns the sound of running water.

Edessa, the ancient Aegae, has much history, but little to show for it. First capital of the Macedonian kings,[1] long before Pella, it remained their burial place until the time of Alexander. According

[1] The very rich tomb discovered by Professor M. Andronicos at Vergina (see p. 217) in the autumn of 1977 has been identified by the excavator as that of Philip of Macedon. If this is so then Aegae, the ancient capital of Macedonia, must have been at Vergina and not at Edessa. (Ed.)

to Herodotus, it was founded by the Temenid Perdiccas and his two brothers, who were exiles from Argos, on the strategic bluff guarding the Emathian lagoon (now the plain). The royal brothers, direct ancestors of Philip and Alexander, personally tended their flocks in gardens where, adds Herodotus, wild roses grew into 'wonderful blooms, with sixty petals apiece, and sweeter smelling than any others in the world'. The early Macedonian kings were homely people and the queen did the cooking. In 336 BC it was the scene of a splendid ceremony in honour of the marriage of Philip's daughter to an Epirot prince, but the festivities ended in disaster when the assassin's knife was thrust into the king's back as he entered the crowded theatre between a double row of statues of the gods. Thus perished the man who inherited a kingdom, writes Crote, confined to 'a narrow territory around Pella' and left Macedonian ascendency 'established from the coasts of the Propontis to those of the Ionian Sea'. In medieval times the town, then called Vodena, was strongly fortified. During the Latin occupation, after the knights had lost what little control they ever exercised over Macedonia, it became a battleground between the armies of the rival exiled aspirants to the Byzantine throne.

The antiquities are insignificant. The Byzantine church of the Koimesis (Dormition), beside the modern cathedral, has some ancient columns and damaged frescoes. Alleys bordered by old Turkish houses with projecting wooden balconies lead to a plateau shaded by silver planes, where a Turkish mosque with a well-preserved porch is crowned by a large tea-cosy dome. Remains of Byzantine capitals and inscriptions are displayed within. A minaret with a crumbling circular balcony casts an oblique shadow across the dusty wasteland; in summer children squat in the shade eating cherries or peaches, while dogs scavenge hopefully among piles of garbage.

But most people – trippers from Salonica – come to Edessa to visit the **waterfalls**. On the plateau behind the escarpment the Voda divides into two streams which flow between weeping willows before cascading into the plain which stretches eastward in a haze of fruit orchards and poplar groves. A cool shadowy public garden, neatly laid out with flowerbeds and filled with rustic belvederes and kiosks at which hideous souvenirs are sold, overhangs a vertical bluff. Down its sides roar the waters of the Voda, their spray drenching the leaves of walnut, pomegranate and wild fig trees sprouting from mossy ledges thick with maidenhair.

Returning to the fork at Skydra, one follows the road skirting the foothills of Mount Vermion. In spring a blaze of pink peach blossom stretches for miles across the orchards.[2] At the end of a side road to the right lies the hamlet of **Leucadia**, where useful information (if not the services of a custodian) can be obtained regarding a visit to the temple tombs concealed among plantations of peach trees. After Alexander's spectacular obsequies at Babylon the tradition of burying the Macedonian kings at Aegae came to an end. This pastoral fringe of the Emathian plain is now thought to be littered with as yet unexcavated sepulchres containing the ashes of princes and generals who fought fratricidal wars for the mastery of the East, when they brought back the Orientalizing influences that characterize so much of the art and architecture of the Hellenistic period.

The first tomb, built of ashlar masonry, and of the mid third century BC, is visible from the road. The façade, covered with a thin layer of marble, is crowned by a frieze, six yellow metopes and a cornice with painted moulding. An antechamber, around which runs a narrow bank with traces of floral decoration, leads into a vaulted sepulchre, also once painted.

More impressive is the so-called **Great Tomb** (also signposted), the original of which is dated to the period of Alexander the Great, also surrounded by peach trees. Although protected by a modern cement roof, this quasi-Oriental monument makes an astonishing impact. After plodding across well-tended orchards, one is suddenly confronted with a two-storeyed structure, composed of large stone slabs set in regular courses (rendered slightly concave by age), emerging, like some Babylonian temple in miniature, out of an excavated pit. On the first storey two columns *in antis* and four engaged Doric ones frame panels painted with life-size representations unique in their layout both in monumental painting and sculpture: (left to right) (i) the deceased, holding a spear and the sheath of his sword; (ii) Hermes in his role of conductor of the dead to the Underworld (his other functions being those of herald, musician, thief, liar, diplomat, inventor of astronomy, boxing, weights and measures and cheating); (iii–iv) Aiacus and Rhadamanthus, Lords of the Elysian Fields, who, according to Plato, were the respective judges of the European and Asiatic souls of the dead and whose responsibility it was to decide whether the departed should cross to the Isles of the Blessed or be condemned to eternal punishment in Tartarus. On the second zone of the first storey sculptured metopes depict the battle of the Centaurs and Lapiths between blue-painted

[2] The westbound road from Edessa across the Western Macedonian highlands is described in Chapter 15.

triglyphs. The third zone is decorated with a sculptured frieze, also painted, of skirmishes between Persians and Macedonians (the former being identified by their breeches and hoods, the latter by their armour) – which probably refer to the campaigns in the East by the deceased prince or general whose mausoleum this was. The second storey consists of six Ionic half-columns alternating with painted doors within frames in the shape of the Greek letter π. Little remains of the architrave and pediment. Beyond the façade an antechamber leads into the vault, on the walls of which engaged columns alternate with painted panels. As an example of both architectural complexity and the Hellenistic attachment to the outward symbol of human mortality, nothing could be more arresting than this grotesque monument.

The entry into the **Tomb of Lyson and Callicles** (second-century BC), so-called after an extant inscription on the doorway, is less imposing but more curious. Brushing aside a fretwork of branches and brambles, the custodian opens the metal lid of what looks like a well-head flush with the ground. After him the traveller descends an iron stairway – it is an awkward descent and the shaft so narrow that it leaves little room for manoeuvre for a person of more than average girth – leading into a man-made subterranean cavern, once the sepulchre of a princely Macedonian family. The walls are painted with garlands, effigies of arms and an altar on which writhes a snake, symbol of the Underworld. Twigs and pomegranates painted on either side of the columns *in antis*, just below the capitals, give the impression of being suspended on hooks. Outlines of towers and ramparts decorate the ceiling of the vault. Twenty-four ossuaries can be counted in niches on the walls. Of the gold objects offered to the dead none remains – the result of age-old loot – but some arms still hang from nails, one of which is decorated with a star within a border of laurel leaves. There is little oxygen in this macabre folly of a charnel-house, and it is a relief to spiral up to the orchards and the light of day.

About five kilometres west of the tombs a track climbs the foothills between banks of campion and golden drop, skirted by sheets of butterfly orchids, to Eisvoria (or Kephalari), **site of ancient Mieza**. It is best to leave the car at a confluence of little streams and walk up a path bordered by moss-covered boulders and clusters of giant mullein whose blooms are still used as fish poison. Opposite rises a wall of cliff divided into just perceptible ledges, believed to be the **site of Aristotle's Academy** founded by Philip of Macedon within the precinct of a sanctuary of the Nymphs.[3] Here the thirteen-year-old Alexander, far from the palace intrigues of Pella and the overpowering influence of his mother, could be instructed in a more tranquil atmosphere in the art of government and kingship and his 'passion for pre-eminence', quoted by Plutarch, tempered by the philosopher's counsel. He was taught ethics, physics, politics and geography; and the relationship formed between master and pupil in the colonnades of the Nymphaeum, where fountains trickled among ornate statues, survived the tremendous events of later years. In the encampments spreading across the wastes of Asia, it is said that he never went to bed without a well-thumbed copy of the *Iliad*, annotated by Aristotle, and kept in Darius's jewelled casket beside his unsheathed dagger. In practice, he paid little attention to the application of his tutor's principles on the art of government, but the seed of the love of learning, implanted at Mieza, prevailed throughout that brief meteoric career. Although the 'stone seats' mentioned by Plutarch, in which Aristotle sat meditating in the course of his botanical and zoological investigations, are no longer visible, the boscages of planes and willows are still there; and the grassy glades where Alexander and his companions – Ptolemy, Cassander, Harpalus and the beloved Hephaiston – hunted and exercised. Some fragments of mouldings, carved in shallow relief with leaf-like designs, as well as Roman coins have been found, and in the small caves pitted in the escarpment there is evidence of the grotto with stalactites mentioned by Pliny. There are also remains of a Hellenistic stairway and of structures including an Ionic portico at the top of the ledge from which water cascades into copses of birch, walnut and Judas trees. (In the course of recent excavations carvings of gorgons, lions' heads and floral decorations have been found).

A branch road ascends the foothills to **Naousa,** whose once famous vineyards have been replaced by apple orchards. An esplanade with flowerbeds and a belvedere and cafés, shaded by great pines, overlooks all that part of the cultivated plain which was formed centuries ago by the silt of numerous streams pouring down from the sides of the Vermion range.

Regaining the main road, one ascends the escarpment again: this time to **Verroia,** the ancient Beroea, spreading across a ledge of the foothills. As in many Macedonian towns, a somewhat muted air prevails: a lack of the usual Greek ebullience, not to say stridency.

[3] The belief is founded on preliminary excavations and the topographical evidence of ancient writers.

Instead of the usual Greek dust there is running water; instead of brilliant light an opalescent haze. Outlines are blurred and rounded. It is a painter's, not a sculptor's scene. Some old Turkish timber-framed houses put up a brave show among the cheap modern buildings.

The **museum**, situated on a ledge overlooking the orchard country, houses a collection of Roman sarcophagi, column bases, Roman and Early Christian carved plaques from neighbouring sites and fragments of idols and axes ascribed to the impressive date of 6200 BC from Nicomedia, the oldest Neolithic site in Greece, situated in the plain below. Some fine icons from Byzantine churches are soon to be displayed here too.

Vestiges of **Roman fortifications** – a ruined tower of the third century AD is conspicuous – crown the hill at the entrance to the town where Pompey spent the winter assembling his legions before the battle of Pharsalia. St Paul also stayed here for three months, converting large numbers of the inhabitants. In Byzantine times the town was a bulwark guarding the western approaches to Salonica, and consequently one of the first objectives in the lightning campaign waged by Theodore Angelus II, Despot of Epirus, in the thirteenth century, when this fiery claimant to the Byzantine throne freed all northern Greece of Franks, Bulgars and other foreigners.

Post-Byzantine churches and timber-framed chapels are tucked away in secluded courtyards, where Christian devotions could be performed in the privacy of the family circle without drawing undue attention from hostile pashas and fanatical imams. Ayios Spyridinos, near the Hotel Vergina, has a bishop's throne carved with effigies of stags' heads, painted woodwork and sculptural fragments, including a slab of a winged horse, inlaid in the paved floor. At Ayios Stephanos, in Elis Street, there is an attractive women's gallery, at Ayia Paraskevi (in the same street) a sculptured doorway crowned by a Roman capital, at Ayios Nikolaos, in Megalou Alexandrou Street, a fine carved iconostasis and a pavement inlaid with re-used marbles. More important is the fourteenth-century **Church of Christou** (Christ) in a sunken garden in Kontoyiorghaki Street, a single aisle basilica with **frescoes** by Callerghis, who is described in an inscription as 'the best painter in Thessaly'. His style is elegant and fluent, probably influenced by that of icon painting, and his faces are remarkable for their liveliness of expression. In the Descent into Hell, Christ, wearing luminous yellow garments instead of the usual scarlet mantle, is more the gentle saviour of mankind than the formidable judge of the souls of the dead so dear

216

to earlier Byzantine iconographers. The same limpidity of outline prevails in the Crucifixion. The Dormition of the Virgin is rendered with little originality but with an impressive blend of colours. In the Annunciation, the Angel, seemingly propelled by some inner force, advances eagerly towards the Virgin under a triumphal arch.

The maze of the ramshackle upper town is dominated by the curious basilica of the **Old Metropolis** (Kentrikos Street), now undergoing restoration, whose original structure goes back to the fifth century. On the north side of the spacious naos, entered from the narthex between chocolate-coloured pillars, a colonnade is laid out in three groups of ninth-century columns, two in each. Brick inlay of a later period surrounds the exterior of the apse. The last transformation was made in the fifteenth century when the frescoed walls were whitewashed, Christian symbols ripped off the desecrated sanctuary and a Moslem congregation shuffled shoeless across the naos, now thick with Turkish carpets, to the *mihrab*.

At the south-western apex of the plain, ten kilometres east of Verroia, extends the debris of the large Hellenistic site of **Vergina**, of which we know next to nothing,[4] except that it is named after a legendary queen of ancient Verroia. Ignored by mythographers and historians alike, it remains an archaeologists' domain. Descending through fertile country, the road crosses the reed-fringed Haliacmon flowing between banks bordered by copses of poplars out of a chasm between the Vermion and Pieria ranges. West of the modern village of Vergina the plain is studded with mounds, often no more than twelve feet high, each of which is a burial place, the oldest being dated to the Early Iron Age (1000–700 BC). In these tumuli were buried the tribesmen who dwelt on the wooded Pierian slopes, which Hesiod and Apollonius respectively believed to be the birthplace of the Muses (as opposed to their home on Mount Helicon) and of Orpheus, offspring of a Thracian king and one of the nine goddesses of song and poetry. Later the place became a vast Hellenistic necropolis, and the fact that women were interred beside the men suggests the mounds served as family vaults.

Climbing to the palace site, south-east of the village, one suddenly encounters a well-preserved **Macedonian royal tomb**. The façade resembles that of a little Ionic temple, with four half-columns, a frieze of painted flowers and a pediment. Marble slabs, which formed part of the doorway, lie across the floor of the antechamber. In the barrel-vaulted burial chamber are a grave, a bank on which the urn containing the deceased's ashes were placed and the damaged

[4] See footnote on p. 211. (Ed.)

but imposing throne of a Macedonian king of the early third century BC.[5] The arm-rests are supported by carved sphinxes. Traces of painted griffins devouring a yellow stag against a red ground are visible on the sides and footstool.

The ruins of the **palace**, built of buff-coloured limestone, and designed round a colonnaded court, cover an area of approximately five hundred by three hundred and fifty feet. The dimensions alone suggest royal pomp of the first magnitude. Archaeologists date this huge palace to the early third century BC; it is consequently reasonable to suppose it to be the residence of Antigonus Gonatas (so-called from the Macedonian word *gonatas*, after the iron-plated knee-cap worn by the king as a piece of defensive armour).

The ruins are scarcely more than shoulder-high, but the architectural layout is clear: more so with the aid of a ground plan. Shade is provided only by a large oak tree at the north-east end. You enter from the east, like the courtiers and palace attendants did, through what was a pedimented portico, flanked north and south by four long rectangular chambers, followed by the propylaea – the small Ionic columns decorating the upper storey are now strewn about the ground – and thence into the court once bordered by sixty massive Doric columns, now littered with pieces of cornice and architrave, drums and capitals eroded and fossilized by time and weather. South of the propylaea are the foundations of a circular chamber believed to be the ceremonial room in which the king received ambassadors and generals. One of the chambers of a succession of five, which constituted the south wing running along the base of the scrub-covered hillside, is covered with a beautiful well-preserved **floor mosaic** with foliate designs radiating outwards from a central star and enclosed within a medallion with decorative borders – almost Saracenic in style, like an Arab tile – and four female figures wearing a calathus on their heads in each corner. Judging from traces of Erotes and Tritons riding dolphins in the floor decoration of the side chambers, archaeologists believe that representations of erotic scenes were removed later by more prudish inhabitants, mindful of Early Christian susceptibilities with regard to licentious representations in art. The west side consists of three small and three larger chambers paved with small marble plaques joined by red mortar, with a drainage hole in the centre. Excavations at the southwest end of the palace have revealed a colonnaded open court beyond which were porticoes and chambers forming an annexe to

[5] The fact that the tombs at Leucadia contained no thrones supports the theory that they were the burial places of princes or generals.

the tetragon of the palace proper. The north side, now completely destroyed, overlooked steep sloping ground and is thought to have been a covered terrace overlooking the Haliacmon as it flowed through the mountain cleft and the strange necropolis of burial mounds extending across the plain.

In the absence of historical references and literary allusions it is difficult to conjure up a picture of what the original site must have looked like or of the people by whom it was inhabited, other than that they admired architecture in bulk and were profoundly influenced by the interaction between the Greek heritage and the more sumptuous art of the Orient. In its dimensions alone, thrusting aggressively from the ledge above the plain, the palace, in its now somewhat naked geometric state, still remains a very impressive ruin. Vergina was partly destroyed by the Romans; some sections of the palace survived, however, to serve different – probably religious – purposes during later periods.

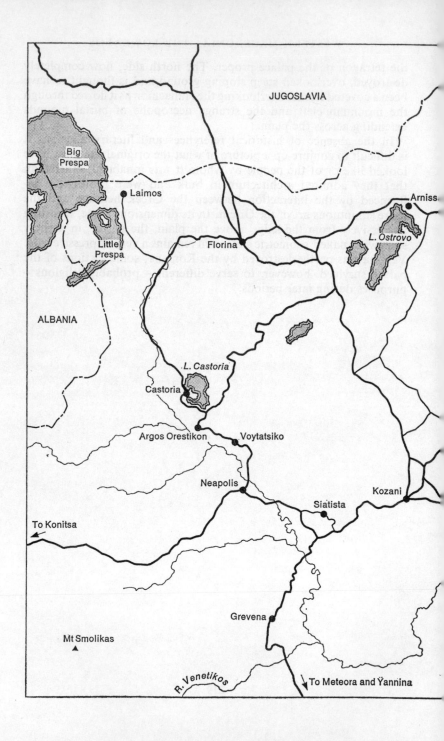

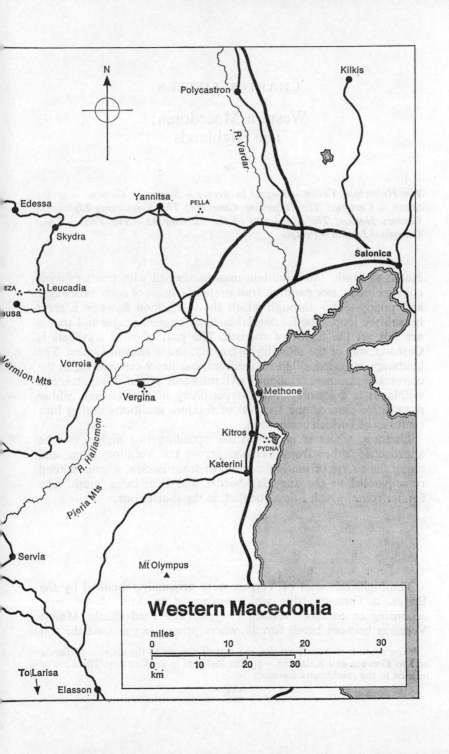

Western Macedonia

miles
0   10   20   30

0   10   20   30
km

CHAPTER FIFTEEN

Western Macedonia:
The Highlands

❧

The Haliacmon Valley – Kozani to Servia – Siatista – Grevena – to the
South – Castoria: The Byzantine Churches; The Seventeenth-Eighteenth
Century Houses; The Monastery of the Mavriotissa – The Voda – Lake
Ostrovo – Florina – Prespa

North to south, the mountain mass is seamed with tracts of agricultural land – rice paddies, fruit orchards, fields of corn, beet-sugar
and poppy-seed – through which the Haliacmon flows in a great
horse-shoe loop. The forests, lakes, snow-capped ranges and passes
are not yet the haunt of tourists. The goal of most travellers is
Castoria, one of the most important Byzantine sites in Greece. The
landscape is varied, often magnificent, but never classical or, in the
conventional sense, 'Hellenic'. At no point is the Mediterranean
visible. It is a journey into the periphery of the Balkans, whose
remoteness ensured the survival of folklore traditions during four
centuries of Turkish occupation.

Castoria, where it is worthwhile spending two nights, can be
approached either from Verroia, across the Vermion range and
along the course of the Haliacmon, or from Edessa, whence a road
runs parallel to the Jugoslav border and then turns south. The
former route, which I describe first, is the shorter one.[1]

I

The highlands west of Verroia were originally inhabited by the
Briges, a Thracian tribe which emigrated to Asia Minor, and,
according to Strabo, founded Phrygia. The road climbs Mount
Vermion between beech forests, where primroses grow. At the top

---

[1] The route is shorter, provided the two diversions to the south – to Servia
and to Grevena and Kalabaka – are not included in the itinerary. These are of
interest to the southbound traveller.

of the pass there is a tremendous aerial view of the **Haliacmon valley**, with the river winding between green banks against a prodigious background of the wooded Pieria ranges rising to 7000 feet. The scale is immense. A long dizzy descent in hairpin bends terminates in wheatfields around the unattractive town of Kozani, a road junction in the plain of Ptolemais, where lignite mines have brought prosperity to the region.

South of Kozani the Pieria range forms an unbroken backcloth to undulating countryside. A southbound road crosses the Haliacmon flowing between chalky cliffs. A gap suddenly appears in the mountain barrier, with a group of twisted outcrops of rock guarding the entrance to a profound defile. At their foot lies the sleepy little town of Servia, originally founded by Serbs settled here by the Emperor Heraclius in the seventh century to defend the strategic pass into central Greece. Opposite the needle-shaped rocks a hill is crowned by the ruined towers of a Byzantine fortress overlooking a loop of the Haliacmon. Little else survives of the military fortifications of this former key-town, where Michael II Angelus, the violent hotblooded Despot of Epirus, met his pious consort, Theodora, and carried her in state across the mountains to his capital at Arta. Beyond Servia, a number of narrow passes are succeeded by tracts of inhospitable moorland whence the road descends into Thessaly at Elasson (see p. 145).

To visit **Siatista**, seat of a remote feudal society that flourished in the twilight era after the fall of Constantinople, one turns right at the twenty-fourth kilometre west of Kozani, just before the junction of roads from Castoria and Grevena. The branch road climbs into limestone mountains with fine structural forms uncommon in these parts. The multi-coloured houses of Siatista spread across a line of broken hills. Once inhabited by rich furriers, Siatista seems to have been left unmolested by the Turks. Straddling no centre of communications, it was a retreat to which wealthy merchants retired, untroubled by Turkish tax-collectors, and dwelt in lofty houses with projecting third storeys supported by wooden brackets and painted with stylized flowers and foliate patterns below the cornices. The chief interest of the timber-framed houses, now abandoned and falling in ruins, lies in their elaborate Oriental-style interiors and frescoed walls, evocative of a rural seignorial way of life swept away in the holocaust of the War of Independence. There is no feeling of continuity here. Unlike Edessa, Verroia or Castoria, Siatista has no roots in Macedonian history. A phenomenon of the post-Byzantine age, it was the product of its own inaccessibility.

Only two old houses, virtual museums of folklore art, are easily accessible.[2] First the **Nerantzopoulos house**, which is still inhabited. As in most large residences of the Turkish period, storerooms and wine-cellars are on the ground floor, sleeping quarters on the first, reception halls on the second. The exterior walls are whitewashed, pierced with windows protected by coffered shutters and wrought-iron gratings fashioned in squiggles and spirals. The nail-studded gate is secured at night by a heavy bar, intended to keep out the brigands who once roamed the encircling mountains. The interior painted decoration is primitive and rustic, with still-life compositions on different courses: bowls of apples and pears; slices of water melon studded with black seeds. On the lower courses stylized flowers, red and blue, spread across gold and pale yellow backgrounds.

The **Manoussi house**, also eighteenth-century, is more impressive. The exterior walls of the third storey, protected from rain and sun by wide eaves, are painted with geometric designs which create an impression of faience, reminiscent of the ceramics embedded in the exterior apses of chapels in the Pelion area. Despite the ravages of damp and woodworm, numerous chambers still preserve a faded image of the work of generations of rustic interior decorators who plied their crafts in itinerant workshops throughout Macedonia in the seventeenth and eighteenth centuries. The woodwork is admirably carved, and the variegated shapes of the banisters add a further touch of fantasy to the architectural embellishment. A maze of little galleries and panelled halls on different levels leads to the spacious low-ceilinged reception chamber, reserved for night-long death laments chanted by choruses of black-draped crones, for formal name-day celebrations and wedding festivities conducted with all the pomp dear to a peasant community. Accompanied by violin, clarinet, lute and drums, a frieze of figures would move in stilted measures across the creaking floor-boards, jangling with bejewelled amulets and necklaces of coins and chains studded with cameos and pendant agates: the men in fur-lined waistcoats with filigree plaques like mail breastplates, the women in embroidered shifts and sequin-studded cloaks bordered with twisted silken cords.

The walls of the sun-parlour, its bay windows supported by columns like a miniature loggia, are adorned with mock-heroic frescoes: a stag hunt with black birds perched on tree-tops or

[2] Enquiries for the custodian should be made at the café in the main street. Other houses worth looking at (if admittance can be gained) are those of the Poulkos and Hadjimichaili families.

Delphi: the Theatre and Temple of Apollo.

Delphi: the Tholos.

flying across a lemon yellow sky; a kilted hunter with long black moustaches drawing his sword preparatory to killing a lion which sticks its tongue out at him; a panorama of Constantinople, Queen of Cities. The drawing is that of a child, and like a child's, it has a dream-like quality. Islamic influences are evident. The bedrooms are distinguished by a curious architectural feature: fireplaces in the form of apse-shaped pyramids with bases surrounded by a marble kerb and surmounted by a cone capped by a cross, like some Christian version of a Moslem monument. Immense cupboards with carved panels painted with tendrils terminating in calyxes line the walls. In them were stacked the precious heirlooms: embossed silver buckles, chaplets hanging from filigree plaques studded with coloured stones, embroidered belts, Gospel books bound in embossed metal covers, and elaborate national costumes and chains of coins of different foreign currencies worn by women both as talismans and adornments.

Most of these folklore objects,[3] wrought in gold or silver and often ornamented with semi-precious stones, were the products of Macedonian and Epirot workshops, and so great was the renown of Greek peasant silversmiths that their creations found lucrative markets throughout the Balkans. Needleworkers too, especially from Kozani, would emigrate to Vienna, where their embroideries were greatly prized. The arched windows of the Manoussi house are filled with panels of stained glass set in stucco: an importation from the Danubian states, with which the local furriers and wine merchants traded. Perched on the top floor is the minute and only lavatory – Turkish style, a hole in the floor – projecting above the neglected garden. The whole affair is a gigantic doll's house – it must have been a fantastic place to live in, set against a background of desolate mountains from which jackals descend at night to shriek in the stony wastes around the village.

A descent between slate-grey hills brings us again to the main north-south road: to Castoria and Grevena respectively. As an alternative route into Thessaly and the south, the way through Grevena has little to offer but its spectacular climax. In summer heaps of different kinds of melons are piled up in gigantic pyramids in the main square of **Grevena** – I know of nothing else to recommend this dreary provincial town. The road crosses the ravine of the

---

[3] Specimens of these objects are displayed in the Benaki and Greek Popular Art Museums in Athens, as well as in rudimentary folklore museums in many Macedonian towns, including Salonica and Yannina. Copies (skilful or otherwise) are on sale in tourist shops in the main tourist centres throughout the country.

Venetikos, its rocky banks eroded into strange forms above pools of ice-green water into which peasant boys dive. This is the ancient country of Elimeiotis, across which the nineteen-year-old Alexander, just crowned king and flushed with a resounding victory over the Illyrians, force-marched his army at a pace as yet unknown in military history in order to reach southern Greece and chastise the rebellious Thebans. Descending gradually across a barren melancholy mountain tract, one is rewarded by a novel and superbly theatrical view of the Meteora rock-pillars barring the way into the Thessalian plain. To the west the Pindus mountains rise sheer, with dark chasms biting deep into the range. Between awesome heights, the road, by contrast, follows a lovely fertile strip traversed by a stream which feeds the Peneius. Plane trees shade a jungle of brambles, wild fig and mulberry orchards, the long grass sizzles with the chirping of cicadas, and hornets and dragon-flies whirr crazedly in the sun-drenched foliage. The road enters the plain at the base of a cluster of obelisks and pinnacles of stratified conglomerate, rent by gloomy caverns leading into the heart of the valley of the Meteora. To the west another road scales the Pindus to Metsovo and thence to Yannina, capital of Epirus.

Back at the junction of the main northbound road to Castoria and the Siatista branch, one continues along the upper valley of the Haliacmon, famous in antiquity for its destructive inundations. Westward runs the spine of the northern Pindus, capped by the formidable snow-capped peak of Smolikas (8640 feet). At Neapolis a branch road to the left leads to Konitsa and the Albanian border. Groves of poplars spread across shallow gullies through which mountain streams feed the Haliacmon. The village of **Voytatsiko**, built on seven hills, surrounded by oak and beech woods, overlooks the river valley. Barns with thatched roofs suggest the increasingly northern character of the country. The road by-passes **Argos Orestikon**, named after an ancient city allegedly founded by Orestes, when he fled from Argive Mycenae, pursued by the avenging Eumenides, to what were then believed to be the furthest confines of the world. The village is now the centre of a trade in sheepskin rugs. Soon the road is winding along the shore of a mountain lake. Mist clings to the banks in the early morning, and wild fowl skim the placid waters in long arrowhead lines.

The houses of **Castoria** rise from the twin shores of an isthmus on to a rocky headland. Among the highest, the Hotel du Lac (or Limnis)[4] commands a prospect, beyond a foreground of dark

[4] Cheaper accommodation can be found in the lower town (Celetron, Orestikon).

pines, of the ice-blue lake and poplar-fringed shore against a screen of wild mountains piling up towards Albania in the west, Jugoslavia in the north, dominated by the cone-shaped peak of Vitsa. Byzantine churches and chapels spread fan-wise round the hotel, which is a good starting-point for sightseeing.[5] A full day is required to visit the main churches (which have unusual and decorative features) scattered among abandoned tower-like eighteenth-century houses overlooking derelict courtyards. The climate is harsh and northern. In winter the lake freezes; in spring adders glide in the undergrowth; summer does not come till June. A thriving fisheries industry (perch, pike, eel) is undergoing rapid development. But it is the fur trade which has brought prosperity to Castoria, for centuries a recognized dumping-ground for strips of mink and other pelts discarded by the more fastidious furriers of Europe and America. Teenage workers, heirs of the original fur-traders who came from Siatista, crowd the two hundred workshops. Seated in rows in front of trestle-tables, they scrub mangy fragments of tails and paws with a razor-like implement, sort them out, snip, trim and join them together with a long needle and finally overseam the whole piece on a machine. The furs are then re-exported and sold as stoles, wraps and coats at relatively low prices in Athens, Germany, Holland, Belgium and to a lesser extent in the United States.

The history of the town, the ancient Celetrium, is uneventful until the Middle Ages when a succession of invaders made it into an important staging-post on the way to the East. Among the first were Robert Guiscard, 'the Weasel', Norman Duke of Apulia and Calabria, who opened the eyes of Western princes to the glittering prospect of dismemberment of the Byzantine Empire, and his son Bohemond, Prince of Taranto, a gigantic ruddy-faced yellow-haired adventurer, who spent the Christmas of 1096 here and requisitioned all the pack-animals in the region to swell his army marching on Constantinople. Later, during the Frankish occupation, Michael Angelus II, Despot of Epirus, conducted a guerrilla war in the neighbouring hills against the Eastern aspirant to the Byzantine throne. Then came the Albanians, and finally the Turks who stayed for over six centuries, and the Jews who developed the fur industry. In 1947-9 insurgent Communists armed by Eastern bloc governments waged a two-years struggle against the American-equipped

[5] On a recent visit to Castoria I found that admittance into the churches was only possible by applying for the keys to the custodian at the Church of Ayios Nikolaos Kasnitzi (Omonoia Square). This somewhat inconvenient measure is probably of a purely temporary nature.

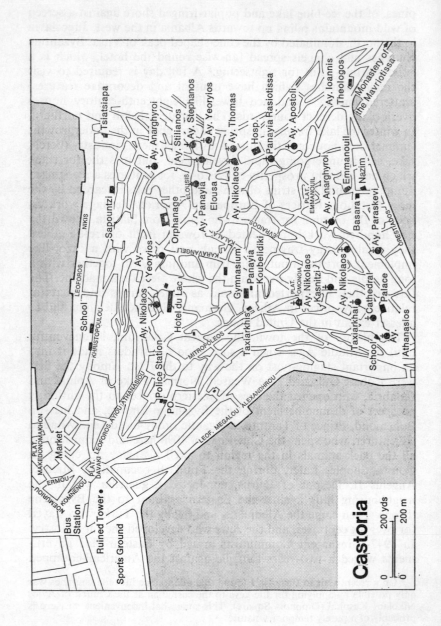

Castoria

0   200 yds
0   200 m

Greek army from hideouts among the surrounding villages, whence they abducted thousands of children whom they dispatched across the frontiers for indoctrination in Marxist ideology.

The monuments are wholly Byzantine, but there is no evidence of the multiple domes that crown the edifices of the Palaeologue epoch; here the more austere basilica form endures almost un-challenged, the angular planes of its sloping roofs conforming more harmoniously with the northern setting. On summer evenings, however, the elaborate brickwork decoration of the exterior walls glows with a warm roseate hue. Of the seventy-two Orthodox churches and chapels commissioned by pious Castorians, at least six are worth visiting. They belong to the eleventh to fourteenth centuries.

At the entrance to the public garden, beside the Hotel du Lac, stands the little eleventh-century church of Ayios Nikolaos, with some sixteenth-century frescoes, of which the most striking (left on entering) represents a melancholy youth wearing a fez, probably a relative of the donor, who died at an early age. His bereaved mother laments beside him.

A sharp descent in a northerly direction leads to the small tenth-century **Basilica of Ayios Stephanos**, with single columns separating the nave from two diminutive aisles. Its unusual height and narrow dimensions, together with the charred surface of the walls, produce a sombre effect. The frescoes, desecrated by Moslem fanatics, are too blackened to charm. More interesting is the brickwork decoration of the exterior, a conspicuous regional feature. Earlier, cruder and more provincial than the designs that girdle the walls of the Holy Apostles in Salonica, the decoration is none the less ingenious, with its complex interplay of cubes, crosses, lozenges, half-moons and (above the narthex entrance) wheel-spokes within sun-discs.

North of St Stephen is the more attractive **Basilica of Ayioi Anarghyroi** (SS Cosmas and Damian), the oldest in Castoria. Across the bay, above the lakeside belt of vegetation, the flanks of barren mountains reflect the drifting clouds. Cries of farmyard animals rise from neighbouring kitchen gardens. Destroyed, it is said, by the Bulgarian Tsar Samuel in the tenth century, the church was re-founded by the Emperor Basil II when he spent the autumn of 1018 in Castoria, celebrating his triumph over the Bulgars in the company of their captive queen and those members of her staff who were spared decapitation.

The **exterior walls** are decorated with an intricate pattern of brick inlay: rhombuses, triangles, rows of X's and dentilated bands. Two sun-discs frame an arched window divided by a colonnette above the apse. Symmetry and picturesqueness are nicely blended. Eleventh-to twelfth-century exterior frescoes – another provincial feature – break up the monotony of the west façade. Figures of St Peter and St Paul flank the doorway; on either side of them the two patron physicians, Cosmas and Damian (portrayed again in the arched niche above the doorway) stand protectively. The interior is so dark that it is advisable to ask the custodian to open both the narthex and south doors. The figures in the blackened frescoes of different periods (the overlays are often apparent) then assume identifiable forms. In the narthex a grim bearded St Basil with a nasty turned-down mouth reflects an unusual aspect of the beneficent bishop who devoted his life to relieving the miseries of the poor. In the later frescoes of the naos the faces are softer, more fleshy, the garments less rigid. In a haunting vision of the Pentecost rays of light rain down on the heads of the apostles grouped on either side of a double arched window divided by a colonnette.

Abandoned **tower-like houses** of the seventeenth and eighteenth centuries, once the grandest in Macedonia, and the homes of prosperous furriers, extend along the north shore of the lake. Bats and cockroaches are now in sole possession of the frescoed sun-parlours and panelled halls, where painted ceilings are streaked with damp, carved balustrades and ornamental doorways cracked and warped beyond repair and fragile shutters swing dangerously above courtyards overgrown with nettles. The three-storeyed Tsiatsiapa house, in a lane behind the waterfront (Nikis Avenue), is now a fretwork of rotting timbers. Remains of latticed windows, of recessed balconies and wooden brackets suggest the once ornate exterior. Cobbled alleys lead (west) to the less ruined Sapountzi house, architecturally very formal and symmetrical, approached through a court. The first two storeys are of stone, the third timber-framed, shaded with eaves that protect the walls from the drip of melting snow in spring. All around rise the gaunt shells of abandoned mansions. Sometimes, when a fresh wind blows across the lake, splintered beams crash down among the heaps of rubble.

Fragments of Byzantine ramparts, which protected the isthmus from the west, are visible from Davaki Square. From here Ayiou Athanasiou Avenue climbs to the Hotel du Lac, and thence, within a short walking distance, to another group of churches on the steep southern slope of the headland. Below the Gymnasium (Secondary School), conspicuous for its neo-classical façade, stands the ancient and picturesque little **Church of the Panayia Koubelidiki**, so-called after the Turkish word *kouben*, meaning a dome, which, in this instance, is disproportionately tall. The usual exterior brickwork decoration – cubes, crosses, triangles, rectangles – is tidier though less inventive than elsewhere. The fifteenth-century frescoes (Elijah fed by the raven, St John about to be beheaded while Salome dances before Herod) of the exterior walls of the narthex give a coquettish air to this little architectural folly.

To the west, the eleventh-century **Basilica of the Taxiarchoi** (Archangels) produces an almost barn-like effect, in spite of a jigsaw puzzle of brick inlay, after the extravagance of the Koubelidiki. Frescoes, with the Archangels flanking the entrance and two pigmy-like figures of the donors, a Bulgarian prince and his half-Greek mother, cowering at St Michael's feet, spread across the façade. The fourteenth-century frescoes in the interior have unmistakable affinities with the southern Serbian school of Byzantine painting. There is a realism and fluidity of movement, a suggestion of three-dimensional style foreign to the classical, more static, iconography of Constantinople. At this time Serb invaders were pouring across the northern borders. Cultural relations with the capital were disrupted and weakened by a succession of wars that broke up ethnological groups. Iconographers in remoter provincial centres, such as Castoria, consequently drew inspiration more freely from local sources and traditions. In the naos of the Archangels, for instance, we see a painted border depicting icons of saints hanging on hooks: a pictorial device unknown to Constantinopolitan iconographers.

South of the Archangels Metropoleos Street enters Omonoia Square, a confined space, lively at night with open-air tavernas on different levels crowned by the little single-chamber Basilica of Ayios Ioannis Prodromos (St John the Baptist). More important is the twelfth-century **Church of Ayios Nikolaos Kasnitzi**, named after the donor, which repeats the familiar architectural and decorative pattern of the Castorian basilica. In the fine thirteenth-century **frescoes** the well-known figures play their accustomed liturgical roles. In the apse the Virgin *Orans* is flanked by two angels (one in coral robes, the other in faded green) bearing kerchiefs. Their movements are free and articulate. Above the apse presides another effigy of the Virgin, this time of greater dignity, approached by the Angel Gabriel with an alert expressive face. Above the west door the Dormition of the Virgin is crowded with mourning figures in pastel-shaded garments grouped around the bier on which lies the corpse in a matt inky-blue shift. Above the Dormition the Transfiguration is crowned by an emaciated Christ with matchstick legs (a common device of provincial iconographers anxious to emphasize the asceticism and other-worldliness of their holy figures), his white garments fluttering in the breeze. Full-length figures – St Nestorius, St Mercurios, young warrior saints and a noble St Nicholas in pink and blue robes – line the south wall. The frescoes of St Nicholas Kasnitzi are not among the great masterpieces of Byzantine painting; but they possess freshness and vigour, tempered by an engaging rustic simplicity. Religious feeling is roughly expressed and the symbolism crude, but sympathy for the tragedy of the Passion is genuine and deeply felt.

The way down to the waterfront leads past another group of *archontika* (houses of the archons or notable citizens), their roofs crowned with storks' nests. The **Nazim house**, preceded by a little loggia, is the best preserved in Castoria. A musicians' gallery, its walls painted with garlands of flowers, overlooks a reception room, where engagements and marriages were celebrated. The *saloni*, or drawing-room, and halls are elaborately frescoed, and the decoration has all the story-book whimsicality of Siatista: the same nostalgic evocation of Constantinople, the effigies of lions bearing bowls of fruit on the tips of their tongues, and friezes of houses amid poplars, willows and stylized cypresses. The rooms are surrounded by low settees, on which the archons reclined, gazing across the lake through stained-glass windows.

The south shore (Megalou Alexandrou Avenue) is bordered by plane trees. Flat-bottomed fishing-boats with blunt-shaped bows and sterns glide across the slime-covered waters of the southern bite of the lake. In the evening, loaded with perch and carp, they emerge ghost-like out of the mist, nosing their way towards wooden jetties. After skirting a sandy beach littered with hulks of half-constructed boats, the narrow road, bordered by weeping willows, becomes a favourite strolling-ground, with cyclists and holiday-makers bound for lakeside tavernas where hunks of meat, sold by weight, are served on strips of oilpaper. Between the shore and a rocky hillside the **Monastery of the Mavriotissa** nestles in the shade of plane trees. A landing was effected here by a Byzantine army led by Alexius I, astutest of Comnene emperors (and consequently most detested by the Crusaders), who laid siege to the Normans occupying Castoria. The Emperor probably founded the monastery later. It was considerably rebuilt during the fourteenth-century Serb occupation.

The church, chapel, some cells and a belfry spread along the lakeside. It is a secluded place, once the haunt of Byzantine and Slav princes who came here to worship. The exterior side wall of the chapel of St John the Divine is painted with crude post-Byzantine frescoes of saintly figures. But in the Last Supper (interior north wall) there is a charming arrangement, totally devoid of perspective, of glass and cutlery, plates, goblets and bowls laid out on a half-moon table.

In the main church (the Dormition of the Virgin) a single-aisle basilica with narthex, the **frescoes** of the late twelfth (or early thirteenth) century are, in spite of clumsy execution, vigorous in conception, with detached groups of figures depicted in a state of semi-arrested movement. On the exterior south wall of the narthex we see saints (Demetrius, George), prophets, emperors and a Tree of Jesse on whose branches Christ's ancestors are framed among stylized foliage. Within the narthex there is a crude but animated Last Judgement, crowded with militant avenging angels and deformed cringing creatures representing the various categories of sinners: slanderers, moneylenders (hanging upside down), and harlots with long black ringlets.

A wooden door carved with crosses and diamond-shaped lozenges leads into the naos. The dominating fresco is the **Dormition of the Virgin** (west wall) which is grand and tragic, the figures stilted but expressive, the mourners' faces turned obliquely towards the bier so that the focus is on the centre of the picture, with the lamenting women in the niches of the toy-like architectural background forming a framework for the formidable, almost masculine, corpse on the bier. In the apse, above the Evangelists who meditate over the composition of their Gospels, an impervious Virgin is seated on an ornamental throne, holding the Child, who has an absurdly mature face, flanked by Archangels in star-spangled robes. At her feet crouches the diminutive monkish figure of the donor. Above the Virgin is a grand **Ascension**: first a frieze of apostles between stylized trees, with the Virgin *Orans* in the middle; then Christ, with a terrible Messianic expression, a protruding stomach and short legs, seated in a glory supported by two contorted angels. Neither faulty drawing nor clumsy execution deprives the composition of power or intensity of feeling. Throughout the church the sacred personages are represented as symbols, crude and uncompromising, with forceful, heavily lined faces, often frowning, sometimes menacing, and bodies depicted in stilted jerky attitudes. Provincial painters took great pains to inspire awe, if not terror, in the hearts of worshippers.

The numerous post-Byzantine chapels scattered about the headland are objects for walks. The walls of many, both interior and exterior, are frescoed. In the Apazari quarter (north shore), the church of Ayios Ioannis Prodromos is worth visiting, if only to look at the frescoes in the women's gallery. Examples of crude popular art of the seventeenth century, they are, like so much post-Byzantine painting, didactic in purpose. Demons are seen torturing the malicious gossiper, cheating miller and female usurer; an adultress suffers ignoble torments inflicted by a demon in the form of a snake, while the most shocking treatment of all is reserved for the harlot.

II

The beginning of the longer western route from Edessa to Castoria may pardonably be associated with that vaguely defined geographical area known in antiquity as the 'Gardens of Midas', which supposedly extended around the Macedonian kings' flowery capital of Aegae. The configuration of the land, with its wooded sliced ledges ascending the Vermion range, has none of the dramatic quality of the central Greek mountain formations. Everything is tamer, somewhat lacking in definition. The upper reaches of the Voda, which the westbound road follows, possess all the fertility of the Emathian plain, without any of its domesticity. There are no towns, few villages. Planes, mulberries and wild figs add a pastoral touch to the rolling upland stretch, with weeping willows bordering the tributary streams which wind round rocky islets. The route must be the one followed by Alexander when, weary of the rumbustious brawling of family life at Pella, he retired to sulk in Illyria.

After leaving the Voda valley the road crosses a plateau of rushes surrounded by ilex-covered hills. Below, to the west, beyond the maize fields, appear the sparsely inhabited shores of **Lake Ostrovo**, the ancient Begoritis, mentioned by Livy, its pale blue inlets making deep inroads into arid mountain sides. At the north-east end of the lake a huddle of habitations is all that remains of ancient Arnissa, once a station on the Via Egnatia, better known as medieval Ostrovo which was fiercely disputed by the armies of rival claimants to the Byzantine throne when Frankish Greece was beginning to fall apart. In the general confusion of civil war on different levels – Frank against Frank, Greek against Greek – the shores of Ostrovo were often littered with the abandoned impedimenta of defeated armies. There are ruins of a Turkish mosque on an islet off Arnissa: once the centre of a village said to have been submerged in the lake.

Sparsely inhabited valleys follow; and highlands of scrub where the armies of the Emperor Basil II and the Bulgar Tsar Samuel contended for the strategic prize of Ostrovo in the early eleventh century. The Bulgar forts, dismantled by the 'Bulgar-slaying' Byzantine emperor during his victorious campaigns, are now replaced by abandoned stone-built villages: a melancholy scene. But the descent leads into a warmer climate, with a fertile plain running north to south between hazy mountain ranges. To the north, at the head of the broad strip of cultivation, lies **Pelagonia**, where the Byzantine emperor in exile decisively defeated the Frankish armies, commanded by that engaging but meddlesome French Champénois prince, William de Villehardouin, in a battle which preceded the expulsion of the Crusaders' descendants from Constantinople by only two years. More recently, in the twentieth century, Balkan and German invading armies have poured down the gap in the mountains – known as the Monastir Gap, after the Jugoslav city (now Bitolj) at its northern extremity.

Across the 'gap' the garrison town of **Florina**, fought over during the First World War and destroyed during the Communist rebellion in 1947–9, stands in a commanding position at the outlet of a mountain valley.[6] This is the ancient land of Lyncestis, famous for its waters said to possess intoxicating qualities, and whose royal house married into that of the Macedonian kings only to find the connection used as a pretext for the annexation of their country. There is little to say about Florina; unsmiling square-faced peasants bring their produce to market, and bored-looking soldiers stroll along the unattractive streets. Both seem as remote from Mediterranean Greece as the Balkan landscape itself. But there is one last lap: to the Prespa lakes.

The road climbs a flank of the mountains west of Florina above a fertile valley. At the watershed, beyond the oak and beech forests, there is a military check-point. Otherwise the country seems uninhabited, muted. One senses the proximity of frontiers: of an end to all things Greek. After passing another check-point and winding between puce-coloured hills, one is suddenly peering over the rim of a great bowl surrounded by mountains. The configuration is confusing. North to south runs the lake of **Little Prespa**, appendix-shaped: a Greek-Albanian lake, its surface a cold hard blue. Beyond an isthmus extends **Big Prespa**, whose waters are shared by Greece, Albania and Jugoslavia, heart-shaped in the north, tapering at the southern

---

[6] The traveller who wishes to visit the Prespa lakes before descending to Castoria is obliged to spend the night at Florina, where there is adequate accommodation.

end into an inlet which runs parallel to Little Prespa, biting deep into Albanian territory. To the west rise the stark Albanian mountains, at the foot of which wound the Via Egnatia. The descent is through domesticated but deserted country, the red soil contrasting sharply with the naked grey mountains on whose ridges snowdrifts lie in crevices. The scale and range is immense, the desolation grandiose. I know of no more inhospitable place than this meeting-point of three countries, where Alexander defeated the Lyncestrian tribes whose subjection ensured the safety of his rear, at a time when he was concentrating the bulk of his forces in the east for the passage into Asia. In the late tenth century the Bulgar Tsar Samuel established his military headquarters and a court, noted for its savagery, in this inaccessible area, from which he waged a long, defiant and ultimately hopeless struggle for the possession of northern Greece against the invincible Emperor Basil II.

Along a level stretch of shore washed by Little Prespa extends a **bird sanctuary** in the process of development, to which birds from all over south-eastern Europe migrate – 177 species have been recorded – and the only site in Europe where pelicans are known to nest. The erection of a watch-tower is planned for the benefit of birdwatchers. We saw some birds – but no human being, until we reached a place called Koula, where a couple of tourists were bathing off the rocks in the ice-blue water. At the western end of the isthmus a soldier barred our way; he pointed at the hills directly in front of us. 'Albania,' he said. On the islet to the south of the isthmus, somewhat quaintly named St Achilles, after a Roman martyr-soldier or Orthodox prelate (the Church does not seem to have made up its mind) there is a Byzantine church, founded in the tenth century by the Bulgar Tsar Samuel, with remains of contemporary frescoes. I was at Prespa during a period of political crisis, rumours of imminent war with one of Greece's neighbours were catching up on us. My failure to get a permit from military headquarters in Florina prevented us from visiting the church. We continued along the north-east shore of Big Prespa in search of a village. We needed petrol. We found it at Laimos, at the foot of beige-coloured hills, the last village this side of the Jugoslav border: a bucolic place with houses scattered among poplars in which myriads of birds twittered. One heard villagers talking Serbo-Croat as well as Greek. This was obviously the end. We turned back: towards Greece.

After re-crossing the line of hills above the Prespa basin one comes to a fork. The road to the south runs through a shut-in wooded country. Donkeys stand tethered to tree-trunks in groves of silver planes and goats browse in terraced glades where the parched grass of summer replaces the banks of narcissi of early spring. We saw soldiers – lonely recruits from some neighbouring frontier post – splashing about in streams that unite and separate forming shady pools where the water freezes hard in winter. The whole place is alive with bird-song. In antiquity the Orestae, a barbarian tribe, dwelt here, more happily blessed by nature than many of their neighbours, until they were subjugated by Philip II and their well-watered valleys annexed to 'Greater' Macedonia. The road climbs through beech woods and then winds down in successive loops, each of which affords a more entrancing view of the northern shores of Lake Castoria, the tall houses of the town strung out along the isthmus and the mallet-shaped headland projecting into the shallow waters.

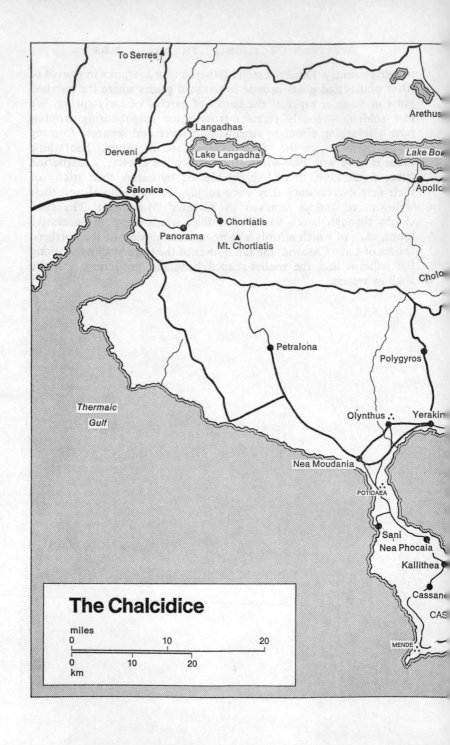

To Serres

Arethus

Langadhas

Derveni

Lake Langadha

Lake Bo

Salonica

Apollo

Chortiatis

Panorama

Mt. Chortiatis

Chol

Petralona

Polygyros

Thermaic
Gulf

Olynthus

Yerakin

Nea Moudania

POTIDAEA

Sani

Nea Phocaia

Kallithea

Cassan

CAS

MENDE

The Chalcidice

miles
0   10   20

0   10   20
km

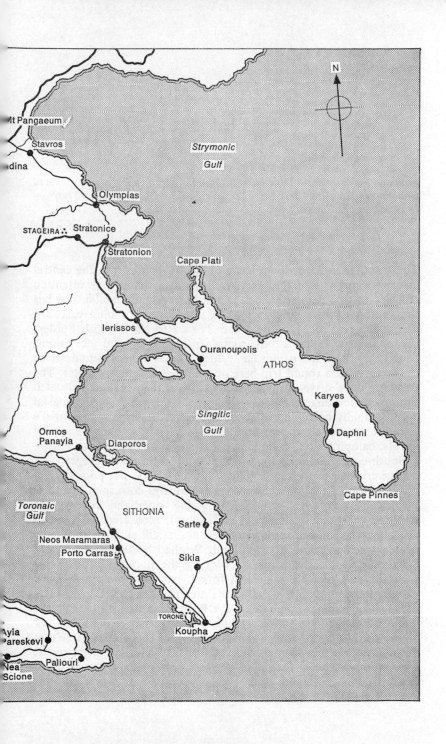

CHAPTER SIXTEEN

The Chalcidice

꙳

Potidaea – Cassandra – Olynthus – Sithonia – Torone – Polygyros – Mount Cholomon – Stageira – Ierissos – Xerxes's Canal – Ouranoupolis – Stavros – Langadhas: The Firewalkers

The traveller in Macedonia has a choice of routes into the central and western parts of the country. But much that merits attention still lies east of Salonica. Back in the Macedonian capital, one has the option of two itineraries: (i) the highway running eastward across the rest of Macedonia and Thrace to the Turkish border; (ii) a somewhat circuitous route, including several deviations, round the Chalcidice peninsula – which I have attempted to describe in the form of a round trip based on Salonica, in this chapter. The two long days' drive can be broken at any of the new hotels situated on, or overlooking, beaches of the finest sand. Much of the coastal area is rapidly becoming what the brochures describe as a 'tourist's paradise', with all the amenities of new roads, anchorages for yachts, camping sites, swimming pools and even conference centres.

South-east of Salonica the Chalcidice juts out into the Aegean like a huge crustacean with three jointed lobster-claws. The poor state of preservation of the antiquities does not always correspond to their historical importance, and much of the woodland country (as opposed to the bungalow-pocked beaches), across which Xerxes's army marched in the summer of 480 BC, is still sufficiently off the beaten track to recall a virgin land. Washed by the Thermaic and Strymonic Gulfs, the peninsula has, by the nature of its strange contours and sparsely populated forest, remained a self-contained geographical unit, with a character different from the rest of Macedonia. The original inhabitants, the Paeonians, a rustic people cut off from the two-way traffic of trade and ideas that crossed the neck of the peninsula, developed independently of the Thracians. Herodotus says that they claimed descent from the river god Scamander, with whom Achilles fought in single combat below the walls of Troy. But in the eighth and seventh centuries BC the coast was

The Bronze Charioteer belonged to a quadrign placed on the terrace of the Temple of Apollo at Delphi.

Trikkeri, one of the Pelion Villages.

colonized by Euboean settlers from Chalcis who intermarried with the natives. For centuries the forest tracts remained wild and un-inhabited, the thirty cities founded by the colonizers being strung out along the shores of the three prongs. Athens too founded colonies here; Corinth and Sparta objected, and the Peloponnesian War followed; finally Philip II of Macedon reduced the country to subjection. The present inhabitants, mostly woodcutters and fisher-men, are a dark taciturn people; unlike most Greeks, they seem, except in the tourist centres, to be impervious to the presence of strangers, indifferent to their provenance or destination.

From Salonica the road runs through dreary suburbs to the landmark of the nineteenth-century Villa Alatini, situated on a bluff above the sea, where Sultan Abdul Hamid II, 'The Damned', was interned after his deposition in 1909. Just before the villa a branch road to the north climbs Mount Chortiatis to **Panorama**, a summer resort of red-roofed houses amid dark green conifers. There are restaurants and a panoramic view of the city, gulf and western Chalcidice. On torrid summer evenings the air is wonderfully bracing. A five-kilometre stretch of bleak moorland ends at the village of **Chortiatis**. Here, beside the ochre-coloured church, is an unassuming little twelfth-century church of the Metamorphosis, with four niches in the angles which create an optical allusion of an octagon, crowned by a shallow windowless dome, probably a later addition of the Turkish period. The narthex has disappeared to make room for an adjacent hovel. The original Comnene frescoes are unfortunately covered with plaster; vestiges of a fine head of a young saint within a sombre-coloured halo suggest their quality.

Down below in the plain, the south-bound highway skirts crowded beaches linked by a ferry-boat service with Salonica. At the fifty-first kilometre a branch road runs east to the locality of **Petralona**, where the cave of Kokkines Petres (The Red Stones), famous for its refulgent stalactites, is situated on the base of a foothill of the Cholomon range. One day in 1960 a party of visitors, entering the cave, stumbled on a fossilized skull, later identified as that of a Neanderthal woman who probably lived some seventy-five thousand years ago. Greece, it was thus established, was inhabited by primitive man in the Pleistocene age of the world's formation.

The road continues across open country – a golf-course landscape with views of distant cone-shaped hills – which soon contracts into a narrow isthmus. Here begins the geographical area associated with the 'Thracian tribute': the detested levy exacted from the colonies allied under duress to Athens in the fifth century BC. At

Nea Moudania, a fishing village and useful base for an extended tour of the Chalcidice, there is a hotel, fish taverna and café (on the beach) patronized in the evenings by young fishermen off duty, the elaborateness of whose clothes and hair style gives them the air of models about to step out of a fashion magazine. They drink Nescafé in genteel silence, staring with large black eyes at the shabbily dressed foreigners.

At the hinge of the westernmost prong or claw, the site of ancient **Potidaea** extends beyond a narrow canal. Xerxes's fleet anchored here and took provisions. Half a century later the Corinthian-inspired revolt of Potidaea against Athens, to which it owed allegiance, was one of the incidents that triggered off the Peloponnesian War. And here, in the Chalcidice, geographically so remote from Athens and Sparta, were fought some of the decisive campaigns of a war in which the whole Hellenic world from Ionia to Magna Graecia was finally involved. Potidaea was, in fact, the Sarajevo of antiquity. Nothing was ever the same again in Greece after the twenty-seven-year 'Great War'.

Athenian pride, stung by the insolence of Potidaean defection, demanded instant retribution, but neither battering rams nor other aggressive weapons helped the assault troops, led by the brilliant Phormio, to break Potidaean resistance. Blockaded by the Athenian fleet, the Potidaeans were also decimated by the plague spread by reinforcements from Athens, where the epidemic was raging, and the bodies of those who fell on the walls were eaten by the survivors – the very bitterness of the Potidaean defence was an indication of the growing resentment felt by many Greeks at the high-handed policy of Periclean Athens. It took the besiegers two years to reduce the city; the epitaph of those who fell is in the British Museum. In the Hellenistic period Cassander, who had assumed Alexander the Great's mantle in mainland Greece, founded a new city on the site and called it Cassandreia. Its government was modelled on that of a Hellenic state. Although politically less disunited, like so many other equally ostentatious Hellenistic cities it nevertheless possessed no centrifugal pan-Macedonian force from which to draw the inspiration that the southern states found in the Athenian Acropolis, the Delphic Oracle or the Olympic Games. In terms of such comparisons, Cassandreia was an outstanding flop.

Cassandra is now a melancholy fishing village with a muddy canal crossing the isthmus and some shacks dotted about a wasteland. Brightly painted caiques anchor in the creeks where the Macedonian triremes were once built (Livy talks of a hundred vessels at a time being constructed in the docks). I have counted eight ruined towers – all medieval, in which classical masonry has been re-used – extending across the isthmus. Some have been pilfered by the inhabitants in search of building materials for their wretched little maisonettes, and archaeologists have identified ancient slabs among the village refuse. It must have been somewhere along here, in the days of the great siege, that Socrates saved the life of the young Alcibiades, thus initiating – if the story is not apocryphal – his famous friendship with the most controversial personality of the late fifth century BC. The blocks of masonry nearest the sea (west) mark the point where the line of forts guarding the entire headland once began. The substructure close by is possibly of the period of Justinian. Fishermen talk of ancient underwater stairways: visible only when the sea is calm and translucent.

From Potidaea the Cassandra headland (the western prong of the Chalcidice peninsula) runs southward in a series of domesticated, low, neatly sliced cliffs. The green cultivated landscape is difficult to associate with the legendary Phlegra, whose earliest inhabitants, the earthbound giants, aspired to depose the gods of Olympus. For their insolence they were condemned, when vanquished, to dwell in the bowels of the earth, where their tormented contortions caused the earth to shake and lava to belch forth. Every volcano known to the ancient Greeks was consequently thought to be the site of a giant's subterranean prison and each of these monstrous offspring of Mother Earth became a personification of volcanic eruption.

The road follows the east coast of the prong. Above the beaches reddish-brown cliffs are studded with tall pines, whose wood was used for centuries for the construction of triremes in antiquity, and schinus scrub with its many-toothed leaflets. At **Nea Phocaia** a medieval tower crowns a bluff overlooking the little harbour. Until recently inhabited exclusively by sheep-farmers, the countryside is rapidly developing into a complex of camping sites and tourist hotels. Copses among the shady still undesecrated woods are pockmarked with beehives. At **Kallithea** cliffs screen an ugly modern hotel, the Ammon Zeus, situated on a beach of fine sand. Beside it is an ancient ruin: the foundations of a fourth-century BC temple of Zeus Ammon, with a north-south, instead of the usual east-west, axis, strewn with Doric, Ionic and Corinthian capitals. A nearby spring, which provides the hotel with its water supply, is popularly associated with the stream diverted by Zeus to flow underground from Mount Olympus in order to irrigate his maritime sanctuary. Ammon was of course an Egyptian deity, generally depicted as a man with the head of a ram, whose association with Zeus is noted by Servius, the scholiast of Virgil. When Dionysus, in the course of his world-wide travels, found himself parched with thirst in the burning Libyan sands (the Greek word for sand was and still is *ammos*), he invoked his father, Zeus, for help. A ram instantly appeared and led the young god to a spring which it revealed by scraping its foot in the sand. Subsequently Zeus Ammon was always depicted with a ram's horns and identified with the protector of man, just as the ram is the guide of desert herds.

Southward the bungalow compounds continue. The monster luxury Pallini Beach Hotel is succeeded by the Xenias, where the coastline, more broken, offers greater variety. The road turns inland across the saddle of the prong and passes through the village of **Ayia Paraskevi**, where there are traces of the vernacular architecture of the Turkish period. Children playing in pot-holed lanes glance at one and go on with their games; in the cafés, men look up from their backgammon board and continue to rattle dice. But no Chalcidian, for all his lack of inquisitiveness (so rare in a Greek) is likely to be unfriendly when asked for help.

At **Nea Scione**, on the west coast of the prong, below the pine-clad hills, carpeted in spring with shrubs of bright-coloured cistus, is the as yet unexcavated site of ill-fated Scione, where the Athenians took revenge on the inhabitants for welcoming Brasidas, the Spartan leader, as the 'liberator of Hellas', placing a gold crown on his head and decking him with garlands. Retribution took the form of a massacre of the entire male population which had held out against the Athenian siege so long and courageously in 423 BC.

The road skirts another fine beach as far as a wooded bluff crowned by a modern hotel, the Mendi: site of ancient Mende, once famous for its delicious wine and beautifully minted coins of Silenus riding an ass. Here too there was fierce fighting during the Peloponnesian War, while the triremes of Nicias and Brasidas manoeuvred along the coast. The north-bound road back to Potidaea and the isthmus continues across low flat-topped promontories.

North-east of Potidaea the village of **Olynthus** lies at the head of the deep Toronaic Gulf. A track runs through fields dotted with clumps of chestnut trees. The air is heavy with humidity, the drone of cicadas deafening. The ancient city, laid out by Hippodamus of Miletus, the greatest town planner of antiquity, extended across a squat eminence like a table mountain rising sheer on all sides out of the pasture lands, crowned by towers and walls. Lilac-coloured nutty-scented heliotrope spreads around the base. There is no

custodian, no visible habitation: only horses grazing in the groves.
Thucydides says many Chalcidians settled 'inland at Olynthus, to
make that one city a strong place'. By the early fourth century BC
the political prestige and economic prosperity of the Olynthian
Confederacy had become a byword. No compulsion was exercised
on member states, and equal, generous and attractive terms were
offered to all applicants with democratic ideals. Narrow nationalist
motives, however, induced neighbouring Acanthus and Apollonia
to solicit the intervention of Sparta, whose gimlet-eye had long been
fixed on this progressive and potentially powerful state. At first the
Lacedaemonian attackers made little progress and even suffered
humiliating defeats. The nadir of their fortunes was reached when
King Agesipolis died, according to Xenophon, of a 'burning fever',
and his body, 'placed in honey', was carried back to Sparta. But a
sustained blockade (382–379 BC) ended in surrender, and the Olynthians had to accept subjection to Sparta. The destruction of the
confederacy was a blow to Greece and the nascent democratic
ideal. Some thirty years later, Philip II of Macedon unleashed an
avalanche of conquest on eastern Macedonia. Sparta sullenly
refused to raise a finger in aid of her Chalcidian protégé, and
Athenian assistance – fourteen thousand men and fifty triremes –
largely inspired by the oratory of Demosthenes, came too late to be
of use. Shorn of all power by their Spartan 'protectors', undermined
by treachery (the first recorded use of a fifth column in Greece),
the Olynthians surrendered to the Macedonian phalanx. On the
scene of destruction, Philip staged a festival with athletic and – for
the Macedonian king had his softer side – poetical contests.

The climb to the summit of the rocky mound is steep but short.
From here the besieged Olynthians had a grandstand view of their
cavalry charging down the hill against the Spartan helots massed
before the walls. The American School of Classical Studies has
carried out some excavations; but so far little of importance has
been uncovered. Cisterns and substructures seem an inadequate
legacy of a city once so politically mature for its times. The area
covered by the fragmentary ruins, however, gives an idea of the
extent of the town-plan. Vestiges of Neolithic dwellings reveal that
the hill was inhabited as far back as the third millenium BC. To the
west rises an escarpment, brick red in colour, with cleanly sliced
sides and a flat top from which the Spartans watched the assembly
and disposition of Olynthian units within the citadel. Around the
heliotrope belt huge beetles scuttle among the rocks. Strabo says
that near Olynthos 'is a hollow place called Cantharolethron

[Beetle-death] . . . for when the insect called the Cantharos, which is found all over the country, touches the place, it dies'. No apparent trail leads to 'Beetle-death' any longer.

Beyond the Olynthus branch, the road continues eastward, past the tourist beach (and hotel) of Yerakina. At the top of the rise there is a fork in the road. One way leads across the isthmus to the Singitic Gulf, the other penetrates the middle prong of the Chalcidice: hilly wooded **Sithonia**, once scattered with cities of the earliest colonizers. Range upon range of hills of ever-increasing height, sliced with gulleys filled with plane and olive trees, rise from the sandy coves of the west coast. An abandoned dependency of an Athonite monastery – windowless buildings with slate roofs and tall chimneys amid poplars and cypresses – spreads across the mouth of a valley. The beaches continue: pine-fringed. Beyond the harbour of Neos Maramaras and its cone-shaped islet, the large tourist resort of Porto Carras, now under development, suggests the role now destined for the whole coast. From here the road I prefer climbs into the hills, past a huge agricultural estate, its terraced vineyards, olive groves and citrus orchards affording sudden glimpses of sea, wooded spits of land and rocky islets. From a considerable altitude one looks down on an inland bowl which conceals another ruined dependency of an Athonite monastery. The descent to the coast leads through alleys of mulberries and pine-fringed lagoons. To the south rises the hatchet-shaped bluff of Vigla. Black mountain goats graze in the shrubbery bordering the beach. At the southern end of the crescent-shaped bay another bluff, which repeats in miniature the forms of Vigla, marks the site of the acropolis of ancient **Torone**. There is not much to see, but it is one of the most evocative places in northern Greece. Torone was the chief settlement of the early colonizers. During the Persian Wars the inhabitants Medized and provided the Great King with arms and supplies; during the Peloponnesian War, although officially allied to Athens, the city welcomed Brasidas and his Spartans as liberators, but when Cleon, the Athenian demagogue-general, recaptured it, the Toronians paid for their fickle behaviour. The male population was deported to Athens and the women and children sold into slavery.

Vestiges of Byzantine fortifications can be identified along the line where the ancient ramparts extended, and Hellenic masonry is embedded in the soil of the strip of land connecting the acropolis with what must have been the ancient town. The visible blocks of granite probably formed part of Hellenic edifices. As yet, it is a remote and undeveloped place. The only sound we heard was the cry of a shepherd calling to his goats on the slopes of Vigla.

Immediately to the south the deep inlet of Koupha is cunningly concealed by the northern arm of the Vigla promontory which scythes round to create a lovely landlocked bay with a sandy beach and perfect anchorage. Thucydides calls it the harbour of the Colophonians. It was also known as Cophis (deaf) because of its protected nature, for the sound of waves breaking on the open shore could never be heard here. Theophrastus, the Aristotelian philosopher, who had a taste for botany, says the Egyptian bean grew in a nearby marsh which I have identified.

The road now climbs into hills covered with heather and arbutus. Vultures perched on rocky ledges suddenly flap their wings, wheel, hover and swoop down to peck at the carcase of a dead goat. The east coast is very rugged, less wooded, more sparsely inhabited than the western shores. From above the bay of Sikia there is a spectacular view of the Athos peninsula running north to south, with the tip, Cape Pinnes, crowned by a conical peak which is repeated, at a much greater altitude, in the dramatic summit of the Holy Mountain itself. Monasteries, hermitages and maritime arsenals are discernible along the length of the tremendous backcloth.

North of the bay and beach of Sarte, the coast becomes grander, its broken forms more intricate. Pine-clad spits project into the still waters of the Singitic Gulf. Poplar-lined lagoons girdle the low sand-fringed islet of Diaporos. At the cove of Ormos Panayia one turns westward back to the point where the road penetrated the Sithonian headland.

At the head of the Toronaic Gulf, not far from the Yerakina beach, a road climbs the Cholomon range, the central massif of the peninsula, winding between hills of increasing height covered with arbutus, whose wood was used for making flutes, and whose large red berries are supposed to – but do not really – taste like strawberries. **Polygyros**, a pretty village with red-tiled roofs, spreads among poplars in the folds of hills where myriads of birds sing. Hereabouts, according to Xenophon, was the site of Apollonia, one of the two Chalcidian cities which undermined the Olynthian Confederacy by inviting Spartan intervention. Beautiful silver coins, showing the head of Apollo on the obverse, the god's lyre bound with a fillet on the reverse, minted at Apollonia, are one of the few surviving legacies of Chalcidian art.[1] The road to the east climbs and dips, winds around oak-covered ridges to the summit.

[1] Specimens of these coins are exhibited in the British Museum and the Numismatic Museum in Athens.

The landscape is unlike any other in Greece. The massif is cut by no deep valleys, conceals no high-lying plains; there are no bold dramatic contours, no vast perspectives. Foreground and background melt into each other in gentle undulating folds; a faint opacity tinges the light; wisps of smoke spiral up from woodcutters' fires. The descent in hairpin bends through silent chestnut forests has an elegiac quality. A muted feeling seems to hang over the village of **Arnaia** and its large triangular square bordered by lime-washed houses with balconies ablaze with morning glory and climbing roses. Around here once stretched a tract of virgin forest, where lions roamed in packs and attacked the caravans of camels loaded with Persian stores in 480 BC.

The road descends towards the village of **Stratonice**. On the right a marble statue of an ancient Greek figure holding a scroll stands commandingly on a ledge. Wooded hills roll towards the Sithonian prong which vanishes in the sea-haze. The effigy, which is modern, glossy and without artistic merit, represents Aristotle, and the terraced ground, surrounded by walnut trees, is the site of Stageira, the philosopher's birthplace. The son of a local physician, he spent his childhood roaming the woods, absorbed in the study of natural history. He never forgot his native city. After the Chalcidice had been laid waste by Philip, he persuaded his pupil, Alexander the Great, to rebuild Stageira, of which he always remained a citizen, but by the first century Strabo found the city totally abandoned. Substructures of Hellenic masonry can be identified around the terraced ground. There are also ruins of a tower and an edifice with built-in arches of a later period.

The road reaches the coastline of the Strymonic Gulf at Stratonion, below a forbidding cliff, where the mines, now rich in magnesite, provided the silver for Chalcidian coins. Sandy beaches littered with grotesque outcrops of rock stretch southward as far as **Ierissos**, once Acanthus, the jealous and mischievous rival of Olynthus. Beyond the village, the last prong of the trident culminates in the peak of Athos, hidden by the headland of Cape Plati. The mole, which affords shelter to small craft from the winter gales and etesian squalls that lash the Thracian sea, is built on Hellenic foundations.[2] Ancient marble slabs and square-granite blocks are scattered across the hill above Ierissos, where the acropolis once stood. Here Xerxes was received with pomp during his westward march, and Brasidas, who, according to Thucydides, was 'not a bad speaker for a Lace-

[2] From here a caique sails daily to the monasteries on the east coast of the Athos peninsula. Hence the potential importance of Ierissos to the traveller.

daemonian', once again won over the local inhabitants to the Spartan alliance by his 'seductive arguments'. Vestiges of tombs of the classical necropolis have been excavated on the sands. But the modern fishing village has little to offer, other than its fine beach and a hotel, the Athos, useful to travellers bound for Mount Athos. A prevailing air of melancholy is only relieved on summer nights when the seashore tavernas are visited by an itinerant bouzouki orchestra.

The road across the mile and a half isthmus roughly follows the course of the canal dug by Xerxes's engineers to allow the passage of the Persian fleet – two triremes abreast. There is evidence of substructures of walls and some man-made mounds. The ditch itself is now filled with soil. Men of all nations were employed in shifts 'and put to the work of cutting a canal under the lash', for, according to Herodotus, the Great King 'wanted to show his power and to leave something to be remembered by'. In charge of this ambitious operation was Artachaeës, the tallest man in Persia (over eight feet), whose voice, the loudest in the world, could be heard from one end of the isthmus to the other.

On the west side of the isthmus the little fishing port of **Ouranoupolis** shelters in a wide tranquil bay skirted by sandy beaches and dotted with wooded islets. A luxury hotel, the Eagles Palace, and a more modest Xenias, both with bar, restaurant and private beach, offer a pleasant refuge for weary travellers. A daily caique carrying a passenger-load of shaggy monks and unshaved pilgrims chugs into the port from the monasteries of the west coast of Mount Athos. Occasionally the silhouettes of water-skiers skim the shimmering skyline, weaving a trail of silvery wash around the islets. The village, built in 1923 by refugees from Cappadocia on the site of a Hellenistic city, founded by Alexarchus, brother of Cassander and inventor of a form of slang rare in the Greek language, is tidier and more attractive than Ierissos. The five-storeyed **Tower of Prosphori** with gun-slits and wooden balconies dominates the landscape from a bluff above the mole between two coves. Once a lay dependency of the Athonite Monastery of Vatopedi, the abandoned tower was bought in the 1920s by an Anglo-Australian couple who converted the ground floor into a workshop where peasant girls now weave knotted rugs decorated with traditional Byzantine patterns.[3]

[3] See *Athos, The Holy Mountain* by Sydney Loch, Lutterworth Press, London, 1957. The local weaving industry, largely promoted by Mr and Mrs Loch, has developed rapidly, and the attractive rugs of Ouranoupolis are now sold in expensive Athenian shops and exported to foreign markets.

From Ouranoupolis a north-west wheeling movement through Stratonion completes the circular tour of the Chalcidice. Leaving the road to Stageira to the left, one climbs a seaward spur of Cholomon and descends in hairpin bends to the northern shore of the Strymonic Gulf. Beaches of white sand are broken up by rocky inlets. Chestnut forests spread across the flanks of the valleys, and ice-cold streams trickle through shallow gullies to the sea. The smell of iodine and wet sand is mixed with that of pungent evergreens. To the east rises the outline of mountainous Thasos. As yet there is little traffic: only woodcutters leading convoys of donkeys laden with logs. Occasionally a solitary figure standing on a spit of rock in the middle of a deserted cove casts a fishing line. There is probably no finer series of beaches in Greece – soon, one is told, to be dotted with box villas, Xenias hotels and camping grounds. At **Olympias**, the ancient Caprus, port of Stageira, a wooden jetty projects into the poplar-fringed bay, where rowing-boats moored to an island mentioned by Strabo rock in the oily swell.[4] At night flotillas of brightly painted fishing-caiques put out to sea, their carbide flares, which attract the fish into the nets, strung out across the dark waste in phosphorescent garlands and S-shaped formations. On the eve of the summer solstice (feast of St John the Divine, 24 June) smoke trails above the tree-tops from dozens of bonfires over whose embers villagers, young and old, leap in order to be cured of all ailments and enter a better year. To the north-west, where the Strymon flows into the sea through a wide estuary, looms Pangaeum, the mountain of gold. At **Stavros** plane trees skirt the shore and a broad walk is lined with cafés. The little port was discovered by the British army based on the Strymon valley during the First World War, when it became a rest camp, provided with swimming facilities and tennis courts in summer, woodcock shooting in winter. The tennis courts are no longer identifiable but there is always the song of nightingales in the cool dark arbours formed by the giant planes.

The road veers westward through a lush ravine to the village of **Rendina**. A track to the north leads to Arethusa, where the aged Euripides, driven out of Athens by a campaign of calumny provoked by his cynical questioning of the gods' infallibility, was torn to pieces by the dogs of the Macedonian king, set upon him by rival poets. According to another version, the dramatist, still lusty at the age of seventy-five, was attacked by stray wild dogs on his way to keep an amorous assignation. In Athens the news of his death

---

[4] From Olympias a rough but beautiful mountain road climbs through dense forests to Stageira.

caused Sophocles, then over ninety, to appear publicly in mourning. Later Arethusa became a staging-post on the Via Egnatia. There is nothing to see there now.

Beyond Rendina the main road follows the course of the Via Egnatia across a featureless plain. To the north stretch the shallow waters of Lake Bolbe, whose perch were much relished by Archestratus, the Magna Graecian author of an epic poem on the art of cookery, facetiously called 'the Hesiod of gluttons'. On the southern shore lies the village of **Apollonia** (not to be confused with ancient Apollonia through which St Paul and Silas passed when they left Philippi after the earthquake. Another lake, Langadha, is equally without scenic distinction. Herodotus says the original inhabitants of this lake district, notorious for their polygamous habits, dwelt in houses perched on piles approached by planks. Trap-doors opened on to the lake below and the feet of babies were tied to hooks to prevent them from falling into the water through these frail contraptions.

At **Derveni**,[5] where much of the treasure exhibited in the Archaeological Museum at Salonica was discovered in the fourth-century BC burial chambers, there is a crossroads. The road to Serres leads to another fork. The branch to the right crosses the plain through alleys of poplars to **Langadhas**, where a macabre religious rite is performed by a sect of Thracian firewalkers on the feast of SS Constantine and Helena (21 May). It is a shabby place, smelling of kebab, over-ripe vegetables and **kaimak** (cream skimmed from milk) ices. The firewalking rite, manifestly pagan in origin, translated into thinly veiled Christian terms, and carried out to the accompaniment of wailing fifes and beating drums, has recently received the blessing of the Church. So the slaughter of animals, the burning coals and primitive music are now invested with all the trappings of officialdom, and the ceremony, held in a waste-ground near the cemetery, draws increasingly large numbers of visitors from Salonica and foreign tourists.

The origin of the Christian rite goes back to the mid thirteenth century, when the church of St Helena in a remote Thracian village caught fire, and the icons, licked by destructive flames, groaned so loudly that the villagers plunged into the blazing building and rescued them without suffering a single burn. The holy images were then handed down from generation to generation. In 1914 they turned up with some Thracian immigrants at Langadhas, where

[5] From Derveni the main road continues to Salonica, twelve kilometres to the south.

they have since remained – artistically undistinguished and blackened by smoke.

The ceremony begins in the morning. A garlanded calf with candles stuck in its ears is led out, to the accompaniment of ritual dances and the thud of drums. Clarinets wail; occasionally there is a fanfare of trumpets. The moment the knife is plunged into the squealing animal, a great moan escapes from the crowd. Women's shrieks pierce the air. In the afternoon the bonfire is lit, and the *Anastenarides* (so-called from their groans, i.e. *anastenazo*, to groan), bearing the holy icons, caper shoeless on the red-hot coals, to the accompaniment of banging tambourines. In the tavernas wine and ouzo flow. Sometimes the firewalkers interrupt their tripping measures to shout and leap in the air. Doctors are said to have testified that the soles of their feet are neither blistered nor discoloured.

The pagan context – the shackling of the garlanded calf, beloved of Dionysus, the ululations recalling the cries of the demented chorus in the *Bacchae* of Euripides – needs no underlining. Even the gestures of the firewalkers are said to derive from an ancient myth which tells of oak trees swaying in dance patterns to the accompaniment of tunes played on the lyre by Orpheus. The whole ceremony seems to be a mixture of Dionysiac and Orphic – orgiastic and musical-religious – elements. Like their pagan forbears, the Thracian firewalkers invest a basically religious idea with all the accessories of calculated hysteria. The lutes, the jigging measures, the burning embers and flying sparks stem from the same Dionysiac belief in a mystic experience gained through uncontrolled intemperance. It is strange that such a barbaric rite should have succeeded, by means of a pretty story of wailing icons, in being admitted into the calendar of feasts of the most Orthodox of Christian Churches.[6] After 21 May Langadhas lapses for another year into the routine of agricultural domesticity. Only cinders remain scattered over the waste-ground until the autumn rains turn them into squelching mud.

---

[6] From year to year there are variations in the order of events and in the composition of the musical instruments. On one occasion, for instance, no trumpets were heard; the drum, however, remains predominant, its remorseless beat setting the tone for the whole proceedings.

CHAPTER SEVENTEEN

Mount Athos: Historical Outline and Practical Information

❧

This second paradise or starry heaven or refuge of all virtues . . .
Imperial charter of the Emperor Andronicus II Palaeologus (1282–1328)

But however wondrous and picturesque the exterior and interior of the monasteries, and however abundantly and exquisitely glorious and stupendous the scenery of the mountain, I would not go again to the ἅγιος ὄρος for any money, so gloomy, so shockingly unnatural, so lonely, so lying, so unatonably odious seems to me all the atmosphere of such monkery . . . The name of Christ on every garment and at every tongue's end, but his maxims trodden underfoot . . .
Edward Lear to Chichester Fortescue, August 1856

The thousand-year-old monastic republic of Athos, independent of the Greek state although policed by its officers, extends along the eastern prong (the Akte of antiquity) of the Chalcidice peninsula. Fortified medieval monasteries fringe the wooded coast, and hermitages and eyries cling vertiginously to the sides of vertical cliffs. Some settlements are abandoned, others still inhabited by a handful of monks who celebrate daily and nocturnal services in frescoed churches filled with wonder-working icons, golden candelabra and carved gilded iconostases. Outwardly it remains the truest extant image of Byzantine monasticism; in reality, it is a twilight place, nostalgic, muted, dying of apathy and dereliction.[1]

The fertility of the promontory is legendary, and the landscape, with the Holy Mountain soaring to a tapering peak at the southern extremity, could not be more splendid. The Virgin herself found the prospect so bewitching that she fell in love with it when she was forced to land in the Bay of Iviron, after her ship, bound for Cyprus, where she and St John were about to pay a visit to Lazarus, had

[1] Since the author's last visit, there has been some revival, to the extent that a shortage of accommodation for new recruits is reported, the result of earlier neglect of vacant buildings. (Ed.)

been blown off course. Enchanted by the shady forests and flowery meadows, she annexed the peninsula, declared it her private garden and forbade any member of her sex to enter it, whereupon all the pagan idols fell off their pedestals and destroyed themselves. The whole spiritual development of the community stems from the worship of the Mother of God; and her mantled form, the monks say, still haunts the groves and coppices below the walls of woodland monasteries.

The earliest hermits came in the eighth century, seeking refuge from the persecutions of Iconoclast emperors. The first recorded solitary was Peter the Anchorite in the ninth century. Beset by demons and wild beasts, he dwelt in a cave on the marble mountain for fifty years. The influx of anchorites increased, and in 872 the Emperor Basil I granted them a special charter of protection. The future pattern of the republic was established by St Athanasius, a Bythinian monk, who founded the first monastery, the Grand Lavra, and reaffirmed the Virgin's injunction that no woman or female animal should enter the holy territory. Pious men, anxious to escape from the world of temptation, flocked from the Orthodox countries and founded monasteries, financed by princes and statesmen. Artists from Constantinople, Salonica and Crete were commissioned to fresco the walls of churches and instruct the monks in the art of iconography. While preserving their independence, the new foundations acknowledged the suzerainty of the Byzantine emperor. Under Constantine IX Monomachos (1042–55) regulations governing the administration of the communities – monasteries, sketes and *kellia* – were drawn up; and in the reign of Andronicus II Palaeologus (1282–1328) the various settlements passed from the imperial to the patriarchal authority. The best brains in the ecclesiastical world gravitated to the Holy Mountain, which gradually became the symbol of the Church's undisputed influence over every sphere of the national consciousness. Religious learning and scholarship flourished. In the fifteenth century the idiorrhythmic system, which meant that each monk fed and clothed himself from his own resources, was introduced in several monasteries where the rule was milder than in the cenobitic or communal (and more austere) establishments.

During the centuries of Latin, Slav and Ottoman occupation the monasteries preserved the prestige of Byzantine religion undiminished, and when the War of Independence came in 1821 Finlay was justified in saying that Mount Athos 'held a more revered place than the memories of Marathon and Salamis' in the minds of ordinary Greeks. But in the nineteenth century the wealth that poured in from Tsarist sources was turned into an instrument of Russian foreign policy and the number of novices from Slav countries threatened to exceed those from Greece and Asia Minor. The Russian Revolution put an end to that. After the Second World War the flow of recruits from all Slav countries was cut off at source. Where there were once forty thousand monks, there are now about a thousand, and narrow Greek nationalism paralyses any form of theological stimulus in a twentieth-century context. Most of the monasteries, filled with treasures of religious art, provide little more than a refuge for aged monks of peasant origins and limited education, a place where men who have proved to be failures in the world may retire to live and die cheaply. All artistic activity has ceased; the fields and vineyards owned by the idiorrhythmic orders are largely abandoned; parasitic plants wind poisonous shoots round trunks of fruit and nut trees; deforestation is rife, and the bracken grows so high that it is difficult to locate the shady mule-tracks that once linked one monastery with another.

What remains then to be seen? Just some decaying monasteries inhabited by a few aged illiterate monks? No. Each monastery is a castellated stronghold. The architecture, if not always good, is either striking, picturesque or spectacular. Many of the libraries and treasuries possess priceless works of silverware, icons and illuminated manuscripts, as well as a variety of other religious works of art wrought in gold, bronze, jasper and marble, including the holy relics so dear to the Orthodox faithful. There are also some mosaics. Detailed catalogues of the collections of works of art, which represent five hundred years of Byzantine civilization and its long drawn out post-Byzantine aftermath, were made in the nineteenth century by the Russian, Greek and French scholars, Uspensky, Lambros and Millet. In every instance, the monastic buildings gravitate round the main church, which is cruciform (Greek Cross plan) with varying numbers of side chapels. All contain frescoes (mostly of the late Byzantine and post-Byzantine periods – some very good, others indifferent).

It is helpful to bear in mind the uniform iconographical arrangement of an Athonite church, which, generally speaking, applies to every Byzantine church in the country. Above the world, in the dome of heaven, reigns Christ Pantocrator, surrounded by worshipping angels, while the Virgin and St John the Baptist intercede on behalf of mankind; in the central apse (there are three) the Virgin and Child sit enthroned within a golden aureole above the altar. Around this focus of divinity, in the pendentives and vaults, unfold the scenes of the Twelve Feasts and the Passion (these sometimes overflow into the narthex). On the lower register – the terrestrial one – prophets, saints and holy men are ranged in strict order of precedence. Finally, on the historiated pavements assemble the monks and lay worshippers. The church thus represents the universe in miniature. As regards the frescoes, every rule and regulation, every technical and aesthetic device, is meticulously codified in the *Painter's Guide*, compiled from much earlier manuals by Dionysius of Phourna, an eighteenth-century monk.

But no mistake should be made about it. Hardship and frustration, an unappetizing diet and (sometimes) dirty sheets are the lot of the traveller. He may even encounter something unique in Greece – unfriendliness. But the loneliness and tranquillity, the emphasis on superstition and demonology, the obsession with the past and indifference to the future, the sheer anachronism of it all, produce in one a state of almost traumatic fascination. The journey may be the most arduous in Greece; it is also probably the most exciting. The lover of dramatic landscape will find little in the whole country to match some of the prospects encountered.

Formalities

Only men, but not 'beardless boys', are allowed to cross the frontier which runs north to south across the neck of the peninsula. A recommendation for a residence permit of four days is issued to foreigners, if supported by a testimonial from their Embassy or Consulate, by the Ministry of Foreign Affairs in Athens or the Ministry for Northern Greece in Salonica. Control of passports is effected at the port of Daphni. At Karyes, the capital, the document issued by the Ministry of Foreign Affairs is exchanged for a residence permit signed and countersigned by the Holy Synod and the Nomarch, the local civil authority. This permit must be presented to the guest-master of every monastery at which the traveller wishes to stay.

Method of Travel

Caiques leave daily from Ouranoupolis and Ierissos. They put in at the arsenal of every monastery – and any skete or hermitage on request. Private caiques can be chartered at Ierissos, Ouranoupolis, Daphni and some of the larger monasteries. From the arsenal there is generally a steep climb (ranging from a quarter of an hour to an hour) to the monastery. There are seldom mules for hire. One has to carry one's own baggage. It is essential to travel light.

Accommodation

Monastery gates are shut at sunset, after which it is possible to gain admittance only under exceptional circumstances. It is important to make friends with the guest-master (*archontaris*), a key personage, who allocates beds (often in a dormitory) and regulates hours of meals (a gratuity is accepted). Applications to visit the Library, treasury and various chapels should be made to the Librarian through the guest-master.

Organization

The Julian calendar (thirteen days behind the Gregorian) is kept in all monasteries except Vatopedi. Byzantine time is also kept, and 12 o'clock is at sunset. In the cenobitic (communal) foundations, travellers share their meals with the monks in the refectory. Lunch is usually at 9 a.m., dinner at 5 p.m. In the idiorrhythmic establishments, where discipline is milder, meals for visitors are served in the guest-house (*archontariki*) at more conventional hours. During fasts (which are frequent) food is likely to consist of boiled vegetables. At other times it can be more varied – and perhaps nastier. Visitors would do well, while travelling light, to take a supply of tinned foodstuffs, biscuits, processed cheese, etc. At the monasteries of Vatopedi and the Grand Lavra, biscuits, cigarettes and *loucoumi* (Turkish delight) are sold. There are grocers at Karyes and Daphni.

Itinerary

A one-day visit is ruled out. A three-day tour enables the traveller to visit either Iviron and Vatopedi or Iviron and the Grand Lavra, the three senior monasteries, and cast a quick glance at the frescoes of the Protaton at Karyes en route. Yachtsmen, after going through the usual formalities at Karyes (reached by bus), can sail round the peninsula, visiting any monastery (or indeed all) at will.

On my last visit I worked out what seems to me to be a practicable eight-day tour by caique, starting at Ouranoupolis.[2] This is the minimum time required to visit the ten most important monasteries (a summary of the history and contents of the remaining ten is given at the end of Chapter 18).

[2] The residence permit obtained at Karyes is now valid for four days only; but one can also go back to Karyes to renew the permit officially. Foreign tourists are admitted at a rate of ten daily. (Ed.)

In describing the journey, I adopt the method of a personal journal, hoping it will give the traveller some useful hints as to what to expect from Athonite habits and monkish idiosyncrasies. Mount Athos is not the mere sum total of its monasteries and hermitages. It is a way of life; to begin to try to understand it requires a little insight into the character of its strange inhabitants.

CHAPTER EIGHTEEN

Mount Athos: A Traveller's Journal

✢

Karyes: The Protaton – Chilandari – Vatopedi – Iviron – The Grand Lavra –
The Sketes – Dionysiou – St Paul – Gregoriou – Simopetra – St Panteleimon
– Xenophontos – Docheiariou – The Lesser Monasteries

21 August

We left Ouranoupolis at ten o'clock by the public caique. Among the
passengers were three elderly monks who had been visiting relations
in what they call 'the world'. A profound, almost reverential silence
descended as we sailed into holy waters below pine-clad cliffs
fringed by sandy beaches. Occasionally an abandoned hermitage
appeared in a clearing in the woods. Somewhere along here was the
site of ancient Dium, one of the few Chalcidian colonies which
refused to fall for Brasidas's blandishments and join the Spartans
in the great war against Athens. In the south the peak of the Holy
Mountain, a pyramid of white limestone, was wreathed in wispy
clouds, its tapering form repeated in a similar cone at the tip of the
promontory. Strabo calls it 'breast-shaped'.

Arsenals – fortified tower-like structures, surrounded by disused
port installations, which serve as landing-stages for the monasteries
– began to skirt the shore. The first was that of Zographou, where
logs of wood were laid out in rows along the beach, awaiting export,
and from which the *arsenaris* (arsenal-keeper) waved to us from a
projecting balcony; then those of Docheiariou, crowned by a
crenellated tower flanked by cypress trees; Xenophontos, its wooden
galleries overlooking the placid bay; St Panteleimon, with its lime-
green onion domes and derelict warehouses; Xeropotamou, an
inland monastery.[1] We were soon entering the port of Daphni, a
huddle of hovels at the foot of a steep hill.

After showing our passports and having lunch (an oily stew
served stone cold) in a taverna under a vine trellis, we took the
afternoon bus to **Karyes**. The passengers included two men wearing

---

[1] For Zographou see p. 297. St Panteleimon, pp. 289–91.
Docheiariou, pp. 293–5. Xeropotamou, p. 296.
Xenophontos, pp. 291–3.

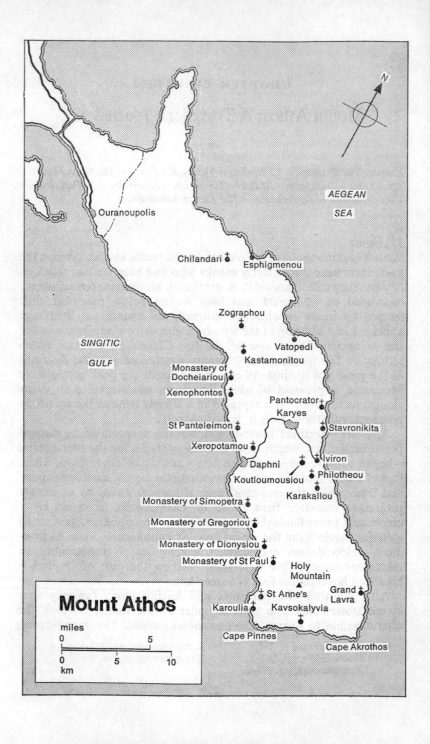

Chilandari

Esphigmenou

AEGEAN
SEA

Ouranoupolis

Zographou

SINGITIC

GULF

Vatopedi

Kastamonitou

Monastery of
Docheiariou

Xenophontos

Pantocrator

Karyes

St Panteleimon

Stavronikita

Xeropotamou

Iviron

Daphni

Koutloumousiou

Philotheou

Karakallou

Monastery of Simopetra

Monastery of Gregoriou

Monastery of Dionysiou

Monastery of St Paul

Holy
Mountain

Grand
Lavra

St Anne's

Karoulia

Kavsokalyvia

Cape Pinnes

Cape Akrothos

Mount Athos

miles

0   5

0   5   10
km

caps with the badge of the double-headed eagle – emblem of the ecclesiastical police force. Climbing potholed hairpin bends, we passed the Monastery of Xeropotamou which spreads across a shady ledge with deep ravines on either side, and ascended through a jungle of shrubs. The smell of sun-baked myrtle was pungent. The forest now closed round on all sides, and we drove through a tunnel of trees, whose trunks, entwined in creepers speckled with purple berries, grew out of a bed of ferns so dense that no path has ever been cut through it. After crossing the watershed the road descends into a bowl-like valley, seamed with verdant gullies and scattered with nut groves and farm-houses. 'Karyes!' cried the driver with a flourish, and we observed the domes of churches and ecclesiastical colleges crowned with crosses glistening in the afternoon sun.

In Ayion Pneuma (Holy Ghost) Street, where the bus stops, there are grocers', cobblers', the only post office on the peninsula and a shop filled with postcards, rosaries, wooden wine-jugs and eucharistic bread-stamps carved by monks in outlying sketes. Respect for the Holy Ghost precludes smoking, wearing a hat or short-sleeved shirt in the street.[2] We climbed a cobbled lane between well-watered gardens to the house of the archimandrite, to whom we had a letter of introduction. Pigeons piped in the surrounding orchards. A white-bearded *yerondas* (servant of a senior cleric) brought us coffee and ouzo – they call it *raki*, the Turkish word, here – in a courtyard filled with roses, oleanders and hydrangeas. He told us he had not been outside Karyes for forty years. The archimandrite, who was more worldly (an iconographer and landscape painter) conducted us to the authorities who issued us with residence permits.[3] We looked at the Assembly House of the Holy Community, where novices hurried across marble halls carrying cups of coffee to high-ranking prelates, while the archimandrite fetched the key of the church which is the chief glory of Karyes.

The **Protaton,** or Church of the Holy Community, joint property of all the monasteries, is a basilica (the only one on Mount Athos) of the tenth century, restored in the thirteenth and sixteenth. The belfry with striped bands is a later addition. The exterior is plain enough, but the walls of the naos are covered with early fourteenth-century frescoes of the Macedonian School (a group of Greek artists working throughout Northern Greece and the Balkans). The best of

[2] The same rule about smoking and personal attire applies to the main courts of all monasteries on Mount Athos.
[3] The owner of the inn where one puts up for the night will inform the traveller how to carry out the formalities.

them are probably by Manuel Panselinos, an enigmatic figure of Thessalonian origin, whose work is characterized by sturdy modelling, depth of expression and a new realism apparent in both portraiture and detail. In the *Painter's Guide*, Dionysius of Phourna compares Panselinos to 'the moon in all its splendour', the word *'panselinos'* meaning full moon.

Unhampered by the architectural complexities of the Greek Cross plan, the master painter was able to achieve an unusual unity of composition across large surfaces. The painted decoration is divided into four distinct zones, with the topmost reserved for standing figures of, for the most part, Christ's ancestors. Across the third zone (from the bottom) spread the noble groupings from the lives of Christ and the Virgin in a flowing, frieze-like continuity. In the **Birth of the Virgin** St Anne's exhaustion after the pangs of labour is suggested in the support she seeks from her attendants while trying to take some food. In the **Presentation of the Virgin in the Temple** a timid little Virgin, led by St Anne and Ioachim, appears before the hoary old priest, followed by maidens carrying lighted candles. Puckish figures in the form of Hellenic river gods personifying the Jordan and the sea retreat before the Lord's displeasure in the **Baptism**, while three children dance across the bridge spanning the river. Architectural backgrounds are used to stress the unity of the compositions, as in the **Incredulity of Thomas**, in which Christ stands axially in the central arch, the apostles in the other two. A similar symmetry of arrangement, both of figures and architectural features, is apparent in **The Last Supper**. Harmony becomes the keynote. In the scenes from the **Deposition from the Cross** and **Lamentation over the Body of Christ** (both are unfortunately badly damaged) which follow the **Crucifixion** and **Descent into Hell**, human suffering is depicted with great intensity, the representation of St John in the former achieving truly dramatic heights as he raises the dead Christ's hand to his cheek. The mood in the **Dormition of the Virgin** above the west entrance is more Italianate and the figures are less heiratic.

Representations of Evangelists, prophets, military saints, bishops and martyrs extend across the two lower zones. An austere spirituality haunts the faces of the ascetic saints, each of whom is depicted with a distinct individuality rare in Byzantine iconography: particularly the white-bearded **Euthymius**, who lived to be ninety-six, his sunken eyes reflecting the disillusioned wisdom of his years; **Hosios David of Thessalonica**, whose gnarled knobbly features recall those of generations of Greek monks; **St John the Baptist**, tragic in the force and intensity of his expression. In the north and south corners of the nave **St John Damascene and the monk Cosmas** are represented as hymn-writers, holding scores; in the south aisle, across the breadth of the long arches before the sanctuary, the tall figures of **Melchezedek and Moses** are depicted, clad in bejewelled robes, the former with a long white beard, the latter as a young man holding the tablets. In the prothesis, within the sanctuary, there is an unusual portrait of a **youthful Christ**, full of vigour and freshness. Throughout the church the colour scheme is remarkable for its glow of different shades of pink and red (coral, flame and claret, pale and ruddy flesh tints) set off by sea blues, ambers and silvery greens. Shading is effected by black or indigo-blue and green brush-strokes. The use of yellow against white produces a bold effect. Everywhere luminosity and chromatic harmony prevail.

In the Protaton we saw the holy icon of *Axion Estin* ('It is meet and right'), found in a cell near Karyes, where a tenth-century monk was visited by the Archangel Gabriel and instructed how it was 'meet and right' to glorify the Virgin. On Easter Monday the image, shaded by an umbrella, is borne in procession to the homes of the local representatives of each monastery, who sprinkle rose water and incense over it while church bells ring and spectators shout, 'Long live the Virgin!'

It was too late to visit the nineteenth-century Russian skete of St Andrew – a fantasy of onion domes and coloured roofs, crosses and towers – among groves of hazelnut trees north of the village. Its most important possession is a relic of St Andrew – part of his forehead. We went to the inn for supper. I do not remember what we had to eat (perhaps it is as well), but there was resinated wine. We slept in a room with six beds, after asking for clean sheets (very damp). Washing arrangements were confined to a cold water tap in the court where we dined. But the view from the rickety wooden balcony outside our room was unforgettable. The steep eastern side of the Holy Mountain rose sheer above woods and vineyards, haunted, it is said, by seductive Nereids who have trespassed into the Virgin's garden. The whole countryside was mantled in a velvet sheen of moonlight. Occasionally, the shriek of a jackal broke the spectral silence.

22 August

We got up at 6 a.m. to catch the bus to the Bay of Iviron. The cobbled alleys of Karyes were deserted. The absence of women's and children's voices had begun to make an impact. Some travellers find it grows stronger the longer they stay on the Holy Mountain, until they finally become aware of a great void at the heart of things. It is hard to get used to the idea that nobody has been born here for over a thousand years. The road wound down to the coast, past the Monastery of Koutloumousiou,[4] its crimson church surrounded by high walls. The gullies seaming the Virgin's garden were a paradise of vegetation: oleanders, mulberries, olives, walnuts and hazels; ferns, ramblers, spiky shrubs, deciduous and evergreen, and thick coverts where jackals hide. The smell of aromatic herbs drifted across the hillside. To the south, a wisp of cloud formed a perfect halo round the peak of Athos. At the landing-stage of Iviron the caique had just put in.[5] A high sea was running, the *meltemi*, the etesian wind that funnels through the Hellespont and hits the Aegean with redoubled force, breaking the waves in sprays of foam against a primitive sea wall. We hurled ourselves and our luggage into the pitching caique. One of the passengers, a policeman, his complexion the colour of his uniform (pea-green) groaned and leant, gurgling, over the rail.

The coast is wild, grand and rocky, fringed with bluffs and crags from which a succession of monasteries overhang the sea: the medieval tower of Stavronikita crowning a huddle of abandoned monks' cells, 'like a Gothic castle', says Curzon, 'perched upon a beetling rock';[6] Pantocrator, astride a cliff lashed by waves so high that our caique could not enter the minute harbour; Vatopedi, largest of all monasteries, a fortress sprawling across a sea-washed woodland; Esphigmenou, compressed, as its name (The Squeezed-together One) implies, within a narrow green valley.[7]

About mid-morning we reached the arsenal of **Chilandari**, the first monastery on our itinerary. The way inland is up a gentle incline. It took us three-quarters of an hour to walk – carrying our bags. On our left a fine thirteenth-century watch-tower commanded the maritime approach. The country is green and open; we did not pass a single human being, not an animal. Beside a thick grove of cypresses, into which no shaft of sunlight ever penetrates, a shrine with a Slavonic inscription commemorates the spot where Stephen Dušan, who had crowned himself 'Emperor of the Serbs and Greeks' at Skopje, was greeted by the monks of Chilandari when he visited

[4] For Koutloumousiou see p. 297.
[5] For Iviron see p. 273–5.
[6] For Stavronikita see p. 297.
[7] For Pantocrator see p. 297.
    Vatopedi see p. 268–73.
    Esphigmenou see p. 297.

the monastery in the fourteenth century. At last we saw kitchen-gardens; then the encircling walls of the great Serb monastery within a ring of hills covered with pine and chestnut trees and dark cypresses thrusting their tips through latticed olive branches. The only sound was the piping of wood pigeons which nest in the arbours of ash and plane.

The monastery (idiorrhythmic) was founded in the twelfth century by Stephen Nemanja, unifier of the Serbs, who donned a monk's habit and died here. A century later, when it was the fashion for Slav princes to marry into Byzantine ruling families and found churches, hospitals and charitable institutions on Greek territory, the monastery was enlarged by Stephen Milutin, son-in-law of the Emperor Andronicus II Palaeologus. Chilandari soon became a cradle of Slav culture, visited by Serb kings and national heroes. It is now inhabited by some twenty monks, mostly anti-Communist refugees from Jugoslavia. Relations with Belgrade, however, are not severed, and Marshal Tito presented the house with a tractor.

We passed through a frescoed gateway into the **court**, the loveliest on Mount Athos. The layout of the monastic precincts is more or less identical throughout the peninsula: a central court, varying in size, with the church in the middle, and the refectory, cells, chapels, oratories and sometimes cloisters grouped round it, the whole enclosed within high walls. Fan-shaped, the court at Chilandari is a perfectly composed complex of tall brick edifices (considerably rebuilt after a fire in 1722), with whitewashed upper storeys supported by wooden brackets. A fourteenth-century tower, with windows within arched frames, overlooks slate roofs of a dull pink colour and domes crowned with crosses. In the late afternoon a roseate glow is reflected from walls striped with tiles of different brick-red shades. In the centre of the court stands a seventeenth-century octagonal *phiale*, a basin for blessing the holy water, with a jet in the form of a cross with foliate patterns and roofed by a domed canopy. The interior walls are frescoed. Beside it rise two tall ancient cypresses, in whose foliage the monks once hid their treasure of relics, icons and manuscripts, when Latin pirates attacked the monastery. Nature (or Providence) came to their rescue. A clammy fog rose suddenly from the valley, enveloped the pirates as they scaled the walls and completely confounded them. Others lost their bearings in eddies of white mist and in their panic they slaughtered each other. Only three survived; they were succoured by the monks and converted to the Orthodox faith. Their portraits adorn the walls of the refectory.

The guest-master led us up to a cool spacious gallery with settees ranged along walls hung with photographs of the Karadjordjevič dynasty. We were offered ouzo, coffee and *loucoumi*, and shown our sleeping quarters – an enormous dormitory, all to ourselves. The primitive lavatory overlooked a sun-dazzled glade surrounded by cypress and olive trees thrumming with cicadas. We had lunch – boiled marrows, tomato and onion salad, gherkins, bread and wine – with the abbot, who was fond of his glass of wine, and a theology student from Athens University who gave Greek lessons to the Serb monks during the summer vacation. After a siesta we started sightseeing, conducted by the librarian.

The **Church of the Presentation of the Virgin** is of the twelfth century, enlarged in the fourteenth, with later additions and transformations. The exterior brick decoration, largely composed of striped bands and arched surrounds, tends to obscure the purity of the architectural ensemble, with its five domes, apses, arches and barrel vaults. You enter through the rectangular *liti*, a virtual exonarthex – a feature of all Athonite churches, whose layout is uniform: *liti*, large square narthex, cruciform naos, gilded iconostasis pierced by three doors, and tri-apsidal sanctuary. At Chilandari the naos is distinguished by a beautiful twelfth-century **pavement of Opus Alexandrinum**: slabs of verd-antique within a border of petals and concentric circles of different marbles – grey, blue, green and off-white – superimposed with cubes and rectangles within larger rectangles. Most of the frescoes (*c.* 1300) are ruined by tasteless nineteenth-century repainting. Noteworthy exceptions are the untouched portraits of Stephen Nemanja, the founder, and King Stephen Milutin, the thirteenth-century benefactor, on the southwest pilaster above the former's tomb.

Beside the Bishop's throne hangs the miraculous icon of the Virgin Tricherousa. The face, brown with age, is surrounded with gold and votive gifts (jewelled crosses, strings of coins). The icon, the monks say, belonged to St John Damascene, who wrote such fiery denunciations of the Iconoclasts that the Emperor's agents punished him by cutting off his right hand. The severed member was hung on a wall and left to wither. But the Virgin visited him in a dream and undertook to restore his hand if he promised to use it exclusively in writing panegyrics in her honour. On waking, the holy father pressed the dried-up stump to the Virgin's lips in the image, after which arm and hand were promptly united by supernatural grafting. As a votive offering, he placed a commemorative silver hand below the Child's feet, whence the icon derives its name of Tricherousa, 'the Three-handed One'. Scholars, however, attribute the icon to a period much later than that of Iconoclasm. Next to the Tricherousa is a bejewelled staff belonging to the Emperor Andronicus I Comnenus, who paid for his crimes by being strapped to a camel's back and paraded through the hippodrome where he was torn to pieces by an angry mob in 1185. Above the Bishop's throne is a set of charming thirteenth-century miniatures set on cloth stretched across gold plate.

In the **Library**, situated within the tower,[8] we saw an eleventh-century edition of the homilies of St John Chrysostom, hundreds of patriarchal sigilla and chrysobulls, and a fourteenth-century **illuminated Book of Gospels** of Serbian origin with letters of gold and silver and large rounded semi-uncials drawn on white parchment, much admired by Robert Curzon, who, travelling on Mount Athos in 1837, seems to have had no scruples about extorting precious manuscripts from ignorant monks in exchange for a few drachmae.[9] It is to the credit of the monks of Chilandari that they did not fall for his usual blandishments. We look at a small **mosaic panel of the Virgin and Child** (portative mosaic icons of this kind are rare) in the grand austere manner of the twelfth century (although it may be of later workmanship). But our unstinted admiration was reserved for a set of superbly painted **icons of the fourteenth century** (probably the finest on Mount Athos): four contemplative Evangelists holding bejewelled Gospels, clothed in mantles of subtly matched purple, olive green and smoky blue shades; a Deisis – Christ, authoritative and compassionate, between the Virgin and St John; the Archangels (Gabriel in blue and green robes, with wings of dull gold shaded with grey-blue brush strokes). A softness of texture and limpidity of outline, suggestive of Slav influences, distinguishes these beautiful panels.

The refectory, largely disused, is less interesting. Apsidal and T-shaped, its walls are covered with seventeenth-century frescoes representing *inter alia* the life of St Sabbas, the pious son of Stephen Nemanja. The figures are loutish and lifeless. The Last Judgement, which always figures prominently in the apses of refectories, is more attractive, with its semi-circular architectural background of arches and fancy towers.

Descending into the court, we saw an old monk with a flowing

---

[8] The objects in the Library are soon to be moved to a neo-Byzantine building under construction near the tower.

[9] The Hon. Robert Curzon, *Visits to the Monasteries of the Levant*, John Murray, London, 1865 edition.

white beard beating the *simandron,* an oblong wooden board on which the performer taps with a mallet to summon the community to prayer. The whole place, the weed-grown court, the flimsy wooden stairways, the maze of cells and chapels, echoed with the repetitive beats which obviously derive from a set score, the introductory *lento* passage working up to a lively *vivace* climax, only to die down and begin all over again. Soon we heard the rise and fall of a feeble voice chanting the litanies in Slavonic. As it grew dark the cypress trees flanking the *phiale* stood out like sentinels guarding the isolation inviolate.

We dined with the friendly abbot and the theology student. By the time we went to bed (about nine o'clock), the galleries overlooking the court were empty. No light showed anywhere, except a kerosene lamp fixed in a bracket pointing the way to the lavatory. A bat was making frenzied gyrations round it.

23 August

The abbot placed Marshal Tito's tractor at our disposal to carry our bags to the arsenal. We bathed and had a picnic lunch on a sandy beach. Later the abbot, who was on a visit to the *arsenaris* and had exchanged his cylindrical hat for a floppy straw one, trailed across the sands and presented each of us with a little bunch of sea-daffodils. Except at Dionysiou we were not to meet with such friendliness again.

The caique left at two. The theology student, on his way to post letters at Karyes, was seated next to me. As we pitched and rolled in the trough of huge waves, he inveighed against the iniquities of British foreign policy in Cyprus, British ingratitude (it would have been American ingratitude had I been an American) to Greece which had saved the Western world from Communism, etc. etc. Illogical, rhetorical, cliché-ridden, the discourse continued relentlessly. Typically, we parted the best of friends. Politics and heroics apart, he was the type of Greek who can be both charming and intelligent.

The climb from the landing-stage to the **Monastery of Vatopedi**, screened by wooded hills watered by streams, is steep but short. A squat watch-tower overlooks the arsenal and a huddle of wood-cutters' huts. A crescent-shaped bay sweeps northward at the foot of hills seamed with valleys where pomegranates and Japanese medlars grow between hedgerows of blackberry bushes festooned with clematis and wild vine. On late summer evenings caravans of mules wind down the paths to the monastery gates where logs of wood (the monks' sole supply of fuel in winter) are unloaded. You enter

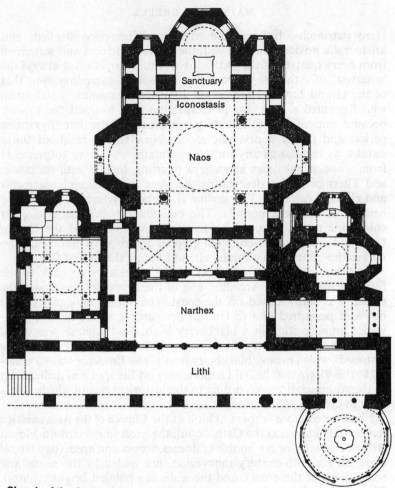

Church of the Annunciation, Mount Athos

through a porch in the shape of a canopy guarded by an icon of the Virgin. A Turkish soldier once had the temerity to shoot at her hand. The Virgin retaliated swiftly. She drove the Turk so mad that he hanged himself from a tree whose branches withered and died.

After a long wait in the guest-house, a sulky guest-master offered us coffee (no *ouzo* or *loucoumi* here). We wandered round the polygonal **court** – larger than that of Chilandari, less well composed, but suffused with an even brighter glow from crimson stuccoed walls and brick courses with fantastic geometric designs. A warren of cells, chapels, storerooms extends across a slope within fortified walls.

Here patriarchs, bishops and archimandrites once strolled, and aristocratic novices mingled with the suites of princes and statesmen from every quarter of the Orthodox world. Vatopedi was always the 'smartest' of Athonite monasteries, its wealth exceeding even that of the Grand Lavra. Here stayed John Cantacuzenus, a statesman who fomented a civil war in Constantinople, usurped the throne, became one of the outstanding emperors of the late Byzantine period and finally a nomadic monk. Now there are about thirty monks, as bigoted as any on the mountain, who stare suspiciously from wooden balconies at modern pilgrims, loaded with rucksacks and Thermos flasks, desecrating the place with unseemly garments and clicking cameras. The skyline is broken by turrets, domes and belfries of different periods. The octagonal *phiale* has a circular colonnade and a frescoed baldacchino. A painting of the Eye of God and a chocolate-coloured puppet figure of a Saracen, who strikes the hours on a church bell, add the final touch of fantasy.

In Athonite legend the origins of the monastery go back to the fourth century, when Arcadius, son of the Emperor Theodosius the Great, was shipwrecked off the coast. The Virgin took pity on the boy and permitted him to land in her garden, where he was afterwards found resting in a blackberry bush. So the place was called Vatopaidi – 'blackberry bush boy' (the spelling however is now Vatopedi, which means 'blackberry field'). The Emperor was so grateful to the Virgin that he built a monastery on the spot and dedicated it to the Annunciation. According to the historical record, the house is a tenth-century foundation. It is of the idiorrhythmic order.

I had time before vespers to look at the **Church of the Annunciation** (commonly known as the Catholicon), the most important on Mount Athos. The exterior is a jumble of domes, arches and apses (two lateral ones, an eleventh-century innovation, are added to the north and south arms of the cross), and the walls are painted bright crimson. The interior of the colonnaded *liti* is covered with eighteenth-century frescoes, whose whimsical folklore character is epitomized in the coy expression of the damned souls floundering in the river of Hell. Above the doorway into the narthex are three mosaic panels: a severe, unsmiling Deisis of the eleventh century, flanked by the Virgin and the Angel of the Annunciation (fourteenth century). The figures are heavy and forceful, in the monumental style. Magnificent fourteenth-century **bronze doors**, decorated with designs of leaves and birds and figures of the Virgin and Gabriel in relief, lead into the narthex, where the early fourteenth-century frescoes are distinguished by a pink glow reminiscent of the Protaton. The resemblance, especially in the grouping of figures, between the Betrayal and Duccio's rendering of the same scene in the Opera del Duomo at Siena is striking. Foreboding and tension, a whirlwind of movement, characterize both compositions. Even the awkwardly stylized trees are repeated – in more evolved forms – by the Sienese painter, who is thought to have studied under a Byzantine master.

From the narthex I passed through sixteenth-century ivory-inlaid doors into the **naos**, which is paved with lavish polychrome marbles laid out in geometric designs. The dome is supported by granite columns with (possibly fifth-century) brass rings. The **frescoes**, despite restoration in the eighteenth and nineteenth centuries, are among the supreme achievements of the Macedonian School of painting in the early fourteenth century. An important new trend, later developed in other Athonite frescoes, is observed for the first time. A series of individual pictures seems to replace the strict liturgical sequence of symbolical scenes. Overall uniformity is sacrificed to narrative. Episodes, groups, individual figures jostle each other within their own spatial limits, with less of the old feeling for majestic order within a unified whole. The detached statuesque symbolism of the past is diversified by appeals to piety, pity, wonder – to human emotions. The colours are colder than usual: perhaps owing to restoration. An austere blue predominates and the familiar figures of the Dodecaorton pursue their tragic destinies in an inky haze, through which it is not always easy to distinguish the detail.

The grandest compositions are the **Entry into Jerusalem** and the **Crucifixion**, both larger than life-size. An atmosphere of expectancy prevails in the Entry. Christ in luminous dark blue robes rides the donkey sideways, as he listens to the arguments of the Apostles, while the people of Jerusalem pour out of the ornamental city gate. The branches of the palm tree wave in the breeze. The background is a tortuous complex of domes, roofs, cornices and pediments, red against an inky star-studded sky. In the Crucifixion the use of rigid straight lines – in the draperies of the stricken Virgin, the handkerchiefs of the lamenting angels, the anatomical details of the figure of Christ, who seems to stand on the Cross rather than to be nailed to it – heighten the sense of anguish. Only the figure of St John is conventional and unconvincing.

Two thirteenth-century icons flank the sanctuary: a Holy Trinity, disfigured by flashy haloes executed in gold filigree, and a Virgin and Child, also faced with filigree but distinguished by the poignancy of the Virgin's expression. Above are dark mosaics (probably eleventh-century) of the Virgin and Angel of Annunciation, protectors of the church, guarding the entry into the sanctuary. The eighteenth-century iconostasis is very elaborate: the work, probably, of some monkish woodcarver with a love of pastoral life. Stags, hunters, boys picking grapes frolic among flowers, pine-cones and vine-sprays.

It is important to get permission to enter the sanctuary. Here are kept a tenth-century gold- and silver-sheathed icon of the Virgin and Child, surrounded by scenes from the Dodecaorton; a superb (also tenth-century) **steatite icon of St George**, depicting the saint, clad in warrior's attire, holding lance and shield, standing between two columns under a canopy emblazoned with heraldic devices; a set of very small mosaic icons, interesting for their rarity; two fourteenth-century icons of the Virgin and Child and the Archangel Michael, who has a touchingly affectionate expression. Some of the most venerated **relics** in the Orthodox Church are also kept here and only shown to the visitor on request (and under strict surveillance). They include parts of the True Cross, the index finger of St John the Baptist, the skull of St Gregory of Nazianzus, a ninth-century gold and silver reliquary embossed with scenes from the life of St Demetrius, which contains a piece of blood-soaked earth from the public baths at Salonica where the martyr was speared to death, and the 'Icon of the Dolls', a ninth-century diptych, once the property of Theodora, wife of the Iconoclast Emperor Theophilus, who, when found worshipping secretly in front of the image, archly declared she was playing with her dolls. The Emperor hushed up her idolatrous offence. But the most revered relic of all is an enamelled silver box studded with gems containing a fragment of the Virgin's girdle: a piece of russet-coloured ribbon woven with gold thread and sewn with seed pearls by the Empress Pulcheria, a cultivated Athenian lady of the fifth century. Dropped by the Virgin on the site of Golgotha, it changed hands several times, was carried from country to country, allaying epidemics of the plague and finally presented by a fourteenth-century Serb prince to Vatopedi. When Curzon visited Vatopedi in the 1830s, he says, afflicted persons were allowed, in return 'for a consideration', to kiss it and be cured.

We dined in the guest-house with some itinerant monks. The fare was vegetarian, without wine. There was no conversation: not even polite formalities. We went to our room, overlooking the mysterious velvety hills. It was about eight o'clock. We talked for a while in whispers. Suddenly there was a loud knocking at the door and the angry voice of the guest-master was heard inveighing against our irreverence in this house of God.

Meteora: the Rousanou Monastery at sunset.

Salonica, Church of the Holy Apostles: Mosaic of the Transfiguration.

24 August

We got up at six and breakfasted on biscuits and Nescafé (our own). We visited the beautiful church again and persuaded a relatively amiable monk to let us see the Library and refectory. Visitors need waste no time on the latter. It is cross-shaped with marble-topped tables and ugly frescoes of the eighteenth century. The most striking object in the library is an extremely elegant specimen of Byzantine silverware: a **jasper cup** of the mid fourteenth century on an octagonal stem with silver gilt decoration and the monogram of the donor, Manuel Cantacuzenus, Despot of Mistra, inscribed on the base, and handles in the form of beautifully moulded griffons holding the rim in their claws. Among the six hundred manuscripts (over half on parchment) are an eleventh-century psalter with the monogram of the Emperor Constantine IX Monomachos, an octateuch (also eleventh-century) with fine miniatures which preserve much of the ancient tradition of book illumination, including personifications of the sun and moon, the seasons, night and day and the signs of the zodiac, and part of an eleventh-century edition of Strabo's *Geography* (one of the few illustrated copies in existence) with a crudely drawn but extraordinarily accurate map of the course of the Nile.

We looked at the ruins of the Theological School which spread across a wooded ridge above the monastery, and descended along lanes between ilex, arbutus and Judas trees to the crescent-shaped shingly beach, where we ate a picnic lunch. Horseflies and wasps plagued us, while striped butterflies fluttered among the blackberry bushes. We then took the south-bound caique and sailed to the Bay of Iviron.

The ascent from the arsenal to the **Monastery of Iviron**, which spreads across a densely wooded ledge, is easy by Athonite standards. The monastery (idiorrhythmic) was founded in the tenth century by three Georgian monks (they called themselves Iberians and gave the monastery its name). Its maritime situation invited pirate raids and the monastery suffered much from Saracen attacks. In the fifteenth century the King of Georgia financed its reconstruction. But fire and earthquake took their toll, and most of the surviving buildings around the large irregular court, including belfry and *phiale*, are of the seventeenth century and not particularly distinguished: some of the chapels are painted red and one bright mauve. The south buttress wall, cracked from top to bottom by an earthquake, supports a ruined tower, one of the five that formerly crowned the walls.

Before the sun went down we looked at two of the smaller churches.

First the **Chapel of the Portaitissa,** situated where the Virgin addressed the pagan inhabitants and forbade any woman or female animal ever to enter her private garden. Ivory-inlaid doors lead from a hideously frescoed narthex into a small naos where the miraculous gold-sheathed icon of the Portaitissa (The Virgin of the Gate) is kept. The dark brown face is discernible through an overlay of gold decoration, surrounded by votive gifts. The monks of Iviron claim it to be the work of St Luke. According to a popular Athonite legend the icon, cast into the sea by its owner during the Iconoclast persecution, appeared seventy years later in the Bay of Iviron, standing upright on the waves. Above it a column of fire rose to heaven. The monks set out in rowing-boats to rescue it, but each time they approached the image, it retreated and a celestial voice was heard saying that only Gabriel, a Georgian anchorite who dwelt in a cave above the monastery, was worthy of recovering it. So Gabriel was summoned from his eyrie; after walking on the waves, he grasped the image and carried it lovingly, followed by the entire hierarchy of monks, to the church. But every night the image moved of its own accord to the monastery gates, until the Virgin told the perplexed monks in a vision that she had not come to Mount Athos to be protected, but to protect them, and when they were all gone she too would leave her beloved garden. So a chapel was built near the gate, and the icon has stayed there ever since.

The second chapel, that of St John the Baptist, supported by four columns of green serpentine, is built, superstition has it, on the site of the pagan temple where the idols fell down when the Virgin landed here. Disappointment awaited us in the **Library,** where all the illuminated manuscripts (several hundred) were packed and ready for removal to a new museum. From what I vaguely remember from a previous visit and find confirmed by other writers, I recommend the traveller to look for two leather-bound folios of the Bible, written in Georgian on parchment by St Euthymios, one of the three founders; two Gospels of the ninth and twelfth centuries; a particularly fine Book of Gospels of the eleventh century; several fifteenth-century editions of ancient Greek works set to type for the first time by the Venetian Aldine Press; and the imperial robe of Emperor John I Tsimisces (969–76) who, although a soldier and regicide, was also a champion of monastic life on Mount Athos.

Our sleeping quarters overlooked a steep slope of woodland – the drone of insects and cicadas in the hot airless valley was deafening – with just a glimpse of the Holy Sea beyond. The room was primitive, but there was no sign of the 'numberless tribes of vermin' which tenanted Curzon's chamber in the mid nineteenth century. A tap at the end of the gallery provided us with washing facilities. For dinner (served in an annexe of the kitchen) we had boiled beans and bread soaked in rancid olive oil, supplemented by our own processed cheese and *loucoumi*. There was as much wine as we wanted. We sat up late, talking to the guest-master, who was an authority on Athonite legends. It was all very pleasant after the regimentation of Vatopedi.

25 August
In the morning we visited the **Church of the Koimesis** (Dormition of the Virgin). The frescoes of the *liti* and narthex are over-restored and unattractive, but a set of beautiful Nicaean tiles inlaid in the exterior wall of the *liti* serve as a curtain-raiser to the quasi-Oriental lavishness of the naos: a scene of exceptional opulence, with pendant silver censers, bronze candelabra from which lighted tapers flicker in front of a gilded iconostasis, a huge chandelier, frescoes on the upper register, icons with gold backgrounds hanging on walls and pillars. The tenth-century **pavement of Opus Alexandrinum** – marbles of orange, pink and mauve blending with ophite, porphyry and verd-antique – is contemporary with the original foundation, the bronze band round the medallion in the centre bearing the inscription of the Georgian founders. The great chandelier, a trophy captured by a Byzantine emperor in a campaign in the east, is carved with pigmy-like effigies including an allegory of Love, a Buddha-like deity and Persian soldiers; the immense enamelled corona, which surrounds it, decorated with crosses, double-headed eagles and arched frames for icons, came from Moscow in 1902. In front of the sixteenth-century iconostasis, which is crowned by an ormulu gilt cross, there is an extraordinary early nineteenth-century object: a silver lemon tree, also of Muscovite origin. Russian donations to Iviron were traditional, and in 1654 the Tsar Alexius underwent a miraculous cure through the agency of a duplicate icon of the Portaitissa. In his gratitude he presented the monks with lands near Moscow which greatly added to their revenues. (A jewel-studded Book of Gospels weighing twenty-seven kilos, the gift of Peter the Great, its cover embossed with religious scenes and floral designs, is now displayed in the museum). Behind the iconostasis there are ampullae, chalices, crucifixes, pyxes and a beautiful **silver gilt cross**, a masterpiece of Byzantine silverware. The whole church is lambent with copper, brass, gold and silver; the effect is almost barbaric in its splendour. It is not easy to forget its Georgian origins.

Frescoes cover every inch of wall space on the upper register. The finest is the **Pantocrator** in the dome (probably twelfth-century) set against a gold fan-shaped background ribbed with lines like the spokes of a wheel, the hub of which is Christ's head. His expression is haggard but serene, and thin gold brush-strokes emphasize and fill out the folds of drapery. Below him are the Virgin *Orans* and the Archangels (fifteenth-century).

The church is rich in icons. Portative images hang on walls, some obscured by age, others new and gaudy, all with the familiar attributes of monkish iconography: crude symbolism, robust colour schemes, picturesque detail. The devotional icons, placed on stands or on the iconostasis, include an early image of the Virgin holding the Child surrounded by angels set in a rococo frame (north transept) and a magnificent **Deisis** (south-west transept) overlaid with gold plate so finely embossed that the draperies recall the work of some ancient sculptor. More icons, some of which are ancient and a few beautiful, adorn the walls of the restored refectory.

After lunch I walked over a shoulder of steep woodland north of the monastery and looked down on the coastline: at the castellated pile of Stavronikita and the waves breaking on the cliff of Pantocrator. Higher up in the valley, abandoned hermitages were scattered among copses of poplars, and the domes of Karyes glistened in the sun.

The caique for the Grand Lavra arrived at about four; the wind had dropped and the Holy Sea was smooth, with just a faint swell. As we chugged southward the coast became more abrupt; forest smells drifted across the water which turned from indigo blue to aquamarine and pearl grey. The peak of Athos, divested of its nebulous corona, tapered into the clear air. A waste of sea stretched east and south. Beyond the arsenal of the inland monastery of Philotheou (see p. 298) we caught a glimpse of Karakallou and its handsome tower surrounded by cypress trees and nut groves (see p. 298). The coast, almost unbroken, became more wild and desolate. Suddenly we were sailing into a hidden creek, like a pirate's lair, in the shadow of a concrete tower – the arsenal of the **Grand Lavra**. I thought of Curzon landing here in the nineteenth century and telling his dragoman: 'Well . . . we are at Mount Athos; so suppose you walk up to the monastery, and get some mules or monks, or something or other to carry up the saddle-bags. Tell them the celebrated Milordos Inglesis, the friend of the Universal Patriarch . . . kindly intends to visit their monastery; and that he is a great ally of the Sultan's, and of all the captains of all the men-of-war

that come down to the archipelago: and . . . make haste now . . .'
Alas, we did not possess Curzon's credentials. We climbed for over
half an hour up a steep hill pock-marked with bushes of holly-oak
and arbutus, along the path that St Athanasius climbed when he
first landed here, fighting prowling demons all the way, to found the
first monastery.

In the failing light we discerned grey stone shapes ahead: a tower
and rampart; then the wall-girt buildings of the idiorrhythmic
monastery stretching across a ledge surrounded by vineyards and
dominated by a rocky spur of the Holy Mountain, on a ledge of
which was situated the fourteenth-century hermitage of St Gregory
Palamas, champion of the Hesychasts. The sun had just set and we
heard the creak of wood on ancient hinges as the gates were slammed
behind us. We passed through a domed porch and entered what
seemed to be a small medieval town: a maze of cobbled alleys,
vaulted passages and small courts surrounded by low buildings with
cupolas and slate roofs. Monks were chatting with lay labourers.
A German student, who had left Iviron early in the morning and
walked all day across the wildest stoniest part of the peninsula,
told us of views of 'unparalleled splendour'. But his shoes were in
a terrible state. We had dinner in the guest-house – over twenty of
us, all lay visitors. By nine o'clock everybody had gone to bed.
From the gallery above the court, speckled with shadows of lemon
trees, I could hear jackals shrieking in the vineyards. Gradually the
unearthly whine drew nearer until I had the impression that entire
packs of these scavenging beasts were prowling below the walls,
hunting for carrion.

26 August

Early in the morning the court was full of animation. Monks were
unloading baskets of marrows from the backs of braying donkeys,
gardeners carrying picks and shovels, accompanied by boys shouting,
as they set out for the fields and vineyards. Fruit trees and vine
trellises, beds of straggling zinnias and pots of flaming salvias give
the Lavra a rustic village-like air. There is little order in the layout
of chapels, cells, arched troughs, wooden stairways and turrets, all
surrounded by grey walls within an area of several acres. The court
preserves something of the original *lavra*, a community of hermitages
which existed before the monastery was built in 963. The foundation
arose out of the friendship between Athanasius, a Bithynian ascetic,
to whose pioneering spirit the future theocracy owes so much,
and the dour puritanical general, Nicephorus Phocas. At the outset

of the Cretan campaign (961) the general persuaded his pious friend to bless Byzantine arms. As soon as victory was won, he vowed, he would himself become a monk. But after inflicting a decisive defeat on the Saracens, Phocas found the prospect of usurping the throne more attractive than fulfilling his promise. So he placated Athanasius by founding the monastery which was to retain precedence over all others on Mount Athos. It was further enriched by John I Tsimisces, Phocas's assassin and successor on the throne. Unlike most Athonite monasteries, the Grand Lavra has never been destroyed by fire and the main tower is part of the original tenth-century foundation.

We first looked at the eighteenth-century **Chapel of the Panayia Koukouzelissa** (The Virgin of Koukouzelis), which is associated with another popular Athonite legend. Koukouzelis was a thirteenth-century goatherd who had a beautiful voice. As he roamed the slopes above the monastery singing hymns, his flock would stop browsing and trip round him in dancing measures. The omnipresent Virgin was so delighted with the youth's melodious warblings that she pressed a gold coin in his hand while he slept in front of her icon, which now hangs in the chapel and is named after him: a jewel-studded silver gilt image in rather dubious taste. It afterwards acquired wonder-working properties. In 1945 a forest fire spread dangerously near the Grand Lavra. The icon was carried to the gates and the flames retreated. In the minds of simple Greeks thaumaturgical icons are still regarded as the most efficacious antidotes against misfortune, ill-health and natural calamities.

The librarian conducted us round the sights. The **phiale**, a seventeenth-century restoration of an earlier construction, shaded by two ancient cypresses planted by St Athanasius, is the most beautiful on Mount Athos: a tea-cosy dome (frescoed within) resting on arches filled with brick inlay and supported by little columns crowned with block capitals. The balustrade is composed of marble panels carved with designs of rosettes, birds, leaves and pine-cones; the bronze jet is decorated with animals surmounted by an eagle. At Epiphany the holy water is consecrated in the huge porphyry basin before the whole community of monks. The **Church of the Koimesis**, whose architectural pattern – Greek Cross flanked by two cruciform chapels – became the model for all Athonite churches, is not without blemishes. There is a squatness about the proportions, with weighty vaults and massive apses; the cupola is the largest on Mount Athos; the exterior walls are painted bright puce. The frescoes of the *liti* and narthex are tasteless examples of early nineteenth-century work. Impressive metal-faced oak doors of the Middle Byzantine period, elaborately decorated in *repoussé* technique with rosettes, petals, scrolls, vine leaves and crosses studded with gems, open into the naos, which is less splendid than that of Iviron. The two columns at the west end are part of the original tenth-century structure. On the screen, a nineteenth-century castellated stone monstrosity, hang two splendid **icons**, gifts of the Emperor Michael IX Palaeologus (1293–1320): the Virgin with doe-like eyes and convex cheeks; Christ, with aquiline features and deep, penetrating expression, holding a Book of Gospels. Part of the main apse is hallowed ground, and no human foot is allowed to tread on the spot where St Athanasius fell, broke his back and died, while helping to raise the dome. The Chapel of the Forty Martyrs (left) contains his silver-encased tomb draped in a mauve cloth decorated with crosses. The walls of the Chapel of St Nicholas (right) are painted with sixteenth-century frescoes by Frangos Catelanos, a Theban educated in Italy, executed in a somewhat bogus Venetian manner.

More important, though restored, are the **frescoes** of the naos, the work of Theophanes, a master of the Cretan School of painting, who died at the Grand Lavra in the early sixteenth century. Crete was then occupied by Venetians, not Turks – an important distinction. While open to Italian stylistic innovations, Cretan painters remained faithful to the old tradition of formalism and symbolism. In spite of an advance in technique, a new interest in the dramatic and picturesque, conservatism still holds Byzantine religious art in firm, if slightly loosened, shackles. Theophanes's work seems more monkish and mystical than human and emotional; but his draughtsmanship and feeling for clarity are apparent in the grandiose Dormition of the Virgin, dominated by the noble figure of Christ holding the Virgin's soul (above the main doorway). For an agreeable blend of colours one should turn to the Transfiguration, with its ochre rocks and mauve-tinted draperies, to the brown angels with gold haloes below the Pantocrator, to the procession of saints and fathers of the church with glittering nimbuses on the lower zone. Every known trick of the brush is used to make the figures identifiable symbols, to heighten the dramatic allegory.

The walls of the disused **refectory**, the largest on Mount Athos, built in the shape of a cross (the fixed marble-topped tables forming a cross within a cross), are also covered with frescoes (also restored) by Theophanes and his Cretan disciples. The Last Supper spreads across the west apse, where the abbot once sat. Other scenes have to do with eating: the miracle of the loaves of bread, the supper at

Emmaus, Elijah fed by the raven. More moving is the **Dormition of St Athanasius** (north apse), a lyrical scene filled with mourning figures within a semi-circular rampart, with a pink church symbolizing the dome that caused the saint's death at the apex and monastic dependents kneeling in worship in the folds of undulating hills beyond the walls. The south transept is filled with a panoramic vision of the **Last Judgement**, a confused assemblage of figures, incidents, allegories. The layout follows that of most Byzantine Last Judgements: on the top band, angels, apostles, the Virgin, Christ in Glory from whose feet flows the River of Fire; in the middle zone, groups of prophets, patriarchs, bishops, martyrs, choirs of holy women; on the lower register, sinners, devils and the grisly Monster of Hell into whose gaping jaws avenging angels energetically cast damned souls, depicted as puny naked figures.

To the right (north) of the refectory, a huge *simandron*, twelve feet long, beaten only on the most solemn occasions, hangs from metal chains beside a bell-tower. We passed the goldfish basin which St Athanasius dragged up the hill in the form of a block of unhewn stone as he warded off the assaults of demons who broke his ankle but were finally driven off by blows from his iron-tipped staff. The spot where the saintly foot was imprinted on the rim in the course of the skirmish is marked by a cross.

The librarian, anxious to hurry us on, and inclined to gabble his information (obviously learnt by heart), led us to the **treasury**, which possesses the gifts of the two Emperor-benefactors of the tenth century: the chasuble of Nicephorus Phocas, which he wore over a hair-shirt (he believed in self-mortification), his imperial crown studded with pearls, precious stones and gold leaf and surmounted by a jewelled cross, and his **Book of Gospels** with a superb cover on which Christ is depicted standing on a dais under an arch within a rectangular frame of precious stones; an early **mosaic icon of St John the Divine**, set within a frame of mosaic medallions in each of which a saint is portrayed, presented by John I Tsimisces, together with an exquisitely wrought jewel-studded **gold cross**, in whose arms splinters of the True Cross are concealed. There are also reliquaries and chrysobulls, brooches and pendants glittering with emeralds, sapphires and amethysts, ecclesiastical stoles of the fifteenth and sixteenth centuries and vestments embroidered with scenes of the Dodecaorton.

The **library** possesses eight hundred manuscripts on parchment. We looked at some leaves of St Paul's Letters to the Corinthians and Galatians from a sixth-century codex, an eighth-century illuminated Book of Gospels, a tenth-century illuminated manuscript of Dioscorides's *Manual of Botany*, an eleventh-century manuscript of Plutarch's *Lives* and a fifteenth-century first printed edition of Homer.

After an early lunch of bean soup and tomatoes, we descended to the arsenal to catch the two o'clock caique. Nothing could be more spectacular, in a sense more forbidding, than the journey round the cape. The wind had dropped, and the sea was smooth, metallic. The caique hugged the coast, which became increasingly abrupt and desolate beyond the arsenal of the Romanian skete of Prodromou. We passed the mouth of the **Cave of the Wicked Dead** high up on the cliff-side. Its fetid chambers, the exile of excommunicated monks, were said to have been littered with bloated corpses with horny talons and hair that grew to their ankles, for the bodies of renegade monks, contrary to the laws of nature, did not undergo decomposition. We doubled **Cape Akrothos**. The bases of towering screes were fringed with gigantic boulders that have hurtled down in primeval landslides, composing into ramparts of contorted stone sliced by horizontal fissures formed by millennia of erosion. Grottoes were made up of a succession of arched tunnels in which the water swished and gurgled. Around here Mardonius's fleet was dashed to pieces in a storm in 492 BC and the Persian sailors were 'seized and devoured', says Herodotus, by 'man-eating monsters' that infested the waters.

Sailing between razor-edged reefs, we saw two seemingly inaccessible *kellia* (solitaries' eyries), perched hundreds of feet above the sea, and the formidable ravine up which Peter the Anchorite, the first hermit, climbed single-handed. The Eastern mystical tradition of attaining the good life through the purest asceticism is easily comprehended in this savage setting. Another cave, until recently inhabited by a solitary, overhangs a dizzy ledge, forming part of the eyrie of St Neilos, from whose corpse myrrh trickled down the side of the scree and floated on the waves in patches of luminous gold so that sailors came to collect it and afterwards sold it to pious worshippers. Six thousand feet above towered the limestone crest of Athos, crowned by a white chapel. Strabo says people who scaled the final peak could 'see the sun rise three hours before it rises on the seaboard', and its shadow is supposed to be cast across the Aegean as far as the island of Skiathos ('in the shade of Athos').

Suddenly the desolation is relieved by a glimpse of human habitation. The skete of **Kavsokalyvia**, a dependency of the Grand Lavra, winds vertically up the side of a fertile gulley. Chapels with domes and

slate roofs and whitewashed cottages, inhabited by monkish iconographers, are surrounded by clusters of bay trees from whose leaves
laurel oil is pressed. Here dwelt St Akakios, who took flight one
day in a religious transport and floated up to the summit of Athos
where he met the Virgin. We passed two rowing-boats propelled by
black-robed hermits with white beards. They waved and went on
fishing.

As we rounded Cape Pinnes, where the screes acquire a deep
pinkish, almost fiery, hue, the skete of **Karoulia** burst into view: a
chain of eyries straggling up a perpendicular streak of vegetation
and connected with each other by a cobbled track (just wide enough
to allow the passage of a single mule) which has replaced an ancient
system of communication whereby the hermits, on visits to each
other, clung to the ropes or chains passing over makeshift pulleys.
Little shelves of soil are terraced one above the other, planted with
vegetables and a few vines, surrounded by cacti. It is like the
Ladder of Heaven in the Last Judgement. A blue dome was visible
and some huts where more worldly-minded hermits carve religious
souvenirs and crosses of deer-horn which are sold at Karyes. The
next skete was **St Anne's**. Each shelf in the vertical succession of
eyries is connected with the next by primitive aqueducts made of
hollowed-out trunks of pine and cypress through which streams
cascade from one vegetable plot to another. Modern icons are
painted by the inhabitants of these vertiginous abodes. In the
church of St Anne there is a venerable relic: St Anne's left foot. We
had now doubled the promontory and put in at the Nea Skete, an
eighteenth-century dependency of the Monastery of St Paul, where
the woollen socks worn by Athonite monks are knitted by hermits.
The slope of the mountain was less abrupt and there was a green
foreshore, with some modern houses, like suburban maisonettes,
scattered among orchards.[10]

We sailed into the Singitic Gulf. On our starboard, high up on
the mountainside, rose the fortress of the Monastery of St Paul
(see pp. 286–8). The coast was still steep, but wooded and more
broken. One could imagine men dwelling in this country. We were
chugging towards the **Monastery of Dionysiou**: four storeys of
whitewashed cells with projecting balconies, roofed with slate tiles

---

[10] On request the caique will put in at the port of any skete. St Anne's, Karoulia
and Kavsokalyvia are the most important. It is impossible, however, to include
them in the eight-day itinerary outlined in this chapter. They possess no art
treasures. The hermits are generally friendly. Accommodation is extremely
primitive.

and crowned by a medieval tower, soaring above an immense foundation of wall that rises like a stone pier from an isolated bluff above the shore.

From the arsenal we climbed a cobbled path, between plane and walnut trees, overhanging the torrent-bed of the Aeropotamos (The Windy River), so-called because sudden currents of cold air whistle down it from the mountain. Terraced kitchen-gardens were bordered with oleanders and we noticed peach trees heavy with golden fruit. By the entrance gate there is a fountain of cold water and a belvedere overlooking the peaceful gulf.

It was five o'clock and we were hustled off to dinner in the refectory. The rhythm would be different now. We were in a cenobitic house – one of the friendliest and most beautiful on the peninsula. The monks here are not just refugees or vagabonds from the world, anxious to secure free board and lodging in return for gabbling parrot-like praises of the Lord in a haze of incense. The spirit of contemplation and communion still exists here, and frugality has some relation to godliness.

The rock on which the monastery is perched allows no room for outward expansion. Cells, storerooms, galleries pile up, supported on struts, one above the other. At the summit of the pinnacle is the crimson-painted church within its cramped court. The origins of the monastery's foundation go back to an eremitical vision. In the fourteenth century a hermit called Dionysius dwelt in a neighbouring eyrie. One night he noticed flames leaping heavenward from the bluff above the sea. Every night the supernatural blaze grew brighter. Interpreting the message correctly, he begged his brother, a Trapezuntine bishop, to persuade the Emperor Alexius III of Trebizond to build a monastery on the holy spot. And it was called after him – Dionysiou.

The beautifully proportioned **refectory**, entirely frescoed, is T-shaped, with arches at the point where the arms join the stem. As we ate – a Lucullan feast by Athonite standards (pilaff with fried squid, tomatoes stuffed with rice and garlic, peaches, bread and rough red wine) – a deacon mounted the brightly painted pulpit and read from the menology, while we gazed round the frescoed walls. Shafts of light, slanting through the windows, fell on gruesome scenes of martyrdoms: severed heads surrounded by gold nimbuses rolling on marble floors, ferocious Roman legionaries brandishing blood-stained swords, bodies clad in nothing but loin-cloths, hanging upside down. The principal frescoes are of the sixteenth to seventeenth centuries: the Last Supper in the east apse above the abbatial table;

scenes from the life of Christ and the Virgin on the upper register, saints and ascetics as usual on the lower band; a vast **Last Judgement**, reminiscent, in its multiplicity of detail and grouping of figures (but not in artistic merit), of Giotto's rendering of the same scene painted over two hundred years earlier in the Arena Chapel. The Ladder of Heaven is full of animation and comings and goings. Figures in mauve and yellow garments anxiously scale the celestial rungs, urged on by officious angels. At the top they are received by Christ standing against a star-studded sky. The ones who drop off are pounced upon by spiteful demons. At the bottom of the pit wind the coils of the snake-like Monster of Hell with two expressionless eyes set wide apart; a damned soul dives head first into its gruesome maw.

The cool pleasant cloister of the refectory is frescoed with lively apocalyptic scenes: the Four Horsemen, martial and purposeful, conscious of the power that 'was given unto them over the fourth part of the earth, to kill with sword, and with hunger, and with death, and with the beasts of the earth';[11] the Earthquake, with the roofs of buildings collapsing in a strangely geometric fashion, while stars rain down from garlands of soap-bubble clouds framing discs of the Sun and Moon which have smug patronizing expressions.

We attended vespers in the dark frescoed church, spellbound by the voice of a young beardless monk chanting the litanies in a soaring tenor, while hoary old men, bent double with fatigue and infirmity, muttered *Kyrie Eleison! Kyrie Eleison!* ('Lord have mercy! Lord have mercy!'). They then kissed the holy images, which represent the one visible and palpable manifestation of Heaven on earth, and shuffled out, removing the veils they attach to their hats during the liturgy. There was little to do but to retire to our bedroom on the top floor of this complex eyrie of corridors and projecting balconies. From the windows there was a drop, absolutely sheer, of hundreds of feet to the base of the bluff fringed by a rocky shore.

28 August
In the morning an amiable librarian took us sightseeing. The **Church of Ayios Ioannis Prodromos** follows the usual Athonite plan. The sixteenth-century **frescoes** possess a harmony and homogeneity, a fluidity of design and freshness of colour rare in the grandiose wall-paintings of the ancient and more venerable churches of Vatopedi and Iviron. Less opulence in the way of gold and marble decoration also creates an atmosphere of greater restraint and concentration. The artist is Zorsi, a native of Crete, possibly of Venetian origin.

[11] Revelation, VI, 2–8.

His work is more Italianate, less monkish, than that of his compatriot Theophanes (see p. 279). His draperies billow and swirl and his architectural backgrounds are more integrated. On the debit side, the loss of rigidity entails a corresponding loss of sturdiness. But the softness never degenerates into insipidity.

From the dome the Pantocrator blesses mankind. Angels, standing on a green lawn, surround him. In the pendentives the Evangelists write their Gospels among pink and blue shadows, surrounded by desks, lecterns and footstools. Opposite the Nativity (barrel vault of south apse) St John baptizes Christ, who is immersed in the waters of Jordan, against a star-studded sky. In the Transfiguration (south apse) the ethereal figure on the pinnacle of Mount Tabor is clad in a pale blue robe with a coral pink glory, its triple aureole reflecting the Hesychast doctrine of 'Uncreated Light' emanating from all three persons of the Trinity. In the Descent into Hell (north transept) the three main protagonists, Christ, Adam and Eve (both in imploring attitudes), are boldly projected against a background of Limbo. In a barrel vault of the north transept there is a beautiful Incredulity of Thomas, a strangely static composition, with a serene Christ standing in the central arch of the colonnade. The mourners in the Dormition of the Virgin (above the main doorway) emerge out of a haze of funereal colours: dull blues, greys and mauves. In the Betrayal 'lanterns and torches and weapons' are borne aloft by the 'band of *men* and officers from the chief priests and Pharisees'[12] and the grouping of figures is strikingly Giottesque (it is not impossible that the Italo-Cretan Zorsi was acquainted with the Arena frescoes in Padua).

In the **library** we saw the famous **chrysobull of Alexius III of Trebizond**, the imperial charter confirming the foundation of the monastery, which Finlay calls 'one of the most valuable monuments of the pictorial and calligraphic art of the Greeks in the Middle Ages'. On the piece of parchment (more than twelve feet long and eight inches wide), on which the scarlet of the imperial ink vies with the golds and bluish-greens of uncials entwined with tendrils, a majestic Christ is depicted in the act of blessing Alexius and his Empress. Among the manuscripts are a twelfth-century Book of Gospels with a cover decorated with enamelled interstices and a figure of Christ on the Cross between the Virgin and St John, and another of the thirteenth century with an earlier cover minutely carved in wood with scenes from the Dodecaorton.

After nine o'clock lunch in the refectory, we chartered a caique

[12] St John, XVIII, 3.

to take us to the Monastery of St Paul. From the jetty we saw baskets of peaches, dangling at the end of long ropes, being hauled up by monks on a balcony that projected above the great supporting wall. We struck a bargain with the caique-master and chartered his boat for the next two days. This would enable us to visit the last group of monasteries on the west coast without having to spend a night in each of them.

From the arsenal of the **Monastery of St Paul** we walked for over half an hour up a stony path in a wild and rocky landscape. The monastery straddles the mouth of a savage ravine against a background of terrific precipices, its walls rising like a vast medieval stronghold out of the scrubland. To the east a lofty crenellated wall protects the monks' cells from the icy blasts that funnel out of the ravine in winter. The approach is strewn with boulders washed down by torrents or hurtled across the thyme-scented mountainside by landslides. The last lap of the painful ascent is along a cobbled path, trellised with vines. Beside the gate there is a pergola where we rested, listening to the gibberish of a lay vagrant – one of the many who roam the peninsula in search of a bed and free meal – whose limbs shook as though he were struck with the palsy. Fumbling in the pockets of his verminous clothes for a Book of Gospels, he then read several passages aloud, looking up occasionally to leer obscenely at us. Wandering through empty courts and galleries, we finally tracked down the guest-master who led us to a spacious guest-house overlooking the stony waste and offered us plum jam, coffee and *ouzo*.

The original establishment was founded in the tenth century by a hermit named Paul, a contemporary of St Athanasius, who heard an unearthly voice instructing him to build a house of God on the site of his cave. The monastery, now cenobitic, was largely destroyed by fire in 1902. Monkish carelessness, the lavish use of woodwork for constructional purposes, candles burning beside holy images, have all contributed to the outbreak of these devastating conflagrations in which much of the original structure of numerous Athonite houses has perished. At St Paul only the Chapel of St George, the sixteenth-century tower (the tallest on Mount Athos), and the great east wall survive. The other buildings are modern and of little interest.

We climbed a series of wooden stairways to the **Chapel of St George,** built (allegedly on the site of the hermit Paul's rock-dwelling) into the fortified wall which forms a backcloth to the monastery against a further screen of stupendous cliffs. The chapel, overlooking the domes of the Church of the Presentation of the Virgin, is small: a barrel-vaulted basilica with a narthex. An inscription, possibly spurious, dates it to 1423, but the **frescoes** are more closely related to the Cretan School of the sixteenth century. Whatever their date, they have the distinction, rare among frescoes on Mount Athos, of being wholly unrestored. In their freshness and luminosity, in the subtlety, delicacy and transparency of their colour tints – light yellows and greens, whitish and roseate hues – they compare favourably with the best work of the late Byzantine period.

The tone is set immediately by the saints and ascetics ranged round the walls of the narthex. Each figure stands out as an individual. The frescoes of the naos, battered though untarnished, still glow with much of their original variety of colour. The faces are expressive and the garments lavish. The space is so confined that there is no difficulty in identifying the scenes. The mood of the **Nativity** is serene and pastoral, with a relaxed Virgin reclining on a faded pink couch, while the Child lies swaddled like a little mummy in the crib, and a white dog crouches in the shade of a silvery olive tree. The rocks in the background are the colour of pale honey. In the **Presentation of Christ**, the figures in mauve, aquamarine and brown robes move across a background of a plum-coloured canopy supported by rust-coloured columns. A bejewelled Bible, its pages edged with pink, lies on a table between the Virgin and Simeon, who receives the Child. The **Transfiguration**, though ill-proportioned, reveals the artist's virtuosity in blending non-primary colours. In the **Raising of Lazarus** white-bearded figures in robes of dove grey and various shades of pink, framed between yellow rocks, watch the unwinding of the mummy's shroud against a snow-white castellated background under a sombre sky. Across the vault are **medallions of the Virgin and Child and six prophets**, each a compelling portrait. On the north wall SS Peter and Paul are depicted in the act of embracing. Notice also Paul, founder of the monastery, depicted with a very mangy beard – an allusion to the fact that he was a eunuch.

We walked down to the arsenal in the sizzling heat. Lizards scuttled among scorched shrubs. We swam off a pebbly shore in what are said to be shark-infested waters. Centuries ago the inmates of Dionysiou, perched on their highest balcony, watched a shark frustrated in the act of swallowing a monk bathing in the cove below. Stretching his arms outwards, the holy man arranged his body in the shape of a cross so that the shark was unable to devour him. No sea monsters disturbed the translucent water on this occasion. The boulders and cliffs rising sheer above were horizontally seamed with brightly coloured stratifications: puce and brown, amber, olive green and pink.

We got back to Dionysiou to find the monks in a state of unusual animation. It was the eve of the feast of the Assumption of the Virgin, and the beardless chorister whose voice had impressed us the night before wandered round the monastery beating the *simandron* with his little mallet. The tinkling tune echoed across the galleries girdling the crimson church, which now represented a microcosm of the Kingdom of Heaven, towards which the Virgin's soul was being borne aloft by angels. There was a strong smell of incense. The service lasted all night, without a break. We went into the church several times. Some of the weary, hungry monks (they had not touched meat or fish for a fortnight) slept as they leant on their staffs. Others sneezed when a deacon swung a censer under their noses. There was no formality – the absence of pews in an Orthodox church tends to make clergy and congregation wholly unselfconscious. Priests came and went. Hour after hour the Divine Office went on, to the accompaniment of the plaintive eight-tone chant. In the cloisters and passages veiled black-robed figures lingered, whispered for a moment and disappeared into the church, crossing themselves.

29 August

Early in the morning we sailed in our chartered caique to the cenobitic **Monastery of Gregoriou**. Like Dionysiou, though less beautiful and interesting, it is perched on a bluff above a creek. A ruined tower and wilted palm tree crown the pile of buildings, whose wooden balconies of different colours overhang the sea.

We were received by the abbot who led us to an ugly refectory, where we lunched with all the monks on pieces of dried cod-fish fried in the most rancid oil I have ever tasted, followed by custard, washed down with vinegary wine. We soon recovered our spirits, however, in an airy gallery with walls painted sky blue, from which there was a prodigious view of the wild abrupt coastline stretching southwards. A heavy bank of cloud was settling on the peak of Athos.

The monastery was founded by Gregory, a hermit of Mount Sinai, in the thirteenth century. Fire destroyed it in the eighteenth, and all the buildings are relatively modern. The exterior walls of the church of Ayios Nikolaos are painted blue, and dark magenta drums support grey metal-sheeted domes. The eighteenth-century frescoes of the interior are without distinction. At the north end of the naos

Pella: the Lion Hunt Floor Mosaic. The attitudes of both men and beast form a perfectly balanced composition.

Castoria: houses in the old town.

The Nazim House at Castoria: wall paintings in the small salon

there is a venerated but not very ancient icon of the Galaktotro-
phousa (The Virgin Giving Suck), in which the Virgin is depicted
with a sour peevish expression offering her breast to the Child. Her
mantle of red, orange and gold is very effective.

By mid-morning we were sailing northward below the fourteenth-
century **Monastery of Simopetra**, seven storeys of strut-supported
wooden galleries crowning a foundation wall twice as formidable
as that of Dionysiou, soaring into the air out of dark green woods a
thousand feet above sea level, and joined to the mountainside by
an imposing aqueduct with a double tier of arches. During a great
fire in the sixteenth century panic-stricken monks hurled themselves
over the balconies and were dashed to pieces on the boulder-strewn
vegetable plots below. From the arsenal it is about an hour's steep
climb to the monastery. Simopetra's façade may be the most theatrical
on the Holy Mountain; otherwise it has little to offer, except an
aerial view of the peninsula and gulf.[13]

Beyond the arsenal of Simopetra the scenery becomes tamer. We
put in at Daphni, our original starting-point, in time for a late lunch,
then hugged the coast, the most domesticated on Mount Athos.
The sky had become overcast and by the time we reached the
arsenal of St Panteleimon drops of rain were falling on an oily
grey sea. A gentle ramp leads from a waterfront of tall, gutted
warehouses and woodcutters' shacks into a fantasy Russian town in
miniature.

The **Monastery of St Panteleimon**, commonly called Roussiko
(The Russian One), is one of the most extraordinary sights on
Mount Athos: not because of its antiquarian interest – it has none
– but because of its decayed splendour, with spires, bell-towers and
paved courts on different levels, its thirty churches and chapels,
their red roofs crowned with onion domes and gold crosses, forming
a vast Russian enclave in an Aegean setting of pine-woods, cypress
thickets and olive groves.

The early foundation of the twelfth century was dedicated to St
Panteleimon, a court physician and convert to Christianity, whose
martyrdom in the reign of Diocletian was distinguished by the
extraordinary resistance shown by his head to every attempt at
severance by the most stalwart executioners. It finally succumbed,
wreathed in a resplendent halo, to the blows of the mightiest axe in
the Roman Empire. He remains a popular patron of doctors and
medical institutions. After the Byzantine era the monastery fell on
bad days and it was not until the early nineteenth century that the

[13] For the Monastery of Simopetra see also p. 298.

influence of Mother Russia, head of Christian Orthodoxy since the fall of Constantinople, reached the Aegean and led to a rapid influx of Russian monks. The Russian Government, always eager to secure support in Greece against their traditional common enemy, Turkey, exploited the link between the sister Churches and showered wealth on the Holy Mountain, and on St Panteleimon in particular. At the turn of the century it was the largest and most active monastery in the whole Athonite community, and the number of Slav monks on the Peninsula amounted to two thousand, as against three thousand Greeks. This was the culmination of a connection between the Byzantine and Slavonic worlds begun a thousand years before when St Cyril and St Methodious left Constantinople to convert the first Slavs to Christianity. But after 1917 few novices found their way to St Panteleimon. Less than a dozen monks, flat-faced Russian peasants, have survived to drag out their last senile years in this decaying nineteenth-century stage-set.

We carried our bags along tiled paths, past deserted chapels covered with lichen, until we reached a large unkempt court. An old monk with matted red beard, prominent cheek-bones and light-coloured rheumy eyes was crouching on the ground. As we drew nearer we observed that he was feeding armies of ants with bread-crumbs. We addressed the monk in Greek. He replied in Russian, but seemed to understand what we wanted. Arranging his breadcrumbs in a little pile on the ground, he shuffled off, returning after a few minutes with a lay guest-master who led us through a gloomy gallery to a shuttered drawing-room filled with peeling leather armchairs and sofas covered with antimacassars. Photographs of the Tsar, Tsarina and Tsarewich and related royalty (Edward VII, the Kaiser) hung on the walls. The ritual coffee and *ouzo* were produced.

Later, shafts of sunlight, penetrating the cloud bank, shone on gold crosses and green domes, as we wandered along trellised passages, across tiled courts, up and down stairways with ornamental balustrades, past neglected flowerbeds shaded by limp palms. We saw a fountain and a chapel with columns crowned with Corinthian capitals and pedestals with cornucopias from which dusty ferns drooped languidly. The exterior of the church of Ayios Panteleimon is pleasing: its walls painted coral pink, its domes sheeted with grey metal. The interior is a mass of gold and gilt, with an outsize chandelier and corona. The frescoes would do credit to the illustrator of a children's book of Bible stories published in about 1910. The liturgy is celebrated in Slavonic, and the choir was once the most famous on Mount Athos. Across the inner court, opposite the church, is a huge refectory (1500 monks used to dine here), in the shape of a basilica with barrel-vault aisles and an apse at the west end. A belfry on three stepped levels, culminating in a lime-green spire, surmounts the edifice.

On the highest level, crowning the whole fantastic pile, are the two enormous **Chapels of the Protection of the Virgin and SS Alexander Nevsky, Vladimir and Olga,** which virtually form a single large cathedral, all gilt and ormulu and gold crosses and rococo columns, capable of accommodating a congregation of two thousand. The walls are hung with hideous icons, and marble pillars with Ionic capitals support the gallery. We then visited the official reception hall of the guest-house, filled with gilt-framed photographs of Tsars and other royalty, of Rasputin and famous abbots. All that was lacking, one felt, was an empty ballroom, ghost-like, echoing with familiar tunes from *Swan Lake*.[14]

Although this is a cenobitic house, meals are no longer served in the refectory. We dined by candlelight in the kitchen of the guest-house. Afterwards there was nothing to do but wander across the empty courts and watch the sheet-lightning flash across the southern sky above the Holy Mountain. Stumbling along a dark gallery, I heard mice scuttling about and thought I saw a gigantic spider hanging from a beam in the ceiling. No other monastery on Mount Athos has such a haunted air.

30 August
Early in the morning we walked to the cenobitic **Monastery of Xenophontos**: two storeys of projecting balconies, crowned by domes and broken towers, supported by strong walls, overlooking a sandy beach. It is a peaceful place, surrounded by green hills. A convoy of donkeys, carrying loads of wood, wound through the groves. The monastery owes much to Balkan benefactors. Founded in the eleventh century by a pious Byzantine nobleman called Xenophon, it was restored in the sixteenth by Moldo-Wallachian princes, in the eighteenth by Romanian hospodars.

Steps lead up from a sloping irregular court to the **Church of Ayios Georghios (St George)**, frescoed by two sixteenth-century artists of the Cretan School, Antonios and Theophanes (not to be confused with the more important Theophanes who worked at the Grand Lavra).[15] Their work is somewhat cold and hard – in a way typical

---

[14] Since my last visit to the monastery, fire has once more ravaged several buildings described here. Restoration work is in progress.
[15] The frescoes were restored in 1902 – on the whole, judiciously.

of the Cretan School – but that of Antonios is also bold and original, and the large scenes on the upper zone merit attention. The tragedy of the **Crucifixion** is stressed by sharp angularities, by hooded effigies of the sun and moon reflecting the darkness that fell over the earth between the sixth and ninth hours. A macabre quality haunts the **Lamentation over the Body of Christ**, in which a Virgin of unprecedented austerity mourns over the livid-hued body of Christ, and the attendant women, half-crazed with grief, tear their faces with their nails. In the **Dormition of the Virgin**, the Virgin's body lies horizontally on an ornate bier; a rigid vertical Christ is surrounded by angels; bishops are clad in gorgeous vestments and mourners in swirling robes, while the apostles arrive across the sky in soap-bubble clouds. The **Entry into Jerusalem** has a quality of starkness, an absence of architectural and incidental detail rare in this composition. Antonios's skill as a draughtsman may be halting, but he possesses remarkable virtuosity in the manipulation of colour; in the violence of his contrasts he is often extremely original, using pitch black (instead of indigo blue) skies as a background for his favourite Siena reds, corals and claret hues. Here, more than anywhere else on Mount Athos, it is possible to discern the origins of that explosion of luminosity and dramatic impressionism which was to distinguish the masterpieces of El Greco less than half a century later. In comparison, the work of Theophanes in the same church (a triple Crucifixion, another Entry into Jerusalem, an Ascension) seems trivial and insipid.

As the monastery grew in size and importance, the church was found too small and a larger edifice, also dedicated to St George, was raised in the early nineteenth century further up the slope. It is unfrescoed but possesses a fine collection of icons, a reliquary containing a drop of St John the Baptist's blood and two magnificent **mosaic panels** (portative icons) of the thirteenth century, representing St George and St Demetrius. They are executed in the minutest tesserae. Both faces emerge as portraits: young men of nobility, virile, sensitive and chivalrous.

Descending the ramp to the beach, we noticed a little stream of fresh water trickling through the pebbles on the spot where an icon of St George (now hanging on the south-east column of the new church) was found by monks centuries ago. Roughly man-handled by Iconoclasts, the icon oozed blood from a crack in the panel and was thrown into the sea. Months later it was tossed up on the shore of Xenophontos, whereupon the holy spring, whose waters are said to be purgative, gushed forth for the first time.

We began the last lap of our journey and were soon casting anchor off the landing-stage of the idiorrhythmic **Monastery of Docheiariou**. From the sea Docheiariou composes into one of the finest architectural ensembles on the peninsula, its buildings and dependencies spreading fan-wise against a background of hills speckled with pines and cypresses. Balconies overhang stout walls with elliptical blind arches, and a geometrical pattern of belfries, chimneys and slate roofs is dominated by a tower flanked by cypresses. A frescoed porch leads through a labyrinth of cool shady passages painted with murals into a small court. Pomegranate trees grow in the shade of walls covered with flowering creepers.

The monks say the monastery was founded by Euthymius, superintendent of stores (*docheiarios*) at the Grand Lavra and personal friend of St Athanasius. According to the historical record, the site was purchased from the monks of Xenophontos in the eleventh century and the church dedicated to the Archangel Michael, a staunch champion of Athonite holy men against Saracen pirates. The monastery enjoyed imperial benefaction and later that of Moldo-Wallachian Voivodes who restored the church after its destruction by corsairs in the sixteenth century.

In the shadow of the great tower, crenellated, machicolated and dated to the early sixteenth century, the wooden loggia of the charming eighteenth-century guest-house overlooks roofs and domes on different levels. After the usual refreshment, we visited the **Church of the Taxiarchoi** (Archangels), the largest and one of the most beautiful on the Holy Mountain. The exterior is of brick – a welcome change from the usual crimson stucco – and the blind arches are inlaid with dark wedge-shaped tiles between outer and inner curves. The interior is covered with sixteenth-century **frescoes** of the Cretan School, possibly by Zorsi, who worked at Dionysiou. Mid nineteenth century restoration has not deprived the paintings of their original liveliness, although there are some hard glossy tones and over-smooth surfaces which render the faces waxen and insipid. Across the north wall of the exo-narthex there is an enchanting representation (probably unrestored) of the **Dormition of St Ephraim**, the Mesopotamian bath-keeper who became one of the most popular hymnographers of the fourth century.[16] The mourners are grouped fan-wise round the bier. Long white beards, draperies and striped vestments form a symmetrical pattern of vertical lines.

[16] The hymns, 'Receive, O Lord, in Heaven above/Our prayers' and 'Virgin wholly marvellous' are translations into English from the original Syriac of St Ephraim.

The conch-shaped centrepiece is framed within bucolic scenes of eremitical life: hermits praying, reading holy books, riding donkeys, tending fields. A stylite perched on an ornate column casts a rope to haul up a basket of provisions. Flowers, stylized shrubs and trees sprout from the ground. The range of colours is subdued: dove greys, dull greens, browns. An air of muted serenity pervades the composition, and the lyrical mood recalls the Dormition of St Athanasius at the Grand Lavra.

In the narthex the Archangels flank the main doorway into the naos; to the left, the Virgin enthroned holds the Child clad in gold robes. Beside her St Nicholas, wearing an elaborate vestment, presents a reliquary. A complementary panel on the south wall represents Christ with an open Book of Gospels and St John the Baptist unfolding a scroll. On the same wall bunches of grapes hang from the Tree of Life. Scenes from the Old and New Testaments, framed within medallions formed by tendrils, decorate the north wall and a naked Adam tames wild animals: a lion, panther, elephant, stag, monkey.

The **naos** is lofty and beautifully proportioned, the tall central drum supported by four granite columns. A slab of green marble on the pavement commemorates one of the Archangel's miracles. A shepherd boy of Sithonia, who had found hidden treasure, was assaulted by monks possessed by demons. They tied a marble slab to his neck, dropped him in the sea and made off with the treasure. Floundering in the waves, the boy called on the Archangel for help. St Michael promptly came to his rescue, carried him tenderly to the shore and laid his body, dripping wet, on the floor of the church at Docheiariou, where he was found by a monk beating the *simandron* just before matins. As in the two narthexes, every available inch of wall space is frescoed. In the **Transfiguration** (south lunette), Christ, a white wraith, radiates 'Uncreated Light' from the summit of the stepped rocks of Mount Tabor. On either side, Moses and Elijah stand on desolate plateaux seamed with symmetrical crevices. The same sense of order and symmetry prevails in the **Descent into Hell** (north lunette), in which Christ bestrides the shattered gates of Hell strewn with broken locks, and a diminutive angel fetters Beelzebub with chains. On the gilded iconostasis, a typically fussy example of eighteenth-century wood carving: biblical episodes intermingle with bucolic scenes and hunters stalk their prey among stylized bushes.

Outside the church we admired the charming *phiale*, the interior of whose dome is frescoed with scenes of monastic vessels pursued by Saracen fleets and defenceless monks rescued from corsairs by the Archangels (the monastery, rising directly from the water's edge, was always an easy target for maritime marauders). A cool frescoed colonnade, where slanting rays light up figures in once opulent draperies against faded architectural backgrounds, leads to the sombre little **shrine of the Panayia Gorgoepeiköos** (The Virgin who grants requests quickly), which possesses a wonder-working tenth-century icon of the Virgin strung with votive offerings. A careless monk once allowed the smoke of his candle to blacken and disfigure her face. The Virgin commanded the monk to be more careful. Forgetful by nature, he repeated the offence. This time the Virgin, acting like an outraged Athena or Artemis, instantly blinded him. The stricken man pleaded for mercy, whereupon the Virgin (always ready – again like an Olympian deity – to pardon an offence after the infliction of physical punishment) appeared to him in a vision and declared, 'Monk, your prayer has been heard, and you shall see again as you used to, for I am the Ready-Listener.'[17] Only the smoky faces and hands of the Virgin and Child show through the gold leaf with which the icon is sheeted. Throughout the country, Orthodox supplicants, anxious for a swift answer to their prayer, address their appeals to icons of the Gorgoepeiköos.

The refectory is frescoed with apocalyptic scenes, slightly earlier in date than those in the church, of which the most remarkable is a strange representation of **God Enthroned** against a background of lighted arches: an elderly haloed figure with a homely expression, holding the bejewelled book 'sealed with seven seals' which could only be opened by the Lamb with seven horns.[18] The white ram is depicted here with green horns; it stands on its hind-legs, about to receive the book from God.

We left Docheiariou and its atmosphere of tranquillity with regret. The sea was calm, the sun hot, as the caique chugged north-ward – back to the world. We bathed off a sandy beach at the foot of a pine-clad cliff crowned by the ruined buildings of a deserted skete. The shore was littered with pebbles of different colours – onyx and porphyry, amber and russet, marble streaked with green veins and tesselated greys – smoothed into oval and elliptical shapes by the endless friction of waves. In the late afternoon we saw the Tower of Prosphori (see p. 249) rising above the port of Ouranoupolis. On landing we found the car caked in dust, parked under the shadow of the tower. We sat at a waterfront café. A few tables away, two boys in jeans and striped shirts fiddled with a transistor which emitted

[17] Sydney Lock, *Athos, The Holy Mountain*, Lutterworth Press, London, 1957.
[18] Revelation, V, 1.

snatches of the duet from the first act of *Traviata*. A girl in a multi-coloured cotton dress brought us iced lemonades. The sudden realization of what had happened, of where we were, was breathtaking. A child was cuffed by another and began to howl. Its cries drowned the last echoes of wood pigeons piping in the copses of the Virgin's empty garden.

*

Travellers wishing to visit the remaining ten monasteries must plan for a considerably longer visit (at least two weeks) and accordingly obtain the necessary permit at Karyes (see p. 259). Less important than those described above, the other monasteries are all beautifully situated, and the inland settlements provide opportunities for enchanting walks. I list them below in a topographical sequence which roughly follows the route described in the previous pages, i.e. Daphni to Karyes, Iviron to Chilandari and back, and round the peninsula to Docheiariou.

Xeropotamou (idiorrhythmic)
Inland. Situated on a plane-tree-shaded plateau above the Singitic Gulf, just off the Daphni-Karyes road. Founded in the tenth century, burnt by pirates and rebuilt *c*. 1600. The church of the Forty Martyrs possesses two important artistic objects: (i) the largest piece of the True Cross on Mount Athos set amid jewels in a silver-gilt reliquary, once the property of the Emperor Romanus I Lecapenus (919–44); (ii) a beautiful twelfth-century **steatite patera of St Pulcheria**, carved with a design of the Virgin surrounded by angels in vestments of deacons and mounted on silver. Water placed on it overnight is said to boil over by the morning. It then serves as an antidote against snake-bite.

Koutloumousiou (cenobitic)
Inland. A quarter of an hour's walk from Karyes. Pastoral situation: cornfields, olive groves, kitchen-gardens. Founded by a thirteenth-century Turkish prince, converted to Christianity, who became an Athonite monk. The church of the Metamorphosis has sixteenth-century frescoes and a good icon of St Nicholas.

Stavronikita (idiorrhythmic)
East coast. Situated on a wooded eminence, crowned by an imposing tower, above the rocky shore. Superb view of the Holy Mountain.

Founded by a tenth-century Byzantine officer. The church of Ayios Nikolaos was frescoed in the sixteenth. A panel on the south-east column conceals the icon of St Nicholas-of-the-Oyster, recovered from the sea in the sixteenth century with an oyster embedded in the Saint's forehead. When the oyster was removed blood poured from the gash in the wood made by a fanatical Iconoclast before throwing the image into the sea. The oyster's outline is discernible on the right of the Saint's forehead. At present this monastery seems to attract relatively young monks with fairly progressive views.

Pantocrator (idiorrhythmic)
East coast. Perched on a rock above the sea with a fine view of Stavronikita and the Holy Mountain. Founded in the fourteenth century; its fortifications strengthened in the sixteenth. The dark red church of the Transfiguration (with a whitewashed porch) possesses restored sixteenth-century frescoes and an icon (north-west pillar) of the Virgin Yerondissa (depicted as a nun) from whose eyes oil once flowed when the monastery's supply had run out and a sick priest was in need of a healing unguent.

Esphigmenou (cenobitic)
East coast. Within easy walking distance of Chilandari. Derives its name, 'The Squeezed-together One', from its position at the mouth of a narrow valley. An eleventh-century foundation, destroyed by Crusaders, pirates and fire. Most of the undistinguished buildings are of the eighteenth century. The church of the Analypsis (Ascension), striped red and white, possesses a fragment of the True Cross and an early miniature mosaic of Christ.

Zographou (cenobitic)
Inland. Within easy walking distance of Chilandari or an hour's climb from its arsenal on the west coast. A Slav (largely Bulgar) foundation of uncertain date (possibly tenth-century), which rose to prominence in the thirteenth century. Architecturally undistinguished. The church of Ayios Georghios, striped red and white, possesses a fifteenth-century miraculous icon of St George (Italianate in style) which flew of its own accord from Palestine to Mount Athos and was painted by a divine hand – hence the monastery's dedication to the anonymous 'Zographos' (painter).

Kastamonitou (cenobitic)
Inland. Within walking distance of Zographou. Surrounded by

gardens, vineyards and myrtles. An eleventh-century foundation, restored in the fourteenth. The church of Ayios Stephanos, rebuilt in the nineteenth century of local marble, possesses parts of the True Cross, a wonder-working icon of St Stephen and relics of St Andrew and St Stephen which are said to exude a delicious smell to the sinless, non-smokers and little boys.

Philotheou (idiorrhthymic)
Inland, overlooking the east coast. Situated among gardens and vineyards. Allegedly founded by the tenth-century hermit Philotheos. Only the eighteenth-century church of the Evanghelistria (Our Lady of Good Tidings) and the refectory escaped the fire of 1871. The church possesses relics donated by the Emperor Nicephorus III Botaniates (1079–81), who abdicated the throne in order to become a monk. These include an icon of the Panayia Glycophylousa (The Sweetly Kissing Virgin) on the north-east column: one of the many attributed to St Luke by monkish superstition.

Karakallou (cenobitic)
One mile inland overlooking the east coast in the beautiful Provata country: chapels, farmhouses, wells, kitchen-gardens and hazel woods. Founded in the eleventh century, and not, as the monks believe, by Caracalla (whose portrait is included in the church frescoes). The church of SS Peter and Paul is of the sixteenth century. The frescoes are of a later period. A fine crenellated tower dates from the sixteenth century.

Simopetra (cenobitic)
West coast. Situated a thousand feet above the sea. Most spectacular position in the whole peninsula. Otherwise of little interest. Founded by a hermit Simon from whose pores myrrh flowed and who was guided by a star to the wild spot where the monastery was subsequently built. Destroyed by fire in the sixteenth century. The church of the Yennesis (Nativity) is late nineteenth century. Images of saints and demons are frescoed on the walls of rock-hewn passages.

CHAPTER NINETEEN

Eastern Macedonia

❧

The Strymon – Serres – Amphipolis – Mount Pangaeum – Kavalla – Philippi – The Nestus

North and east of the Chalcidice lies eastern Macedonia, originally the country of the Thracians, annexed by Philip II to the Macedonian Empire after a series of lightning campaigns in the mid fourth century BC. Fertile, but less beautiful than the Chalcidice, it is full of military associations. The return journey from Salonica to the border of the modern province of Thrace can easily be accomplished in one day; but it allows for few deviations, one of which at least, to Philippi, is of outstanding interest. Spending the night at the attractive port of Kavalla, one can also visit Serres and Amphipolis and then either return to Salonica or penetrate deeper into the Thracian plains.

In antiquity the natives, noted for their barbarous character, inhabited all the country south of Mount Haemus, from whose summit the ancient Greeks imagined they could see both the Euxine and the Adriatic Seas. Rivers flow north to south through marshy estuaries into the Aegean. The climate is one of extremes, and the winters are of unparalleled coldness by Mediterranean standards. Xenophon refers to soldiers wearing fox-skin caps, to wine being frozen in vessels. Oxen and cattle, now as then, are plentiful; so are the eels in the river mouths.

Much has been written about the savage customs of the Thracian tribes that descended from the north to plunder the food-producing plains. Disloyal and faithless, they did not hesitate to sell their children for money. They spoke an uncouth non-Hellenic tongue, were idle by nature, drunken by predilection, but could be hospitable on occasion, offering boys, white horses and rough carpets as presents to strangers. Noblemen were tattooed, and cannibalistic women wearing horse-masks ate their Sacred King at the conclusion of his reign (by whom its date was fixed is not recorded). Today the inhabitants, by contrast, are thrifty peasants and tobacco merchants; they have also made an important contribution to the

299

professional classes throughout the country.

The road from Salonica to Serres, after crossing a rolling feature-less landscape, descends to the west bank of the river **Strymon**, whence blew Pindar's 'lord of the winds', and Aeschylus's 'Northern blast'. According to Apollodorus, the river was navigable until Heracles rendered it shallow by casting boulders in its bed in one of his fits of uncontrollable exuberance. Throughout Greek literature the omnipotent character of the river and currents of air that blow across its spacious valley, affecting the weather of the whole country, are emphasized. Modern meteorologists still carefully note the force and direction of winds funnelling through the Strymonic Gulf before making their weather forecasts for the whole country. In 1916–18 the river constituted the demarcation line between the armies of the Allies and the Central Powers. In 1941 German tanks streamed down the valley from the Bulgarian frontier to reach Salonica within three days. To the north extends a rich granary through which the river meanders between poplar-lined banks. East of the bridge, at the foot of Mount Vrontous (Mount Thunder-claps) lies **Serres**, the ancient Sirris, where Xerxes left large numbers of sick and wounded during his retreat after the battle of Salamis.

The modern town, seat of a bishopric and a tobacco-growing centre, is distinguished only by a pleasant rectangular square (Plateaia Eleutherias) bordered by poplars and weeping willows, with a basin in the centre around which peacocks strut; at the west end stands a large abandoned mosque crowned by six domes. In summer tobacco merchants and their families pace up and down the square in the ritual evening **volta**. But Serres was important in medieval times. At the foot of the castle hill the **Metropolis**, dedicated to the Holy Theodores, rises out of a depression surrounded by maisonettes. A large brick basilica, somewhat cumbersome in outline, its date is uncertain, but the mosaics of the interior apse, largely destroyed by the retreating Bulgarians at the end of the Second Balkan War in 1913, have been assigned to the eleventh century. The little domed chapel of later date at the north-west end was connected with the medieval keep by an underground passage used by Stephen Dušan, the Serbian national hero, who conquered large tracts of northern Greece in the fourteenth century. He made it the seat of a pretentious little court on the Byzantine model and wrote to the Doge of Venice that he now considered himself 'master of all the Empire of Romania'.[1]

[1] Ioannis Cantacuzenos, Historiae III, quoted by A. A. Vasiliev, *History of the Byzantine Empire*, Basil Blackwell, Oxford, 1952.

The interior can be visited only by permission of the Bishop (Secretariat in Kyprou Street), who deputes a deacon to show visitors round. The walls are bare, and only two of the original six grey marble columns of the aisles are preserved, but the proportions are lofty and harmonious. There are some finely carved bas-reliefs lying about: a Pantocrator in low relief, griffons and horses, elaborate crosses. Fragments of an eleventh-century mosaic of the Last Supper, said to have been of outstanding quality, can be discerned in the apse.

A single bastion crowns the remains of the Byzantine, later Frankish, Serbian and Turkish, castle on the summit of a pine-clad hill overlooking the city. In the early thirteenth century Theodore Angelus, Despot of Epirus, made the castle at Serres his base for the liberation of Macedonia from the Franks. In the fourteenth century the fall of the castle to the Serbs was considered a disaster of the first magnitude to Byzantine arms, already suffering shattering defeats at the hands of the advancing Ottoman armies.

Pine trees shade the castle hill. Southward, beyond the ugly urban agglomeration, extends the cultivated plain in a pale yellowish-green haze. It was at some point along here that Xerxes abandoned the Sacred Chariot of Zeus, which, among his other formidable impedimenta, was too cumbersome to transport all the way to the Athenian Acropolis. More intriguing is the view to the north, where chalky cliffs and shallow ravines filled with pines and evergreens mount in a series of rugged forms towards the desolate heights of Mount Vrontous, among whose snow-capped peaks the thunder is said to roll louder than anywhere in the world.

About halfway down the east slope a side road leads through the wood to the little fourteenth-century Byzantine **Church of Ayios Nikolaos**. Recently restored, its red-brick walls bright against the dark green of pines, it is something of an architectural extravaganza, with an exo-narthex wider than the main body of the church and crowned at each end by domes. A belfry is attached to the southern end. Three absurd little cupolas surmount the narthex and a well-proportioned drum the whole edifice. The interior is without interest. But it is a secluded place, and the air is balmy with the scent of resin.

From Serres the road runs eastward across tobacco and wheat country, its monotony relieved only by the snow-capped shape of Mount Pangaeum to the east. Before descending towards the mouth of the Strymon, a signposted road winds up to the village of **Amphipolis**, where the services of a local inhabitant should be engaged to conduct one round the scattered ruins of this once important ancient city.

The flying-ants are a pest, the brushwood thick and prickly, and the distances between the groups of unidentifiable foundations considerable. But one is impressed by the sprawling dimensions of the site and its commanding position controlling all the ways of communication between the Strymonic Gulf and the interior plains, with the river winding in two wide loops round the hill before flowing through a lagoon into the gulf. To the east rise the spurs of Mount Pangaeum, whose gold and silver mines and forest tracts (which provided timber for the local shipyards) contributed so much to the prosperity of the city. In the west the wooded Chalcidice massif dips down towards the isthmus; beyond it, the headland is crowned by the magical peak of Athos.

The history of the place, originally called Ennea Odoi (The Nine Ways) because it was the junction of nine strategic roads, is eventful. Herodotus says that when the Persians, in their westward march in 480 BC, learnt the name of the place they seized nine native boys and girls and buried them alive as a propitiary sacrifice. During the period of Athenian imperial expansion a new city was founded on the site and it was renamed Amphipolis. It was colonized by Athenian settlers who lost no time in exploiting the mineral and agricultural resources of the region. Thus Amphipolis came to be regarded as one of the chief jewels of the Periclean maritime empire.

During the Peloponnesian War this commercial prize was bitterly contested by Athens and Sparta, and it finally fell in 422 BC to Brasidas. The Athenian defeat became an undignified rout and Thucydides, in command of the Athenian triremes, failed to re-capture it. The 'dismay felt at Athens at its loss', writes Grote, 'was greater than had ever before been experienced'. Indignation was so great that Thucydides was banished. To make matters worse, Cleon, the rugged Athenian leader, who had assumed the now somewhat tarnished mantle of the dead Pericles, was killed while fleeing by a mercenary peltast in the service of the Spartans. But in the battle of Amphipolis, a Spartan victory of the first magnitude, Brasidas, the architect of the triumph, was also killed; and the defeated Thucydides, with his usual magnanimity, wrote of the Spartan hero, whose probity and moderation were equal to his military resourcefulness, that he was 'buried at the public expense of the city . . . and the Amphipolitans . . . ever afterwards sacrifice to him as a hero and have given him the honour of games and annual offerings'. After the fall of Amphipolis Athenian prestige was never to stand so high again; and moreover, the double event of the Athenian defeat and the death of Brasidas made such an impact on Hellenic consciousness that it increased the influence of the pacifist parties, enabling them, a year later, to negotiate the abortive Peace of Nicias, celebrated by Aristophanes in his comedy, the *Peace*, in which he represents his winged hero in the form of a dung-beetle mounting to heaven with the aid of every Greek who wished to end the interminable war. Over half a century later Amphipolis fell to Philip of Macedon.

So much history, and how little to show for it! Of scientific excavation there has been a mere scratching of the ground. At intervals, across the cornfields of the rolling eminence, you see truncated pedestals of grey marble, white unfluted columns lying in hollows, a trench in which broken pillars stand in a row, fragmentary remains of walls, of a cyma and cornice, some Corinthian capitals and, far removed from any other vestige of antiquity, the legs and buttocks of a large marble horse gleaming white amid the green corn. Some of the foundations have apse-shaped east ends: remains of the Early Christian township that rose on the debris of the pagan city.

East (left) of the fork on the main road, a path climbs a mound: a natural tumulus, out of whose exterior the sepulchre of a Macedonian prince has been carved. Steps descend into a barrel-vaulted chamber with an L-shaped stone couch (or tomb), sufficiently large and imposing to have been the last resting place of a person of considerable distinction.

Reaching the west-east highway, you turn west and cross the bridge spanning the wide-bed of the Strymon, famous for its eels. Here Xerxes too built a bridge across the river – 'cables some of papyrus, some of white flax', says Herodotus, '. . . being prepared for the bridge . . .' – and the Persian Magi 'tried to propitiate the river by a sacrifice of white horses, and after performing many other magical tricks in the hope of winning the river's favour . . .' The dread in which the Strymonic river god was held by local inhabitants seems to have been transmitted to their Asiatic conquerors. Thence the Great King continued his march, and his prodigious army inspired such awe in the natives that they never again dared to plough the fields over which it had passed.

On the east bank of the river the **Lion of Amphipolis**, a colossal lion couchant, with magnificent mane and gaping predatory mouth, re-assembled from late fourth- (or early third-) century BC fragments, stands on a stepped pedestal in a wispy pine grove. Its eyes are fixed across the estuary at the flat-topped acropolis of Amphipolis. Cars, buses and lorries bowl along the highway, below the impervious gaze of the superb animal guarding the mouth of the river. In Hellenistic times these monumental lions, symbolic of virility, were generally raised as war memorials. At Amphipolis it is thought to crown the tomb of some distinguished Macedonian prince.

East of the estuary the highway follows the base of Mount Pangaeum, whose ancient gold mines were the goal of every invader and would-be conqueror. From the earliest times the mountain's bulbous spurs and knobbly summits – one is exactly in the shape of a female breast with a clearly defined nipple – has exercised a powerful hold over the Greek imagination, both as a haunt of the deities and a source of economic wealth. Mythographers say that Orpheus was the first man to dwell among its wild ravines and swaying oak trees: not the gentle lyre-playing lover of Eurydice, but a more enigmatic figure of Thracian origin, who instituted savage cults and stood every morning on the topmost summit to greet the sun-god as his chariot of fire cast the first rays of light across the plains. But then Dionysus, the riotous god of wine, came to Thrace and saw the possibilities that the glens and forests offered for the indulgence of his bacchanalian orgies and bibulous festivities. Jealous of Orpheus's attachment to his own half-brother, Apollo, he set his train of raving Maenad women on his rival. After tearing Orpheus to pieces, the drunken creatures cast the severed parts of his body into the Hebrus river. Henceforth, Dionysus, ivy-crowned, waving his thyrsus from his panther-drawn chariot, lorded it over the mountain; and the bestial cries of his revelling Satyrs and Maenads echoed from crag to crag. But Dionysus was basically an effeminate character, having been reared as a girl until the age of puberty, and he also liked beautiful things; he fed on honey, and, during his reign on Mount Pangaeum, roses, famous all over Greece, bloomed on its slopes. He also established an oracle in one of its less rugged glens.

The gold mines also figure in mythology, for the wealth of Cadmus, founder of Thebes, is supposed to have come from the precious ore of Mount Pangaeum. The deposits – gold, silver and other metals – were situated on the lower slopes which rise directly above the road. The coins minted from the silver of Mount Pangaeum in the cities of the 'Thracian Tribute' bore effigies of lions and bulls in combat, of nude horsemen and ithyphallic mules, crows, cocks and octopus, as well as representations of Dionysiac Satyrs and Maenads.[2] At

---

[2] Specimens of these coins are displayed in the British Museum and in the Numismatic Museum in Athens.

The Tower of
Prosphori dominates
the landscape at
Ouranoupolis.

Lion of Amphipolis – a
colossal lion couchant,
with magnificent mane
and gaping predatory
mouth, re-assembled
from late fourth-
century BC fragments.

Naupactus: the Venetian castle overlooks the port.

(or near) **Eleutheroupolis,** now a tobacco-growing centre, Thucydides had an estate, whose soil was seamed with veins of gold and to which he retired after the debacle at Amphipolis. Plutarch claims it was here, under the shade of a plane tree, that he began to write his history of the war. When the mines were exhausted is not established, but as late as the first century AD Strabo refers to the inhabitants finding nuggets of gold throughout the country between the Strymon and the plains of Philippi.

Beyond Eleutheroupolis the road skirts the southern end of the plain of Philippi and zigzags down a wooded hillside, affording an enchanting view of the amphitheatrical port of **Kavalla,** protected by a headland crowned by crenellated Byzantine walls. Colour-washed houses rise steeply up the pine-clad slopes, and ferry-boats ply between the port and the offshore island of Thasos.

Colonized by Thasians, it was called **Neapolis** in antiquity. During the campaign of Philippi the galleys of Brutus and Cassius were anchored in the harbour. St Paul, after seeing the vision in which '. . . a man of Macedonia . . . prayed him, saying, Come over into Macedonia and help us', took 'a straight course to Samothracia, and the next day to Neapolis'.[3] In the fourteenth century Neapolis was the starting-point of the Catalan Grand Company's turbulent march across the country. An emporium for the tobacco-growing plains of the hinterland, the port has long been a bone of contention between Greece and Bulgaria. In both wars the Bulgarians seized and occupied it, without leaving a trace of a Slav minority to substantiate their claim. Today it is the second largest town in northern Greece; and its gaily painted houses (pink, blue and white), interspersed with a few crumbling neo-classical nineteenth-century mansions, mounting in terraces up a crescent-shaped screen of wooded hills, the picturesqueness of its old Turkish quarters, its animated waterfront, combine to make it the most attractive of Greek provincial towns.

A day in Kavalla is well spent. The **museum** lies near the tobacco warehouses, west of the waterfront. In the Neapolis hall (first on left) are fragments of seventh-, sixth- and fifth-century BC pottery, terracotta figurines in showcase No. 7 (notice the maiden with a serene expression and a missing leg concealed by folds of drapery) and two squat fifth-century BC fluted columns with elaborated Ionic capitals from the temple of Parthenos, the virgin goddess of Neapolis. The Amphipolis hall (second on the left) is more rewarding. There is a delicate black mid-fourth-century BC ewer with two gilded

[3] Acts, XVI, 9–11.

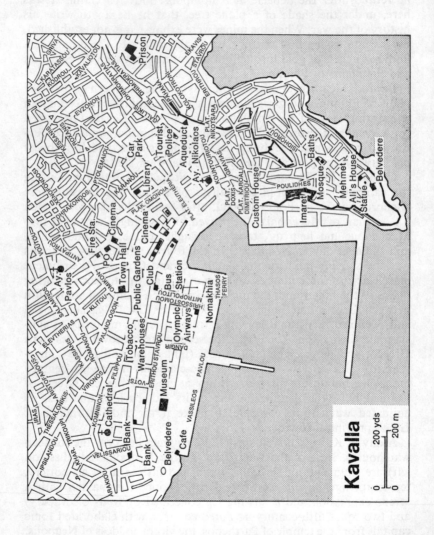

Kavalla

0   200 yds
0   200 m

wreaths, a fourth-century BC statuette of a siren in a state of exaltation, a vase with a lively painting of Hermes, a Satyr and Aphrodite
riding a horse in a bacchanalian procession, a fourth-century BC
stele (among others of inferior quality) of a funeral banquet in
which a reclining male figure (the departed soul) is surrounded by
his mourning wife, children and attendants, a small well-proportioned
gilded cantharus and more attractive glazed vases of the fourth and
third centuries BC. But the most impressive object is a restoration of a
Macedonian tomb from Amphipolis faced with fragments of
original frescoes in Dionysiac figures, thyrses, lions and other
beasts, and plants indigenous to Mount Pangaeum. A gold wreath
and a beautifully shaped silver hand-mirror, found in the tomb, are
displayed in a special showcase. Like the exhibits in the museum at
Salonica, they all tell the same story. The sculptor's art in northern
Greece never achieved the perfectionism that distinguishes the
creations of southern Greek classical statuaries and handicraftsmen;
but in the Hellenistic age the Macedonian artist's observation of
nature, his sense of fantasy and delight in variety seldom fail to
charm. Ceramics and jewellery are displayed in the third, less
interesting, hall (first floor) as well as a third-century BC statuette
(among later Roman ones) of a chubby naked baby with an extraordinarily precocious expression playing with a goose.

'Old' Kavalla is worth visiting, and it can be seen in a leisurely
two hours' walk. It is best to start from Eleutheria Square and bear
east along Omonoia Street to the conspicuous landmark of the
Turkish aqueduct, known as the Kamares, straddling an isthmus
which joins a fortified bluff to the mainland. Built in the mid sixteenth
century – when even the most backward Turkish engineers might
have been expected to be more advanced in the science of hydro-
statics – this anachronistic structure, which now dominates a
crowded bus terminal, consists of a double row of twenty tall
double arches, those of the higher tier alternating with two smaller
superimposed ones.

From the aqueduct one returns to the old port, filled with caiques,
and follows Poulides Street, climbing the west side of the headland
along whose ridge run well-preserved Byzantine walls.[4] This is the
heart of the old Turkish quarter: a maze of steep alleys and sudden
unexpected declivities. On the right extend low shallow-domed
buildings which compose into the Imaret, an almshouse for the aged
and needy (and impecunious students): all wretchedly dilapidated.
Unfortunately Greek nationalism precludes the conservation, let

[4] The keep is at present a military area, into which entry is forbidden.

alone restoration, of the monuments of the centuries of subjection. But in spite of the decay and neglect, the Imaret still reflects a forgotten aspect of a vanished Moslem world. Secluded and soporific, it could not be more worthy of its Turkish epithet, *Tembel-henneh* (the place of the lazy). A colonnade surmounted by eighteen metal-sheeted tea-cosy domes surrounds a sunken irregular-shaped courtyard. Here the aged turbaned figures would wander, when they were not snoozing in the cells which contained three hundred divans. At the southern end of the court a convex projection like a bastion, surrounded by a water conduit, where the old men performed their ablutions, supports a domed mosque with a portico overlooking the court. A second colonnaded court, square this time, full of the sound of cooing doves, has remains of fretwork screens between square columns. The sunken courts are now deserted. A place of oblivion – barely a hundred years old.

Beyond the Imaret Poulides Street mounts between rotting Turkish timber-framed houses to a belvedere overlooking the island-studded Thracian sea. A pedestal is crowned by a bronze equestrian statue of Mehmet Ali, his scimitar drawn, mounted on a splendidly caparisoned horse impatiently pawing the ground. A prosperous Albanian farmer, born in Kavalla in 1769, Ali was to become Pasha of Egypt and founder of the Egyptian royal dynasty which ended with Farouk. Beside the statue is **Mehmet Ali's birthplace**, a rambling Turkish house in an excellent state of preservation, thanks to the care and money expended on it by the Egyptian Government. From the kitchens and storerooms of the ground floor, one ascends to a harem with latticed shutters. Here are ranged the broad divans where the little ladies, showing nothing but their dark doe-like eyes above their yashmaks, reclined, eating syrupy sweetmeats; and panelled cupboards, where their embroidered garments and quilted bedding were kept; an apse-shaped fireplace, tapering in a slender cone, projects from the fourth wall. The primitive bathroom, in which the ladies stood while attendants poured water over them, is only surpassed in stark simplicity by the lavatory – a triangular hole in the ground. In Mehmet Ali's study, which communicates with smaller chambers where his scimitar-armed bodyguard kept watch, one relic remains: his writing-desk, adorned with framed photographs of all the members of the dynasty. An elaborate tomb carved with rosettes and foliate designs, in which Mehmet's mother is buried, embellishes a shady garden full of birds and well-tended beds of tulips and stocks.

Fifteen kilometres inland, the **ruins of Philippi** extend across a fertile plain at the foot of a pyramid-shaped hill. From no other point is Mount Pangaeum, a huge isolated cone rising out of the aspen-studded fields, seen to better advantage. Originally Crenides, the place was renamed Philippi and fortified by Philip of Macedon, who needed the gold of Mount Pangaeum to wage the wars that would make him master of Greece. But Philippi did not become famous until 42 BC, when the two largest Roman armies ever engaged in hostilities against each other manoeuvred across the chequerboard plain, much of which was then a marsh and swarmed with bees, while birds of prey, whose shadows formed, in Cassius's words, a 'canopy most fatal', hovered overhead.[5] The strategic value of the position chosen by the rival armies for the decisive test is self-evident, for it guarded that part of the Via Egnatia which passes through a narrow defile and ensured the security of Neapolis and the maintenance of maritime communications with Asia Minor.

The battle, inevitable result of the struggle for power following Caesar's murder, consisted of two separate engagements, both fought west of the town between the marsh and the eastern ring of hills: both initiated by the Republican leaders, who seem to have repeated Pompey's mistake at Pharsalia, provoking an untimely head-on clash instead of trying to wear the enemy down. In the first engagement Octavian, feeling wretchedly ill, was completely routed by Brutus's legions, which were conspicuous not only for their republican ardour, but for the splendour of their gold and silver arms. The sickly future master of the world only escaped capture by fleeing to Antony's camp. But in this engagement Cassius, warned by unfavourable omens, was worsted by Antony and, in his despair, committed suicide.

Deeply distressed by the death of his friend, Brutus decided to 'try fortune in a second fight'.[6] But this time Antony's legions infiltrated the Republicans' position and Brutus was trapped and overwhelmed, whereupon he 'retired to a hill', says Suetonius, 'and slew himself in the night'. Although Shakespeare makes Antony pay a handsome tribute to his defeated opponent – 'the noblest Roman of them all' – Suetonius adds that Octavian, more vindictive, sent 'Brutus's head to Rome, to be cast at the feet of Caesar's statue'. Thus perished the Roman Republic on the marshy fields of Thrace. The way now lay open for the final struggle between the two victors of Philippi. After Actium Octavian, now Augustus

[5] Shakespeare, *Julius Caesar*.
[6] Shakespeare, op. cit.

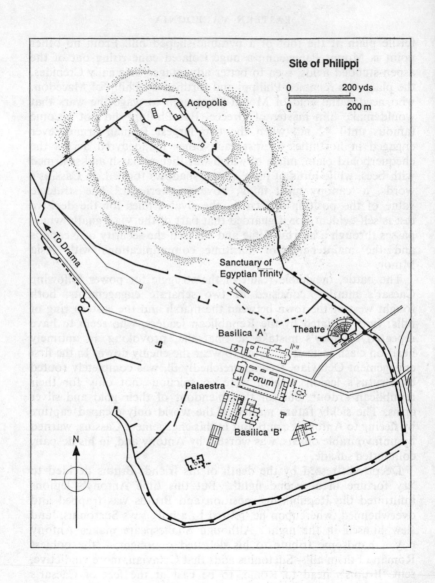

Site of Philippi

0 — 200 yds

0 — 200 m

Acropolis

Sanctuary of
Egyptian Trinity

Theatre

Basilica 'A'

Forum

Palaestra

Basilica 'B'

To Drama

N

Caesar, remembered the strategic value and agricultural wealth of the plain and sent colonists to Philippi, so that by the time of St Paul's visit it was a completely Roman city, its wide and beautiful streets crowded with strutting praetors, lictors and magistrates.

The religion, a form of primitive obscurantism, was still that of the indigenous Thracians, who worshipped the goddess Bendis, an Underworld deity, and the heroic Thracian Horseman in whose dual personality were combined the attributes of a dashing hunter and solemn high priest. Scythian undertones were not lacking. The official faith of the governing class, of course, was that of pagan Rome. Such was the religious background which St Paul found when he reached 'the chief city of that part of Macedonia . . .'[7] and met Lydia, the 'seller of purple', beside a stream, thought to be the one crossed by the Via Egnatia two kilometres west of the site. But, in spite of his conversion of Lydia and her household, neither the Thracian multitude nor the Roman magistrates took kindly to the Apostle's exorcism of a soothsaying damsel's evil spirit; so they rent his and Silas's clothes in the market place and cast them into prison.

The ruins, Early Christian rather than Roman, are extensive, impressive and easy to identify. From the entrance gate (immediately right of the road from Kavalla), you climb a stairway and turn north (left) to reach a confusing mass of rubble which has been labelled **Basilica A**, probably destroyed in an earthquake.[8] Dated to the fifth century, it is T-transept in shape, with a semi-circular apse. Among the debris are several fragments of the sculptural decoration that once adorned the interior: acanthus leaf Corinthian capitals, pieces of cornice, plaques carved with crosses, rosettes, garlands, spirals and two peacocks drinking at the Source of Life against a background of stylized trees, stepped pedestals, chancel slabs and column bases. The marbles, grey and Thessalian, must have added splendour to the scene, as the sun's rays, piercing the clerestory below the timber roof, fell obliquely across the colonnades separating the aisles. The interior is thought to have been a typical example of Early Christian taste, somewhat austere, but inspired by a deep emotional exaltation. With the eclipse of the Roman Empire in the West, the Via Egnatia had declined in importance, and Philippi may no longer have been an important commercial centre; but the size of its churches and their surviving decoration provide evidence

[7] Acts, XVI, 12.

[8] In the absence of any indication of the dedication of the Early Christian basilica of Philippi, scholars have given alphabetical symbols.

of the city's prominence as a place of pilgrimage, the first in Europe at which the Gospel was preached.

Immediately below Basilica A a barrel-vaulted chamber, with traces of wall-paintings (probably of a later date), is said to have been the **prison of St Paul**. But nothing remains of the doors that the earthquake caused to open. It rocked the foundations of the cell and loosened the prisoners' bonds, whereupon the panic-stricken guard was promptly converted and baptized, and the Romans, both frightened by the earthquake and tired of the Apostle's nuisance-value, let him and Silas go unmolested on their way to Amphipolis.

From here a path climbs to the terrace of the **Sanctuary of the Egyptian Trinity** – Isis, Serapis and Harpocrates – where more than one cella and the vestigial remains of stuccoed walls are discernible. It is difficult to avoid a feeling of historical and geographical dis-orientation. The sacerdotal Thracian Horseman and the infernal Bendis – yes; the Olympian deities and the martial gods of ancient Rome – certainly; St Paul and the Early Christian martyrs – of course; they are all germane to the religious history of Philippi. But then suddenly the moon-goddess of the Nile, a Memphian taurine divinity, and the weakly son of Osiris, mystic child of silence, enter the scene. The incongruity is bewildering. Flying insects sting one and lizards slither across the path as the ascent grows steeper until it reaches the summit of the conical hill which dominates the ruined city. Traceable fragments of the medieval enceinte are superimposed on the fourth-century BC walls, with three towers silhouetted against the skyline.

Starting from Basilica A again and following a southerly course one passes a series of curious rock-hewn chambers: tall vertical niches, possibly connected with the worship of Bendis; then Latin inscriptions of the third century, also rock-hewn, dedicated to Silvanus, the Roman god of woods and fields, where women were forbidden to worship, agriculture being considered an exclusively male vocation; then a railed-in enclosure with a well-preserved chequered marble pavement and two tall columns crowned with impost capitals. Finally one reaches the **theatre**, originally a Hellen-istic edifice (the side entrances, through which the chorus entered, date from this period). It was remodelled in the second century AD to suit Roman tastes, with an unusually large orchestra to allow sufficient room for gladiatorial shows. The original Greek proscenium was also removed to make way for more showy imperial embellish-ments. There are about half a dozen Roman tiers of limestone, the rest of the cavea having been somewhat tastelessly restored in the late 1950s. From the topmost tier, alongside which ran a vaulted gallery, there is a fine view across the agricultural plain to a ridge of wooded hills separating the hinterland from the sea.

But the more impressive ruins lie east of the road, opposite Basilica A, on flat ground. First there is the large rectangle of the **forum**, on a truly Roman scale, much of it dated to the reign of Marcus Aurelius. Little remains standing above waist-level, but many of the stone and marble slabs, carved with Latin inscriptions, are of great size. With a little patience and imagination, one can identify the main features: the foundations of two temples at the north-east and north-west angles; a library on the east side; to the north a stepped tribune, whence St Paul probably preached the word. Around it lie fragments of Roman statues. At the south-east end fluted columns stand on huge plinths; at the west end is a well-preserved stretch of paved road, flanked by a parapet with a row of slender unfluted columns. The havoc and destruction is nightmarish. In spring sheets of forget-me-not carpet the ground and the clusters of asphodel that sprout from crannies in the shattered masonry only seem to emphasize the totality of the city's ruin. Recent excavations have revealed the foundations of an Early Christian octagonal church, comparable to that of St Vitale at Ravenna, which had an altar on one side and colonnades on the other seven.

Immediately west of the forum extend the ruins of Philippi's chief glory, **Basilica B**, the warm cream-coloured stone of its surviving piers dominating the ruins. Dated to the reign of Justinian, it suggests the work of architects and sculptors of Constantinopolitan (or at least Thessalonian) origin. The plan in itself must have been exciting: a domed basilica with an additional cupola above the sanctuary, taller and higher than the shallow one crowning the aisles which were lighted by a clerestory and preceded by a vaulted narthex with three entrances. The east apse was spacious, and two smaller ones appear to have been added to the north and south sides. It was an intriguing experiment, representing a transitional period in church architecture when the Hellenistic-style basilica with all its Eastern undertones was gradually developing into the true Christian basilica of Byzantium. But disaster intervened before it could be completed. The great dome above the sanctuary collapsed, and, for reasons unknown, the architects lost heart; the would-be great church remained unfinished and was never consecrated.

The sanctuary arch, a perfect ellipse of brick, is flanked by piers composed of rectangular slabs of re-used ancient masonry. At the north-east end rises another pier with courses of carved decoration.

On the east side stand two truncated columns of tesselated marble. The sculptured decoration is of the highest order (of the period), and all the Early Christian love of zoological and botanical detail, inherited from Hellenistic Asia and pagan Rome, is exploited. Notice the carving of the pilaster courses, the fishes, birds and flowers on plaques, the rosette designs on atrium capitals and chancel slabs, the hearts (or leaves) on a fragment of the altar and, most beautiful of all, the **two nave capitals and imposts** which crown pieces of a pillar and a base. The acanthus leaves, which appear to grow organically from roots embedded in the impost, are carved in such deep relief that light and shade effects confer on them an air of reality. Other fragments include a chancel slab carved with a medallion enclosing a four-armed cross, and an altar slab with a cross with six arms in the form of ivy leaves. Wandering around once, I saw black clouds billowing across the crest of Mount Pangaeum, which the Turks called Pilaff-Tepeh (the pilaff mountain), alternately blotting out and revealing its snow-capped peak and the breast-shaped cone of a lower level; then, as the snow-clouds were blown westward, shafts of sunlight slanted across the aspen groves, warming the masonry of the piers into a rich creamy pink, accentuating the exquisite ornamental relief of the acanthus leaves of the two great capitals.

Passing through the horseshoe-shaped sanctuary arch of the basilica, one enters the pagan **palaestra**. Apart from a fine acanthus leaf capital, the debris of this ancient exercise ground for Macedonian and Roman youth means little to the unprofessional eye. At the south-west end there is a remarkable if unbeautiful monument of Roman times. Seven steps descend to a doorway crowned by a well-preserved lintel leading into a rectangular sunken court which served as a latrine. The marble seats are ranged in rows along the sides of three walls. I counted more than twenty in a tolerable state of preservation.

East of the ancient enceinte extend the foundations of the **Basilica 'Extra Muros'**, littered with slabs, some carved with crosses growing out of ivy tendrils, which may have been a fourth-century edifice, subsequently restored and modified. Its main interest lies in the sixteen crypts below what was once the nave and which, according to epitaphs discovered *in situ*, were the sepulchres of distinguished Philippian prelates. Fragments of floor mosaic are also preserved. Against red or white fields we see birds, dolphins and blue-edged crosses, astragalos, blue meander and other geometrical designs, all set within squares.

East of Kavalla the road crosses open country as far as the village of **Paradeisos,** where there are some attractive Turkish-style white-washed houses with wide eaves, overlooking the Nestus as it flows between poplar-lined sandbanks out of a narrow gorge against a background of wooded hills. No road as yet penetrates the labyr-inthine intricacies of the **Nestus gorge** – only a railway, designed in the nineteenth century by the Turkish rulers of Macedonia to follow a course that would not lie within range of the guns of the Greek fleet or those of Greece's protecting powers. It seems an extra-ordinarily roundabout way – obviously conceived in purely military terms – but it gives the traveller by rail the opportunity to see a whole part of 'Balkan' Greece that is not covered in the normal itinerary by car. At first the defile is sombre and constricted, with the river flowing swiftly between precipitous cliffs eroded into strange architectural forms studded with evergreens. As the gorge opens out, the aspect becomes grander; the banks are lined with poplars; the higher levels with ilex, pines, Judas trees. A procession of wooded conical mounds recedes northwards.

Drama, the ancient Drabescus, where the Athenian colonizers of Amphipolis, venturing too far inland, were cut off from their base and slaughtered by Thracian tribesmen, lies at the foot of Mount Phalakro (The Bald One). The town has little to offer – only an important Tobacco Research Centre. Southward extends the tobacco-growing country, the so-called 'golden plain'. The line runs south-west, under the shadow of Mount Pangaeum, buttressed by subsidiary ranges. One obtains a strange bird's-eye view of the stream of the Anghites flowing hundreds of feet below between dark vertical cliffs which never see the sun. At Serres the line turns sharply to the north, towards **Sidirocastro,** picturesquely situated at the foot of rocky hills, one of which is crowned, as the town's name implies, by an 'iron castle'. To the north rise the gloomy ranges of Bulgaria, the Beles mountains, at the base of which the line crosses the upper reaches of the Strymon where it emerges from the **Rupel Pass**: a strategic point for every invader, commanding the wedge-shaped Strymonic basin, key to all eastern Macedonia. The pass became famous (or infamous) in the First World War, when the country was split by two opposing factions: the pro-German Royalist Government of King Constantine I and the pro-Entente Liberal opposition headed by Eleutherios Venizelos. As a gauge of Greece's benevolent neutrality to the Central Powers, the Govern-ment surrendered Fort Rupel, which defends the pass, to the Bulgar-ians. So great was the revulsion of feeling of the major part of Greek public opinion that the 'Rupel' incident proved the mainspring of a chain of events culminating in the formation of the Provisional Government under Venizelos at Salonica, the exile of King Constantine at the point of the gun – more precisely, the guns of British and French battleships – and the entry of Greece into the war against the Central Powers.

The railway then fringes the east shore of Lake Doiran, where scattered hamlets spread across the confines of Greece and Jugoslavia, turns sharply to the south, and, beyond Kilkis, a garrison town at the foot of the Krousia mountains, descends towards Salonica along the banks of the Gallikos river.

CHAPTER TWENTY

The Thracian Plains

Xanthe – Abdera – Komotini – Alexandroupolis – Trajanopolis – Pherae: Church of the Dormition – The Hebrus – Didymoteichon: The Turkish Border

East of the Nestus extends the modern province of Thrace, which remained under Turkish rule until 1913. Cornfields and tobacco-growing plains, unrelieved by groves, woods or vineyards – only the occasional poplar or aspen – are enclosed between the sea and the Rhodope mountains. Painted carts rattle along side roads and groups of dark-skinned Sarakatsans, members of self-contained ethnic communities scattered all over northern and western Greece, stand in silent sullen groups in the level fields. The miniature shanty towns are often largely inhabited by turbaned Turks and women in un-relieved black, their faces hidden behind yashmaks. Greek subjects, they still speak their own tongue, attend their own schools, worship in their own mosques.

It can all be seen in a day. If the traveller, motoring to or from Turkey, wishes to spend a night in a Thracian town, Alexandroupolis seems the obvious halt; it has best hotels (and an airport). It is a journey into an incongruously un-Greek world. The prairies, traversed by muddy streams, the barrier of Balkan ranges shrouded in haze or cloud, have little in common with the shimmering plains of Greece encircled by grandiose mountains. The light, landscape, architecture, even the people, herald a new climate. It is, in fact, a prolonged frontier region, with the Turkish border as the goal.

Xanthe is the first stop. Vasileous Constantinou Square, with its little hamman, clock tower and rows of shoeblacks, is the town's main hub. Even the kiosks have Turkish-style pointed roofs once crowned with crescents. North of the square a fruit market extends across a depression bordered by rows of bright red *kilims*, tied to ropes hanging out to dry.[1] Pigeons pipe in acacia trees, and rivulets

---

[1] *Kilims:* thin handwoven rugs, brightly coloured, the oldest known form of carpet, probably of ancient Egyptian origin; popular throughout the Balkans; the older and finer specimens are also used for mural decoration.

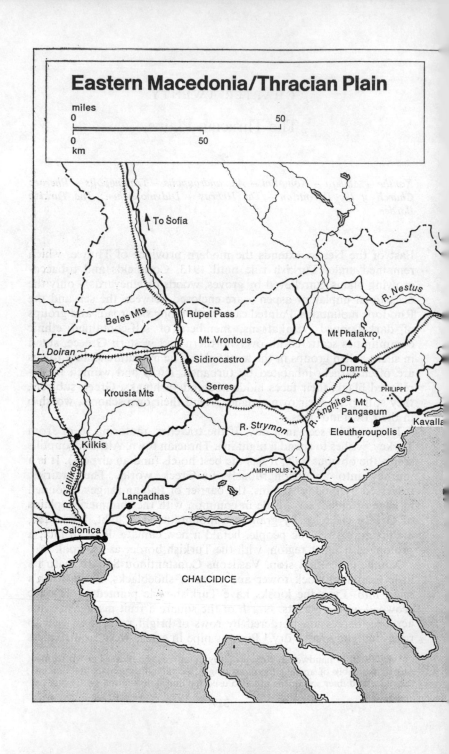

Eastern Macedonia/Thracian Plain

miles
0   50

0   50
km

To Sofia

R. Nestus

Beles Mts

Rupel Pass

Mt Phalakro

Mt. Vrontous

L. Doiran

Sidirocastro

Drama

PHILIPPI

Serres

Krousia Mts

R. Anghites

Mt Pangaeum

Kavalla

R. Strymon

Eleutheroupolis

Kilkis

AMPHIPOLIS

Langadhas

Salonica

CHALCIDICE

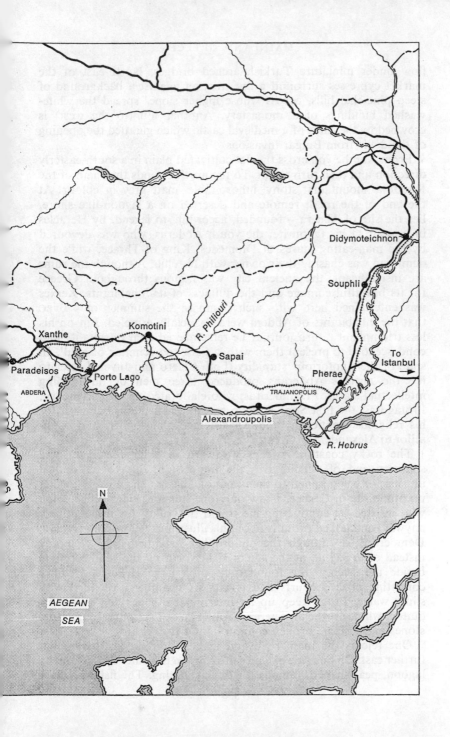

flow under miniature Turkish arched bridges. North-east of the market cypresses surround a fine minaret against a background of steep pine-clad hills, across whose higher slopes spread the white-washed buildings of a monastery. Another hill (to the west) is crowned by the ruins of a medieval castle which guarded the opening of the defile from Bulgar invasions.

From Xanthe you cross the flat cultivated plain in a south-easterly direction and then turn south. To the north extends the chain of the Rhodope mountains: stony, inhospitable, matt grey in colour. At the end of the road, remote and deserted on a lagoon-like shore, lies the site of **Abdera** – founded, according to legend, by Heracles in honour of his favourite, the youth Abderus, who was devoured by the man-eating mares of Diomedes, King of Thrace, while the demi-god was chasing their owner with his club. Although the ruins are insignificant, the ancient city was famous throughout Greece for its beautiful coinage and the dullness of its inhabitants. Xerxes was entertained here with such pomp in the summer of 480 BC that the inhabitants of Abdera were financially crippled. But on his less triumphant return journey he remembered their hospitality and condescended to present them with 'a tiara and scimitar of gold'. In spite of their notorious stupidity (both Cicero and Juvenal refer to it), the ancient Abderans produced three men of outstanding intellectual stature: Democritus, who elaborated an atomic theory; Protagoras, the first Sophist, who was impeached and banished for his religious scepticism; and Anaxarchus, philosopher, and counsellor to Alexander the Great.

The rocky coastline sweeps westward in a large crescent, the southern end of which gives the impression, due to an optical illusion, of being joined to the island of Thasos. There is no lonelier maritime site in Greece. I saw only one human being: a fisherman who insisted on conducting me round the 'ruins' (easily identified, anyway) and talked proudly about his illustrious fellow-countryman, Democritus, as though the philosopher had died only yesterday instead of in 357 BC at the age of 109. North of the road terminal beside the sea are the foundations of a large Hellenistic edifice consisting of two courts and twenty-six chambers, all filled with slimy water. Frogs keep up an interminable squeaking and mosquitoes whine overhead. There are some slabs of masonry, foundation stones and a single broken column – little else.

One rejoins the main road and makes for the coast again, but further east. On one side extend salt-pans, on the other a huge muddy lagoon, pear-shaped, famous for duck-shooting. The fishing village

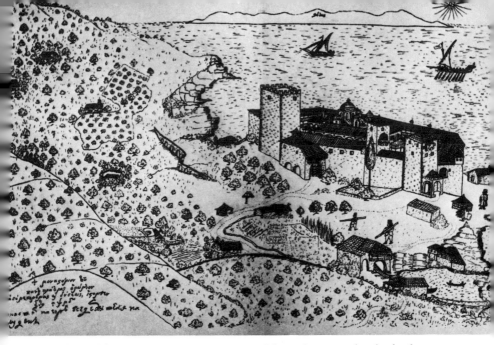

Mount Athos: Pantocrator Monastery, an eighteenth-century drawing by the Russian monk Vasili Barsky.

Mount Athos: the Protaton – Presentation of the Virgin in the Temple, attributed to the master painter Panselinos.

The Monastery of
Simopetra on Mount
Athos, soaring out of dark
green woods a thousand
feet above sea level.

The Monastery of
Dionysiou, one of the
friendliest and most
beautiful on the peninsula.

of Porto Lago is remarkable for the intricacy of the channels joining the lagoon with the sea and its church of Ayios Nikolaos, with a belfry, squatting on an islet in a shallow inlet. Waterfowl fly overhead, and innumerable causeways cross the lagoon; it is all strangely disorientating. The road then veers inland across cattle-grazing ground to **Komotini**, capital of Thrace.

A market centre for tobacco and agricultural produce, it possesses the largest Turkish minority in Thrace; in streets and cafés the strident peahen screech of Greek women contrasts strangely with the soft lilting cadences of Turkish men. The tempo is slower than elsewhere. But if the atmosphere is Turkish it possesses little Oriental glamour. The tiny minority of Bulgarian-speaking Pomaks, a swarthy taciturn people – the Bulgarian frontier lies only fourteen miles to the north – make little impact. In Hephaestus Street, appropriately lined with coppersmiths' shops, the Mosque of Yeni Djami, with a wide dome crowned by a gold crescent, is bordered by a grove of seedy-looking cypresses. Turbaned Turks in baggy black breeches pace up and down the entrance court, exchanging agricultural gossip; others, removing sweat-soaked shoes, pad across striped kilims to kneel in worship before the *mihrab*. The Mosque of Eski Djami in Chrysanthos Square is less picturesque: box-shaped, with yellow walls pierced by white arched window frames. The minaret is striking – and, like all minarets, beautiful in itself – with two balconies carved with elaborate fretwork. For the traveller coming from Turkey, however, neither mosque is really worth bothering about.

The Komotini-Alexandroupolis stretch is remarkable only for a Roman bridge crossing the Philiouri stream, followed by the almost wholly Turkish-speaking village of **Sapai**, where there is a curious minaret, belly-shaped in the centre, beside which we saw Turkish boys playing volley-ball. The Rhodope chain recedes to the north, towards the western spurs of Mount Haemus, among whose uninviting fastnesses the Thracian Dionysus had a sanctuary. Somewhere in this grey wilderness too was the shrine of Rhesus, at whose altar oxen, wild boar and gazelles came out of pure love for the handsome son of the river god Strymon and the muse Euterpe to present themselves to the executioner's axe. After climbing scrub-covered hills the road descends through olive groves – a rare sight in north-eastern Greece – to a flat unbroken coastline and the town of **Alexandroupolis**. Originally named Dedeagatch by the Turks after a hermit who lived in a tree, Hellenized Alexandroupolis has little to offer but some wide streets and a claustrophobic provincial air. It is however, a useful base for leisured travellers bound for the Hebrus valley.

One continues along the course of the Via Egnatia. Fifteen kilometres east of Alexandroupolis a hill to the north, said to be an extinct volcano, marks the **site of Trajanopolis**, an important station founded by Trajan. The scattered masonry on the northern bank of the stream of the Tchai (Turkish 'tea') is Roman, incorporated in Byzantine defence works, designed purely for military purposes. All this country was once peppered with Roman forts and strategic points guarding the vital highway. Seven kilometres beyond Trajanopolis a signpost points the way to **Doriscus**, where there are no ruins, but where Xerxes built a fortress and stopped to count the troops of his mammoth army. The grand total, says Herodotus, probably exaggerating, 'turned out to be 1,700,000'. The counting, he continues, 'was done by first packing ten thousand men as close together as they could stand and drawing a circle round them on the ground; they were then dismissed, and a fence, about navel-high, was constructed round the circle; finally other troops were marched out into the area thus enclosed and dismissed in their turn, until the whole army had been counted'.

Beyond the fork to Doriscus the road veers north, up the Hebrus basin, with the mountains of Turkish Thrace rising in the east. It is worth stopping at **Pherae**, a dusty (alternatively muddy) village which is entered across a ruined aqueduct with a Gothic arch. The village is centred round the twelfth-century Byzantine **Church of the Koimesis**. The country around here enjoyed considerable prosperity, with a corresponding increase of population, for the Comnene emperors rightly considered it a vital area guarding the approaches to Constantinople from the west. Most of the exterior of the church is unfortunately now covered with puce-coloured wash. Its proportions are sturdy and harmonious, with five domes, a spacious apse and three recessed blind arches reinforced by four buttresses. Traces of tile decoration, both in the apse and on the small southeast dome, as well as a plaque with an effigy of a heraldic eagle on the wall below the south-east dome, indicate that the church was no mere provincial house of worship. In the interior four granite columns are crowned with Theodosian capitals; there are also vestiges of frescoes, obviously not the work of a hack provincial iconographer; rows of holy figures; a good head of a haloed youthful saint on the north wall, surmounted by two equally impressive heads on the arch; and bishops holding scrolls on the south wall.

Above Pherae the road leaves the highway to Constantinople,

which follows the Via Egnatia – featureless country associated only with the march of countless conquerors ever since the Persian steamroller, composed of dark-skinned little men wearing soft felt caps, embroidered tunics and coats of mail, and armed with spears, cane arrows and wicker shields, tramped across the prairies. Soon the wide streak of the Hebrus appears winding between fields and orchards: a frontier made by geography, it would seem, to end the ancient feud between Greek and Turk. The road passes through **Souphli**, centre of the silkworm trade, a green hill overlooking mulberry orchards, often flooded by the fast-flowing river, in whose eddies the head of music-loving Orpheus, his body torn to pieces by Dionysus's raving Maenads, floated, still singing, towards the islet-studded delta, seven miles wide, whence it was borne on the crest of a foam-tipped wave to the island of Lesbos. The banks are fringed with reeds which the inhabitants cut into strips in order to make brooms. Among its sandbanks gold was once found, says Pliny, and nearly two thousand years later a French nineteenth-century traveller saw men searching the sands for grains of gold that were washed down from the river's Bulgarian sources.

At last, out of the flat watery expanse rises the circular hill of **Didymoteichon**, crowned by the ruins of its medieval **castle**, surrounded on almost all sides by tributaries of the Hebrus. This is the end – ultimate objective of the traveller in north-east Greece. Beyond lies Turkey. The climb up the castle hill is steep, short and rewarding. It is best to start at the little church of Ayia Marina, on the west side, where crumbling bastions covered with lichen overlook the tree-lined banks of numerous streams. Passing through an arched gateway you wind up the slope, pitted with caves in which ragged dark-skinned gipsies dwell, surrounded by barking watchdogs, while crows squawk overhead. There are well-preserved fragments of walls (inner and outer defences), of Roman, Byzantine and Turkish masonry, for the history of Didymoteichon is not uneventful. Originally named Plotinopolis, after Plotina, Trajan's wife, it became the medieval Demotica, a corruption of Didymoteichon (the twin walls). In 1189, during the Third Crusade, Frederick Barbarossa, on his way to engage Saladin in Syria, held the town hostage while he negotiated his passage through Byzantine territory; in the fourteenth century the usurper John VI Cantacuzenus proclaimed himself emperor here; soon after Sultan Murad I captured the castle by infiltrating a fifth column through the twin walls and established his temporary capital here. It was in one of the rock-hewn chambers of the hill that Charles II of Sweden, conqueror of Denmark, Poland, Saxony and the Ukraine, is alleged to have dwelt when he sought asylum in the Sultan's territories after his crushing defeat by the Russians on the field of Poltava (1709). Otherwise, under Turkish rule, it is the same old story – decay and oblivion. The grassy summit is littered with fragments of unidentifiable masonry. The view embraces patchwork fields and fruit orchards – Greek and Turkish – with the streams of the Hebrus meandering in loops in all directions. There seems to be water everywhere. On a hill to the north-east, across one of the tributaries, khaki-clad figures are seen bustling about parade grounds, barracks and other military installations, while sentries perched on rocky outcrops stand on watch 'o'er Hebrus's silver tide'.[2]

Little is left of the town – a mere frontier-post inhabited by a dwindling mixed population of Greeks and Turks. Beside Demarcheion Square there is a block-like mosque, and a tall minaret. Better still there is a striking view of the castle hill with its ruined towers and walls mounting the east slope in oblique parallel lines. In Katsandonis Street, a perfectly preserved exterior of an abandoned Turkish timber-framed house – a ruin inside, crawling with vermin – is one of the finest examples of Turkish domestic architecture in the country. After that there is nothing left to do but turn one's back on the east.

[2] Euripides, the *Hercules Furens*.

CHAPTER TWENTY-ONE

The Approaches to the West

❧

*(I) The Locrian coast – Naupactus – Antirrhion; (II) The Locrian massif;
(III) The Pindus spine – Metsovo*

Western Greece is a series of formidable massifs more or less
parallel to and west of the Pindus spine, fringed by fertile coastal
strips and washed by the Ionian Sea (and the Corinthian Gulf in
the south). Variety in landscape is matched by the immense chronological span of the historical sites: ancient, medieval and Ottoman.

There are four main ways of approach, although one lies beyond
the confines of this book. It is the obvious route, from Athens
through Corinth and along the northern shore of the Peloponnese
as far as Rhion, which is linked by a ferry-boat service with Antirrhion
on the mainland coast. I propose to describe here the three remaining routes:

(i) the way from Delphi through Galaxeidi, virtually in the centre
of the country (see map on p. 334-5);
(ii) the longer, more devious route from Delphi to Naupactus by
way of Amphissa, which penetrates the mountainous heart of
Ozolian Locris (see map on p. 334-5);
(iii) and finally the route from Kalabaka, further north, which is
perhaps the most spectacular (see map on p. 376-7).

I

From Galaxeidi the road skirts the northern shore of the Corinthian
Gulf, at the foot of the mountain barrier of Ozolian Locris, so-called
in antiquity because the inhabitants, the Ozolae (the word is believed
to derive from the verb *ozó*, 'to stink') wore undressed animal
hides next to the skin and consequently exuded a nasty fetid smell.
After Galaxeidi comes **Eratini,** spreading across a green maritime
strip; here Sir Giles Eastcourt, one of the earliest English travellers
in Greece, companion of the more ubiquitous Sir George Wheler,
died in the seventeenth century. Ferry-boats ply across the inland
sea between Itea and the Peloponnesian port of Aeghion. The

Delphi Beach Hotel, gaunt and barrack-like, rises incongruously from a shore of spiky rocks. Fishing hamlets are set amid little oases and cypress groves, with low islets dotted about the crescent-shaped bays. Soon the austere mountains recede, making room for the river Mornos to flow through an alluvial valley into the sea; they then advance again, leaving **Naupactus** to extend, cramped and ribbon-like, along a reed-fringed coast.

After the Third Messenian War (464–59 BC), in which the Messenians were once more routed by their formidable Spartan neighbours, the Athenians somewhat provocatively established Messenian settlers here. Filled with hatred of their conquerors, who were also the Athenians' chief rivals in the struggle for the leadership of the Greek world, the Messenians gladly manned this strategic naval station which commanded the approach through the narrows into the Corinthian Gulf from the west. It was in these confined waters, between the Peloponnesian and Locrian massifs, that Phormio, the Athenian admiral, engaged the entire Peloponnesian fleet in the third year of the Peloponnesian War (429 BC). Commanding twenty swift triremes, he coasted boldly round the larger enemy fleet, constricting its manoeuvrability so that many Peloponnesian vessels fell foul of each other. Then he attacked, forcing the Peloponnesian vessels to retire. Unwilling to admit defeat, the Lacedaemonians and their allies, says Thucydides, 'remained opposite . . . practising and preparing for battle'. At one point the Peloponnesians succeeded in driving the Athenians so close inshore that Phormio was forced to deploy his vessels in a dangerously attenuated line. But handling his small fast squadron with dash and discipline, he broke through the more cumbersome Peloponnesian triremes and routed them. There was no second round. Timocrates, the disgraced Lacedaemonian admiral, threw himself overboard and was drowned in the harbour of Naupactus.

In medieval times Naupactus was ruled by Angevins, later by Venetians who built the great castle, made it 'the strongest bulwark of the Christian people', and stayed for nearly a hundred years. An island in a Turkish sea, the wall-girt city, then called Lepanto, suffered violent siege, with Turkish cannon balls raining down for weeks on end. It fell in 1499: the last Venetian stronghold on the Greek mainland. Its loss was such a blow to Venetian pride that Grimani, the admiral (and future doge) who effected the surrender, was lampooned by popular versifiers and street urchins in Venice as 'Antonio Grimani, the ruin of the Christians'.[1]

[1] William Miller, *The Latins in the Levant*, John Murray, London, 1908.

The little Venetian **port**, filled with painted caiques, is oval-shaped, defended by two towers at either extremity on the breakwater – a perfect stage-set. From here the Turkish fleet of Sultan Selim the Sot, who preferred women and wine to battle, set sail one October morning in 1571 to engage the combined Papal, Spanish and Venetian squadrons of two hundred galleys commanded by Don John of Austria which were cruising west of the strait. In a cabin of a Spanish galley, Cervantes, a private soldier, lay prostrate with fever. But the moment the alarm was sounded, he did not hesitate to take up a position of great danger in a boat slung to the galley's side and received two gun-shot wounds. One of his hands was permanently maimed, and he always referred to it as a token of the proudest moment of his life. Within hours the Turkish defeat was total and 'many of the Turks, blinded with fear, casting away their weapons to escape the fury of the enemy, threw themselves headlong into the sea, among the already dead and half-drowning'.[2] They lost over a hundred galleys and thousands of men. Christendom, it was proclaimed, was saved, the invincibility of Ottoman power proved a myth. But the battle was not decisive. The allies fell out among themselves and Venice made a separate peace with the Sultan. Turkish dockyards, working overtime, made good the losses. By the seventeenth century Naupactus had become a second Algiers and the Crescent once more fluttered unchallenged throughout the eastern Mediterranean.

A steep cone-shaped hill, girdled with a triple line of walls, overlooks the port. A road, passing below a line of well-preserved fortifications, winds up to the Venetian **castle**. Passing on foot through a series of arched gateways overlooked by a crenellated bastion, one enters the bailey, now a shady pine-wood. A slippery path, thick with pine needles, mounts to the chapel of Prophitis Elias (Prophet Elijah), once the site of a pagan sanctuary. On Sundays Naupactians stroll up here and picnic under the resin-scented arbours. Fragments of look-out posts, built on ancient Hellenic foundations, form belvederes. A wall-walk north of the chapel commands a view of a steep pine-clad slope falling away into a ravine. The outer line of defences makes a fine sweep to meet a transverse wall. Further down, another transverse wall runs impressively along the entire width of the enceinte. From here it is easy to perceive the general design of the castle which is divided into five successive wards on different levels. Below, the little town clings to the side of the hill, with the oval harbour, guarded by its two

[2] Richard Knolles, *The General Historie of the Turkes*, Adam Islip, 1638.

diminutive bastions, in the exact centre of the picture. On either side extend the sandy reed-fringed beaches. Across the strait rise the Peloponnesian ranges.

Beyond Naupactus the road runs westward along a well-watered coastline, along which the Messenian hoplites marched in support of Phormio's squadron and cheered the rout of the Lacedaemonian fleet. **Antirrhion,** terminal of the ferry-boat service from Rhion, is little more than an agglomeration of port installations, distinguished by a low fort, known as the Castle of Roumeli, built by the Turks on the site of a medieval defensive position and crowned by a lighthouse. The wash of ferry boats, crammed with buses and lorries, streaks the blue channel – the Turks called it the Little Dardenelles, for it is little more than a mile wide. The sea is often choppy, for the wind is funnelled through the channel between high ranges. Eastward extends the inland sea of the Corinthian Gulf; westward the Peloponnesian and mainland shores fan out and the mass of Cephalonia, with Ithaca behind it, emerges out of the Ionian Sea. In the south, the eroded hills of Mount Panachaecus pile up towards the Peloponnesian heights.

Everything beyond Antirrhion may be said to form part of western Greece proper.

II

From Amphissa the road to Naupactus climbs the bare elephantine flanks of Mount Ghiona, providing prodigious views of the arena of mountains enclosing the Sacred Plain. Continuing in a north-west direction – the desolation is relieved only by a rash of battery chicken farms – we reach **Lidhoriki,** so-called from the medieval Ledorex, a Catalan stronghold guarding the approaches to the Spanish Count's capital of La Sol, i.e. Amphissa. Situated at an altitude of nearly two thousand feet in an unproductive, sparsely populated wilderness, the village was a hide-out during the Second World War of a group of guerrillas known as the 'Golden Resistance' from the number of sovereigns they secured from the British Government in order to fight other differently orientated political groups rather than the common enemy. It is pleasant to break one's journey at Lidhoriki for refreshment (*ouzo*, coffee, fried eggs – there is little else). The air is crystalline, the inhabitants blond, ruddy and friendly. Thence begins the grand meandering descent to the coast. The mountain configuration acquires an increasingly intricate character, the range alternately forming canyons, sunless valleys

328

and hollow gorges. One insulated crag is crowned by a white chapel. Soon the road is running beside the Mornos, the ancient Hylaethus, at first a crystal-clear stream bordered with plane trees, winding between great cliffs and fir-clad slopes. Joined by numerous tributaries, it then turns into a wide muddy torrent forcing its way around the numerous obstacles raised by the mountain complex in order to reach the sea.

A dirt road to the right (the signpost says 'To Krokillion' – a minor deviation of seven kilometres) ascends steeply above the confluence of the Mornos and one of its tributaries. With the increasing altitude, the vistas become more awe-inspiring, especially in autumn when the lower forest belt is ablaze with colour. Beside a plane tree at **Kria Vrisi** (The Cold Spring) there is a monument raised to the memory of Makriyannis, one of the ablest and most extrovert generals of the War of Independence. The site is said to be that of his birthplace, his mother having been taken in her labour pains while gathering corn in the fields. After distinguishing himself in some of the most notable exploits of the war, Makriyannis fell for the heady delights of political conspiracy. Soon out of favour with the State Security Police, he devoted himself to the composition of his memoirs, written in an alternatively naïve and lapidary style which still makes lively and informative reading. After having the book illustrated by an untrained peasant painter, whose style matches that of the martial author – aerial views of set-piece battles fought on land and by sea – the hardy mountaineer, turned general, politician and man of letters, was sufficiently pleased with his literary achievement to send a copy of the text and illustrations to Queen Victoria. The illustrations are now in Windsor Castle.[3]

Less than one kilometre beyond the monument is the abandoned village of Isvora, where Makriyannis spent his childhood and youth fostering his flamboyant patriotism and hatred of the Turkish oppressor. More striking is the red-roofed village of **Krokillion** (the terminus of the branch road) below a fearsome peak. The terrace of the village church overlooks a narrow wooded valley, beyond and around which rise successive ranges capped by nodular peaks and crags.

The main road to the south continues through the Mornos valley, surrounded on all sides by the architectural forms of heights at

[3] A complete set of the delightful Makriyannis prints can be seen in the Gennadeon Library in Athens. An admirable English translation by H. A. Lidderdale of the *Memoirs*, a standard work on the Greek War of Liberation, has been published by the Oxford University Press, 1966.

different levels; after a final descent through a valley of orchards and vineyards planted with alleys of needle-shaped dwarf cypresses, it reaches the northern shore of the Corinthian Gulf. The road turns westward. One crosses a bridge spanning the Mornos and enters Naupactus.

III

Scaling the Pindus range at a tremendous altitude, the westward road from Kalabaka leads to Yannina, capital of Epirus. From the Kalabaka-Grevena fork it ascends in wide loops; below, to the south-east, the Peneius winds through a wide wooded valley, with the tusks and obelisks of Meteora composing into a grotesque gateway leading into the level plain. Ahead, westward, loom range upon range of mountains. Occasionally a village with ugly corrugated-roofed houses spreads across hillsides of apple and fig orchards. The deeper one penetrates into the massif – into the actual spine of the whole country – the wider, dizzier and more confusing become the loops followed by the road, with the wooded heights pressing in on all sides. The holm-oak belt is succeeded by the stone pine – a Christmas tree scene, with the watershed dominated by a beetling crag. At the top of the formidable pass – the Katara (the Damned One) – a large hollow arena opens up to the south-east, its rim circled by the road which gradually descends the slopes of fir, box and beech into the heart of the bowl, where the twin villages of **Metsovo** (Prosilion and Anilion) so called because the former faces towards the sun and the latter is supposedly condemned to eternal shade, cling to the sides of precipitous cliffs.

Metsovo, reputedly one of the show villages of Greece, is by the very nature of its position claustrophobic (the mountain in configuration makes walking, indeed strolling, an exhausting recreation limited to back-breaking ascents and dizzy vertical descents). It remains the centre of the Koutsovlachs; Roumanian-speaking Vlachs who, it has been suggested, may be the descendants of Roman legions stationed in the bleak strategic passes of the Pindus mountains (alternatively of Pompey's army after its rout at Pharsalia). Other historians believe them to be ancient immigrants from Dacia. During the Latin occupation and in Byzantine times Metsovo, always populous in spite of its remoteness, was administered by a Wallachian governor. Under the Turks the inhabitants did not suffer the worst of depredations. A seventeenth-century Vizier, fleeing from the Sultan's displeasure, took refuge here. When pardoned, he became Grand Vizier. In recognition for the hospitality offered him by the inhabitants, he granted them special privileges in the form of grazing rights and tax exemptions. The prosperity of the village never diminished, and today it is famed for its carpenters, among the best woodcarvers in Greece, goldsmiths and silversmiths, for its ski-fields, its trade in tourist souvenirs (bedspreads, fleecy sheepskin rugs and carved wooden bric-à-brac) and its excellent if moderately expensive smoked cheese.

Narrow cobbled alleys descend between tall houses – the older ones roofed with grey slate – and tourist shops, to a large poplar-shaded square where in summer the inhabitants stare wide-eyed at open-air television, as the sun sets over the mountain peaks. On feast days round dances are performed here, the men, their ruddy faces set in stony expressions, wearing black kilts and black *tsarouchia*, the women in dresses embroidered with flowers and sleeveless, generally crimson-edged, black cloaks, pigtails hanging down their back from under black kerchiefs. Adjoining the square is the **Church of Ayia Paraskevi**, a sixteenth-century foundation in basilica form, with a clock tower crowned by a cross which the departing Turks, after their defeat in the First Balkan War (1912), believing it to be made of gold, tried to shoot down and carry off as loot. The church's main interest lies in its wooden iconostasis, dated to *c.* 1730, in which the Epirot woodcarver has attempted to render representations of God and the Expulsion from the Garden of Eden. Animal designs, an elegant swan and a fox scratching its ear, are carved on two wooden columns framing the south door of the sanctuary. South-east of the square is a playground perched dizzily over the bowl-like valley across which the great peak of Peristeri, towering over the whole central mass of the Pindus, casts its shadow.

The **Tositsa house**, which serves as a museum of local regional popular art – it is signposted – is a replica of a typical grand old Metsovo house, restored by Baron Tositsa, member of a local family of public benefactors. The layout is similar to that of the archons' mansions of the Turkish period at Ambelakia, Siatista and Castoria: armoury and wash-house on the ground floor, bedrooms on the first, reception rooms surrounded by wide low divans in the form of banquettes on the second. The floors are carpeted by fine locally woven *kilims* and the bedroom cupboards are filled with elegantly cut cloaks worn by the gentlemen and the bridal dresses worn by their ladies.

Another agreeable visit is to the **Monastery of Ayios Nikolaos.**

A dirt road descends into the ravine of the Metsovitikos stream at the bottom of the sombre mountain bowl. To the south Anilios spreads, in its alleged permanent shade, across the cliff-face to the south. The short ascent to the monastery is along a path bordered by ferns. Hens peck among beds of dead leaves under an arbour of walnut trees. Pansies, snapdragons and geraniums create a blaze of colour in the monastic courtyard. Here there is serenity. The ring of awful mountains is out of sight. The church, restored in 1960, by M. Evangelos Averoff, a distinguished politician and scion of another Metsovo family of public benefactors, is in basilica form. The post-Byzantine frescoes, also restored, cover every inch of wall space: small panels, rather than the usual grand compositions which create an effect more colourful than arresting. A band of saints' heads amid vine tendrils round three sides of the interior is attractive, but the carved wooden iconostasis must surely be too fussy for even the most enthusiastic admirer of this form of Epirot church decoration. Taped recordings of the liturgy, switched on the moment the visitor enters the church, strike an incongruous, if not synthetic note. In the narthex, converted into a miniature museum, are displayed icons, the most striking of which is one of St Matthew, a dark figure depicted in the act of composing his Gospel, while an angel in red garments stands beside him, inspiring him.

Glad as one is to have visited Metsovo and penetrated the heart of the lonely central Pindus massif, it is agreeable to be relieved of its claustrophobic atmosphere and take to the road again. The west-bound way into Epirus continues to offer an impressive spectacle. One crosses torrent beds with huge boulders, ascends and descends slopes of scrub-oak, circles round eroded hills. It is in this deserted country, at the locality called Peristeri, that the Greek Prime Minister, Tsolakoglou, signed an armistice with the Axis forces in April 1941. After spanning a Bailey bridge, the road climbs the foothills of the barren limestone barrier of Mount Mitsikelli and descends one of its southern flanks, past the Monastery of Panayia Dourahan, founded by an infidel Turkish pasha as a token of gratitude to the Virgin for protecting him during a nocturnal ride across the frozen lake of Yannina. A panoramic view then opens up: the opaque lake, its wooded islet, and the city's mosque crowning the citadel of Yannina surrounded by hazy beige-coloured hills. One enters Yannina from the marshy east end of the lake.

CHAPTER TWENTY-TWO

Western Roumeli

.✤

Calydon – Misolonghi – Pleuron – Aetolikon – Oeniadae – Agrinion – Boucation – Thermon – The Acheloos – Stratos

Beyond Naupactus and Antirrhion variety is the keynote. North of the channel separating the Peloponnese from the mainland rise mountain ranges, from whose gorges streams, swelling into rivers, flow across the plains into lagoons. All this country, loosely termed Western Roumeli, includes the ancient provinces of Ozolian Locris, Aetolia and Acarnania (for Eastern Roumeli, see Chapter 8).

The plains are scattered with rocky knolls and ridges, some of which were once sites of well-fortified Hellenistic cities. Extant walls recall their military importance. Three days (two nights at Agrinion where there are the best hotels) is the minimum time required to see all the places described in this chapter. The direct route, without deviations, provides the traveller with glimpses of the acropolis of Calydon and the Heroes' Garden at Misolonghi. The ramparts of Pleuron can be identified from the highway which also runs below the walls of Stratos in the Acheloos valley. But the two most rewarding sites, Oeniadae and Thermon, lie well off the main road.

Beyond Antirrhion the road loops westward round the formidable mass of Mount Klokova, the ancient Taphiasus, which rises three thousand feet sheer above the sea. The springs at its base are associated with the legend of the evil-smelling waters fed by the poisoned blood of the Centaur Nessus, who was slain by Heracles for attempting to rape his hard-won bride Deianeira, and subsequently buried on the mountain-top. After overhanging the sea at a great height the road winds through a wooded valley filled with Judas trees and crosses the shingly bed of the Evenus, the original boundary between Ozolian Locris and Aetolia, flowing in serpentine streams between steep shrub-covered banks at the point where mythographers suggest Heracles rescued Deianeira from the unwelcome attentions of Nessus.

Aetolia was always a wild country, its mountains scarred with rugged ravines, inhabited by warlike tribes dwelling in scattered unprotected settlements, unlike most Greeks who were basically a

333

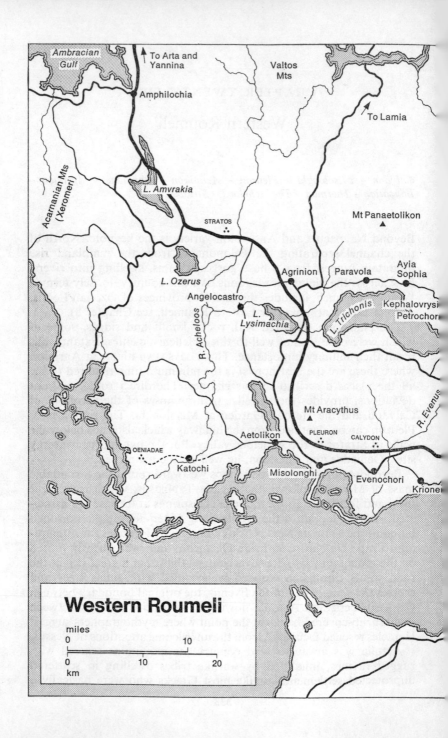

Western Roumeli

miles
0   10
0   10   20
km

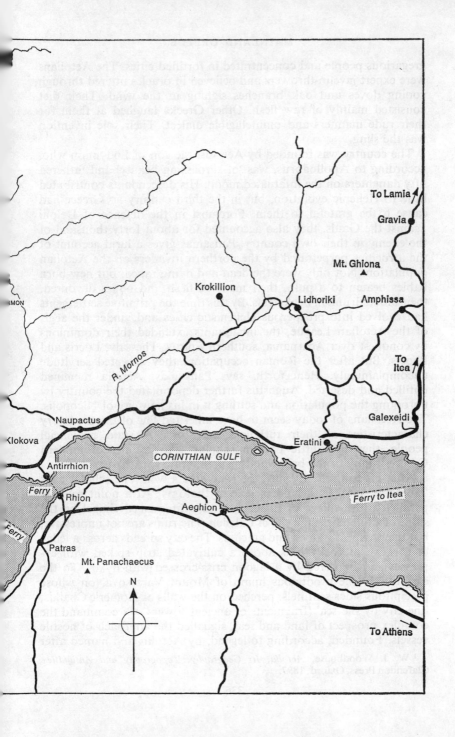

gregarious people and concentrated in fortified cities. The Aetolians were expert javelin-throwers and believed in oracles uttered through cooing doves and oak branches sighing in the wind. Their diet consisted mainly of raw flesh. Other Greeks laughed at them for their rude manners and unintelligible dialect. Their sole invention was the sling.

The country was founded by Aetolus, the son of Endymion who, according to Apollodorus, was 'of surpassing beauty' and fathered fifty daughters on the infatuated moon. His descendants contributed little to Hellenic evolution, but in the third century BC Greece had cause to be grateful to them. Foremost in the defence of Delphi against the Gauls, they also accounted for about forty thousand of the enemy in their own country. Pausanias gives a lurid account of the atrocities perpetrated by the northern invaders on the Aetolian population. Not only were the dead and dying raped, but new-born babies beaten to a pulp, their mangled flesh and bones devoured, their blood drunk in beakerfuls. By this time the primitive settlements had evolved into prosperous Hellenistic cities and, under the aegis of the Aetolian League, the inhabitants extended their dominions by conquest over Acarnania, southern Epirus, Thessaly, Locris and Phocis. But after the Roman occupation, they accepted servitude uncomplainingly. Henceforth, says Pausanias, Aetolia remained untilled and deserted. Augustus further depopulated the country by uprooting the population and settling it in his new city of Nicopolis. The Aetolians of today seem to have inherited few of the predatory characteristics of their turbulent ancestors. A staid provincial people, they take little part in shaping the destinies of modern Greece. Many of the backwoodsmen emigrate to America.

After crossing the Evenus, the road enters what one scholar calls 'Homeric Aetolia': a land of epic mythology.[1] At a point roughly parallel to the village of Evenochori, a whitewashed chapel on the slope of a hill marks the **site of Calydon**. The ruins are not impressive, but the prospect is open and gracious. The city spreads across a ledge of a range of rocky hills above a cultivated strip spiked with cypresses and bordered by a lagoon criss-crossed with dykes. To the east towers the prodigious hump of Mount Varassova, on whose precipitous sides sentinels, perched on the walls of Homeric Chalkis, 'the city by the sea' (fragments of ancient towers still command the complex prospect of land and sea), signalled the approach of hostile vessels. Founded, according to legend, by Aetolus and named after

[1] W. J. Woodhouse, *Aetolia, Its Geography, Topography and Antiquities*, Clarendon Press, Oxford, 1897.

his son, Calydon was the home of many famous mythological figures: of Oeneus, father of Meleager and grandfather of Diomedes, who received the first vine from Dionysus; of Thoas, who went to the Trojan War in a fleet of fifty black ships; and of Oxylus, king of Elis, who, some say, founded the Olympic Games.

A path climbs the hillside; a signpost points to the Heroon, the Heroes' Sanctuary. Ancient slabs litter a wispy olive grove, with vestiges of chambers constructed with rectangular blocks (only a course or two survive) grouped round what must have been a peristyle court surrounded by a colonnade. Beside an adjacent wall steps descend into a vaulted passage which led to a burial chamber (*c.* 100 BC) directly under the court. On the west hill, beyond a farmhouse, overlooking the main road, are the remains of the sanctuary of Artemis Laphria, goddess of the chase, who was worshipped above all other deities at Calydon, a land of huntsmen. The outline of the stylobate of the fourth-century BC temple with cella, colonnades and porch, buttressed with the rectangular blocks of an earlier (and later restored) retaining wall, are clearly identifiable. The temple once contained the famous chryselephantine statue of Artemis Laphria, afterwards removed to Patras. Beside it is the site of a sixth-century BC temple of Apollo: a mass, to the un-professional eye, of unidentifiable outlines. Of the towers and walls that enclosed a city, powerful though never distinguished for its architectural elegance, only shattered plaques are scattered across the wind-blown hillside, where the Calydonian sentinels stood on guard, ready to signal the approach of an enemy rounding the hump of Mount Varassova.

Behind the Laphrian sanctuary the barking of fierce watchdogs now echoes from the barren hills where the heroes chased the Calydonian Boar across the mythical hunting-grounds. The hunt was contemporary, says Apollodorus, with Jason's quest of the Golden Fleece and Theseus's journey from Troezen to Athens -- an age when all men were heroes and all their actions epic exploits; a time before man of the classical era, in his quest for nationality, had reduced his own image to life-size. The legend's origins stem from a typical act of personal vindictiveness on the part of one of the Olympian deities. According to Homer, Oeneus, King of Calydon, forgot to make a harvest-offering to Artemis, who promptly retaliated by sending a monstrous boar to ravage the land. Thereupon the king's son, the red-headed Meleager, organized a great hunt, enlisting the aid of heroes from other parts of Greece: Jason and Admetus from Thessaly, the Dioscuri from Sparta, Theseus and

Amphiaraus from Attica; even wise old Nestor, who came all the way from Pylos, was personally attacked by the boar and had to scramble up a tree in order to avoid being gored by it. No participant, however, was more glamorous than Atalanta, a virgin huntress, suckled by one of Artemis's she-bears, who ran faster than any mortal. When the hunters closed round the trapped boar, she inflicted the decisive wound with an arrow aimed at the beast's ear, thus enabling Meleager to deliver the *coup de grâce*.

Meleager chivalrously offered the spoils – the boar's tusks and pelt – to the intrepid Amazon, but his mother's brothers stole them, and in the ensuing scuffle were killed by their nephew. Meleager's mother, the brooding vengeful Althaea, promptly recalled an old and sinister prophecy. At her son's birth, she had been visited by the Fates who predicted that the red-haired child would live only as long as the log burning in the brazier took to be reduced to ashes. She had consequently hidden the brand in a chest. Determined now to avenge her brothers, even at the cost of her son's life, she hurled it into the blaze. As soon as it was burnt out, Meleager dropped dead. At his funeral all the female mourners, shrieking at the tops of their voices, were transformed into guinea-fowl by the infuriated Artemis. In the violence of its dénouement, in the incontinence of the passions displayed by Artemis, Althaea and Meleager, Calydonian drama has an almost Mycenaean ring, worthy of an Aeschylus or a Sophocles. We have to be content with Swinburne.

It is a short drive from Calydon to **Misolonghi**, its shacks and hovels and gimcrack villas surrounded by shallow water ('the belt of death', Trelawny called it). Flourishing with fisheries, trading in *avghotaracho* (fish-roe pressed into a cylindrical shape and enveloped in a rind of yellow wax – an expensive delicacy), the historic little town remains mosquito-infested, smelling of sedge and salt, rain-lashed in winter, burning hot in summer. At sunset the lagoon, across which flat-bottomed boats skim between rows of piles, reflects an impressionist blend of colours that recall Turner's rather than Canaletto's Venice: bands of amethyst, grey and lavender speckled with coils of green, yellow and pink formed by patches of floating oil. A reef of islets separates the lagoon from the sea.

The leaders of the War of Independence, headed by Alexander Mavrocordatos, first President of the National Assembly, chose this melancholy place for their headquarters because, strategically, it occupied a position similar to that of Calydon in antiquity, controlling both the entrance to the Gulf of Corinth and all communications between the mainland and the Morea. It was also the first place in western Greece to be liberated (and the first in which the Moslem population was exterminated to a man). To it flocked patriots and upper-class Greeks educated in Constantinople – all, says Finlay, 'eloquent in ignorance . . . stiff in their opinions and dilatory in their actions'. It seemed the best place for Byron, as representative of the London Committee, to try to unite the rival factions and persuade them to fight the enemy rather than each other. He arrived on 2 January 1824, wearing the scarlet uniform of the Eighth Regiment of Foot, surrounded by kilted Suliot guards. Guns fired salvoes, and wailing klephtic tunes were played on lutes and clarinets as he was received by the assembled dignitaries: the *banditti* turned politicians, the gorgeously robed clerics, the sallow aquiline-faced aristocrats aping Western manners. Drainage was unknown at Misolonghi and pools of stagnant water lay around the houses. Most of the inhabitants, clad in goatskins, dwelt in hovels among the long reeds. A fetid smell rose from the motionless water.

Byron showed unaccustomed patience, endeavouring to instil some notion of constructive patriotism in the vain and mercenary men who paid lip-service to him, because he had gold to give away and a title which impressed them. But his greatest contribution to the cause of Greece was his death, which occurred, aptly enough, in the course of a violent thunderstorm, after a ten-day bout of malarial fever. The flamboyance of the end matched the record of the past. Not only Greece and England were moved by his sacrifice; all Europe suddenly became conscious of the Greek struggle for liberty. The flow of volunteers from France, Italy and Russia increased. He died, in fact, to quote his own words, that 'Greece might still be free'. In the minds of the ordinary Greek people he was – and indeed still is – not only the greatest Englishman who ever lived, but a symbol of all those qualities their own leaders sometimes lack: disinterestedness, eccentricity allied with reliability, authority enveloped in an aura of aristocratic glamour. When his body was taken back to Newstead the inhabitants pleaded that some part of his mortal remains should remain with them. So his intestines were enshrined in four jars and placed in the church of St Spyridon. They have subsequently been lost. The house in which he lived and died is no longer standing.

The **Heroes' Garden** lies at the north-west end of the town, shaded by dusty pines, palms and eucalyptus trees. The nozzles of old cannon project from gun-slits in the Turkish walls which run along two sides of it. The monuments to the heroes of the war – Byron's occupies the place of honour – are outstandingly ugly, the palm going to that of the anonymous philhellenes: a pile of conglomerate and cannon balls crowned by an urn. But it is pleasant to sit on a shady bench. The smell of resinous pines and disinfectant eucalyptus drives away the saline odours rising from the lagoon.

It was from this landward side that the famous sortie was made. After Byron's death the siege of Misolonghi began in earnest, and a Turkish army under Reshid Pasha surrounded the rampart. The town was defended by a garrison of four thousand Greeks and armed peasants, and a thousand civilians and boatmen. After nearly a year's siege, Ibrahim Pasha brought up his Egyptian army from the Morea and launched flotillas of flat-bottomed boats to attack with musketry and fiery missiles across the lagoon; but every attack was thwarted by the Greeks, who refused an offer of mediation from Sir Frederick Adam, Lord High Commissioner of the Ionian Islands. From Zante, Dionysios Solomos, Greece's national poet, watched the fires of the siege light up the night sky and cried, 'Hold out, poor Misolonghi!' The heroism of the defenders was prodigious, but with the Turks in command of the lagoons it was no longer possible to supply the garrison. So in April 1826 the decision was taken to make a mass sortie through the labyrinth of ditches, dykes and pools surrounding the rampart. As the soldiers sprang forward, writes Finlay, 'Neither the yataghan of Reshid's Albanians, nor the bayonet of Ibrahim's Arabs, could arrest their impetuous attack.' But for the information supplied by a traitor to the Turks the Greeks would have got away, together with all their women dressed in fustanellas and children armed with pistols. But they found the roads blocked by Turkish cavalry. Hunger, wounds and fever took their toll of the surviving groups which straggled up the mountain paths. As the Turks entered the shattered town the few remaining Greeks blew themselves up. Misolonghi is justifiably a national shrine. Throughout the history of the Greeks there is one shining thread of continuity. When their leaders fall, as they sometimes do, below the standards of high responsibility, when they prove themselves to be corrupt, pusillanimous or incompetent, the common people are capable of rising to the greatest point of human sacrifice, dignity and nobility. As Finlay rightly says, the siege and sortie of Misolonghi await their Thucydides.

Misolonghi has one more claim to fame. Costi Palamas (1859–

1943), one of Greece's leading modern poets, spent his childhood here. He afterwards immortalized the weird atmosphere of the waterlogged place in a haunting poem, *The Lament of the Lagoon*. His portrait hangs in the Town Hall beside that of Byron.

West of Misolonghi a line of ancient walls descends a chain of hills rising abruptly out of the plain. A stony track (to the right) climbs Mount Aracythus. In order to visit **Pleuron** it is essential to have a local guide.[2] The deviation is worthwhile: the Hellenistic walls are among the finest in Greece. In the prehistoric age, says Strabo, the place was ruled by Thestius, father of Althaea, the savage Queen of Calydon, and was once an 'ornament' of Greece, though deserted in his own day. A new Hellenistic city rose up on a more inaccessible site in the third century BC, during the wars between the Macedonian kings and the Aetolian League.

The impregnable enceinte, a circuit of about a mile and a half, is a lozenge-shaped quadrilateral, protected to the north by an abrupt spur of Mount Aracynthus, and falling away, east, south and west in rocky declivities. High on a steep slope are several tombs which form a kind of extra-mural necropolis. Descending through a hole in the ground, we entered a vault consisting of two chambers, one of which possessed a stone bench decorated with a volute. The well-preserved stone wall had a lovely smooth patina. It may have been the tomb of some senior garrison officer, for Hellenistic Pleuron was primarily a military stronghold; it was ruled by no great kings and claimed no distinguished citizens.

The entry into the enceinte is from the south-west. Huge rectangular blocks of limestone litter the ground, carpeted in autumn with pale pink crocuses (*Colchicum cupani*) which were believed by ancient apothecaries to produce a deadly poison. A massive lintel, twelve feet long and three wide, is propped up against the wall. From here it is best to follow a roughly south-north direction across the windswept ledge. First, to the vestigial remains of a theatre, the smallest in Greece, built into the west rampart, where the garrison troops were probably entertained with the farces of Aristophanes and Menander. It had only eight tiers and was entirely unornamented. Next comes a strange sunken structure, known as 'The Prisons', believed to have been a huge cistern containing the main water supply of this barren inaccessible place. The pit is approximately one hundred feet by sixty, its sides overgrown with ivy, and crossed

[2] One can generally find a man or boy who knows the way round the ruins, locally called the Castro of Ayia Irini, at one of the farmhouses on the way.

by four parallel walls which may have supported a roof. Each of the oblong chambers formed by these walls is connected with the other by a curious triangular aperture.

To the north, at the apex of the lozenge, extends a deserted ledge, site of the agora. The outlines of the foundations are somewhat incomprehensible. The strictly military nature of the citadel, a formidable observation post dominating the plain, may account for the fact that there is not a fragment of a capital, a column, nor any decorative moulding. A parapet surrounds the north side; immediately below it the well-preserved east gate, with clearly discernible holes on which the door pivoted, overlooks the bleak slopes of the Zygos range.

Turning south-east in order to complete the circuit, one passes the base of an apsidal edifice and the sunken foundations of a square chamber into which a stairway descends, and then skirts the line of the **east walls**, six feet thick and in a good state of preservation: as impressive an example of third-century BC military architecture as any in the country. The line extends unbroken, generally six courses high, sometimes as many as fifteen, composed of massive quadrangular blocks crowned at intervals by low rectangular towers (originally there were over thirty). Vestiges of steps by means of which sentinels mounted the *terreplein* are discernible. In autumn clusters of deep pink cyclamen grow in the shade of the great blocks. Alternating perspectives advance and recede in a wide arc running east to west: the cliff of Varassova, like a huge beast crouching above the plain; the lagoon of Misolonghi intersected with causeways; the fields and cypress alleys of the coastal strip streaked by the highway; a shoal of islets, the Echinades, off which the battle of Lepanto was fought, strung out along the shore where the Acheloos winds through sandbanks to the sea.

From the Pleuron fork the main road runs parallel to a narrow-gauge railway, bordered by pink sea-lavender, which serves the Aetolo-Acarnanian lowlands between Krioneri on the coast and Agrinion. The country is a complex of lagoons and salt-pans, with the Zygos chain forming a barrier to the east. A narrow inner lagoon bites deep into the land, spanned by a causeway, with the colour-washed houses of Aetolikon reflected in the motionless water, looking under a cloudy sky like some Mediterranean version of Vermeer's *View of Delft* in miniature.

To visit Oeniadae one takes the branch road to the west through Aetolikon into a domesticated countryside of maize and cabbage fields. Low rocky humps emerge out of olive groves dotted with the rush and wicker wigwams of the Sarakatsans, a nomadic people who for centuries have migrated between the Epirot highlands and Roumelian lowlands. The road passes through Katochi, whose brightly painted houses climb the side of a knoll overlooking the reed-fringed banks of the Acheloos, and enters a reclaimed marsh-land. Originally Lake Melita, it was connected with the sea by a channel. Knobbly insulated hills rise out of the pampas country like jointed fingers, their bases fringed with reeds and luxuriant thistles. All evidence of the lake has vanished. A low flat-topped range, a sort of miniature sierra, locally known as Tricardo, the **ancient Oeniadae**, one of the strangest Hellenistic sites in Greece, runs north to south, its slopes, abrupt but of no great height, studded with olive trees, on the higher level with oaks. The debris of polygonal walls is discernible through dense thickets. Grunting pigs root for acorns, and horseflies plague the sightseer. Anything up to two hours is required to see the main features of this confusing site.

The legendary founder was Alcmaeon (see p. 346), who named it after his son Oeneus. It subsequently acquired considerable fame for its impregnability. An Athenian army, commanded by Pericles, was unable to scale its well-defended sides in 453 BC. In the Pelopon-nesian War Oeniadae sided with Sparta, and in 428 BC twelve Athenian triremes sailed up the estuary of the Acheloos, but the hoplites were unable to reduce the citadel. In Hellenistic times the hill was encircled with strong new fortifications, and the arsenal and harbour on Lake Melita were joined to the citadel by ramparts. Thus fortified by nature and man, it occupied a strategic position, near the mouth of the Acheloos, dominating the Acarnanian low-lands. But, like other Hellenistic cities of the western littoral, it contributed little to the evolution of Hellenic civilization. In fact the only great name associated with Oeniadae is that of Hippo-crates, who came here once in his medical capacity.

The whole eminence, obviously once an island, is peppered with fragments of polygonal walls (originally a circuit of three miles), gates, cisterns, posterns, sally-ports and foundations of houses, all buried deep in brushwood and difficult to locate. It is best to begin at the north end, where the contours of the port – once a sinuous creek biting deep into the limestone cliff-side – are discernible, enclosed within parallel ramparts running south to north. A fine polygonal wall and tower overlook the former lake. From here one can climb the hill parallel to the eastern harbour rampart. There are

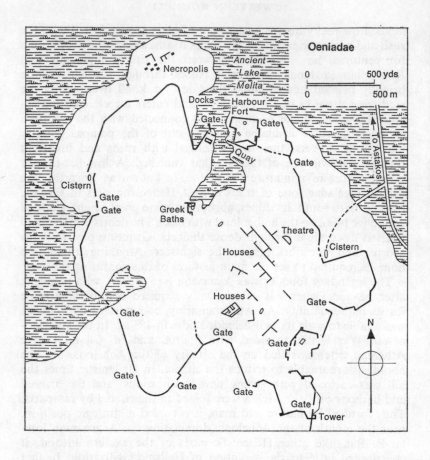

Oeniadae

Necropolis
Ancient
Lake
Melita
Docks Harbour
Fort
Gate
Gate
Quay
Gate
Cistern
Gate
Gate
Greek
Baths
Theatre
Houses
Cistern
Houses
Gate
Gate
Gate
Gate
Gate
Gate
Gate
Gate
Gate
Gate
Tower

To Astakos

0   500 yds
0   500 m

N

paths, but they are confusing. It is best to keep bearing south-east among the oak trees, whose branches shade a thick undergrowth of Jerusalem sage and butcher's broom ablaze with red berries. Rustling sounds are made by great snuffling sows, and snakes glide in the long grass.

A juvenile swineherd directed us to the **theatre**, which is excitingly hidden in a thicket of oak trees. Fragments of more than twenty tiers survive and part of the orchestra is discernible. The cavea was divided into eleven sections and there were twenty-five rock-hewn seats in the front row for notables. From the highest tier there is a memorable view through a tracery of oak branches. The southern extremity of the hill slopes towards the serpentine estuary of the

344

Acheloos, flowing through green fields and shoals of silt. East of the river mouth a group of hills with craggy crests complete the Poussin-like composition: serene, classical and pastoral. Carrying the Poussin analogy a little further, one is struck by the similarity in the disposition of detail, in the spatial relation between foreground and background, in the clarity and balance of the design. The familiar cerulean blue sky is there, and the winding river with grey mountains in the distance. Only the apricot flesh tints of the heroic figures are absent (Oeniadae is a very deserted place). There are few views in Greece which approximate more closely to a French seventeenth-century conception of a classical landscape.

East of the theatre is a large cistern, followed (south-east) by remains of what could have been an important, probably the main, gate. From the theatre a north-west descent leads to the former quay, where the narrow bottleneck of the creek opens out into a large inlet in which the triremes anchored. At the southern extremity of the creek are the ruins of the second-century BC baths: a rectangular edifice with a stone tank and two circular rooms containing basin-like hollows ranged in a circle, where bathers stood as hot water was poured over them from cauldrons.

Following the base of the hill northwards you reach the **docks,** situated on the north-west tip of the promontory. The site is unique in Greece. Below a massive polygonal wall (west of a tower) there is a depression, its cliff-face covered with plain walling, polygonal on the higher course. Tall parallel buttresses between which ships were berthed are easily identifiable; traces of the slipways, once latticed with wood in order to protect the keels of the triremes, are just discernible, but I have failed to locate the rings to which the ships were moored. There is an uncanny feeling of unreality, of something one cannot quite believe in, about these ancient port installations, barely distinguishable from the rock out of which they were hewn, with no visible sign of the sea for miles around.

Continuing east along the base of the harbour fort, past our original starting-point, one can climb the hill again to look into a huge lamia, or pit (in mythology these lamias were the lairs of dragons and other monsters sent by the gods to ravage the earth in revenge for some affront to their pride committed by a feckless mortal). The echoing cavern is hollowed out of the steep wooded hillside and the bottom is filled with stagnant water. Squawking crows wheel around in the gloomy shade.

One road from Aetolikon to Agrinion continues along the east shore of the inner lagoon and then follows a northerly course along the valley of the Acheloos between the range of the Xeromeri (Dry Mountains) and the Zygos chain: a country of scrub-covered, sometimes olive-clad, hills. The village of **Angelocastro,** once the second capital of the Despots of Epirus, is crowned by a ruined Byzantine tower. After crossing a saddle of hills the road descends into the green bowl of the Acarnanian plains, dotted with lakes and traversed by the streams of the Acheloos, with the jagged spurs of Mount Panaetolikon massing up behind Agrinion.[3]

The history of Acarnania is much the same as that of Aetolia. Thucydides dismisses its inhabitants as a primitive uncivilized people, rude and brutal like the Aetolians, although very much their junior partners, and not worthy of being considered Hellenes. They nevertheless contended at panhellenic games. The legendary father-founder of the race was Alcmaeon, who killed his mother Eriphyle out of loyalty to his father when, tempted by a bribe of a pretty necklace, she persuaded her husband, Amphiaraus the Seer, to join in the predestined disastrous expedition of the Seven against Thebes. As she expired, she laid a terrible curse on her son, crying: 'Lands of Greece and Asia, and of all the world: deny shelter to my murderers!'[4] The ground Alcmaeon stood on instantly became barren. Like Orestes he was tormented by the snake-wreathed Erinyes, who embody a primitive concept of rough justice and punish all violations of the sacred ties of kinship with their loathsome attentions. The Delphic oracle, however, was optimistic and provided a happy ending by advising Alcmaeon to stand trial on the banks of the Acheloos – a country, according to Thucydides, 'which had not yet been seen by the sun . . . at the time he slew his mother'. Here then Alcmaeon purified himself, pacified the Erinyes, and married Callirhoe, the river god's daughter. He settled on the silt deposits washed down by the winding streams and his sons colonized Acarnania.

Agrinion, a stronghold of Cassander's during his defensive campaign against Aetolian inroads into Aetolia in 314 BC, is the capital of the nome of Aetola-Acarnania, an important market town and centre of the tobacco trade. Linked by a mountain road with Lamia in the east, it is also the starting-point for a visit to Thermon and a tour of Lake Trichonis. Stiflingly hot in summer, the plain of Agrinion is subject to violent earthquakes (the town was completely

---

[3] An alternative and shorter route from Aetolikon to Agrinion (the main highway in fact) is through the hairpin-shaped Kleisoura gorge which cuts through the Zygos range. Magnificent orange-coloured cliffs tower above.

[4] Robert Graves, *The Greek Myths*, Penguin, Harmondsworth, 1955.

destroyed and rebuilt in 1887). There is a lively public square, lined with hotels, restaurants and the usual provincial confectioners. South and south-east lie the two main Acarnanian lakes: Lysimachia and Trichonis. Distant hills and mountains, blue or gunmetal according to the time of day, form an imposing ring round the well-watered plain.

To visit Thermon you take the road along the north shore of **Trichonis**, the larger and more beautiful of the two lakes, once believed to be unfathomable at its eastern end. Cypress thickets and plantations of pomegranates (whose root is said to be a remedy for tape-worm) mount in terraces above the crescent-shaped lakeside, where olive trees dip their branches in the reeds. The route is lined by a succession of prosperous villages between gullies shaded by large planes. Mulberry trees with whitewashed trunks surround open-air wayside cafés. In antiquity all this shore was densely populated. The first place of importance is **Paravola**, where the ruins of a large ancient fortress, possibly Boucation, of whose history next to nothing is known, are scattered across a steep hill between the village and the lake. Hellenistic walls radiate in all directions from the small oval-shaped summit of the citadel. Climbing the north-west side one skirts defence works composed of rectangular blocks, twelve courses high. The entrance to the summit is guarded by two round medieval towers, built of lower courses of Hellenic masonry, from which sentinels could spot hostile armies debouching from the defiles of Mount Panaetolikon. Close by an apsidal basilica has traces of Byzantine brickwork decoration. From this platform, studded with stunted oaks and wild almond trees and girdled by fragments of the acropolis wall which follows the irregular configuration of the eminence, one gets a good idea of the fortified layout; acropolis walls, inner and outer, with steps leading down to the lower town, also defended by inner and outer defence works. A striking semi-circular tower serves as a centre from which three fortified salients radiate. The north-east side of the terrace, where there are two more very ruined semi-circular towers, is buttressed by a fine piece of polygonal wall. A rampart descends in a north-west direction to the village school, whence another line of less well-preserved walls runs southward in the direction of the lake. The enceinte is nearly a mile in circumference.

Further east streams cascade through the pretty village of **Ayia Sophia** under arbours of plane trees, the ice-cold water gurgling round huge contorted trunks. On the hillside, amid pines and cypresses, there is a curious barn-shaped church of Ayios Nikolaos, built entirely of ancient materials – pilasters, columns, capitals, cornices, even inscriptions – plundered from an old temple of Aphrodite at Thermon. North of the church the shell of a little Byzantine basilica with traces of brickwork decoration nestles in the shade of prickly oaks; south of it a minuscule Turkish hammam raises its shallow dome above the tombstones – one of those numerous examples of the juxtaposition of antiquity, Byzantium and Islam which constantly diversify the Greek landscape. To the north, the spurs of Mount Panaetolikon are dotted with fragments of Hellenistic watch-towers and walls which formed a vast crescent-shaped defensive system protecting the prosperous settlements of the lake district.

The **site of Thermon** (south, right of road), just beyond the village of Kephalovrysi, is the most important in Aetolo-Acarnania. Spiritual centre of the Aetolians – to these rough people it was what the Acropolis meant to the Athenians, Delphi and Olympia to all Greeks – it spreads across a terrace of upland valley, its ruins embedded in marshy ground surrounded by cultivated fields. The spruce-covered sides of the Panaetolikon massif, forming a semicircle round the sanctuary, rise to bare, beautifully proportioned peaks.

In spite of the presence of prehistoric buildings and Archaic temples, we know the sanctuary did not acquire nation-wide renown until the third century BC, when it became the headquarters of the Aetolian League, a loose federation of states under Aetolian domination, which tried to dispute the mastery of Greece with Macedonia. All the treasure of the Aetolians – their gold and trophies – was stored at Thermon. In 218 BC Philip V of Macedon, unwilling to tolerate Aetolian pretensions any longer, set out to punish the League. He sacked Thermon, smashed two thousand statues, and hurried off with much treasure, including fifteen thousand suits of armour, while nimble Aetolian peltasts harassed his rear. According to Polybius, twelve years later Philip, infuriated by the Aetolians' provocative alliance with Rome, 'once more defaced all the sacred objects that he had spared in his former occupation of the place'. Henceforth Thermon ceased to exist.

A tour of the ruins, which are fragmentary though not unimpressive, follows a roughly straight line north to south within what was a rectangular peribolus, once flanked by third-century towers. The barbaric note, associated with the character of the Aetolians, is struck from the outset. Several lop-sided slabs of porous stone, projecting from the soil like a miniature Stonehenge, mark the site of a very early temple. Following the side of the embankment, one reaches the foundations of the **Temple of Apollo**, originally of the seventh century BC, but later refashioned. The holiest shrine of the Aetolians extended across a stepless stylobate, and its most unusual feature was its length, with five columns front and back and fifteen on each side, i.e. three times longer than wide, as opposed to the Parthenon's eight and seventeen. A row of twelve columns ran along the centre of the cella (bases of four survive), supporting the roof (one of the earliest ever to be tiled). There was no front porch at the south end and the wooden entablature was crudely decorated with painted terracotta metopes. The massive limestone drums of the north façade give some idea of the heaviness which must have characterized the building. Primitive in conception and execution, it constituted an authentic expression of the backwardness of the people whose shrine it was.

Beside the temple are the outlines of two early pre-Hellenic structures, known as Megaron A and B, which may have served as palaces. Archaeologists call them 'hairpin houses', because of their apsidal shape, consisting of a porch, a large chamber and curved back room. South of the temple's front entrance a pile of stones indicates the site of the altar, once heaped with ashes of sacrificial animals, around which pilgrims, priests and savage tribesmen gathered at the Panaetolian celebrations every autumn. Continuing southward, past a square reservoir with three courses of rectangular blocks, one reaches three successive stoas which form a long rectangle, now choked with thistles and overgrown with *Delphinium junceum*. Land-crabs, on which the local inhabitants fed during the German occupation of 1941–4, crawl among the damp mossy deposits. Until recently the ruins of the stoas were called the *palaeopazari* (the old bazaar), for here were situated the shops and stores where Aetolian merchants sold their wares during the annual assemblies. Well-preserved bases of statues and ex-votos extend in a long line, shorn of the stone and marble effigies hacked to pieces by Philip V's soldiers. The brambles grow thicker, the ground more swampy, and it is not easy to explore the site.

Across the fields, west of the stoa, lay the agora, in which an annual market was held during the Panaetolian festival. An ivy-clad wall, south of the stoa, formed part of the bouleuterion, where the Aetolian notables appointed their magistrates and tabled decrees. In front of it lie triangular slabs identified as trophies: the only surviving token of the military power of a people who could not even speak Greek properly and whose name was associated with every kind of cruelty and outrage.

The **museum** (a modest building) should not be missed. Besides a fine acroterium of a sphinx with a beautiful head and stylized wings, there is a collection of acroteria with heads, gargoyles, grotesque masks sculptured in relief, many with the paint still preserved, originally placed on the edge of the roof of the Temple of Apollo to screen the tile ends. The execution, though not refined, is robust, and not without a hint of coarse peasant humour. There are also figurines and emblems of anatomical features, fingers, genitalia.

At this point, the south-bound traveller may take an exciting little-known short cut to the coast. Beyond Thermon, just before the village of Petrochoria, the road descends. Superb views terminate in a sun-dazzled haze in the west, where a metallic burnished surface betrays the position of **Lake Lysimachia**. A dirt road to the south (admittedly in a deplorable condition last time I drove along it) penetrates a hot shut-in valley which ultimately gets lost in an Aetolian wilderness characterized by the absence of all villages, by scrub-covered mountains of no great height crowding round on all sides. The drifting scents of sun-scorched thyme and agnus castus possess an almost medicinal quality. A feeling of claustrophobia is inevitable; and the absence of any human beings, of any human dwellings, adds to it. The winding descent affords sudden glimpses, tantalizingly interrupted by the emergence of barren eminences, of the bed of the Evenus: a streak of silver water flowing in a beautiful loop between tree-lined sandbanks. Climbing further down into the river valley, we crossed a bridge and stopped to gaze across the torrent bed from an abandoned hamlet surrounded by groves of dwarf cypresses. A crescendo of sound created by the noontide chirping of sun-struck cicadas seemed to mount into a roar. One had the feeling that this was not a place in which to tarry. The road then descends through tamer country, affording glimpses of Peloponnesian ranges, to Naupactus.

The more leisured traveller, anxious to complete a tour of Lake Lysimachia and return to Agrinion, ignores the branch to Naupactus and drives through a string of villages set in lush countryside of mulberry orchards and olive groves; in the evening old men – the younger ones have bicycled into Agrinion to pace the main square and lounge in the plush confectioners' shops – sit in rustic roadside cafés, playing with their worry-beads as they exchange the latest agricultural gossip. Before striking north to Agrinion, the road fringes the shore of the lake. Through clusters of reeds one catches glimpses of flat calm water in which the structural forms of Mount Panaetolikon are reflected.

North-west of Agrinion a bridge spans the wide bed of the **Acheloos**, whose turbid streams, after flowing from their torrent sources in the Pindus, wind swiftly between reed-fringed sandbanks and mounds shaped like molehills which, Thucydides says, lie 'so thick together that they serve to imprison the alluvial deposits and prevent it from dispersing'. In antiquity the river, symbolical of all fresh water in Greece, and infinitely perplexing in its innumerable and erratic changes of course, constantly overflowed its banks and flooded the countryside. Hence arose the myth of the combat between Heracles and the bull-headed river god, whose body consisted of serpentine coils and one of whose horns, wrenched off by the demi-god, was worshipped as the first cornucopia. Strabo says the river was likened to a bull because of the roaring of its waters, to a serpent because of its endless sinuosities.

A Xenias tourist pavilion on the west bank of the river marks the **site of Stratos**, which is scattered over a low ledge overlooking the Acheloos. Thucydides and Xenophon call it the chief city of Acarnania. Its inhabitants were a tough disciplined people. In the Peloponnesian War they sided with Athens; and when the unruly Ambracians from the north were incited by Sparta to attack Stratos in 429 BC they were ignominiously routed by the intrepid Acarnanian slingthrowers, who were considered masters of ambuscades. In the third century BC neither Philip V of Macedon, the sacker of Thermon, nor his more temperate successor, Perseus, was able to capture it.

The ruins are scanty. The fifth-century BC river gate (west of the tourist pavilion), which consists of two large curved slabs covering a postern, leads through thick walls into a bleak shadeless plateau broken up into low eminences. To the north are traces of the agora; east lie the negligible remains of the theatre. Continuing northward, one reaches the site of the acropolis. A more satisfying ruin is the fourth-century BC Temple of Zeus at the west extremity. Limestone drums of Doric columns and pieces of architrave are scattered around the foundations. In effect, Stratos has little to offer but its walls and a view of the curiously cream-coloured streams of the Acheloos flowing through a bed nearly half a mile wide, along which Strabo says vessels used to sail up from Oeniadae.

The road continues northward. Tractors plough wheatfields, and modern agricultural methods, which came to Greece with American aid, are employed throughout this domesticated country. To the west lies the little lake of Ozerus at the foot of the Xeromeri. Soon another lake, Amvrakia, comes into view, its pale blue waters compressed within a narrow basin fringed with tobacco fields. To the east the advancing mountains of the Valtos are bare and forbidding. A causeway crosses the lake which tapers off into a slender apex. A short climb between arid hills is followed by a descent towards the Ambracian Gulf, where the houses of Amphilochia are huddled round a narrow inlet filled with bright-coloured caiques.

CHAPTER TWENTY-THREE

The Ambracian Gulf

❧

Amphilochia – Vonitsa – The Way to Leucas – The East Coast – Arta: The Despots' Capital; The Churches – The Valley of the Aracthus – The 'Red Church' – Voulgarelli – The Castle of Rogoi – Nicopolis – Preveza – Actium

The gulf, entered by a channel no more than half a mile wide, is broken up by bluffs and spits of land, the mirror-like surface of its shallow waters scattered with shoals and reefs; lagoons, crossed by causeways, fringe the northern shore, and many of the creeks are inaccessible to anything but flat-bottomed boats. Two rivers, the Louros and Aracthus, wind through orange groves, forming wide shingly beds, before pouring their waters, which have risen in the Epirot gorges, into the inland sea. On three sides rise mountains, prodigious in the beauty of their shapes: the peaks of ancient Thesprotia to the north; the Valtos spurs of the Pindus to the east; and the abrupt slopes of the Acarnanian Xeromeri to the south. The composition is grandiose yet serene, and there is a pale mirage-like quality about the scene.

A semi-circular tour of the gulf – taking in the principal sights of the medieval fortress of Vonitsa, the thirteenth-century churches of Arta hidden among orange groves, the ruined Byzantine castle of Rogoi and the extensive Roman ruins of Nicopolis – is easily accomplished in two days. Of Actium little remains but the name and the memory. The obvious place to stay at is the Xenias Hotel at Arta. The drive up the valley of the Aracthus in order to see the 'Red Church', overlooking one of the most spectacular mountain prospects in western Greece, would necessitate spending a third night in Arta.

Amphilochia, lying at the head of a narrow creek, its whitewashed houses with red roofs clinging to a steep hillside among mulberry and eucalyptus trees, serves as a curtain-raiser to the new scene, more Western in character. The waterfront is lively, and there are some fish tavernas. On the hill to the east vestiges of ancient walls, probably those of Limnaea, are discernible. The port, where it is pleasant to stop for a coffee or a drink, was founded in the early nineteenth century as a military outpost called Karavassaras, probably a corruption of caravanserai, by Ali Pasha, when the Albanian tyrant's dominions extended all over Epirus and beyond. The pastures north of the ancient walls are one of the several sites associated with Geryon, the three-bodied six-armed monster who lived so far to the west of the known ancient world that it was believed the sun actually set there. Although Geryon enjoyed Hera's patronage, the capture of his famous red cattle was appointed as one of Heracles's labours, and the monster's doom was consequently sealed. After killing him with a single arrow that pierced all three bodies, Heracles drove the beautiful beasts, whose milk yielded only the purest curds, on to a golden vessel in the shape of a waterlily.

Successive creeks and caves between Amphilochia and Vonitsa afford views of flat islets strung out like a chaplet across the motionless gulf. After climbing into the forbidding Xeromeri, the road dips down into a deep inlet, fringed by a little green plain, with the village of **Vonitsa** huddled on the shore, its medieval castle crowning a bluff above the sea.

On the way to the castle one passes two picturesque churches. The small **Basilica of the Holy Apostles** has a wooden iconostasis, more Italianate than Byzantine in style and execution, decorated with coloured designs of rosettes and tendrils. The money-box, in which one drops a few drachmas for the price of a candle, is painted with figures of St Peter and St Paul holding a model of the church. In the larger **Basilica of St Nicholas** (just below the castle) our attention was drawn to effigies of two lions with human faces and curling moustaches supporting the Cross on the summit of the screen. I asked the boy who attached himself to us in the capacity of a guide if he knew the approximate date of the church. There was no hesitation in his answer. 'Oh, it goes back to the time of Cleopatra!' It was exciting to feel the proximity of Actium and how the memory of one of the world's decisive battles still lives, if only in the name of its most glamorous participant, in the minds of the local peasants nearly two thousand years after it was fought.

It takes an hour to visit the **castle**. Originally a Byzantine fortress, guarding the approaches to the inland sea, it passed in 1294 into the hands of Philip of Taranto, son of Charles II of Naples, as part of the extravagant dowry (£44,800 a year) bestowed on him by the Despot of Arta on his marriage to the latter's daughter, the beautiful Thamar. In turn Frankish and Venetian, it was seized in 1362 by Leonardo Tocco of Corfu, whose descendants held it for over a century and who, like so many Latin rulers of Greece, adopted the most grandiloquent titles – in this case, 'Duke of Leucadia, Count of Cephalonia and Lord of Vonitsa'. In the fifteenth century Carlo Tocco, now master of much of the western mainland and islands, bequeathed Vonitsa to his widow, the Duchess Francesca, a formidable lady of much ability and masculine vigour, and divided the rest of Acarnania among his five bastard sons. Even after the Turkish conquest, the fortress remained an Italian outpost in Ottoman territory; but during the War of Independence it fell into ruins. After the establishment of the modern kingdom, a Greek garrison was stationed in the crumbling keep and the military insurrection, which led to the abdication of King Otho and his headstrong queen, had its genesis here in 1862 (there are few changes of Greek political regime in which the military does not have the first word).

The ruins are mostly Venetian with Turkish additions. Little remains of the original Byzantine masonry. You enter the precincts through an outer gate beside a little pine grove and climb southward (left) along an outer rampart to a ruined tower above the maritime plain. A path then winds northward (right) to a well-preserved bastion and through another gateway. The path continues uphill. A turn to the left brings you to the remains of a two-storeyed building, probably the residence of the Turkish commander, whose windows command a prospect of sea, mountains, islets and headlands. On the left is a long low chapel and beside it (to the east) steps lead down to a deep vaulted cistern. All is deserted. Only insects hum in the evergreen shrubs and the wind whistles through the windows of shells of houses. At this point turn right into the keep on the summit of the bluff crowned by a large building (possibly Turkish) with a fine doorway. Here were the vaulted halls and chambers to which Philip of Taranto brought the seductive Thamar from Arta, together with all the gold that came with her fabulous dowry. A low wall with gun-slits and look-out posts surrounds the triangular keep. From it a path descends westward to a line of well-preserved walls from which there is a view of a fiord-like inlet with olive trees dipping their branches into the water and encircled by a grove of giant eucalyptus. Continuing in a circular direction (south) alongside a low ruined parapet one observes an impressive crenellated wall descending on the landward side into another forest of eucalyptus trees, and the village football field beyond. Thence one returns to the outer gate and the village.

West of Vonitsa the road comes to a fork at the village of Ayios

Nikolaos. The northern prong ends in the headland of Actium, whence one can cross by ferry to Preveza. The western prong leads to the Leucadian channel – along the coast there are impressive remains of ruined Turkish fortifications – and to a landing-stage whence another ferry-boat crosses a narrow channel, no wider than a river, to the island of Leucas.[1]

The best course now is to return to Amphilochia and follow the highway along the east coast. Bluffs, thickly wooded with ilex, overhang a rocky shore, and the pastel-shaded gulf seems so spacious that it is often difficult to grasp its configuration. Soon the border-line between Acarnania and Epirus is reached: not the Epirus of the mountain redoubt, but the lowland fringe, a country of orange groves that stretch for miles around Arta. In spring the scent of orange blossom is intoxicating, all-pervasive. It penetrates the privacy of one's hotel bedroom, and I have heard people say that they can taste it in their food and drink. On the left (west) side of the road, gullies filled with parallel rows of fruit trees debouch into shallow shingly coves. Alleys of dwarf cypresses form wind-breaks and huge fig trees provide luxuriant shade.

Six kilometres before Arta a track to the right (east) leads in less than half a kilometre to the **Church of the Panayia tou Vrioni**, least important of Arta's countryside Byzantine churches. But the deviation is short enough to be worthwhile. A lane bordered by honeysuckle and dog-rose, by golden wattle and azure anchusa and wild gladioli, leads to the church; originally a basilica, it was domed and cross-inscribed when the Patriarch of Constantinople made an official tour of Epirus in the thirteenth century. The exterior walls are decorated with lavish brick inlay, inferior in design and execution to that which distinguishes most of the churches in the plain. But the setting – a cypress grove and cemetery full of rose bushes and flowering Judas trees, their trunks entwined with periwinkle – is charming.

Arta, undistinguished though lively, spreads across a saddleback eminence, with the Aracthus winding in an arc round the northern end of the ellipse. The people are friendly and among the best-looking in Greece; the food is execrable. The **Xenias Hotel** is approached through a medieval gateway, and the modern building, strut-supported, dominates the castle precincts, now a public garden, encircled by well-preserved thirteenth-century Byzantine ramparts (immense quadrangular blocks of masonry which formed

[1] For Leucas, see Ernle Bradford, *The Companion Guide to the Greek Islands*, Collins, London, 1963.

part of the ancient citadel are distinguishable to the professional eye). A castellated bastion overlooks the plain to the north. No hotel in Greece is more attractively situated. Bedroom balconies overlook the streams of the Aracthus estuary; beyond the sandbanks stretch groves of orange and lemon trees in a pastel-coloured haze, with clusters and alleys of poplars climbing green foothills against the back-drop of the Epirot mountains: grey, lonely, infinitely diversified in their forms. In summer frogs croak on the banks of the streams and the sandflies which swarm up from the damp gardens and orchards are a pest.

Here is the site of the citadel of ancient Ambracia. First colonized by the Corinthians under Cypselus in the seventh century BC, it was not until the third that fame and lustre were added to the city by Pyrrhus, the Molossian king, who adorned and fortified it, made it his capital and fought so staunchly against the Roman Republic that Hannibal considered him the greatest of all generals. In the late second century BC it fell into the hands of the then all-powerful Aetolians. But the star of Greece, whether Macedonian, Aetolian or Spartan, had virtually set, and Ambracia declined in importance. After the battle of Actium Augustus removed all the inhabitants to Nicopolis.

But Arta's renown, as reflected in the visible remains of its remarkable churches, belongs to the Middle Ages. As capital of the Despotate of Epirus it was, after Thessalonica, the most important city in mainland Greece during the thirteenth and fourteenth centuries.

The rugged nature of the mountains that surround the Ambracian plain and gulf, through which there are few defiles, formed a natural protection against Crusader inroads. In 1204, when the Frankish flood was sweeping Greece, Michael Angelus Comnenus Doucas lost no time in choosing the ancient citadel of Ambracia as his redoubt and making Arta the military and political headquarters of his Despotate. Though a bastard, he was related to all the great imperial families of Constantinople, and married to the widow of a local tyrant. He formed a militia of Ambracian natives and hired mercenaries and soon turned to the offensive. Playing off one Latin state against the other, he maintained Byzantine administration within his Despotate, whose boundaries he extended from Yannina in the north to Naupactus in the south. While feeble Flemish counts tottered uneasily on the great golden throne at Constantinople, Michael and his successors created in western Greece a Byzantine state, with Arta as its capital, which not only

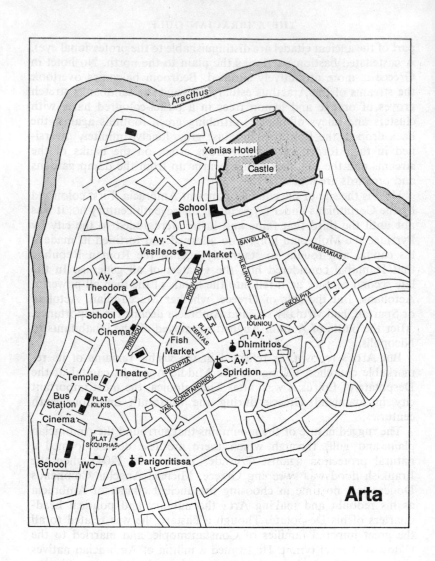

Arta

became a political reality but rivalled in importance the other more 'legitimate' empire in exile set up by the Lascarid dynasty at Nicaea in Asia Minor. In 1215, while campaigning in northern Epirus, Michael was murdered in his sleep by one of his slaves who, some say, was an agent of the Pope, others, of the Franks. Michael certainly had many enemies. His cruelty was notorious, and Pope Innocent III accused him of crucifying captured Frankish knights.

Under Michael's successors, his half-brother Theodore and his son Michael II, the Despots of Arta reached the zenith of their dynastic ambitions. Theodore captured Peter of Courtenay, the Latin Emperor, in an ambush in the mountains of Epirus, and crowned himself Emperor of Byzantium at Thessalonica in 1222. Michael II, an eccentric character, no less violent than his predecessors, made Arta a brilliant capital, conducting an astute cat-and-mouse diplomacy with the Frankish rulers of Greece. He arranged marriages between his daughters and William de Villehardouin, Prince of Achaea, and Manfred, King of Sicily – alliances that strengthened his hand in the kaleidoscopic shifts of Graeco-Latin politics. It was indeed a touch-and-go affair whether the Angeli of Arta or the Lascarids of Nicaea would re-enter Constantinople as emperor when the ridiculous Latin edifice crumbled and the 'God-Guarded city' was restored to its legitimate Greek masters.

After the Nicaean emperor had recaptured Constantinople in 1261, Michael was astute enough to grant a measure of autonomy to the Despotate, the legend of whose vigorous defence of the ideal of Hellenism during a half-century of Latin depredation had taken too strong a hold on the minds of the population of mainland Greece to be lightly dismissed. The subsequent Despots, however, were men of less mettlesome character, and by the middle of the fourteenth century Arta too succumbed to the Serbian flail. Thomas Preljubovič became the Serb 'Prince of Jannina and Arta'. But the Serb empire was also a passing phase, and in 1417 Carlo Tocco, Lord of Vonitsa, moved into the citadel. The curtain came down in 1499 with the Turkish conquest. Ali Pasha, the Sultan's turbulent viceroy of Epirus and Albania, was the last notable personage to stay in Arta's ancient fortress.

The number of churches in and around the city bears witness to its one-time importance. Descending from the castle, we first come to the little **Church of St Basil** in Ayios Vasileos Street. A rectangular single-nave basilica of the early fourteenth century, it is outstanding for its exterior ornamentation, with two courses of inlaid glazed tiles, white and yellow alternating with deep turquoise, which offer a sharp but pleasing contrast to the brickwork decoration on the north and east (apsidal) sides. In each of the windows there is a single unfluted colonnette crowned by an Ionic capital. The church could hardly be smaller, the side apses flanking the central one being positively diminutive, but it sets the tone. This is not peasant architecture. The polychrome effects of faience combined with brickwork are refined and sophisticated, and one immediately gets the impression that the Despotate, insulated from the rest of Greece by geopolitics, was, like the far-away Empire of Trebizond on the Black Sea, a centre of artistic creativity. The interior of the church is now without interest.

More important is the nearby **Church of St Theodora** in Ayia Theodora Square (virtually a children's playground) approached through a gabled arch decorated with brick inlay. Theodora was a straight-laced aristocrat, who came from Servia in western Macedonia as the bride of the Despot Michael II Angelus. In spite of her estimable character she did not enjoy a happy married life. Her husband, infatuated with a notorious courtesan who was also a sorceress and went by the extraordinary name of Lady Gangrene, not only dismissed her from the palace but drove her into exile. The saintly woman kept body and soul together by living on the roots of wild plants, occasionally accepting the hospitality of some remote mountain monastery. Eventually, however, Michael had a traumatic vision. According to the seventeenth-century chronicler of Galaxeidi, Christ appeared to him 'in all the splendour of his divine beauty', denounced him roundly for succumbing to the wiles of Satan's agent, the Lady Gangrene, and threatened to destroy him with 'fire and thunderbolts'. Terrified and conscience-stricken Michael scoured the country for his victimized wife, found her and restored her to her rightful place in the palace. Thanks to Theodora's merciful intercession, instead of the Lady Gangrene being strapped to an ass, as ordered by the remorseful Michael, and exposed to the ribaldry of the inhabitants prior to execution, she was in fact allowed to leave Arta unmolested.

The exterior of the church is charming. The building, which is of the fourteenth century, is low, irregular and architecturally eccentric, the south side, through which one enters it, being faced with a cloister or exo-narthex of four arches terminating in cross-vaults which are returned at the west end by a single bay. In spring the garden beside it (north-west) is a mass of lilac and snowball blooms of guelder rose. Two very dark green cypresses of considerable age, one of which serves as a bell-tower, add proportion and perspective to the scene. The west front, through which the narthex, crowned by a shallow drum, used to be entered, is decorated with lavish brickwork bands: zigzag, dog-tooth and herring-bone. Crosses embellished with carved brick wheel design are ranged above the door of the east wall. The high-placed narthex window consists of the familiar double arch separated by a marble colonnette crowned by a little Theodosian capital. The naos, basilica type, is well-proportioned, with four fine old columns disposed in a square and crowned with acanthus-leaf Theodosian capitals plundered from a nearby Early Christian basilica. The central aisle, higher than the others, is lit by a clerestory. Traces of wall-painting are of a later date and without interest. The narthex is distinguished by a **marble plaque**, believed to be a fragment of Theodora's tomb, sculptured in low relief, depicting the pious woman, who, though crowned and robed as befits a Despot's consort, wears the veil of a nun. Her royal-cum-religious status (she did in fact become a nun) is further stressed by the fact that she holds a royal sceptre in one hand while raising the other in benediction. The diminutive figure beside her, also holding a sceptre, represents her infant son, Nicephorus, who succeeded his father as Despot. Both figures stand under a canopy supported by knotted columns, flanked by two Archangels, while the Hand of God points at Theodora through stars.

Next comes the **Church of the Parigoritissa** (The Virgin of Con-solation), Arta's most imposing monument,[2] now a museum of Christian antiquities which stands on a platform above Skoupha Street, overlooking the orange groves beyond the river. Founded at the end of the thirteenth century by the Despot Nicephorus and his wife Anna Palaeologina, and restored by Count John II of Cephalonia, a snobbish and ostentatious descendant of the Orsini and convert to the Orthodox faith, it is one of the most important if not wholly attractive Byzantine churches in Greece. Three-storeyed, it is in the shape of a tall Greek Cross within a square (the cross is only perceptible in the interior). Drums and cupolas, six in all – an additional one resembling a little pavilion with a dome in the form of a canopy resting on columns above the narthex – seem puny ill-proportioned affairs without any organic relation to the barrack-like cube of stone and brick which they crown.

The interior is impressive, if unusual. The sombre lofty naos is an extraordinary structure, height being achieved by a cumbersome

[2] On the way to the Parigoritissa, notice the substructure of an ancient building, possibly a temple, in Vasileus Pavlos Street.

architectural disposition which creates an impression of a heavy cubic mass suspended in a void (this curious plan was never repeated – presumably because of its impracticability). At each corner of the central square three superimposed courses of columns (in pairs) support high squinch arches forming an octagon on which the drum rests. The columns of the third and highest course are more slender and decorative in effect than structural in purpose. Between each course of vertical columns, which look like organ pipes suspended by pulleys from the apex, are wedged horizontal granite pillars which serve as beams; they are cracked in many places by the sheer weight of the structure. The column-courses are capped by a mass of vaults and arches that fail to cohere aesthetically. Admittedly there is no absence of height and spaciousness – even perhaps of grandeur – but as one modern writer has aptly put it, 'There are moments when this strange church seems to be more like machinery than architecture.'[3]

Turning from architecture to decoration, one's attention is automatically drawn to the dome crowning the lofty square in which a thirteenth-century **Christ Pantocrator** of colossal dimensions is depicted in mosaic, gorgeously robed, and holding an ornamented Book of Gospels. Below are ranged cherubim and prophets erect in beautiful draperies. Fragments of mosaics are also discernible in the pendentives. Most remarkable is the imposing figure of St Sophronius, boldly modelled, distinguished by a violence of contrast in the colour scheme (green shadows, for instance, in the blue beard; an amber-coloured halo) which is unique for a mosaic of this period. Another fragment worth looking at is the rather crude but charming Nativity, full of bucolic serenity, on the topmost north vault. An unusual feature is the depiction of the familiar figures of Joseph, the shepherd and the lamb in the inner band of the arch. The fourteenth-century frescoes of the apse are hopelessly damaged.

From the gallery, reached by a modern staircase, one gets a good close-up view of the amazing architectural intricacies, of the Gothic tracery in one of the squinches, and the fine carving on the north and west arches. One can also examine the beautiful mosaics of the prophets around and below the Pantocrator at approximately eye-level.

Other churches of considerable interest to Byzantine enthusiasts are scattered around the countryside. It is enchanting to walk along the flowery lanes, but unfortunately most of the churches lie in opposite directions, and the smaller ones are not easy to find. It is

[3] Robert Liddell, *Mainland Greece*, Longman, London, 1965.

wiser to drive – and, while constantly asking the way, to be prepared to be misdirected in the maze of orchards, vineyards and straggling hamlets.

One starts south-west of the Parigoritissa. Here the Aracthus, flowing in a series of loops towards the gulf, is spanned by the famous Turkish **bridge of Arta**, the largest and most striking of all these elegant half-moon structures that bridge the rivers and torrents of Epirus and Albania. Built by the Despots on Hellenic foundations and entirely refashioned by the Turks for packhorses, it has four graceful crescent-shaped arches of different dimensions, through which there are lovely views of the metal-coloured mountain barrier to the north. The fact that the highest point (above the largest arch) is not in the centre of the bridge adds further diversity to the construction. According to a legend immortalized in Greek folksong, the thousand Greek masons who built the bridge under the direction of Turkish engineers in the seventeenth century found that the middle pier at which they would toil all day was swept away in the evening by the waters of the Aracthus, at the instigation of the *genius* of the river. Finally, a little bird perched itself on the middle pier, twittered in a human voice and delivered the melancholy message that until the master-mason's wife was buried in the foundations the bridge would never be completed. So the unfortunate woman was induced by a ruse to enter the pier, ostensibly to recover her husband's ring which had fallen inside. Stone and rubble were quickly heaped over her, and the masons set to work to strengthen the pier. Since then the bridge has stood intact. The analogy with the human sacrifices offered by mortals to river gods is obvious. The propitiation of *genii* of all kinds is practised to this day. A cock, goat, ram, even an ox, may be immolated on the site where a building is about to go up. An eminent authority on Greek folklore believes that 'the original conception is doubtless that of the river god demanding a sacrifice, even of human life, in compensation for men's encroachment upon his domain'.[4]

Crossing the modern bridge, from which there is a fine view of the Turkish one, you descend into an orange grove where a tall poplar screens the little Byzantine **Church of Ayios Vasileos tis Yephiras** (St Basil of the Bridge), a charming little extravaganza. The cruciform church is minute, crowned by a cylindrical drum (taller than the main body of the church), which recalls the equally eccentric Panayia Koubelidiki at Castoria. The frieze below the cornice and the brick-

[4] J. C. Lawson, *Modern Greek Folklore and Ancient Religion*, University Books, New York, 1964.

work decoration on the drum are crude but picturesque. The interior is without interest.

Now take the road to Preveza and then the first turning to the left. A dirt road runs through a flat lush countryside. You pass the hamlets and farmhouses of Costakioi and Plisous under an umbrella of green shade. At each successive fork (there are two) turn to the left (it is wise to keep asking the way), until you come to the **Church of Ayios Demetrius Katsouris**, which is surrounded by olive and orange trees, their trunks entwined in ivy. Originally a tenth-century dependency of a Patriarchal monastery, restored under the Despots and finally abandoned in the eighteenth, St Demetrius has no exterior decoration, but the tall drum, the planes of slanting roofs and the three apses (the two outer ones have a particularly shallow convexity) create a pleasing effect. Small, but well-proportioned, this country church has an air of relative loftiness which raises it above the level of a rural chapel. The deserted interior is cross-inscribed. In the middle conch of the sanctuary there is a fine painting of St Blaise, St Modestus and St Polycarp: typically hieratic portraits of holy men, with serene expressive faces, more Constantinopolitan than provincial in style, and assigned to the twelfth century, which means that they are not only older than any other extant frescoes in the Arta region but also reflect the relatively high level of artistic creativeness that existed here even before the time of the Despots. In a side conch (right) we see St Basil and St John Chrysostom, and in the apse the Virgin and Child, the former distinguished by an acid spiteful expression that would do credit to a Medea in one of her nastiest moods. The rest of the frescoes, of little interest, are of the seventeenth and eighteenth centuries.

From St Demetrius Katsouris one drives along lanes bordered by mulberry trees and hedgerows of flowering brambles to the hamlet of **Kirkizates** which is hidden among orange groves shaded by huge fig trees. A boy from the café, where men play backgammon or read newspapers aloud while geese waddle around, will fetch a key from the local priest and conduct you to the thirteenth-century **Church of Ayios Nikolaos tis Rodias** (St Nicholas of the Pomegranate Orchard), now standing impressively isolated in a sunken field. The exterior is distinguished by a tall drum and brick inlay decoration – bands of meander pattern – on the higher courses of the walls (particularly elaborate on the three-sided apse). Effigies of suns ornament the cupola. The interior is cross-inscribed with a barrel-vaulted narthex, and in the naos are two squat marble columns without bases, crowned with well-preserved capitals carved with the device of the double-headed eagle. The frescoes, very damaged, are stylistically of the thirteenth century. A panel on the right side of the iconostasis contains a fine icon of the Dormition of the Virgin, remarkable for the vividness of the red tints. Perhaps provincial in execution, it is nevertheless Constantinopolitan in style – elegant and sophisticated.

From here one returns through shady lanes to St Basil of the Bridge and follows the road to the south (right) to the **Monastery of Kato Panayia**, set in a garden filled with oleanders, pine, olive and orange trees interlaced with creeping vines, which extends across a slope overlooking the Aracthus. Strabo says the river was navigable up to this point. An enormous plane tree dips its branches into the water. The cloistered courtyard and domeless church with its cross-roofs, gables and transverse vault, its frescoed exterior west wall and tall belfry (a later addition), create a complex of subtly graded planes on different levels. Some of the masonry – regular stone courses – is believed to consist of fragments from the ancient citadel of Ambracia. The frescoes of the exterior west wall, shaded by a wide projecting gable which replaced a destroyed narthex, are of a later date and of no particular merit. Left of the doorway, however, there is a lively panel of God swirling across the heavens as he creates the world, and another in which the Almighty, now crowned, creates man in the Garden of Eden. On the right there is another representation of the Creator: this time warning Adam and Eve against Evil, while Satan in the form of the Serpent writhes at his feet and angels expel Adam and Eve from the garden. A multitude of geometric designs, cable and meander patterns, embellish the higher course of the exterior, particularly the apses.

The church was founded in the thirteenth century by Michael II Angelus (his monogram is inscribed in the south wall) as a token of penance for his shameful treatment of his wife Theodora. The interior is less interesting. In some places the overlay of the eighteenth-century frescoes has flaked off to reveal some of the (probably) original paintings. One of the full-length bishops, Anthimus, depicted in the diaconicon, wears a circular scarf round his head tied with ribbons under his chin: a form of head-gear rare in Byzantine hagiography. Capitals of different orders crown unattractive mud-coloured columns of the naos.

There remains the **Monastery of Vlachernae**, most important of Arta's outlying churches. A track to the right of the Arta-Yannina road (north of the focal point of the bridge) winds through fruit orchards and olive groves between the Epirot foothills and the north bank of the Aracthus to a point overlooking a hairpin bend of the river, beyond which the citadel and houses of Arta sprawl across the saddleback hill of Peranthes. Farmyard sounds mingle with the tintinnabulation of sheepbells, and frogs croak intermittently on the river banks.

The monastery was founded at the end of the twelfth century. Originally a basilica, later cross-inscribed and domed, with irregular vaults and three apses of different shapes – one rounded, one three-sided, one five-sided – it creates an architecturally complex effect: varied, assymetrical but not without harmony. There is much brick inlay decoration in the surrounds of the windows of the central dome and apses, where the different designs that embellish each of the irregular projections provide a decorative ensemble full of fantasy and ingenuity. **Sculptural fragments**, the work of Constantinopolitan artists commissioned by Michael II, decorating the exterior walls, add to the general air of diversity (they originally formed part of the marble screen, subsequently destroyed). On the north side an elaborate marble lintel is carved with a design of two plump peacocks, their necks intertwined, surmounted by a cross projecting from a band of stylized foliage. High up on the south front we see a fine marble plaque, carved with a full-length figure representing the Archangel Michael, patron saint of the Angeli, with huge out-stretched wings.

The interior is divided into three aisles by two colonnades of three columns each – the central one thinner than the side ones. Part of the floor is covered with boards which the custodian will remove on request to reveal marble paving-stones decorated with stone tesserae depicting foliate and geometric designs. The high central octagonal dome, painted with a Christ Pantocrator in a bluish-grey mantle surrounded by prophets and apostles with dull yellow haloes wearing mauve and blue garments – a late work of the post-Byzantine period – is flanked by secondary domes, embellishments attributed to Michael II, above the north and south transepts. Another fresco worth noticing depicts the three hierarchs in the conch of the sanctuary. In the south nave lies the alleged tomb – carved slabs pieced together – of Michael II, decorated with crosses, rosettes and stylized foliate bands. Morbidly-minded visitors may slip their hands (if small enough) through a hole in the east end of the sarcophagus and finger the bones of this violent man, whose lust, ambition and ability combined to make him one of the most colourful personalities of thirteenth-century Greece. In the north nave a second equally damaged royal tomb is said to contain the remains of his sons, Demetrius and John, who were quietly put away by their younger brother Nicephorus I. I have not succeeded in tracing the subterranean passage that led from the Despot's palace, after passing under the river-bed and orchard belt. It is said to have been constantly used by Theodora, when, heavily veiled as a nun, she came in procession to worship at Vlachernae, her favourite church.

The 'Red Church' is the ostensible objective of the expedition along the upper valley of the Aracthus to Voulgarelli. East of Arta the road climbs successive spurs of the Tzoumerka massif. Precipitous grey cliffs are sliced by a curious form of erosion into symmetrical, often parallel, courses of bead pattern, egg-and-dart and lozenge bands: in fact, the geologists' 'concertina folds'. This is earthquake country. The road climbs and dips, affording entrancing views of the ice-cold Aracthus, aquamarine in colour, flowing between abrupt wooded banks, of little green hollows and valleys scattered with farmhouses with slate-grey roofs among orchards of quince and almond trees, their steep hillsides covered with giant bushes of heather, dotted in spring with flowering Judas trees. Ever nearer, more imposing, looms the mass of Tzoumerka, cloud-capped, gashed with forbidding ravines filled with snow, its lower slopes dark with evergreens and scrub. Occasionally a shepherd is seen standing on the summit of a ridge against a background of sky. Invariably he waves. Epirots are among the friendliest of Greeks (they also produce public benefactors, men of letters and politicians). Other Greeks say they are stingy – a highland people, one is told, 'like the Scotch, you see'.

Beyond the hamlet of Palaeo Katouni, lying in the trough of a valley, where we saw a field being worked by a primitive harrow wielded by a priest and a boy, the road mounts steeply between groves of almond and Judas trees. Suddenly on the right a roseate glow emanates from the red-tiled roofs of the **Church of the Nativity of the Virgin**, commonly known as the **'Red Church'**: as sophisticated a piece of Byzantine ecclesiastical architecture as one is likely to encounter in a remote highland region. It was founded in 1281 by the Protostrator Theodore (the imperial Master of the Horse). Why here in this mountain wilderness? We do not know. A saddle-back roof has replaced the broken dome of the cruciform edifice. The south front is rich in brickwork decoration, a triple band of red lozenges being particularly effective; also the tile inlay of triglyphs. All the bricks are a bright red, which suffuses the walls with an extraordinary refulgence – especially striking when seen in spring against a background of white and pink blossom of quince and

Judas trees. Windows with triple arches (the flanking ones are blind) on the west front, north and south sides of the narthex and north, south and west barrel vaults of the naos are also filled with red tiles arranged in vertical and horizontal lines. On the three-sided apse, shaded by a plane tree which serves as a bell-tower, more brick inlay outlines the elliptical arches of the windows. The interior, now abandoned, is without interest. Of the vestigial frescoes only the chequered robes of bishops are discernible in the narthex and the dim figures of the founder and his wife on the wall separating the narthex from the naos.

A few kilometres from the 'Red Church' the grey houses of **Voulgarelli** ascend in narrow ledges up a precipitous mountainside on the fringe of the fir belt, above which towers the sombre summit of Tzoumerka. In the last war this Alpine redoubt was the headquarters of EDES, the right-wing resistance organization, whose members spent much of their time, as well as the gold and arms supplied to them by the British Government, in fighting the Communist-controlled ELAS liberation army instead of the Germans. When I visited it we sat at a café on a platform halfway up the terraced village admiring the panorama of the Agrapha range extending southwards, with the elegant cone of Tymphrestus just visible on the horizon. Here the President of the Community, the leading municipal official, was summoned to pay his respects to 'the foreigners'. He offered us coffee and reminisced about the war-time feuds of guerrilla leaders, of enemy bombers swooping down over the defenceless village, choosing their targets at will. Today two unexploded bombs flank the doorway of the main church. Everywhere in the village we were struck by the beauty of the children.

Further up the mountainside the dirt road comes to a dead end. Soon it will join the road under construction from Porta Panayia in Thessaly, and will eventually follow the route taken by the Despots when they set out from Arta to extend their dominions in Thessaly and Macedonia.

Back in Arta one follows the north shore of the gulf to Preveza. After crossing the Louros, the road runs east-west along the fringe of the Ambracian plain. Fifteen kilometres west of Arta an elegant limestone peak rises above the marshy fields on the west bank of the river. It was once crowned by the **Castle of Rogoi**, a strongpoint strategically situated between the river and the main route to Arta, probably built by the Despots on an ancient site to guard their

Church of St Basil, Arta: a rectangular single-nave basilica outstanding for its exterior ornamentation.

The Vikos Gorge: the Monastery of Paraskevi suspended above space like an Athonite eyrie.

The Turkish bridge over the Vikos Gorge.

capital against hostile armies advancing from the coast. Some of the fortifications may, however, be as early as the tenth century. After 1204 and the Latin sack of Constantinople, Rogoi acquired a curious notoriety. After making off with the remains of St Luke from the imperial capital, a Frankish adventurer sold them to the Duke of Cephalonia who placed them in a shrine at Rogoi which lay within his domains. Here they were revered and visited by, among others, that indefatigable fifteenth-century traveller, the scholarly Cyriac of Ancona. After the Turkish conquest, the Evangelist's remains were smuggled to a Danubian fortress.

Remains of strong walls that sometimes reach a height of twenty-three courses stand out impressively around the keep. The foundations reveal Hellenic masonry and part of the ancient circuit is discernible to the north-west. It takes no more than ten minutes to climb in the shade of olive branches to the summit. Tortoises lumber up and down the maquis-covered slope. Wild olive trees and thick shoots of dark green ivy sprout from crannies in the towers and crenellated battlements at the top of the hill, which dominates a fine sweep of the winding Louros. In the distance, herds of cattle graze on the hazy plain. On the north side of the keep there is a single-naved chapel, repaired in the seventeenth century, with moderately well-preserved frescoes of the Virgin, the Archangels and the Dormition.

The northern promontory of the Ambracian Gulf now contracts to no more than three miles at its greatest width: a country of rolling meadows and tall grass, washed to the north by the Ionian Sea and to the south by a complex network of lagoons. Across the isthmus extend the **ruins of Nicopolis** (the city of victory), the most extensive Roman site in Greece. It was built by Augustus to commemorate the battle of Actium, and forcibly populated by immigrants from the towns of Ambracia, Acarnania and Aetolia, whose treasure of statues and marble ornaments were removed to adorn the new city. In conception and foundation Nicopolis is Roman; more than any other Greek colony on Hellenic territory, however, it illustrates the continuity of Graeco-Roman civilization, of the prestige attached by Rome to the memory of a decisive battle fought entirely between Romans in the land of Plato and Aristotle. The whole isthmus is studded with remains of walls and foundations of Roman and Early Christian edifices. It is a perplexing site, pastoral in character, though maritime, capable of producing a feeling of disorientation in the visitor. It is easy to understand how the masses of brickwork scattered about the fields reminded Edward Lear of the Roman Campagna.[5]

For two centuries it was the chief city of western Greece. St Paul spent a winter here, and from it he addressed his moving exhortation to Titus. After Domitian's infamous expulsion of the philosophers from Rome it was here that Epictetus, the lame teacher of Arrian, took up his residence and composed his philosophical discourses. By the fourth century, however, it had declined in importance, and it remained for Julian the Apostate, in one of his transports of pagan fervour, to renovate the city and restore the Actian festival (see below). But in the fifth century the passage of Alaric and his Goths left little but a debris of bricks and smashed statues. In the sixth century Justinian restored the walls, while confining their compass.

The **theatre**, the first monument encountered by the traveller driving from Arta to Preveza, rises against a background of the pale waters of the gulf, broken up by a seemingly endless succession of little bluffs and tongues of land. The orchestra is overgrown with asphodel, and there are sinister rustling sounds among the bushes of wild artichoke. Not only lizards. I have seen more than one repulsively large (probably harmless) snake while making my way across the remains of stage buildings towards the couple of extant tiers on the upper course of the cavea. Peasants say one should beware of asps – a fear perhaps inspired by the ghost of Cleopatra which haunts this country. More homely is the sight of storks nesting in the niches of the upper portico, a semi-circular gallery of arches through which one can look down across the sloping meadows to the lagoon. An ancient geographer says the fish were so plentiful here 'as to be almost disgusting'.

North-west of the theatre lies the outline of the **stadium**, which, unlike other Greek stadia, was circular at each end. Here were celebrated the Actia, the quinquennial festivals founded by Augustus in commemoration of his victory. Sacred to Apollo, the festivals consisted of the usual athletic and musical contests, chariot races and gladiatorial shows, while mock sea-fights re-enacting the battle of Actium were staged in the bay. North of the stadium, just beyond the hamlet of Smyrtoula, rises the hill on which the future Emperor's army was encamped on the day of the battle. After it was all over, according to Dion Cassius, he placed stones round the spot where his tent had been pitched, decorated it with trophies and built

[5] It takes between two and three hours to identify the main extant monuments, most of which lie at a considerable walking distance from each other.

370

a temple of Neptune on the spot. All that remains of it are scattered fragments of the frieze inscribed with huge letters describing the battle (the letters TUNO – viz. NETTUNO – are discernible). They lie round a large block of masonry shaped like a podium, faced with cuttings in which ships' prows are believed to have been inserted.

West of the stadium mounds of rubble indicate the site of Roman brick houses; beyond them extend stretches of low Byzantine walls, broken at intervals by series of triple arches. Opposite the walls against a background of ferns and long grass shelving down to the sea are the ruins of the Early Christian **Basilica of Alcyson** (a local bishop). It has a double aisle, a circular pedestal in the centre and a Hellenistic bas-relief of battle scenes which was later incorporated in the ambo.

Beyond the basilica the sward is littered with more debris of unidentifiable brick buildings. On the landward side of the road, just below the Byzantine walls, which are of inferior construction, composed of rubble between courses of tile, stands the sixth-century **Basilica of St Dometius**. It is outstanding for its beautiful floor-mosaics, masterpieces of elegant design with zoological themes composed of coloured stone tesserae of different sizes: the work of artists, who, if early Byzantine, were clearly influenced by Roman models. One portrays two swans floating under fruit-laden pear trees, with an inscription dedicated to Dometius, the Persian monk who was stoned to death for his faith, within an elaborate border portraying every kind of fish in the sea, including squid, octopus and prawns. There are also representations of sea-gulls and juvenile fishermen spearing tunny fish. In another mosaic men savagely hunt animals within roundels by plane trees.

Following a landward course (west) from the basilica and scrambling over fragments of Byzantine walls, one comes to another Roman edifice, the **odeum**, built of grey stone on a massive substructure. The cavea, almost wholly restored, is one of the most impressive monuments on the site. The position dominates the whole of the tapering peninsula. To the north rise the hills from which Octavian, now confident in victory (the day before, while inspecting his ships, he had met a man riding an ass and having asked his name, received the answer 'Fortunate, and my ass . . . is called Conqueror'), watched the rout of Antony's and Cleopatra's fleets.[6]

Northward, beyond the fragments of the Roman aqueduct which probably traversed the whole of the hilly isthmus, the Epirot moun-

[6] Plutarch, *Life of Antony* (Dryden translation).

tains rise steeply. East and south-east, below the Byzantine walls, a lagoon where herons wade is separated from the main bay by a thread of land.

Returning to the main road, one drives southward under shady poplars. Remains of small arched buildings, probably sepulchres, are scattered about the meadows. In the glades and hollows one catches glimpses of the rush wigwams of nomadic Sarakatsans. Below the road the lagoon is broken up by reed-bordered creeks, where the water lies motionless, slimily stagnant by the time one reaches the wharves of **Preveza**, a sleepy little port on the tip of the promontory. There is a saline fishy smell about the place; but there are some pleasant side-streets bordered with whitewashed houses. Geraniums, hibiscus and bougainvillaea blaze in fragrant courtyards.

The site is that of an ancient city, founded in the third century BC by Pyrrhus and named after Berenice – a wise and virtuous woman, Plutarch calls her – whom the Epirot king courted before becoming her son-in-law. In the Middle Ages it was occupied by Venetians and Turks in turn, until 1797 when it was ceded to France. But Ali Pasha, the Sultan's Albanian satrap, quickly descended upon it, and his executioner, a man of formidable stamina, beheaded every member of the French garrison. Their heads were crated and dispatched as trophies to the Sultan in Constantinople. There are no ancient monuments in the town: only some outcrops of Venetian walls on the periphery, with the ruined citadel (west of the town) overlooking the Ionian Sea. On the whole, Greeks consider Preveza a boring place, and Costa Caryotakis, an early twentieth-century poet of considerable merit, author of *Nepenthe* and a series of caustic, often witty, *Elegies and Satires* exposing the bourgeois horrors of Greek provincial life – the schoolmaster reading his newspaper in the café, the illiterate local magnate totting up his petty profits, the lifeless strollers ambling *en famille* along the shabby waterfront – committed suicide here out of sheer boredom with:

> The olive grove, the sea round and above all
> The sun, death among deaths.[7]

Open-air cafés and modest fish tavernas where I have had the best prawns in Greece spread across a scruffy grove of plane and olive trees overlooking the strait, no more than half a mile wide, which connects the vast three-quarter-moon gulf with the open sea. Empty fishing-boats lie motionless at their moorings in the soporific noon-

[7] Translation by Robert Liddell, *Mainland Greece*, Longman, London, 1965.

tide sun, and caiques and a ferry ply across to the opposite point of Actium. A few sun-tanned children splash about in a shallow stagnant inlet. In the background rise the Dry Mountains of Acarnania and, westward, the majestic outlines of the island of Leucas.

There may be no tangible remains, but it is pleasant to row across the strait in the evening when the waters turn from light blue to mauve and finally a deep purple-grey. Scenically, the point of **Actium** is no more prepossessing than that of Preveza. A spit of land, flat and sandy, all but closing the entrance to the inland bay from the sea, it bears few visible marks of its fame. Slightly to the north are the minimal vestiges of a temple of Apollo Actios of great antiquity, restored and enlarged by Augustus. On the eminence of Anactorium, overlooking the shore, Augustus built a commemorative temple in the Roman style. Strabo says it dominated a sacred grove and harbour where some of Antony's captured vessels were preserved in boathouses. A kind of naval museum, probably.

But the temptation to ponder on the actual course of the engagement, the third and last Roman conflict fought on Greek territory, is irresistible. Of the tactics and strategy displayed by the commanders on 2 September, 31 BC, few historians agree. Antony, whose vessels were larger and more cumbersome, crammed bows to stern in the Bay of Preveza, is thought to have been encamped, with the élite of his army, on the point of Actium, whereas Octavian's lighter and faster galleys were anchored in an inlet well within the Ambracian Gulf. Shakespeare seems to have got the topography fairly correct when he makes Antony tell Enobarbus:

> Set we our squadrons on yond side o'th'hill
> In eyes of Caesar's battle, from which place
> We may the number of the ships behold
> And so proceed accordingly.

More impetuous than his rival, Antony decided to risk all – mastery of the empire – in a battle at sea. The attempt was obviously a failure of colossal dimensions and the engagement, in which Octavian's smaller vessels possessed greater manoeuvrability in these confined waters, was fought in the Bay of Preveza which serves as a kind of ante-chamber to the Ambracian Gulf. The popular version of the debacle is that Cleopatra's unexplained defection with sixty Egyptian galleys, at the crisis of the engagement, turned the scales. Peevish and petulant – as described by Shakespeare (who was after all cribbing North's Plutarch) – the 'ribald-rid nag of Egypt', with 'the breese upon her, like a cow in June' – hoisted her sail and fled, abandoning her infatuated lover, whose lust and 'sleep and feeding' had sapped 'his honour even till a Lethe'd dullness'. Then 'like a doting mallard, leaving the flight in height', he flew ignominiously after the purple sails of the royal vessel speeding towards Egypt.

Abandoned by their eccentric, somewhat hysterical leaders, Antony's captains were pounced upon by Octavian's more manageable galleys which, says Plutarch, sailed 'round and round' and annihilated 'these huge vessels, which their size and their want of men made slow to move and difficult to manage'. Octavian, heretofore imprisoned in the shallow Ambracian trap, had at last broken out into the open sea.

After the disgraceful outcome of the naval battle, the land troops were too dispirited to carry on the fight, and Antony's leaderless legions deserted in droves. The last of the great Roman civil wars was over. In this narrow strait between the Ionian Sea and the lagoon-like gulf, skimmed by wild fowl and ringed around by mountains, the sickly Octavian won the battle of Actium and became Augustus Caesar.

CHAPTER TWENTY-FOUR

Epirus

❧

Cassope – Zalongo – The Acheron – Suli – Ephyra: The Oracle of the Dead – Parga – Dodona – Yannina – Lake Pambotis: The Byzantine Churches – The Cave of Perama – Konitsa – Zagori – The Sarakatsans – Zitsa – Paramythia – Igoumenitsa

Seamed by narrow valleys funnelling out of forbidding gorges, Epirus is well watered by four rivers. Other than the Acherousian plain, there are few open stretches; and slate-coloured mountains, alternatively bare or wooded, sometimes reaching impressive altitudes, achieve a structural perfection, with peaks, screes and ravines composing into an organic architectural whole: highly compressed, though never claustrophobic. In Epirus one has the feeling of sitting on top of the whole of Greece, of being perched on the final crown of this incomparable convulsion of schist, limestone and marble.

In Homeric times, Neoptolemus (alternatively called Pyrrhus), the enterprising son of Achilles, who induced Philoctetes to lend the Greeks the arrows of Heracles considered indispensable for the capture of Troy, settled in Epirus with Andromache, the widow of Hector. He was succeeded by his son Molossus, who gave his name to the future kings of the country which was famous for its dogs, its oxen, and its torrents winding through sunless canyons. The nature of the country gave Achilles's descendants little opportunity to indulge in royal trappings, and the absence of maritime plains retarded, without actually precluding, the process of Hellenic cultural colonization. Although Thucydides dismisses the Epirots as barbarians, Grote considers them 'susceptible of Hellenic influences to an unusual degree . . .'; and it was at the court of one of the rural Molossian kings that Themistocles, the victor of Salamis, chose to take refuge when ostracized by the Athenians for suspected Medism. After the battle of Pydna in 168 BC Aemilius Paulus razed the towns, probably little more than villages, to the ground and condemned the inhabitants to slavery.

In medieval times the mountain redoubt remained out of the main

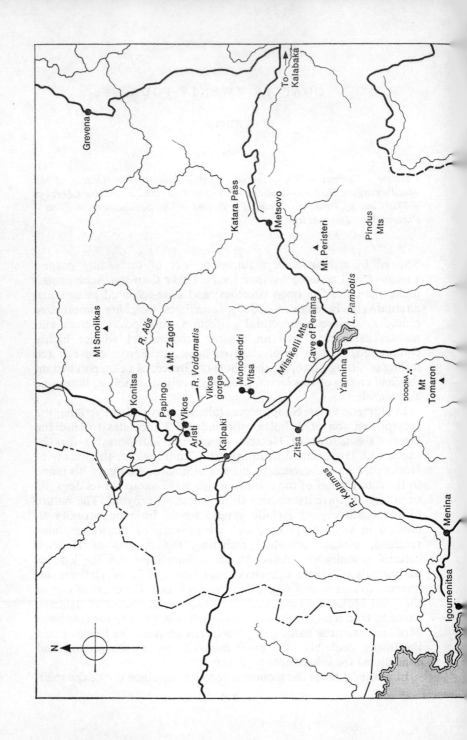

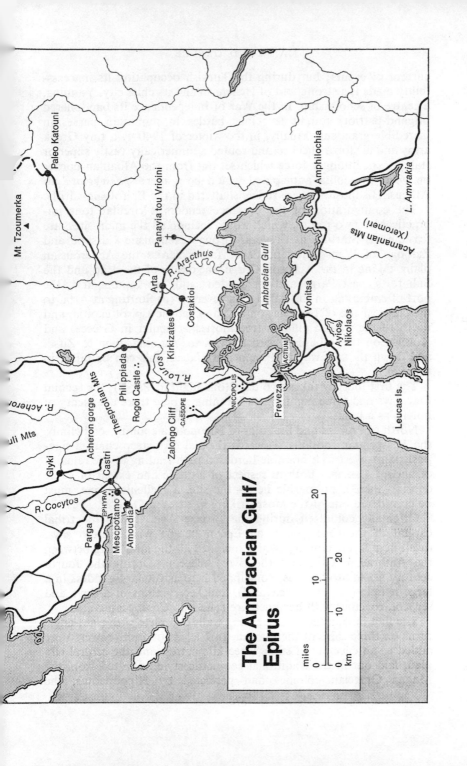

The Ambracian Gulf/
Epirus

Mt Tzoumerka

Paleo Katouni

Panayia tou Vrioini

R. Aracthus

Arta

Costakioi

Kirkizates

R. Louros

Phil ppiada

Thesprotian Mts

Rogoi Castle

Zalongo Cliff

CASSOPE

NICOPO JS

Amphilochia

L. Amvrakia

Ambracian Gulf

Acarnanian Mts
(Xeromeri)

Vonitsa

Ayios
Nikolaos

Preveza

ACTIUM

Leucas Is.

Acheron gorge

Glyki

uli Mts

R. Acheron

R. Cocytos

Parga

Castri

EPHYRA

Mescpotamo

Amoudia

miles 0   10   20

km 0   10   20

current of events; but during the Turkish occupation its inaccessibility made it a stronghold of Hellenism and its chief city, Yannina, a centre of scholarship. In the War of Independence its bandoliered brigand-patriots fought ferocious battles in mountain passes in incredible grandeur. Finally, in the winter of 1940–1, a tiny Greek army and air force checked and routed a numerically vastly superior Italian expeditionary force which set out from the Albanian border on what Mussolini anticipated would be a mere *'passeggiata'* to Athens. His illusions were rudely shattered in the Epirot snowdrifts.

The configuration of the province renders a circular tour impracticable. Two routes, which would include all the main sites, are feasible. (i) Starting at Preveza, through Hellenistic Cassope and Zalongo of War of Independence fame; across the Acherousian plain, taking in the Acheron Gorge, the oracle of the dead and the Suli forts, past Parga and its 'golden sands' to Igoumenitsa, the port of embarkation for Italy (or in reverse). (ii) Starting at Arta, to the classical site of Dodona, on to Yannina, the Epirot capital, and north to the Zagori villages (the most spectacular in Greece) and Konitsa on the Albanian border; back to Yannina, then to Zitsa, and down the highway to Igoumenitsa (again this can be taken in reverse).

The first journey takes two days (one night at Parga); the second four days and three nights, with Yannina, where there are plenty of hotels, as a base.

North of Preveza and the ruins of Nicopolis a country road climbs the Thesprotian foothills. Towards the end of a steep climb a signpost points west to a bramble-bordered path leading to the remains of **ancient Cassope**. Both in respect of altitude and extent of stone debris – there is no marble here – the site, a Hellenistic one, must be considered one of the most striking in western Greece.

Originally colonized during the Bronze Age, it was the tribal capital of the Cassopeans, an Epirot people who, Strabo says, dwelt in a 'fertile country' which included all the land lying between the Ambracian Gulf and the river Acheron. During the fourth century BC Aphrodite was worshipped here as tutelary goddess in a large temple (as yet unexcavated), and her symbols of a dove and serpent, together with her bust, are found on Cassopean coins.

The first inhabitants raised strong walls complete with right-angle turns on three sides of the plateau. In Hellenistic times towers were added to an enceinte of some three kilometres, and the central city plan, laid out in the traditional geometric style imported from the Magna Graecian colonies and perfected by Hippodamus, the

Ionian fifth-century BC town-planner, pivoted on a wide arterial paved way forming an east-west axis in conformity with the configuration of the great ledge across which the buildings spread. To the north the city was protected by tawny-coloured limestone cliffs. Security was thus ensured by nature, and the situation, one of great dominance, enabled the inhabitants to enjoy a bird's-eye view of sea, gulf, lagoons and promontories.

The ruined city can be traced in its entirety within the fortified enceinte. Most of the walls overlooking the formidable southern declivity have unfortunately been destroyed. Immediately left (south) of the main street in the agora area are traces of a long stoa consisting of an outer Doric colonnade and an inner one of square columns. Another stoa ran north to south (west side of the agora); on the east are the remains of an odeum with over twenty tiers carved out of the rock, whence politicians harangued the people massed in the quadrilateral market place: at once the political, administrative and commercial centre of the city.

Opposite the north stoa is the finest extant ruin: the **prytaneum**, or town hall, residence of the city elders and hostel for distinguished visitors. The main walls are of polygonal masonry, and the diagonal interior ones at the four corners of the building constituted a novel feature, probably intended to provide extra support to the upper storey. A large central court was surrounded by Doric colonnades, behind which seventeen chambers, where the town councillors transacted business, were ranged. The upper storey, crowned by a roof decorated with acroteria carved with lotus flowers and palmettes, stopped short on the south side, thus giving the building the shape of a Greek letter π and enabling the dwellers to enjoy the benefits of the mountain breezes. This well-preserved building, the layout of which is perfectly clear to the naked eye, was destroyed by the Romans in the second century BC when they occupied the whole of Epirus and razed seventy Epirot cities to the ground.

Further evidence of the importance – in this instance not military or strategic – of Hellenistic Cassope is provided by the ruin of a large third-century BC **theatre**, where ancient drama was taught. Carved out of the cliff-face immediately north-west of the prytaneum and reached after a stiff climb, it was capable of accommodating six thousand spectators. The gradient is terrifyingly steep. Two huge rocks lying in the centre of the orchestra remind us of the repeated landslides which have buried the foundations of Cassope under successive strata of boulders.

One more ruin at the north-west end of the plateau (it is not easy to identify without the help of the local custodian) completes the as yet inadequate story of Cassope: an underground **burial chamber**, the type of which must now be familiar to the traveller in Macedonia. Stone steps lead to a vaulted passage terminating in a square chamber plundered in the early nineteenth century. Ancient graffiti are identifiable, if not always legible, on the walls of the passageway which, like those of the chamber, were surfaced with marble dust and sand to give the impression of fine marble panels. Situated within the city walls – necropolises usually extended outside the urban perimeter – the chamber may well have been the funerary sanctuary of some Cassopean military hero. As in other Hellenistic sites in western Greece, the emphasis remains on the military aspect. For centuries Greek peasants have referred to the chamber and passage as the *vasilospito* (the king's house). But who was the king? Over what sort of people did he rule? For all its size, and the robust architectural features of its scattered civic buildings, Cassope remains an enigma. Many large edifices whose function is unknown have still to be excavated. Picking one's way among the incomprehensible rubble littering the windswept plateau, one cannot help feeling the inadequacy of archaeological research in this spectacular context.

Immediately east of the signpost to Cassope, the country road dips down to the little eighteenth-century Monastery of Ayios Demetrios. Above it towers the cliff of **Zalongo**, a national shrine, crowned by a group of modern white figures which commemorate a rather over-romanticized incident during the War of Independence. After the fall of the Suli forts in 1822, a number of Suliots fled southwards and took refuge from the pursuing Turks below this prominent eminence. One day children playing outside the church spied a detachment of Ali Pasha's Albanians, bristling with yataghans and muskets, approaching from the south-east. Men, women and children scrambled up the cliff, but the men were ambushed by another Moslem detachment approaching from the north. Caught between cross-fire, they were killed to a man. About sixty women, fearing rape and captivity, reached the summit, whence they hurled themselves, with their children, into the abyss below. It is said the women performed a slow circular folk-dance on the rocky eminence before falling off one by one, at the end of each revolution, as though in execution of some solemn sacrificial rite. A zigzag stairway climbs the cliff-face. Halfway up a little chapel contains the bones of the women whose corpses were found among the boulders. The summit is razor-sharp and one is tempted to wonder whether the dance could ever have taken place in such a confined place. Nevertheless the story remains sacrosanct. The ugly figures of varying height which crown the crag represent abstract forms of the Suliot women in the act of performing their stately gyrations. To the south undulating grasslands shelve down past Nicopolis to the Ambracian Gulf; to the north roll the Thesprotian mountains, compressed into mysterious billowing forms.

Beyond the fork to Cassope and Zalongo, the main road to the north enters a lush wooded valley which contracts into a defile and descends into the Acherousian plain, across which the Acheron flows sluggishly through a series of swamps known as the Acherousian lakes. It was on the banks of the Acheron that the poplar, discovered by Heracles, first grew. Now, yellow iris border rivulets criss-crossing fields of maize and rice-paddies; and buffaloes graze in meadows shaded by poplars, figs and plane trees. In summer the heat is intense, and in antiquity the beautiful but marshy plain, traversed by a loop of the river of Hades, was considered so unhealthy as to constitute the shortest route to Hell. To the north-west the mountain-wall of **Suli** rises sheer to a height of over three thousand feet; arid, forbidding, razor-sharp crests, sliced by vertical crevices.

A branch road leads to **Glyki**, at the foot of the mountains. The deviation is worthwhile. The streams of the Acheron form meres of sun-dazzled water and cafés spread under immense plane trees across what may have been the site where 'the souls of the dead for the most part come', says Plato, 'and after staying there for certain fixed periods . . . are sent forth again to the births of living creatures'. It may also be the site of Homer's grove of tall poplars and 'seed-blighted willows', where Odysseus beached his craft on Circe's instructions, before visiting Hades to consult the shade of Teiresias. It all seems so pastoral now, yet the very name of the river and the terrible mountains running in an unbroken line behind the village give the setting its appropriate infernal quality.

East of the village a track climbs to the entrance of the **Acheron Gorge**. Thence a path penetrates the defile of the dead, which is deep, dark and narrow, with a stream of aquamarine water flowing swiftly between banks of ilex. It was in this sinister setting that Charon, squatting on one of those contorted cream-coloured boulders, lay in wait to ferry the souls of the dead across to the world of shades. If the souls, still in the form of corpses, did not have a coin (the price of the fare) placed behind their ears or laid under their tongues, the avaricious boatman refused to ferry them across to the Asphodel Fields in his 'deeply sounding ferry'.[1] They were then doomed to wait on the banks of the lugubrious river throughout eternity. Rugged heights, from whose parallel ledges tufts of holm-oak sprout in the shade, rise to barren summits dominated by the strange bulbous pinnacle of Kiapha; behind it a higher peak is discerned, and to the south the box-like fort of Kounghi. Rocky bluffs create a zigzag formation as the defile deepens. No gorge in Greece is more macabre. The silence is total except for the flow of ice-cold water between dipping branches of plane trees and occasionally the tinkle of a bell hanging from the neck of a black mountain-goat perched on a jagged rock, like some infernal herald pointing the way to Hell. Once the entrance to the gorge is lost sight of a feeling of constriction, even near-panic, is unavoidable.

Only the deserted forts on the ledges above the path remind us that this mythological gorge was once inhabited by a turbulent people who gave their name to the whole mountain range of Suli. Refugees from Albania, the Suliots, a branch of the Tosks, settled here in the fifteenth century, retaining their Albanian mother tongue and Christian faith. During the early centuries of Ottoman occupation they enjoyed a measure of autonomy, forming a military caste, contemptuous of labour, unconquered by the Sultan's soldiers. They lived by plunder, descending on the farms of Turkish pashas and Greek peasants alike. Towards the end of the eighteenth century their military activities aroused the interest of the Russian Government, and Tsarist agents penetrated the Acheron Gorge to encourage and support the Suliots with gold and arms. Ali Pasha's riposte was a full-scale attack in 1792. But the campaign was a failure and most of Ali's soldiers fell to the pot-shots aimed by Suliots posted in hidden crannies overlooking the gorge, where every shot fired from a higher point must prove fatal. 'A perfect knowledge of the ground,' says Finlay, 'the eye of an eagle, the activity of a goat, and the heart of a hero was required to make a perfect Suliot warrior.' Colonel Leake, more prosaic, calls them plain robbers. Byron, however, says the picturesquely-clad Suliots 'stretch'd the welcome hand' to Childe Harold and his companions.

But the Sultan could not allow this state of affairs to go on indefinitely. The siege was renewed; it went on for years, the Suliot women fighting in defence of the forts. The most formidable was Tzavellena – the parapet she built to serve as part of her lines of communication with the forts is clearly visible on the south bank. As the besiegers increased, however, and the Turkish ring of pennon-

[1] Pindar, *Fragments.*

crowned tents tightened round the entrance to the gorge, Suliot stocks of arms and provisions diminished. When deprived of rain, the besieged would mop up water from the Acheron with sponges let down on ropes from projecting ledges. Eventually these fierce bandoliered brigands – identified with Hellenism by nothing but the Orthodox Church – surrendered, but not until after their leader, the priest Samuel, had blown himself up in the powder magazine of Fort Kounghi. Survivors emigrated to other parts of Greece, but after the outbreak of the War of Independence they returned to their native mountains and once more took up arms against the Turks. The forces of Vrioni, however, were too strong for them and, when offered honourable terms of capitulation in September 1822, they accepted and emigrated to Corfu. Only Marco Botsaris remained in western Greece to carry on the fight. The legend of Suli, probably over-dramatized, remains engraved in the national consciousness, immortalized in poem, folk-song and history book.

Between Glyki and the coast, among the rush-bordered streams of the Acherousian plain, is the village of **Castri**, on a hill fortified by nature. Site of ancient Pandosia, founded in the seventh century BC, its enceinte once included twenty-two square towers, and some rough fourth-century BC polygonal walling (east side). The modern village, past which the Acheron flows towards the sea, is green and pleasant.

Five kilometres to the south lies the village of Mesopotamo, where **Ephyra**, site of a celebrated *necromanteion* (oracle of the dead) crowns a rocky knoll above the Cocytos, a tributary of the 'infernal' Acheron. The excavations lie beneath the eighteenth-century Monastery of Ayios Ioannis. The site, among the most important of its kind in the country, has much in common topographically with the one described by Homer in the eleventh book of the *Odyssey*, in which Odysseus performs the greatest of his feats: the descent into Hell. Archaeologists have indeed demonstrated that Ephyra has a Bronze Age history, and the story is that Neoptolemus sailed here after the Trojan War and ruled thereafter as Molossian king. Here too Herodotus alleges that Periander, the Corinthian tyrant, sent ambassadors to interrogate the shade of Melissa, his murdered wife, who was cold and naked.

The ancient Greeks believed that all hollows and fissures in the earth's crust led to the Underworld where the souls of the dead dwelt and uttered prophecies to enquiring mortals bold enough to search them out. At Ephyra pilgrims had to undergo purification rites, as at all oracles (see Delphi, Trophonius, Dodona). Diet, prayers, ablutions and total silence were among the priority regulations. Sacrifices too. For the dead liked to be propitiated with honey, milk, wine and, above all, the blood of sacrificial animals. The ostentatious solemnity of the ceremonial and the extraordinary gullibility of the consultants – some were only allowed to eat walnuts, others were cleansed with squills by a priest who spat three times in their faces – were the butt of Lucian's satire some nine hundred years later.

The site is an extremely complex one, and the custodian's assistance is indispensable. Walls of thick polygonal masonry – five massive courses of the east wall are preserved – enclose a labyrinth of corridors roofed with heavy lintels and ancillary chambers, the doors of two of which are well preserved. In these chambers we may still see the famous jars – once containers of lupin seeds and Egyptian jonquil given to pilgrims in order to produce hallucinations, flatulence and giddiness. The chambers include a bathroom and dormitories. At the end of the maze of corridors in which the pilgrims submitted to further unusual rites – including the eating of oysters – so that they were worked up into a fit state of psychic hysteria, was the central apartment flanked by three chambers on each side. Here one may still descend through an arched entrance into a gloomy vaulted pit where Hades and Persephone reigned in their infernal 'palace'. Iron wheels and bronze pulley-sheaves, by means of which the shades of the dead were raised in order to gabble their oracles to the open-mouthed pilgrims, lie in the central court. It is worth noting the thickness of the walls (the preserved ones being of the Hellenistic period) which allowed for the priests' movements and 'preparations' being carried out inaudibly. West of this main complex were the storage rooms and more chambers for waiting pilgrims. It is the survival of the props, as well as the pleasant, almost pastoral, setting of the oracle, that tend to produce such an impression of ambivalence in the modern visitor. Frankly, there is nothing in the least infernal about the place. How unlike the gorge of the Acheron.

A short and pleasant diversion may be made along a road bordered by sea lavender and agnus castus which crosses the plain to **Amoudia** (the ancient Glycis Limen, the Freshwater Harbour) and the mouth of the Acheron, referred to by mythographers as the 'forest of Persephone'. The trees that filled the goddess's sacred wood have gone, replaced by a dusty village of shacks; the bay too has been so extensively silted up that it is difficult to believe that this was once the harbour in which an entire Corinthian fleet anchored before

The magnificent theatre at Dodona before and after restoration.

Phthiotic Thebes: a delicately carved capital from Basilica A.

Papingo: snowy spring in the Pindus Mountains.

attacking the Corcyraean flotillas in one of the early moves of the Peloponnesian War (433 BC).

The main road continues to cross the northern end of the Acherousian plain. The awful crags of the Suliot mountains no longer dominate the landscape. We leave the lowlands of walnut, fig and mulberry orchards and climb; winding above a steep wooded coast of red-brick cliffs, we pass a west-bound branch to the lovely **Lychnos** beach, its hotel, its view of the cliffs guarding the Acheron estuary and its plague of wasps; we continue to descend through olive groves to the shore. Here nature and peasant architecture have combined to make the little port of **Parga**, which is in the shape of an amphitheatre, one of the most attractive on the mainland, its paved alleys and stairways mounting steeply between whitewashed houses roofed with slate tiles and courtyards filled with roses, jasmine and orange trees. Tourism has added its contribution: cheap hotels, caravans, camping sites, a plethora of shoddy tavernas. The crescent-shaped waterfront, lined with cafés and souvenir shops, is animated – in the evenings at the height of summer the animation can be overpowering – resounding with the chug and splutter of caiques, the polyglot chatter of mobs of tourists. In the centre of the harbour is an islet crowned with a whitewashed chapel; beyond lies the Ionian Sea and the low flat shape of Paxoi, an offshore island of Corfu. At the northern end of the sickle a pine-clad bluff is littered with the ruins of a Venetian castle. Beyond the bluff, another crescent-shaped bay sweeps northwards, fringed by the 'Golden Sands', one of the finest beaches in Greece (part of which is an enclave of the Club Méditerranée). Thence paths mount through terraced orchards and olive groves dotted with whitewashed chapels and farmhouses surrounded by fig trees. The lower levels are the preserve of campers. Overcrowding is now the lot of Parga.

We do not hear much of it before the fourteenth century, when it was included in the domains of the Despots of Arta, and was famous for its sugar plantations. Under Venetian rule most of its inhabitants were pirates, and the Doge's architects transformed its rocky little fortress into a maritime bulwark against further Turkish expansion. After the Napoleonic Wars, when the Ionian Islands were ceded to Britain, it was supposed to come under Heptanesian administration; but the Sultan persuaded the British to renounce their claim and the little port reverted to the Porte's rule. This surrender was considered an act of betrayal by the inhabitants, who dug up the bones of their ancestors as a precaution against Moslem desecration and publicly burnt them amid loud lamentations. The majority then took off to Corfu in rowing-boats, hugging their children and little else, for Ali Pasha's cavalry had already descended the steep shady paths, occupied the port and sequestered all Greek belongings. This pusillanimous act of British foreign policy is often recalled in lurid oleographs entitled 'The Exodus to Corfu'.

There is no sightseeing. The Venetian castle is very ruined. On the crest of the ridge between the two scythe-like bays cafés shaded by plane trees are enchantingly situated in a whitewashed square. Sea-bathing, underwater fishing, walking in the shade of olive and fruit trees against a screen of rugged mountains constitute the charm of Parga.

To the north of Parga you climb into the rugged hinterland again. Sea and islands disappear from view; the road crosses a saddleback range and enters the **Valley of Margariti**, scene of much guerrilla activity in 1944, which is shaped like an elliptical crater with mountain peaks forming a kind of lunar rim round it. Thick bracken borders the banks of a swamp in which horses wade among water-lilies. A ruined minaret is surrounded by plane trees on the slope of a foothill carpeted with asphodel. The road runs across a little green plain with a cone-shaped eminence in the middle, bounded to the north by strangely eroded hills of bright red rock, and descends to Igoumenitsa.

Beyond the village of Philippiada, the northbound Arta-Yannina highway forces a way through the slate-grey mountains which form a semi-circle round Arta. Ambracian softness is succeeded by Thesprotian ruggedness. Northward winds the narrow claustrophobic valley of the Louros, whose sources lie at a tremendous height in the heart of the Thesprotian massif. Just before we reach the Louros dam – a sheet of pale water surrounded by bare crags – there are vestiges of an ancient water conduit: part of the great aqueduct which supplied Nicopolis with water. Knotted plane branches form an arbour over the stream as the valley contracts. Passing through a tunnel at the narrowest part of the gorge, the road climbs into deserted country where Crown Prince Constantine (later King Constantine I), in command of an army besieging Yannina during the First Balkan War, had his headquarters. The site is commemorated by a monument at the khan of Emin Aga. The encircling peaks become higher, more desolate, dominated to the west by the summit of Mount Tomaron. Eight kilometres before reaching Yannina, a turning to the left leads to Dodona. The road winds up a spur of Tomaron, affording stupendous views of the cruel crevices of the Pindus to the east, of the Mitsikelli massif soaring above the lake of

Yannina. A zigzag ends in an elliptical-shaped valley; three hamlets straggle across the lower slopes of Tomaron, which is speckled with firs and terminates in an elegant snow-capped peak, its sides scarred with screes and pale russet-coloured crevices down which icy torrents must once have flowed.

In the trough of the hollow, immediately facing the back-cloth of Tomaron, are scattered the **ruins of Dodona**, one of the most evocative classical sites in northern Greece, almost Delphic in its solitude and grandeur. But it is not a smiling scene. 'Wintry Dodona', Homer calls it. The Dodonian oracle, dedicated to Zeus, is the oldest in Greece and was consulted by pilgrims long before Apollo took up his abode on the sacred ledge below the Phaedriades at Delphi. Dodona was inhabited by an austere local people who slept on the ground, never washed their feet and elected the god's priests.

It is to Herodotus that we owe the story, told to him by three priestesses, of the oracle's foundation. Two black doves took flight one day from Thebes in Egypt. One alighted on an oak tree at Dodona and spoke with a human voice, instructing the inhabitants to found an oracle of Zeus; the second flew west to establish another at Ammon. The oak on which the Egyptian dove twittered was, according to Pausanias, the second oldest tree in Hellas (the first being the willow in the sanctuary of Hera at Samos, the third the olive beside the Erectheum on the Acropolis). Dodonian Zeus, a Pelasgic deity, dwelt in a tree-trunk, in the hollow of which stood his statue, and his oracular pronouncements were revealed by the rustling of leaves in the wind. Sophocles calls it 'the talking oak'. Gods themselves and epic heroes travelled across the Epirot wilderness to consult the whispering oak leaves: Dionysus, when maddened by Hera, to seek a remedy for his curse; Odysseus, 'to hear . . . whether it were better, after so long an absence, to re-enter fertile Ithaca publicly or privately'. Athena herself removed a piece of the tree's sacred bark which she placed on the bows of the Argo when she accepted responsibility for the expedition of the Argonauts.

As the Pythian pronouncements at Delphi gained international fame and attracted increasing numbers of consultants, Dodona, more inaccessible, declined in importance. Nevertheless poets and writers continued to hold it in high esteem. By the fifth century BC the priests were succeeded by old women whom Herodotus and Sophocles call 'dove-priestesses', who went into transports of ecstasy on the Delphic model. The tragedians laud the oracle's sanctity. Demosthenes quotes its pronouncements and Xenophon recommends the Athenians to hearken to its counsel. Croesus,

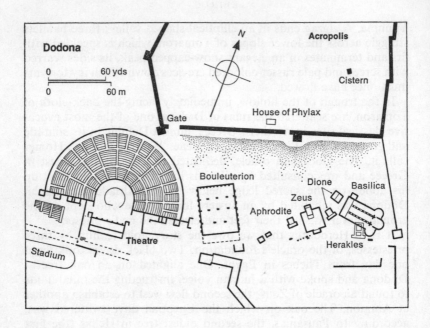

King of Lydia, most enthusiastic of oracle-addicts, did not fail to consult it. As at Delphi, the oracles were extremely ambiguously worded.

Vestiges of ancient walls stand out prominently, and a few holm-oaks are dotted about the valley. Beyond the outline of the stadium (parts of the sphendone are discernible) rises the magnificent semi-circle of the **theatre**, built in the reign of Pyrrhus (third century BC) and recently sufficiently restored to constitute one of the major monuments of its kind in the country. There is no ornamentation left – no statues, friezes, pediments or carved seats for notables – only the harmony and simplicity of the concentric tiers of grey stone. The skene is a muddle of chambers which are difficult to identify. The western parados (side entrance), preceded by a double gate with three fluted Ionic half-columns, leads into the circular orchestra, where the horseshoe-shaped drainage conduit is remarkably well preserved. The large cavea, supported (where it is not recessed, like most Greek theatres, into the hill) by a sturdy retaining wall, is intersected by two diazômai and ten stairways, leaving nine sections for accommodating eighteen thousand spectators on forty-five

388

tiers. One wonders how so vast an auditorium, concealed in a mountain hollow on the virtual roof of the country, could ever have been filled to capacity. Members of the courts of the Molossian kings could not have occupied more than a few tiers. Perhaps the audiences consisted largely of local peasants with ears as well attuned to the cadences of tragic verse as those of their modern counterparts who flock to the festivals of ancient drama held here every summer.

A gateway behind the theatre leads to the acropolis, a sloping quadrilateral within a peribolus crowned by towers. The extant substructures are mostly of the Hellenistic period. Thence a path descends to the **sanctuary**. Scattered heaps of stones, among fields where sheep browse, do not compose into an easily comprehensible layout. Three courses of well-fitted rectangular slabs indicate the site of the bouleuterion, where the Epirot confederacy assembled, and a complex of outlines has been identified as the Temple of Zeus, beside which the mantic oak tree rustled its sacred leaves. The temple was surrounded by tripods supporting cauldrons placed so close together that when one was struck the echo reverberated through the others. Here too was a statue of a boy on a tripod holding a bronze whip which, when blown by the wind, hit the cauldron next to it, setting off a metallic twang that vibrated through all the brazen ornaments. Pyrrhus surrounded the sacred enclosure with Ionic colonnades, but in 219 BC the Aetolians, at war with the Macedonians, destroyed the temple, as well as the theatre – subsequently restored by Philip V of Macedon – and burnt the sacred grove of oak trees.

The last substructure is that of the small temple of Dione, an Oceanid and Zeus's Dodonian consort, which retains some evidence of column bases and calcified shafts. To the right an apse in outline and a marble slab carved with a cross are the only vestiges of a Christian basilica: an indication that Dodona, unlike Delphi, became a Christian sanctuary after the Edict of Theodosius (392).

The short stretch of highway from the Dodona fork to **Yannina**, capital of Epirus, is without interest.

Pylons, maisonettes, roadhouses and petrol stations have obscured Byron's 'lovely view . . . veiled by the screen of hills'. The mountain-girt seat of Ali Pasha, once considered sufficiently important for the British, French and Russian Governments to appoint fully accredited Consuls, remains one of the most animated provincial towns in Greece. The hotels include a good Xenias. A few decrepit horse-drawn cabs trotting across an esplanade, where the inhabitants stroll in serried ranks in summer, provide an air of nineteenth-century picturesqueness and arouse memories of the semi-Oriental city about which Byron enthused and in which Colonel Leake and Pouqueville resided.[2] A garrison (and university) town and centre of communications, it possesses some ugly modern buildings – Divisional Headquarters, Officers' Club, barracks – which heighten the military atmosphere. From the esplanade the town shelves down to a bluff crowned by Ali Pasha's citadel. A few ruined minarets and domes are outlined against the pale waters of the lake. On the opposite shore Mount Mitsikelli, a bleak wall of grey limestone, rises sheer. To the east the perspectives are more intriguing, and mysterious uninhabited valleys wind steeply into the wilderness of the Pindus.

The city's history is purely medieval. Named (the official spelling is Ioannina) after a lakeside monastery of St John the Baptist, it enters the limelight in the late eleventh century, when Bohemond, son of Robert Guiscard, an uncouth but astute Norman invader who, says Anna Comnena, was 'in roguery and treachery far superior to all the Latins who came through', made it his winter quarters, strengthened the walls and plundered the surrounding countryside.[3] During the brief Serb domination, it was ruled by the hated 'Caesar', Thomas Preljubovič, who impoverished the inhabitants by creating monopolies so that all their agricultural produce was traded exclusively by his bailiffs. Given, we are told, to 'unnatural vices', he was murdered by one of his own bodyguard; and his widow (and successor), the delightful Maria Angelina (see p. 168), took as her consort a civilized Florentine of the Buondelmonti family.

Yannina settled down to happier days. But in the fifteenth century the Turks came. In 1611 an irresponsible revolt led by a drunken prelate hardened the mood of the conquerors (see p. 393). The dead hand of the Turks settled on all Epirus. But the inhabitants were more active than other Greeks in keeping the ideal of Hellenism alive by founding schools: some secret, some open. In no other part of the country was the standard of education so high. The schools of Yannina and their teachers – historians, geographers, theologians – provided much of the courage – and a little of the

---

[2] Pouqueville, French Consul at Yannina (1805–17), traveller and historian. His *Histoire de la régénération de la Grèce*, a distinguished work, covers the period 1740–1824.

[3] Anna Comnena, *The Alexiad*, translation by Elizabeth S. Dawes, Routledge and Kegan Paul, London, 1967.

learning – that would make the War of Independence a possibility and modern Greece a reality. Moreover, the inhabitants of Yannina, like most Epirots, were good business men; and by the eighteenth century we hear of them speaking foreign languages and maintaining trade relations with cities extending from Russia to Italy.

In the early nineteenth century Yannina became the capital of Ali Pasha, the cruel, astute and capricious Albanian tyrant who ruled over the pashalik of southern Albania, which included all western Greece, in a state of semi-independence. Then Yannina, a miniature metropolis, knew its palmiest days, with its Oriental little court, its foreign diplomatic representatives, its prosperous trading-houses, visited by merchants, adventurers and travellers from the west. One of these, Frederick S. N. Dawes, a discriminating nineteenth-century scholar, wrote: 'the purity of the diction, the extent of learning, and the knowledge of the world, that distinguishes its society, make Ioannina the Athens of modern Greece'.

The focal point of the modern town is the **esplanade** (Kentriki Square) and adjoining public gardens, whence there is a fine view of the eastern shore of the lake crowned by snow-capped peaks. A few eighteenth-century houses, homes of the grand old families of Yannina, are scattered about the southern urban slope. Unfortunately they are being allowed to fall into even greater decrepitude.

From Kentriki Square **Averoff Street** descends towards the citadel and the lake between rather bogus antique shops and silversmiths filled with buckles, clasps, boxes, etc., inlaid with filigree, for which the craftsmen of Yannina have long been famous. One passes the plane tree from whose branches Ali Pasha's victims, Christian and Moslem, used to hang until the stench from their decomposing bodies was too much even for the local Janissaries. The **citadel**, enclosed within walls of the Turkish period, is a warren of clean whitewashed cottages and some gaudily painted modern maisonettes, crowned by the **Mosque of Aslan Aga** (now the museum). Overhead storks, flapping enormous black and white wings, fly leisurely towards nests perched on ruined minarets. The walled-in area can be entered at several points, and arrows indicate the way to the museum. The simplest approach, perhaps, is from the lakeside, along Tsekouras Street and the first turning to the left (east), whence one climbs past pyramids of cannon balls.

The bluff commands a prospect of the western apex of the lake, which tapers off into a reedy marsh, where land and water fuse into a pale emerald liquescence. A well-preserved minaret stands beside the seventeenth-century hexagonal mosque, which is entered through a glass exo-narthex supported by six columns. The exhibits, of varying quality, displayed under the wide dome constitute a somewhat eccentric miscellany of different periods. It is like wandering through a rather superior Oriental junk-shop. Only the recesses for the shoes of the faithful remind us that the building was once a place of Moslem worship. The antiquities come from various Epirot sites. In the vestibule there is a fine Roman sarcophagus from Paramythia, carved with a procession of nude male figures and clothed women in Bacchanalian attitudes, their drapery blown back by the wind, accompanied by a lion and crouching panther; a tripod, from which flames issue between two griffons, is represented on the reverse side. There are small lead tablets, inscribed with questions put by consultants of the Dodonian oracle: personal queries relating to health, love affairs and projected journeys; also prehistoric pottery and weapons, acroteria and a fragment of a fourth-century BC double-carved moulding – all from Dodona. In a show-case on the south wall are two good icons (probably of the Cretan School of the post-Byzantine period) of St John the Baptist and the Raising of Lazarus. In the gallery there is another fine icon of Christ with a sensitive elongated face, holding a Book of Gospels. Other objects include Epirot costumes and silverware, relics of the War of Independence and Balkan Wars, Turkish carved wooden chairs with mother-of-pearl inlay, and books by authors ranging from Leake to Proust. The whole strange hotchpotch is crowned by an oleograph of Lady Hamilton.

Following an easterly course from Aslan Aga, you approach the disaffected **Fetiye Mosque** through an arched gateway. Its tea-cosy dome and minaret dominate the whole citadel area, from whose fortified parapet the nozzles of old Turkish cannon are still trained across the lake. The plain tomb in front of the mosque is that of Ali himself. Of his Seraglio, where the old Lion of Yannina kept his countless wives, there are only insignificant vestiges. The edifice was destroyed by order of the Sublime Porte after his death.

At this point it is best to turn back and descend to the tree-fringed café-lined landing-stage of **Kyra Phrosyne**, named after the wife of a Greek merchant whose death is immortalized in Greek folklore. The favourite mistress of Ali Pasha's son, she was denounced as a treacherous harlot by the deceived wife, who appealed for vengeance to her all-powerful father-in-law. The beautiful Phrosyne – also noted (among the Greeks) for her wisdom and charity – was promptly locked up in a dungeon, put into a sack and dropped into the lake. Superstition claims that her ghost can still be seen riding a wave in the pale light above the lake. As the wave breaks on the shore the vision fades. From the landing-stage a sandy lakeside road follows the fortifications round the promontory, past memorials to Epirot men-of-letters, and the cave of Dionysius, an unfrocked Bishop of Trikkala, alcoholic and visionary, who dreamed that the Sultan rose from his great divan to pay homage to him. He thereupon decided to liberate Epirus at the head of a band of drunkards who, belching and blaspheming, stormed the city gates. The revolt was crushed and Dionysius, captured in the cave above the lakeside, flayed alive. His straw-stuffed skin was sent as a trophy to the Sultan who rose majestically to receive it. So the absurd cleric's dream came true.

It takes about ten minutes to cross the green waters of Lake Pambotis to the island in the centre, whose reed-fringed shore is surrounded by eel-traps. Its Byzantine churches can be seen in a single morning or afternoon, but there is no more agreeable way of spending a whole day than roaming along the islet's herb-scented paths and cobbled alleys. One can lunch on eels, frogs, trout or crayfish at the taverna of Kyra Vasiliki, named after Ali's beautiful Greek concubine who entered his harem at the age of twelve and later used her influence with the ferocious old pasha with such astuteness that she was often able to intercede successfully on behalf of her oppressed compatriots. The taverna and landing-stage are shaded by plane trees. Little boys pass the time of day prodding wriggling eels they have just caught with bamboo-sticks and other makeshift instruments of torture.

The sightseer's itinerary, which includes five churches, begins at the jetty. One crosses the fishermen's village, its paved alleys bordered by whitewashed cottages bright with flowering creepers, in order to reach the first church on the west shore. The little **Monastery of Ayios Nikolaos of the Philanthropinoi** spreads across a rocky slope where sheep graze among the asphodel. In the courtyard there is a ruined refectory. The church, the most interesting on the island, is a single-nave basilica with a saddleback roof and additional exonarthexes or side chapels of a later date grouped on three sides which endow the rustic edifice with architectural unity. It was founded in 1292 by Michael Philanthropinos, who came to Yannina from Constantinople in the palmy days of the Despotate of Epirus. Michael was the first abbot, in which office he was succeeded by four members of his family. The frescoes, restored in 1963, were painted in the sixteenth century by the brothers Dikotaris of Thebes, who also worked at the Monastery of Varlaam at Meteora. There are no masterpieces: but in spite of the awkward attitudes of the saints, the work is animated. In the south exo-narthex (left of entrance) extends a row of paintings of some of the great figures of antiquity, including Solon, Thucydides, Plato, Aristotle and Plutarch: a not unusual example of the continuity of pagan antiquity in Orthodox religion. In this side chapel too there is a horrific rendering of the Last Judgement. In an arched niche (left) in the narthex we see the donors, the five abbots of the Philanthropinoi, waiting on St Nicholas; above him, at the apex of the arch, reigns Christ, wreathed in a mandorla, with an open Book of Gospels before him. In the north side chapel, believed to be the site of one of the so-called secret schools of Yannina (most of these were actually run openly, the Turks attaching little importance to the preservation of Hellenic culture among their subject peoples), the walls are painted with lively scenes of martyrdom: blood spurting from severed heads; women's breasts being lopped off; truncated limbs lying about in contorted attitudes. On the south wall there is a charming if naïve Creation, full of birds and animals and stylized trees.

South of the monastery we come to the **Church of Ayios Nikolaos of Dilios**, overlooking a grove of poplars, with rushes full of croaking frogs and the lake beyond. The church, basilica-shaped, with a large narthex and half-cylinder apse with traces of exterior brickwork decoration, dates from the early days of the Despotate and takes its name of 'Dilios', alternatively of 'Stratigopoulos', from two prosperous families who financed its restoration. The frescoes are of the mid sixteenth century, and the artists are believed to have been influenced by the work of Theophanes of Crete who painted more ambitious murals on Mount Athos. The Apocalypse above the narthex door is distinguished by a nice blend of colours: yellows, browns and golds. On the wooden iconostasis, said to be the work of the woodcarver responsible for the far more elaborate screen in the Monastery of St Stephen at Meteora, animals browse in a complex foliate setting.

From here one descends to the grove of poplars and follows a shady path in a south-east direction, whence there is an unbroken view across the lake to the mosques, minarets and fortifications of the citadel. The path ends at the **Church of the Eleousa**. Named after a miraculous icon of the Panayia Eleousa (The Virgin of Mercy), it too is dedicated to St Nicholas, patron saint of sailors, whose ubiquity on this rush-bordered islet probably derives from the maritime position of the churches. The architectural arrangement is similar to that of St Nicholas of Dilios, but on a smaller scale. The uncleaned frescoes are too damaged to merit detailed attention.

The Eleousa is a dead end. From here one skirts the swampy shore back to the landing-stage, crosses the village again – but in an easterly direction – as far as the **Church of Ayios Panteleimon** which nestles below a cliff shaded by enormous plane trees overlooking the north-east bay of the lake. A three-aisled basilica of the sixteenth century, it is of little interest except for the architectural oddity of the women's gallery shaped like the dress circle of a theatre. Beside the church is a ramshackle wooden Turkish house, rather pretentiously called the **Museum of Ali Pasha**, scene of the old Lion's dramatic end in 1822. For years Ali's obdurate insubordination had been a growing cause of anxiety in Constantinople. After abortive negotiations with Khurschid, the Sultan's military envoy, Ali retired to his *kioshk* on the island, where he hoped to gain time in which to manoeuvre Sultan Mahmud II into granting him a pardon before taking up arms again in defence of his quasi-independent little Albanian empire. But Khurschid, suspicious of the old wizard's intentions, sent an armed detachment to spy on his movements. Determined not to submit to intimidation, Ali fired on Khurschid's men from the window. In a moment the peace of the soporific little island was shattered by the crack of musketry. Ali, though wounded in the arm, organized resistance among his bodyguard. The regular troops soon penetrated the ground floor and fired through the frail ceiling. A bullet pierced the old pasha's groin. It was a fatal wound. Resistance collapsed. Ali's head was severed and carried in state to the citadel. Thus ended the long and turbulent reign of the Albanian adventurer, the legend of whose amorous and military exploits had thrilled all Europe. The chamber in which Ali was shot has been furnished in the Turkish style with broad divans ranged against the walls, on which hang nineteenth-century prints illustrating the story of Ali and the War of Independence. The most attractive are those by Dupré, a French nineteenth-century pupil of David.

From the museum you pass through a tunnelled passage into a little esplanade overlooking the lake. Here the diminutive sixteenth-century cruciform **Church of Ayios Ioannis Prodromos** (St John the Baptist) is picturesquely built into a rocky recess resembling a cave. The architectural arrangement is consequently somewhat eccentric, with the sanctuary facing north, a saddleback transept replacing the usual dome and two side apses at the east and west ends. The tasteless frescoes are of the eighteenth century.

Four kilometres north-west of Yannina a hump-like eminence rises out of the plain near the airport, its base pierced by the entrance to the **Cave of Perama**, one of the most remarkable in Greece, accidentally discovered by villagers seeking refuge from Italian bombers in 1940–1. Beyond the recess in which they huddled they caught glimpses of vast caverns and galleries. After the war the speleologists came, electricity was installed, and today guides conduct visitors through a complex of fetid chambers, pools of water and twisting tunnels lined with stalactites and stalagmites, often red or dull gold in colour, fashioned by millennia of erosion into shapes that assume the verisimilitude of animals, crosses, exotic plants, Oriental fetishes or disembodied bowels. The more spectacular halls have been given bizarre names ranging from Golgotha, the Dead City and the Ottoman Cemetery to the Artichokes, Marie Antoinette, Niagara and the Marble Forest. Some of the more fragile stalactites, grouped in organ-pipe formations, produce an audible tintinnabulation when struck.

The journey from Yannina to the Albanian frontier should include the diversion to the **Zagorachoria**, some forty-odd villages scattered across upland wastes or perched on crags overlooking the Stygian gorges of the Zagori massif. But the villages have nothing to offer the antiquarian: no monuments; nor archaeology to speak of. A day's drive from (and back to) Yannina gives one time to visit a few of the most strikingly situated villages.

From Yannina the road to Konitsa near the Albanian frontier skirts the flank of Mitsikelli where a branch road to the east ascends a rocky wasteland speckled with poplars and wild pear trees to the village of **Vitsi**, its well-preserved grey stone houses, roofed with tiles shaped like lozenges, ellipses and polygons, clinging to the mountainside. Arched windows in the middle of the ground floor enliven the otherwise unrelieved austerity of these grim rectangular buildings intended to protect their inmates from the elements and to keep wolves and brigands at bay.

The villages are little heard of before the Turkish occupation, when their inhabitants emerge as Christian communities to whom the Turks granted special privileges. By the eighteenth century they had formed a confederacy, dwelling in a state of semi-independence, administered by their own self-elected leaders, exempt from the fiscal extortion that crippled more prosperous communities inhabiting the lowlands (a state of affairs that better suited the Turks who would have found it difficult to police this remote mountain terrain). Many villagers, hard-working and ambitious, emigrated to metropolitan centres within the Ottoman Empire and became members of the professional classes. But they always came back to Zagori (some still do for a brief summer holiday) to bestow wealth and build sturdy houses furnished with fine carpets and furs. After the First World War emigration increased and most of the dwellings now remain firmly shuttered.

Beyond Vitsi the road climbs steeply. Immediately above the village you pass an enclosure containing the rubble of an ancient building and circular hearth recently excavated. The ruins, we are told, date from the ninth to fourth centuries BC. Nothing more. Elsewhere in these mountains, sherds have been discovered and fragments of walled sites (ashlar and polygonal). The role these played in the military history of antiquity – in an area of the Molossian kingdom already superbly fortified by nature – remains an enigma to the layman.

The short ascent leads to **Monodendri**. Architecturally it differs little from Vitsi, for throughout the Zagori massif Epirot stonemasons adopted a uniform plan for dwelling-houses and made use of identical materials. Cobbled mule-tracks are bordered by primitive pavements between stone walls and roofed gates over which branches of almond trees scatter their blossom in spring. As at Vitsi, not a brick roof mars the architectural robustness and austere simplicity of the grey slate tiles crowning the two-storeyed houses.

In the paved square is the church of Ayios Minas, a fifteenth-century basilica with some crude post-Byzantine frescoes and elaborate gilt iconostasis carved with bunches of grapes. Only a few of the fine houses are inhabited: and then only in summer. Once when I was there I saw in the hollow below the square a group of boys, incongruously dressed in the latest and most stylish 'casuals' playing football. It was the only sign of human activity I have ever encountered in this mountain world. To the south extend the summits of the Mitsikelli range: strange shapes like petrified giants caught in the act of executing the most elaborate acrobatics.

Above the village are the pasture-grounds of the Sarakatsans, a migrant people, believed (but not proved) to be descendants of the original pastoral communities of Homeric Greece. Their pointed wooden huts of thatch are often seen scattered about the valleys of Acarnania, Epirus and Thrace. Illiterate, fiercely traditional, with no occupation other than grazing their flocks, they adhere to a strict moral code based on Honour and Family.[4] Between them and the

[4] John Campbell, *Honour, Family and Patronage*, Clarendon Press, Oxford, 1964.

villagers there is often undeclared war: not only the friction provoked by disputes over grazing rights but hostility arising from the
existence of a completely different set of moral values – rigid and
intolerant in the case of the Sarakatsans who consider the villagers
effete, accusing them of frivolity and lack of honour, of indulging in
paederastic practices and having sexual relations with dogs.

From the village square of Monodendri a road to the north-east
descends to a shelf of rock, from which one stares down into the
immensity of the **Vikos Gorge**, at the point where the Voidomatis
and another torrent unite, their confluence forming three mighty
chasms. Travellers who suffer from vertigo should think twice before
gazing into this inferno of desolate flysch. The cliff-walls, absolutely
vertical, speckled with evergreens, are carved with crevices and
shelves – geology becomes geometry, and the stratification is symmetrical to the point of resembling Hellenic masonry. The hum of
thousands of bees echoes up from the boulder-strewn ravines. An
abandoned threshing-floor forms a kind of belvedere, and the little
refurbished monastery of Ayia Paraskevi, built of grey stone with
slate roofs almost undistinguishable from the rock on whose sides
it clings, is suspended like an Athonite eyrie above space. To the
north the gorge widens out and the geometry of the rock formations
becomes even more apparent, with the cliff-face cut up into acute
and obtuse angles, cubes, apices, rectangular cones and arched
niches. Below the path some horse-chestnuts are scattered across
vertiginous ledges.

Back in Monodendri, one can take the road which climbs above
the village into an uninhabited lunar landscape of strange rock
formations, like dolmens, weathered into horizontal, parallel and
angular folds of such regularity and finish that one has the impression
of gazing at a forest of man-made structures of varying sizes. The
feeling of hallucination provoked by this geological phenomenon is
haunting. I recall our relief at seeing a few poppies growing amid the
misshapen rocks, and some bee-hives – although we wondered who
ever climbed up to this dizzy altitude to tend them. When I last
visited the Zagori, this road, along which we encountered neither
man nor vehicle, came to an end at a point overlooking the Vikos
Gorge about midway along its south-north course between Monodendri and the valley of the Voidomatis. From here one looks
across the whole massif, which resembles an uneven tableland – a
huge eruption of flysch – slashed by multitudinous chasms where
bears and lynxes are still said to have their lairs, and by winding

tracks now being converted into well-surfaced roads connecting the various hamlets.

Returning to the Yannina-Konitsa highway from Monodendri one continues north through undulating scrubland. Soon Smolikas, the highest peak of the Pindus, looms majestically in the north-east. On the left of the road a memorial marks the furthest point in Greek territory reached by Mussolini's army in the autumn of 1940. At Kalpaki the road veers eastward, leaving the Albanian foothills behind. At the first fork you take the road to the east and climb through grassland slopes shaded by holm-oaks, horse-chestnuts and Judas trees. At the top of the pass the colossal cirque of the valley of the Voidomatis is suddenly revealed against a wide crescent-shaped screen of summits shaped like fangs. A dizzy descent in hairpin bends leads to the village of **Aristi**, architecturally similar to Monodendri, but less abandoned.

At the bottom of the bowl, a modern arched bridge spans the streams of the Voidomatis (The Ox-Eyed One), where they flow out of the Vikos Gorge. Plane trees line the river banks and *Anenome hortensis* and anchusa carpet the slopes. The waters of the Ox-Eyed One, ice-green between sandbanks, are recommended for the cure of dyspepsia. The peace and serenity of the scene provide a strange contrast to the immensity of the scale. The road then climbs the east side of the bowl and follows a spine of foothills composed of stratifications of schist resembling regular courses of masonry. To the south the jaws of the Vikos Gorge yawn open: cliffs, screes, crags and dolomites, all peppered with caves and arched recesses, against a background of escarpments disappearing into a tunnel of profound gloom. A bluff is crowned by the village of Viko – like a last human outpost before the gates of Hades.

The road ends at the village of **Papingo,** a sheep village and summer refuge of Sarakatsans, its stone houses with squat barn-like roofs and cobbled alleys spreading among almond trees under castellated cliffs which taper off into six monstrous tusks eroded into shapes as weird as the rock formations of Meteora. The highest peak is called the Camel. There is an inn where one can get fresh eggs and rye bread, and the church of Ayios Vlasios (St Blaise), a basilica with a wooden gallery at the west end painted with horizontal bands reserved for the female congregation. Beside the church is a pretty octagonal three-storeyed campanile – a typical embellishment of Zagori churches.

Back on the main north-bound road, one should not omit to take a last look at the heights of Papingo which now acquire the semblance of distorted organ pipes and at the northern outlet of the macabre Vikos Gorge. The savagery of the scene is equal only to its perfection. We descend into a cultivated plain traversed by the Aös which rises in the heights of Smolikas. At the point where the river forces its way through pinnacles and pyramids of wooded rock a **Turkish bridge** – a single wide arch of the utmost elegance – spans the translucent green stream flowing between sandbanks. From the apex of the bridge the view into the gorge is one of precipitous bluffs, either covered in evergreens or bare and eroded, piling up one behind the other, with strange shapes like the organ pipes of Papingo discernible in the more remote depths. Here on the Albanian frontier, as elsewhere in the Zagori, one has the impression that the deities who presided over the architectural landscape of Greece must have decided to complete their task and put away their rulers, dividers and compasses. They certainly ended with a flourish.

At no distance from the bridge **Konitsa**, whose inhabitants suffered horribly in battles between Communists and the Greek national army in 1947–9, spreads across the plain in the shadow of the Albanian foothills. It also has a minaret. It is not a bad place to have lunch in the course of a one-day trip from Yannina. There is an air of muteness about the place and its sorely tried older inhabitants, some of whom speak an Albanian dialect. The influence of the Iron Curtain is omnipresent.

Back in Yannina one now turns to the west. At the twentieth kilometre a branch road climbs up to **Zitsa** (a short and agreeable deviation). Slate roofs spread among Judas trees across the mountainside. At the inn you may try the local Zitsa wine – much commended throughout Epirus. A sparkling rosé, it is sweet and rather sickly. A more rewarding way of spending half an hour is to visit the monastery of Prophitis Elias, situated on a windy plateau surrounded by oaks and pines. The exterior of the church is barn-like with a slate roof crowned by three shallow domes, hardly perceptible from outside, ranged in a straight line, one above the narthex and two above the naos. The frescoes are late post-Byzantine and in no way remarkable. The elaborate iconostasis is a good piece of Epirot woodcarving, with gilded floral designs, surmounted by double colonnades, each with seventeen columns terminating in pointed arches. A commemorative plaque informs us that Byron stayed here in October 1809. From the plateau, along which the poet strolled with the monks, there is a wide view of the Kalamas valley, the ancient Thyamis, one of the four great rivers of Epirus, with ranges of dark green mountains rolling westward. Byron, who fell in love with the place – it was the first impact made on him by the Greek landscape – rhapsodized:

> Monastic Zitsa! from thy shady brow,
> Thou small but favoured piece of holy ground!
> Where'er we gaze, around, above, below,
> What rainbow tints, what magic charms are found!

From the Zitsa fork the highway continues its sinuous eighty-three-kilometre descent to the Ionian shore, following the course of the Kalamas above a narrow gorge through which the river threads its way between juniper bushes. In March violets and primroses grow in the shade of oak trees. Clusters of Judas trees are dotted among pines and ilex, and slate-roofed villages are perched on bluffs below the level of the mountain road. One exhilarating aerial view succeeds another. Emerging from the gorge, the road enters an enormous mountain-girt basin, with the Kalamas, where the right wing of Mussolini's army was decisively defeated in 1940, winding between poplar-fringed banks. There are glimpses of Corfu and the sea beyond.

At the khan at Menina a new road climbs steeply to the south and descends into the northern part of the Acherousian plain, passing through the valley of the Cocythus. **Paramythia,** a village loud with the din of coppersmiths, sprawls across the lower slope of Mount Korillas, which merges into the Suli range. That Paramythia, whose green cultivated valley was always famous for its olives, was an ancient site is confirmed by the discovery of coins and inscriptions and some exiguous Roman remains. In the Venetian era it was known as Castel Donato; and there are fragmentary remains of a castle, with Turkish additions, above the village. The road joins the main Acherousian road network at Glyki.

Along the highway beyond Menina, wayside shells of houses and ugly white monuments commemorate skirmishes between Germans and Greek guerrillas during the Second World War. The journey ends at the little port of **Igoumenitsa,** which has little in common with the rest of Epirus – or indeed Greece. A port of embarkation for (or disembarkation from) Italy, it is distinguished by nothing but its bus terminal and the bustle of arriving and departing ferry-boats and chugging caiques. There are tavernas on the waterfront, and iced drinks at the bar of the Xenias Hotel. Islets, like sprawling porpoises, form a garland round the crescent-shaped bay, beyond which flows the Corfu channel. The scrub-covered hills to the north, above the marshy estuary of the Kalamas, famous in antiquity for its aquatic plants, may be the ancient Sybota isles, off which the Corinthians and Corcyrans fought the great naval battle that helped to spark off the Peloponnesian War. Nevertheless Igoumenitsa retains the impersonality of a frontier town. The traveller's main business is with customs, passports and currency regulations. Formalities are a full-time preoccupation, and the mind's eye is already projected westward – towards Italy, beyond the horizon.

Soon, however, memories begin to crystallize and assume tangible forms: flashes of the tremendous architectural landscape of Zagori; pale reflections of Moslem Yannina and its lakeside Byzantine chapels; perspectives of the 'wintry' valley of classical Dodona; visions of the infernal Acheron Gorge, with the heat-haze hanging over the mythological Acherousian swamp, backed by the Suliot range with its grim forts manned by formidable Amazons – and of all the Hellenic lands that lie beyond, with their marble silhouettes and red-brick domes and medieval bastions; columns, pediments, tombs; amphorae, figurines and Attic profiles; icons, frescoes, floor-mosaics; asphodel waving on windswept slopes and dust lying thick in potholed village streets lined with wispy acacias; the inland seas ringed round by mountains with legendary names; the smell of burning incense and cathartic pine-resin, of scorched herbs and frying mutton-fat; and all the nostalgia for the demise of past genius and affection for an ebullient, contentious, know-all people always ready to be won over by a compliment, joke or wink of complicity. Images take over from memory; the lenses are carefully adjusted; geometrical outlines come into pinpoint focus, and past impressions resolve into imperishable, deeply felt experiences. It was not a Greek who said:

As for you,
Turn over the pages of the Greeks by night and by day.[5]

For those who have known them at all intimately it is difficult to do otherwise.

[5] Horace, *Ars Poetica*, '*Vos examplaria Graeca/Nocturna versa manu, versate diurna.*'

Appendices

❧

Appendices

❧

1. Some Practical Suggestions
2. Hotels
3. Restaurants, Tavernas, Cafés
4. Shops
5. Feasts and Holidays
6. Glossary
7. Chronological Table
8. Table of Byzantine Emperors
9. Tables of Medieval Latin Rulers and Greek Despots
10. Some Books on Greece

1. Some Practical Suggestions

Seasons

JANUARY–FEBRUARY can be cold and wet, with intervals of brilliant winter sunshine. A period of cloudless skies and calm seas in early January corresponds to the ancient Halcyon Days – breeding time of the mythological halcyon birds. Brief falls of snow are not uncommon in Attica and Boeotia (high mountains are snow-covered November–April). In northern Greece, snowfalls and cold spells are of longer duration. Fog is not unknown in Salonica. Woodcock shooting. Almond blossom and first wild flowers (anemones).

MARCH, unpredictable, as everywhere. Hillsides covered with wild flowers. Mid-March to mid-April ideal period for botanists.

APRIL can be showery or idyllic. Good season for travelling with lengthening days. Dirt roads sometimes impassable after spring rains. Scent of lemon and orange blossom intoxicating in orchard country.

MAY, generally fine and warm. Occasional rain. Flowers in profusion.

JUNE, good month for travelling. Not too hot. Sometimes cloudy in the middle of the day.

JULY–AUGUST, very hot. Hordes of tourists. Season of fruits. Crystalline light emphasizes structural quality of landscape. Barren mountains the colour of gun-metal turn a glowing purple in late afternoon. Cooling etesian winds. Macedonia is sometimes intensely humid.

SEPTEMBER, still full summer, but not as hot as July–August. Fewer tourists; fewer local trippers. Quail-shooting.

OCTOBER, in spite of the first rains, generally lives up to the tradition of a 'golden autumn'. Hillsides covered with cyclamen and autumn crocus.

NOVEMBER, unpredictable. Can be a prolongation of the 'golden autumn' or a foretaste of December. Dirt roads often impassable after autumn rains.

DECEMBER, inclined to be cloudy, raw, but not very cold, with some fine spells and magnificent winter sunsets.

Museums

Hours of opening, which are liable to alter and are certainly not uniform throughout the country, should be checked on the spot (hotel receptionists have all the up-to-date pamphlets).

Museums at small ancient sites (sometimes no more than sheds serving as storerooms) have no regular hours of opening. The *phylax* (custodian), who is generally on the spot, has the keys.

All museums throughout the country (including the Acropolis at Athens, the Sanctuary of Apollo at Delphi and other major archaeological sites) are shut on 1 January, 25 March (Independence Day), Good Friday (Orthodox), Easter Sunday (Orthodox), Christmas Day.

Countryside Churches and Chapels

These, even when of considerable historical or artistic interest, are often locked. The keys are generally kept by the local *pappas* (priest) or unofficial *phylax* (the owner of the main café in the nearest village will send a child to fetch either). The child will also show you the way to the church, return the keys to the responsible person and be pleased to receive a tip.

Communications

Enquiries about bus and train timetables can be made at all hotels and travel agencies. Buses are plentiful. The remotest mountain villages are connected with the nearest town by a daily service. Owing, perhaps, to the successive hairpin bend ascents and descents Greek passengers are inclined to be car-sick (nylon bags are provided).

Taxis or private cars (for long journeys) are parked in the main squares of small provincial towns. The price should be fixed in advance.

There are plenty of car-hire agencies (with or without driver) in Athens and Salonica. Travel agents and hotels have all the addresses.

The railway network does not cover the whole country. One can go from Athens to Salonica, and thence to Jugoslavia or Turkey, but one cannot cross the Pindus spine which runs vertically down the length of mainland Greece.

The non-walker who wishes to visit some ancient site, castle or church, to which no passable road leads, may hire a mule or donkey. As usual, the owner of the café in the nearest village is the person to approach for information. Mule- or donkey-riding is one of the most agreeable ways of seeing the countryside, although the saddlebags are sometimes flea-ridden. Riding is particularly recommended when visiting Frankish castles, the keeps of which are perched on precipitous crags.

ELPA (the Automobile and Touring Club of Greece) affords free assistance to members of affiliated associations. It issues maps, leaflets on parking, etc. Its offices in Athens are in the Athens Tower and in Salonica at 11 Constantinou Street.

Travel Agencies

Although the American Express (2 Ermou Street) and Cooks/Wagons-Lits (8 Ermou Street) make all the necessary arrangements for tours, travellers are likely to receive more personal attention and obtain more precise information (hotels, condition of roads, motor coach tours, time involved, etc.) from one of the smaller travel agencies in Athens. Among these are:

HELLENIC TOURS, 3 Stadiou Street (Stoa Calliga)

HEL-PA, 18 E. Venizelou (Panepistimiou) Street

HERMES EN GRÈCE, 4 Stadiou Street

HORIZON, 14 Nikis Street

KOSMOS, 1 Mitropoleos Street (Syntagma Square)

In Salonica among the most centrally-situated agencies are:

COOKS/WAGONS-LITS, 8 Meg. Alexandrou

AMERICAN EXPRESS, 5 Aristotelous Square

Beaches

It would require a small volume to list these. In most parts of the country, the beaches, whether sand, shingle or pebbly, are superb. Those which I consider outstanding are mentioned in the relevant passages in the text.

Transliteration of Place Names

On the highways and main roads the motorist will find signposts in English as well as Greek (off the beaten track there are often no signposts, and one has to keep asking the way). The official transliteration of Greek place names seems to be both arbitrary and quixotic. 'Pireefs' for 'Piraeus', for instance, and 'Olimbia' for 'Olympia'. The present tendency (in Greece) to try to equate the English spelling of place names with modern Greek pronunciation is all very well, but 'Delfoi' and 'Mikinae' look odd, to say the least. In writing this book, I have aimed at keeping usage and common sense as my principal guides in the transliteration of all names.

2. Hotels

Both in Athens and the provinces, hotels are being built so fast that any list given here would be out-of-date (certainly incomplete) by the time this book is published. Nevertheless, the names of a few hotels are mentioned in the text: largely because of their outstanding position.

The monthly publication, *Key Travel Guide for Greece and the Middle East* (obtainable from the more central of the kiosks in Athens or from the publishers at 6 Kriezotou Street (near to Syntagma Square; or consult any travel agent), gives a selective list of hotels (when built or restored), with prices, number of rooms, private bathrooms, whether air-conditioned, etc. It contains similar information regarding pensions and service flats (Athens only), bungalows and holiday camps. Any travel agent will also provide more accurate up-to-date information than is likely to be contained within the compass of a book of this kind.

There may be two opinions about the official classification of hotels by the Greek Ministry of Tourism. By Western standards there are only two real luxury hotels in Athens, the Grande Bretagne and the Hilton, and not eight as at present officially listed. The tendency is to up-grade the various categories. Nevertheless, second and, in many cases, third class hotels are perfectly adequate. Most bedrooms have a shower, if not a bath. The hotels of the government-subsidized Xenias group, found at all the tourist sites, are superbly situated, generally on the periphery of the town or village. Signposts direct the traveller.

3. Restaurants, Tavernas, Cafés

The average Greek has never been a fastidious gastronome. The works of ancient authors contain few references to their repasts. Homeric kings live on bread, wine, olive oil and roast kid. No elaborate dishes are mentioned by the great dramatists or by Plato when Socrates and his companions converse round the dining-table. The same applies to Byzantium. No Byzantine chronicler has left any record of the meals served in the imperial palace or the houses of the Byzantine aristocracy.

The main ingredients in modern Greek cooking are olive oil, tomatoes, onions, garlic, synthetic fats. Most dishes are of Turkish (romantics say Byzantine) origin. In private houses, where the quality of the materials (butter, oil, fats) is good, several dishes can be delicious, such as pilaff, the ubiquitous *mousaka* (minced meat between layers of fried aubergines and onions, with a crust of béchamel at the top) and vegetables (tomatoes, peppers, aubergines, vegetable marrows) stuffed with rice, herbs and minced meat.

The lack of interest in the quality, temperature and presentation of food is not conducive to a demand for a wide range of restaurants. The traveller is likely to be amazed at the paucity of restaurants in a city the size of Athens. Tavernas provide occasions, often delightful, for dining in a relaxed informal atmosphere, but the food (at which Greeks peck leisurely and without the Western concept of an ordered sequence of dishes) is seldom memorable – veal or lamb chops, fried potatoes (soggy), *horiatiki* salad (sliced tomatoes, with peppers, olives, onions and chunks of goat's milk cheese), sometimes a tepid *mousaka*, and, with luck, the delicious smoky flavoured *melintzanosalata* (aubergines worked with oil – occasionally with yoghurt – into a pulp and flavoured with onions).

Travellers with queasy stomachs had best keep to grilled meat (and fish, when obtainable). Most restaurants (but not tavernas) are indoor, even at the height of summer. Service is slapdash, but waiters can be friendly. They often lose their heads, but seldom their sense of humour.

Wines, both red and white, are fair to good, and rapidly improving. Cheeses are variable. Apart from the popular *feta* (white goat's milk cheese), there are several regional Gruyère (Graviera) types, which tend to vary in quality according to the season and even the year; Kasseri (the Turkish Kaskaval); Manouri (Mozarella type) which is good when fresh (winter and spring) and seasoned with pepper and salt; and Metsovo (smoked). The summer fruits (May–September) – strawberries, cherries, plums, yellow peaches, grapes, figs and melons – are beyond praise. Greek beer (lager type) is excellent.

A comprehensive list of restaurants and tavernas would certainly be out of date by the time this book is published. A restaurant (and/ or taverna) with certain pretensions may be open one year, shut the next. A selective list of restaurants is published in the daily English-language newspaper *Athens News* and the weekly pamphlet *The Week in Athens*, which can be bought at any kiosk in the central area of Athens.

The following are a few restaurants and tavernas which seem to be permanent fixtures in Athens (no restaurant or taverna in the provinces apart from in Salonica is worth mentioning). It is difficult to think of a single cheap restaurant which can be wholeheartedly recommended.

Restaurants

BALTHAZAR, corner of Tsocha and Vournazov Streets. Expensive and good. Early-twentieth-century private house converted in good taste into spacious restaurant, with bar (a rarity in Greece).

CORFU, 6 Kriezotou Street, Corfiot and semi-international cooking. Centrally situated, but expensive in view of fare served.

DELFOI, 13 Nikis Street. Mainly Greek dishes. Cheap.

DIONYSOS, 43 Roverto Galli Street (opposite Theatre of Herodes Atticus). Superb view of the Acropolis. International cuisine. Expensive.

FLOCA, 9 E. Venizelou Avenue. Cafeteria atmosphere. International cooking. Expensive.

L'ABREUVOIR, 51 Xenocratous Street. Open-air in summer. French cuisine. Expensive. Good.

LES GOURMETS, 3 Meandrou Street, French style, expensive. Decent.

STEAK ROOM, 4 Aeginitou Street, meats cooked on charcoal. Expensive.

VASILIS, 14A Voukourestiou Street. Greek and semi-international cooking. Relatively moderate prices.

YEROPHINOIKAS, 10 Pindarou Street. Restaurant-cum-taverna. Wide selection of Greek and Oriental dishes. Expensive.

ZONAR, 9 E. Vcnizclou Street. Central. Cafeteria atmosphere. International and Greek cooking. Expensive.

Tavernas

KOSTOYANNI, 37 Zaimis Street. Specialities: Greek hors d'oeuvre (well presented); prawn (or crab) salad. Moderate prices. Crowded, unprepossessing, but decent service and good quality Greek cooking. Decent *carafe* wine (a rarity).

O YEROS TOU MOURIA, 27 Mnesicleous Street. Orchestra. Situated in most picturesque part of the Plaka (see p. 37). Very popular with tourists. Expensive. Noisy.

PLATANOS, 4 Diogenes Street (near Tower of the Winds – agreeable setting). Greek cooking. Unpretentious and cheap.

STEKI TOU YANNI, 1 Troias Street. Wide variety of Greek hors d'oeuvres and good retsinated wine. Piano accompanied by guitarists. Expensive.

TA TRIA ADELPHIA, 7 Elpidou Street. Specialities: Greek hors d'oeuvre (well presented). Moderate prices.

XINOU, 4 Angelos Yerondas Street. Most Greek dishes (and grills). Probably best all-round taverna in Athens. Guitarists. Relatively moderate prices.

ZVINGOS, 41 Ayia Zoni Street. Specialities: pork, lamb and chicken roasted on the spit. Relatively moderate prices.

The larger brightly illuminated tavernas of the Plaka (Athens) – Erotocritos, Vakhous, Palaia Athena, Kastro, etc. – have elaborate floor-shows. The food is indifferent and expensive.

With few exceptions, tavernas do not serve luncheons.

The fish restaurants (taverna type) outside Athens are agreeable – particularly at Tourcolimano (see p. 64) and Glyphada (see p. 65). Here luncheons are served.

The traveller in northern Greece will no doubt observe that the food, i.e. the quality of meat, fish and vegetables, is better in Macedonia than elsewhere in the country. The Olympos-Naousa, Vasileus Constantinou Street (waterfront), Salonica, though wholly unpretentious, has consequently remained the best all-round restaurant in Greece. The same applies to the taverna Krikelas, 284 Vasilissis Olgas Street, also in Salonica (shut in the summer months, May–September).

It might be worth noting that all luxury, first, second and some third class hotels in Athens, and all the Xenias group in the provinces, have restaurants.

Cafés (both indoor and open-air) – they are also confectioners' – proliferate all over the capital, suburbs and provincial towns. The confectionery element is the more popular with Greeks, who have a very sweet tooth. The range of cream-cakes is staggering. The ices are generally good. Many open-air cafés are open until well after midnight.

As in many Mediterranean countries, café life has always played a large role in shaping the people's and country's destinies. In many of the downtown cafés of Athens contracts are drafted, debts contracted and settled, dowries discussed, important new contacts made and plots to overthrow the government hatched.

There is no need to list the cafés. They are there for all to see: in the capital, at every street corner; in small provincial towns, in the main square.

4. Shops

Athens is not a capital for the fastidious shopper, although the quality of goods on sale (both local and imported) is improving rapidly. A weekly pamphlet, published in English and French, on sale at all kiosks in the centre of the city, lists chemists, department stores, discothèques, florists, hairdressers, jewellers, photographers, lingerie shops, perfumeries, etc.[1]

The principal shopping areas are Ermou Street (drapers, lingerie, perfumes) and Stadiou Street (stores, shoes, men's haberdashers). There are expensive boutiques in the Kolonaki and Syntagma Square areas.

Antiques and local handicrafts are more likely to interest the traveller. Antique shops of varying quality proliferate in the Pandrossos Street – Monastiriki and Kolonaki areas.

Travellers should obtain an export licence from the shopkeeper for any purchase of value (if an antique) which they intend to take out of the country. Failure to do so may result in confiscation and payment of a fine.

[1] *The Week in Athens* also contains useful addresses (Embassies, Consulates, banks, car repair services, as well as ferry-boat schedules, timetables of sailings to islands, air flights, etc.).

The best selections of handicrafts are found at:

DIPLOU PELEKIS (The Double Axe), 23b Voulis Street (scarves, bags, handwoven rugs, tablecloths, ashtrays and vases of Cretan alabaster).

THE NATIONAL FUND – 24a Voukourestiou and 10 Stadiou (Stoa Lemou) Streets (handwoven rugs and carpets with old island and Byzantine designs; stoles, tablecloths, bags, embroidered slippers).

Tourist shops, filled with imitation vases, modern icons and plaster casts of famous statues, are centred round the Syntagma Square area. Here are also displayed *tagharia* (woollen bags) and tablecloths, etc., woven with peasant designs. The showcases in the Hilton Hotel give a general idea of the high standard of workmanship of ancient Byzantine jewellery (for addresses of jewellers see *The Week in Athens*). Some of the modern icons (copies of old Byzantine ones) are also of a high standard.

There is a brisk trade in furs. The main furriers in Athens are:

FUR HOUSE, George M. Trakos, 7 Philhellinon Street

VOULA KITSAKOU LTD, 7 Mitropoleos Street

SISTOVARIS FRÈRES, 9 E. Venizelou Street.

The traveller will be impressed by the number of English bookshops, well stocked with standard works and all the latest publications. The main ones are:

ATLANTIS, 8 Korais Street

CACOULIDES, 39 E. Venizelou Street

ELEUTHEROUDAKIS, 4 Nikis Street (the largest)

KAUFMANN, 11 Voukourestiou Street (mainly books on Greece; also old prints)

PANTELIDES, 11 Amerikis Street

LES AMIS DU LIVRE, 9 Valaoritou Street (rare editions of English and French books on Greece).

English and foreign newspapers are on sale at about eight o'clock in the evening, at all kiosks in the Syntagma Square and Kolonaki areas.

Outside Athens and Salonica there are no shops worth mentioning. Villages specializing in regional handicrafts are mentioned in the text.

5. Feasts and Holidays

1 January. Public holiday. Feast of St Basil, one of the most distinguished Early Christian Fathers of the Church. *Vasilopitta* (The Cake of St Basil), a kind of large round brioche, is eaten in every Greek house. It contains a coin which brings good luck to the finder.

6 January. Epiphany. Public holiday. Blessing of the Waters. An official ceremony is held at the Piraeus, attended by high-ranking prelates, flanked by acolytes bearing banners, cabinet ministers and representatives of the armed forces. As the officiating priest throws the cross into the sea and the waters are blessed, ships' sirens hoot and youths dive into the water to recover the cross. Throughout the country wells and springs are blessed.

At Epiphany the earth is rid of *Callicantzari*, puckish demons with red eyes, monkey's arms and cleft hooves, who run amok during the twelve days after Christmas and are probably a Christian version of the boisterous and equally grotesque Satyrs and Sileni who danced attendance on Dionysus. Among the Callicantzaris' favourite pranks are riding piggy-back on frightened mortals, polluting food, making water on fires and flinging pitch on front doors.

February–March
(a) Carnival (the three weeks before Lent). During the three week-ends of the period, children in fancy dress roam the streets, and gipsies, accompanied by performing monkeys, bang on tambourines (into which pedestrians drop coins) at street corners. In Athens, the tavernas of the Plaka are crowded. Streamers and confetti litter the pavements. The most lively Carnival procession takes place in Patras during the third week-end.

(b) *Kathari Deutera* ('Clean Monday' – Monday after last Sunday of Carnival). A public holiday. So-called because it is the first day of Lent. There is a general exodus into the country, and the occasion is one for picnics. Kite-flying begins. In some villages dumb-shows are staged by itinerant mummers. At Thebes there is a lively parody of a peasant wedding, a thinly veiled spring fertility rite, at which the relatives arrive riding donkeys backwards. The bride (a man disguised as a woman) is bedecked with clanging bronze bells round her neck.

'Clean Monday' diet (meatless and served cold) consists of *phasolia piaz* (beans dressed with olive oil and sprinkled with slivers of onion), *taramosalata* (a pinkish purée made of cod's roe, breadcrumbs and olive oil, to which chopped onions and dill may be added), *yalantzi dolmadhes* (rice, currants and pine-nuts cooked in olive oil and wrapped up in vine leaves, flavoured with onion), and *laghana*, flat loaves of unleavened bread.

25 March. Independence Day. Public holiday. Anniversary of the day when Bishop Germanos raised the standard of revolt against the Turks at Kalavryta in 1821. Military parades are held in all towns and villages. The feast of the Annunciation is also celebrated in all churches.

The Easter Cycle[2]

Maundy Thursday. Housewives dye the red eggs which will be cracked and eaten on Easter Day. The first egg placed in the dye belongs to the Virgin; it is regarded as a talisman and must not be eaten. The colour red is supposed to have protective powers. Interiors of churches are decorated with black, purple and white shrouds, and church bells toll throughout the evening.

Good Friday. A day of complete fast, kept by the overwhelming majority of Greeks. Brown wax candles are sold at street corners. Church bells toll and funeral marches and religious music broadcast on all radio networks. Cemeteries are crowded with private mourners laying wreaths on graves.

At about nine in the evening (earlier in the villages), the Epitaphios, the funeral of Christ, the most moving and beautiful ceremony in the Orthodox calendar, begins. Behind the Cross, the body of Christ, in the form of a gold embroidered pall, smothered with wreaths woven out of scented flowers, is borne under a gilded canopy through the main streets of towns and villages. Priests (ranging from mitred bishops in lavish vestments to black-frocked deacons) shuffle behind it, flanked by acolytes in coloured shifts, carrying banners. Then come the officials (civil and military) followed by a crowd of silent dark-clothed worshippers, lighted candles cupped in

---

[2] Orthodox Easter generally falls within the second half of April, seldom before, occasionally in early May. The weather can be showery, but the flowers are at their most prolific, the gardens heavy with the scent of lilac, wistaria, Banksia roses and stocks.

their hands. The procession halts at every street corner where a short prayer is said. By about ten o'clock, when the beflowered bier is borne back to the church and the pall has been kissed by the faithful, all places of entertainment, including many cafés and restaurants, are shut (for a description of the Epitaphios procession in Athens, see p. 37).

Easter Saturday. Nothing could be more striking than the contrast between the solemnity of the Epitaphios and the liveliness of the Anastasis, the Resurrection service, the greatest feast in the Orthodox Church. Throughout the afternoon funereal drapings are removed from churches and replaced with branches of laurel and myrtle, while sprigs of rosemary are strewn across the floor of the naos. White (no longer brown) candles, decorated with white or blue ribbons (the national colours) are sold at open-air booths.

The service begins in a dim incense-laden atmosphere. Gradually more lights are turned on until the whole church is brilliantly illuminated. On the stroke of midnight the priest, in a soaring triumphant tone, chants the words '*Christos Anesti!*' ('Christ is risen!'). The doors of the sanctuary open amid a blaze of light, and the bier, only yesterday borne to the grave, is seen to be empty. Christ has risen. Church bells ring, children shout and let off squibs in the street. Members of the congregation shake hands or exchange the kiss of Resurrection, murmuring 'Christ is risen!' All personal quarrels are (supposed to be) forgiven and forgotten.

The crowds then disperse, homeward bound, holding their candles – it is a good omen to reach the house with the taper alight – and break their fast with a dish of *mayeiritsa* (egg-lemon soup with rice and chopped lambs' liver and entrails, seasoned with dill – rich but delicious) and red-dyed hard-boiled eggs.

Easter Sunday. A day of national rejoicing. In Athens the Head of State and the Cabinet attend the doxology in the Cathedral, while the cannon on Mount Lycabettus fires thunderous salvoes. The paschal lamb is roasted on a spit in gardens and open places, and red eggs are cracked by tapping one against the other. Houses are decorated with lilac: *paschalia*, the flower of Easter.

Easter Monday. Public holiday.

Friday after Easter. Feast of the Virgin Mary who is represented as the *Zoodochos Pighi*, 'The Source of Life'. In villages where the church is dedicated to the Life-Bearing Spring a procession headed by a priest carrying an icon of the Virgin winds through the streets in the late afternoon, as at Acharnae, twelve kilometres north-west of Athens (see p. 74). The procession is sometimes followed by folk-dancing.

23 April. St George's Day. The young Eastern martyr is one of the most popular saints in the Orthodox calendar. Like the no less venerated Demetrius, he represents a Christian reincarnation of the noble ephebe of antiquity.

At Arachova, near Delphi (see p. 111), St George's Day is celebrated with a religious procession, the performance of folk-dances to the accompaniment of drums and bagpipes and athletic contests.

30 April. On the eve of May Day wreaths of flowers – stocks, roses, lilies, pansies – symbolizing the advent of summer, are hung above the front doors of houses, where they remain, brown and withered, until the feast of St John the Baptist, 24 June.

Athenians flock to the suburb of Ano-Patissia, where fireworks crackle and much wine is drunk in tavernas. There is little to eat except hacked pieces of (rather tepid) lamb roasted on open-air spits. The streets are lined with booths, where wreaths of flowers are sold, and late at night the pavements are littered with bruised blooms.

May Day itself may or may not be a public holiday, according to the party line taken by the government in office.

21 May. Feast of SS Constantine and Helena. The feast's importance derives from the aura of veneration attached to the figures of Constantine the Great, founder of the Byzantine Empire, and his pious mother, Helena.

Whit Monday. Public Holiday.

June–July. Festival of ancient drama at Epidaurus.

24 June. St John the Baptist's Feast. The summer solstice. Bonfires are lit in villages on the eve of St John's Day, and the inhabitants dance round the pyre into which the May Day wreaths are cast and leap over the embers, thus purifying themselves of their sins. The cinders, which possess protective and divinatory properties, are collected by housewives. Sea-bathing and the eating of water melon (cheapest and most popular of summer fruits) begin 'officially' on

St John's Day, and the proverb runs 'Do not swim before you see water melon peel floating on the sea.'[3]

17 July. St Marina's Feast. The saint was martyred in Antioch in the third century and her feast ushers in the season of grapes. Peasants flock to the vineyards to cut the first bunches and bear offerings of fruit to the churches.

A fair is held outside the church of Ayia Marina in the Theseum quarter at Athens, where the saint is worshipped as protectress against smallpox (she is also the scourge of all insects).

20 July. Feast of the prophet Elijah, patron saint of thunder, lightning and rain, worshipped on hill-tops crowned with whitewashed chapels where bonfires are sometimes lit (as on Mount Taygetus) and associated with the prophet's ascent to Heaven. As Lord of the Thunder (his thunderclaps are attributed to the rolling of the chariot wheels), he represents a Christian counterpart of Zeus.

15 August. Assumption of the Virgin. Public holiday. After Easter and Christmas the most important religious holiday in the Greek calendar, a symbol of the Orthodox veneration of the Virgin. 1–15 August is a period of fast, which Greeks keep with varying degrees of strictness.

Two great religious pilgrimages are made on 15 August: to the Aegean islands of Tinos (the Lourdes of Greece) and Paros.

29 August. Anniversary of the beheading of St John the Baptist. The malarial fevers that until recently ravaged many of the plains, especially during the torrid month of August, were supposed to be the manifestations of the shock or spasm suffered by the Baptist when he was beheaded to please Salome (a scene much favoured for reproduction in rustic icons). Fairs (*paneghyria*) are held in villages where the main church is dedicated to St John the Baptist.

September. Wine festival at Daphni, near Athens. Entrance charge covers unlimited wine-tasting. Rather bogus folk-dances (see p. 78).

14 September. The Exaltation of the Cross. An important Orthodox feast. In churches a priest presents the congregation with sprigs of basil as a token of the herb that sprouted at the foot of the Cross.

26 October. Feast of St Demetrius, one of the most popular saints

[3] George A. Megas, *Greek Calendar Customs*, Athens, 1963.

in the calendar. All churches dedicated to St Demetrius, a gallant young convert martyred by Galerius in a public bath at Thessalonica, are brilliantly illuminated on the nights of 25 and 26 October.

The weather is usually fine and the last week in October is referred to as 'the summer of St Demetrius' – the Greek Indian Summer. The saint's name day is the occasion for the tasting of new wine.

28 October. Public holiday. Anniversary of the Italian invasion of Greece in 1940, in the course of which a small Greek army routed Mussolini's numerically superior but ill-equipped divisions. Commonly known as *'Ochi'*-day ('No'-day) from the simple negative uttered by the Prime Minister, Ioannis Metaxas, when presented with the Fascist ultimatum by the Italian Ambassador.

6 December. St Nicholas's Day. Commonly regarded as the first day of winter. The saint, patron of sailors, is often represented in popular hagiography dressed in clothes covered with brine, sea-water dripping from his long white beard, after rescuing sailors from sinking ships in winter storms. His affinity with Poseidon is obvious, but he is more benign, less violent, than the Lord of the Trident. He prefers to pacify tempests rather than to rouse them.

Every Greek ship, from the largest ocean-going liner to the smallest caique, possesses an icon of the saint covered with votive trinkets in the shape of vessels.

Chapels dedicated to St Nicholas abound in the islands and maritime districts of the mainland.

12 December. Feast of St Spyridon. The embalmed mortal remains of the Cypriot bishop, martyred during Diocletian's reign, and borne overland from Constantinople to Corfu after 1453 in order to escape Ottoman desecration, are now displayed in an ornamental silver coffin in the church of St Spyridon at Corfu. The saint, patron of Corfu, is greatly venerated throughout the country.

The name Spyridon derives from the word *spyri*, a pimple, and, according to popular superstition, the wonder-working properties of the saint's relics act as an antidote against smallpox, rashes and skin diseases.

24 December. Little boys ring doorbells and ask: *'Na ta poúme?'* ('Shall we tell them?') – in other words, should they sing the *kalanda* (the Greek equivalent of Christmas carols), while they beat a miniature hammer on a little metal triangle, in return for a small gratuity.

In Athens the sale of holly, mistletoe, Christmas trees, turkeys and other Christmas fare follows the Western pattern.

25–26 December. Public holidays.
31 December. Singing of *kalanda* as on Christmas Eve. In the evening all Greeks play cards. It is considered a breach of tradition (if not etiquette) not to try one's luck at the gaming-table on the threshold of the New Year.

6. Glossary

ABACUS – slab crowning capital of a column.
ACROTERIA – sculptured ornamental effigies or mouldings placed at either end of pediment in ancient Greek architecture. Modified form of acroteria may still be seen in some modern Greek architecture (particularly nineteenth-century).
ADYTUM – inner sanctuary and holiest chamber of a temple where oracles were delivered.
AGORA – a Greek market place. Equivalent to Roman forum.
AMBO – pulpit in an Orthodox church.
APHESIS – starting-post of an ancient Greek race-track.
ARCHON – magistrate in ancient Athens, a notable during the Turkish occupation.
ARYBALLOS – ancient flask (swollen in the centre) with a round base, used as a perfume container.

BOULEUTERION – senate house.
BOUZOUKI – a large mandolin with a particularly plangent note.

CALATHUS – a basket.
CANTHARUS – a tall, two-handled drinking cup.
CAVEA – Latin for Greek κοῖλον: the whole part of an ancient theatre reserved for spectators.
CELLA – enclosed inner room of a temple, often containing the cult statue.
CENOBITE – monk living with others in a community.
CHITON – sleeveless tunic, fastened over the shoulder by clasps and round the waist with a girdle, worn by men and women in ancient Greece.

CHLAMYS – oblong outer raiment, smaller than the himation (see below) and even more ornamented, hung from the neck.

CHOREGIC – pertaining to a choregus, administrator and financer of a chorus. Choregoi were wealthy citizens responsible for the training of the dance-chorus.

CHRYSOBUL – Byzantine imperial charter.

CLERESTORY – the upper part of a church with windows above the aisle roofs.

CONCH – the concave surface of the vault of an apse.

CYMA (recta or reversa) – a moulding of S-shaped profile; recta-concave at the top.

DEISIS – representation of Christ between the Virgin and St John the Baptist as intercessers.

DEME – geographical unit for local government purposes in ancient Attica.

DIACONICON – sacristy to the right of the sanctuary in an Orthodox church.

DIAZÔMA – horizontal passage between the tiers of an ancient theatre which served as a foyer.

DODECAORTON – The Twelve Feasts, the principal scenes from the lives of Christ and the Virgin, which (either in mosaic or fresco) decorate the walls of all Byzantine churches.

DORMITION – religious art term applied to funeral of holy personages, particularly the Virgin.

DROMOS – a public way, often lined with statues, temples, etc.

ECHINUS – a cushion-like moulding (ovolo moulding) fitted on top of a column immediately below the abacus. So-called because it resembled the shell of an *echinos* (sea-urchin).

ENTASIS – a convexity of the shaft of a column: an intentional distortion designed to obviate the optical illusion whereby a straight column appears thinner in the centre than at the top or bottom.

EPHEBE – a youth just entering manhood or just enrolled as a citizen in ancient Greece.

EPHOR – inspector, curator.

EPITAPHIOS – flower-decked bier of Christ borne in procession in towns and villages throughout the country on the evening of Good Friday (also a gold-thread embroidery representing the body of Christ after the Deposition).

EREMITE – a hermit.

421

EXEDRA – apsidal (sometimes rectangular-shaped) recess with seats (classical architecture).

EX-VOTO – votive gift.

FIRMAN – an edict or administrative order issued by an Ottoman sultan.

GIGANTOMACHIA – battle between gods and giants on the friezes of temples.

GLYCOPHILOUSA – a type of icon of the Virgin and Child (The Sweetly Kissing One) in which the Child is depicted resting his cheek against the Virgin's.

HAMMAN – Turkish bath.

HELOT – Spartan serf who formed backbone of Spartan army.

HETAIERA – a courtesan in ancient Greece.

HIMATION – cloak of varying texture, colour and embroidered decoration, worn by both men and women in ancient Greece.

HOPLITE – heavily-armed ancient Greek infantryman.

HYDROPHORUS – bearer of pitcher filled with water.

ICONOSTASIS – screen adorned with icons separating the sanctuary from the remainder of an Orthodox church.

IDIORRYHTHMIC – a monastery in which each monk maintains himself independently.

IN ANTIS – two porch columns between two prolongations (*antae*) of the side walls of the cella of a temple.

KATAVOTHRON – subterranean stream flowing under hard limestone rock of many Greek mountains.

KELLIA – retreats of hermits.

KIOSHK – Turkish palace or pavilion.

KORÉ – an ancient Greek maiden. Term commonly applied to statues of young women of Archaic period.

KOUROS – an ancient Greek youth. Term commonly applied to statues of young men of Archaic period.

KRATER – a vessel with wide mouth in which liquids, chiefly wine and water, were mixed.

KOKKINELI – slightly resinated rosé wine.

LECYTHOS – a slender vessel (derived from the domestic oil-flask) with long spout-like mouth, used at fifth-century BC funerals. The base is sometimes rounded.

LINEAR B – syllabic script used for writing the Greek language from *c.*1400 to *c.*1150 BC. (The form of the Greek language written in Linear B is usually known as Mycenaean Greek.)

LITI – a spacious outer narthex in some Orthodox churches.

LOUKOUMI – Turkish delight.

LOUTROPHORUS – a tall ancient Greek vessel used to bring water for the bath, especially at a marriage.

MANDORLA – almond-shaped aureole surrounding depictions of holy personages in Christian art.

MEGARON – Homer's term for the great hall of a palace.

METOPE – one of the square spaces either decorated or plain between triglyphs in the Doric frieze.

METROON – temple of the Mother of the Gods.

MIHRAB – prayer niche indicating the direction of Mecca in a mosque.

NAOS – the main chamber, or inner shrine, of a Greek temple, in which the effigy of the deity was kept. Also the main body of a Byzantine cruciform church, entered through the narthex.

NARGHILE – synonym for Hookah.

NARTHEX – vestibule across the west end of an Orthodox church.

NOME – Greek nomos, administrative division of ancient Attica.

OCTATEUTH – the first eight books of the Old Testament.

ODEUM – concert hall.

OINOCHE – an ancient jug for pouring; with handle.

OPISTHODOMOS – back chamber of a temple, serving as a treasury.

ORANS – representation of the Virgin or a saint with arms outstretched in an attitude of prayer.

ORCHESTRA – circular space below the lowest tier of an ancient theatre where the chorus chanted and performed dance patterns. A small segment of the circle was generally occupied by the narrow stage (see proscenium).

PALAESTRA – an open space for wrestling or athletics in ancient Greece, especially the forecourt of a gymnasium.

PANTOCRATOR – The All-Ruler (Christ), an effigy of whom is depicted in the central cupola of most Byzantine churches.

PARADOS – one of two side entrances into the orchestra of a Greek theatre used by the chorus only. The *parodoi* often had architectural embellishments.

PELTASTS – ancient Greek soldiers armed with a light shield.

PENDENTIVE – a concave section of vaulting leading from the angle of two walls or arches to the circular base of a dome.

PEPLOS – fifth-century BC dress (angle-length, belted up) worn by women on ceremonial occasions. Often elaborately embroidered.

PERIBOLUS – an enclosed precinct, or the wall around it.

PERISTYLE – colonnade surrounding a temple or court.

PHIALE – holy water basin outside a church.

PHYLAX – guard, custodian.

PODIUM – low platform or continuous base carrying a colonnade or building.

PRONAOS – outer chamber (sometimes a portico) of a temple, in front of the naos.

PROPYLAEA – entrance way (generally a monumental gateway) to a sacred enclosure.

PROSCENIUM – narrow stage of an ancient theatre on which the protagonists, but not the chorus, performed.

PROSTYLE – colonnaded portico in front of an ancient building.

PROTOME – bust.

QUADRIGA – chariot drawn by four horses.

SIMANDROM – oblong wooden board outside an Orthodox monastic church which is tapped to summon monks to prayer.

SKENE – back wall of stage of ancient Greek theatre. Sometimes used loosely to mean the whole stage and its embellishments.

SKETE – dependancy of a monastery.

SOFFIT – the under surface of an arch or beam.

SOUVLAKIA – pieces of lamb, veal or pork grilled on a skewer.

SQUINCH – section of vaulting arched across an angle used in reducing a square to an octagon.

STEATITE – soapstone.

STELE – upright stone or marble tablet, often sculptured, placed above ancient graves.

STYLOBATE – continuous base or substructure from which the columns of a temple rise.

TELESTERION – a place of initiation in ancient Greece.

TERMA – finishing post of an ancient Greek race-track.

THOLOS – a circular building, generally a temple.

THOLOS TOMB – circular mausoleum with a monumental approach and a conical beehive roof, covered with earth so as to form a tumulus.

THYRSUS – a staff borne by Dionysus, tipped with a pine cone or sometimes twined with ivy and vine branches.

TRIGLYPH – block of stone or marble carved with three vertical bars placed in the entablature of temples of the Doric order.

TRIREME – ancient Greek galley rowed by three banks of oars.

TSAROUCHIA – Turkish-style red slippers with pompoms.

VOLUTE – spiral ornament, especially the distinctive corner feature of an Ionic or Corinthian capital.

YATAGHAN – a Turkish sabre with a curved blade, an eared pommel and no guard.

7. Chronological Table

BC

Neolithic Period (? *c.* 3200)

Early Helladic Period (*c.* 3200–1900)
c. 3000–2000   Early Bronze Age. Minoan civilization in Crete.

Middle Helladic Period (*c.* 1900–1575)
c. 1900–1575   Middle Bronze Age. Achaeans settle at Mycenae.

Late Helladic Period (*c.* 1575–1100)
c. 1575–1100   Late Bronze Age.
c. 1400–1200   Mycenaean ascendancy on the mainland.
c. 1400   Destruction of Knossos and Phaestos in Crete.
c. 1250–1200   Trojan War.

Early Iron Age (*c.* 1100–750)
c. 1100–1000   Dorian invasion. Destruction of all Mycenaean cities.
c. 900–800   Legislation of Lycurgus at Sparta.
c. 800–700   Fame of Delphic oracle established.
776   First panhellenic games held at Olympia.

Archaic Period (750–480)
c. 750–700	Homer.
c. 730–10	First Messenian War.
c. 700–650	Megarian colonists found Byzantium.
c. 635–20	Second Messenian War.
594–93	Solon's social reforms in Athens.
582	Pythian festival at Delphi transformed into pan-hellenic celebration.
560–10	Tyranny of the Peisistratae in Athens.
530–15	Temple of Apollo at Delphi rebuilt by the Alcmonidae.
514	Conspiracy of Harmodius and Aristogeiton.
510	Expulsion of Hippias from Athens.
508–7	Democratic reforms of Cleisthenes at Athens.
490	Persian expedition led by Datis against Greece. Battle of Marathon.
480	March of Xerxes across Greece. Battle of Artemisium. Leonidas defends Thermopylae. Xerxes in Athens. Destruction of the Acropolis. Battle of Salamis.
479	Battle of Plataea. Persians leave Greece.

Classical Period (480–323)
476–60	Aggrandisement of Athens under leadership of Cimon abroad and Aristides at home.
472–1	Ostracism and flight of Themistocles.
468–56	Building of Temple of Zeus at Olympia.
464–59	Third Messenian War.
462–60	Rise of Pericles.
447–38	Construction of Parthenon.
437–2	Building of the Propylaea.
431	Outbreak of Peloponnesian War.
430	Plague in Athens.
429	Death of Pericles.
429–7	Siege and reduction of Plataea by Peloponnesian allies.
425	Siege of Sphacteria.
421	Peace of Nicias. Dedication of Temple of Niké Apteros.
420	Rise of Alcibiades.
419	Resumption of hostilities between Athens and Peloponnesians.

418	First battle of Mantinea.
415	Mutilation of hermae at Athens. Athenian expedition to Sicily. Recall of Alcibiades.
413	Spartans occupy Deceleia in Attica.
c. 408	Completion of Erectheum.
405	Lysander commander of Spartan fleet. Battle of Aegospotami. End of Athenian naval supremacy.
404	End of Peloponnesian War. Surrender of Athens. Destruction of Long Walls.
403	Thrasybulus overthrows the Thirty Tyrants. Restoration of democracy in Athens.
401	March of the Ten Thousand under Xenophon.
399	Trial and death of Socrates.
371	Battle of Leuctra. End of Spartan hegemony. Ascendancy of Thebes under Epaminondas and Pelopidas.
371–69	Foundation of Megalopolis and Messene.
362	Second battle of Mantinea. Death of Epaminondas.
356	Birth of Alexander the Great.
338	Battle of Chaeroneia. Philip II master of Greece. End of Greek democracy.
336	Assassination of Philip II. Accession of Alexander the Great.
334	Alexander crosses into Asia.
324	Alexander's divinity proclaimed at Olympia.
323	Death of Alexander.

Hellenistic Period (323–146)

323	Outbreak of war between the Diadochi.
323–2	Lamian War. Greeks revolt against Macedonian tyranny.
307	Demetrius Poliorcetes master of Athens.
281	Formation of Achaean League.
226	War between Sparta and Achaean League.
222	Battle of Sellasia. Sparta defeated by armies of Macedonia and Achaean League.
168	Battle of Pydna. Defeat of Perseus by Aemilius Paulus. End of Macedonian monarchy.
146	Sack of Corinth by Mummius. Supression of Achaean League. Greece and Macedonia become a Roman province.

Roman Period (146 BC–AD 330)

88–7	War between Rome and Mithridates, King of Pontus, in Greece.
86	Sack of Athens by Sulla.
48	Julius Caesar in Greece. Battle of Pharsalia.
42	Battle of Philippi.
31	Battle of Actium.

AD

c. 50–3	St Paul's mission to Greece.
66–7	Nero visits Greece.
125–9	Hadrian visits Athens.
132	Completion of Temple of Olympian Zeus at Athens.
313	Edict of Milan. Toleration of Christian worship.
330	Constantine the Great transfers capital of the Empire to Constantinople.

Early Byzantine Period (330–843)

392	Edict of Theodosius the Great proscribing paganism. Sanctuaries of Delphi and Olympia closed down.
395	Gothic invasion of Greece.
467–77	Invasion of Vandals.
588	Slav invasion of the Peloponnese.
726–80	First Iconoclast period.
802–42	Second Iconoclast period.
843	Proscription of Iconoclasm by seventh Council of Nicaea.

Middle Byzantine Period (843–1261)

1018	Byzantine victory over Bulgars. Emperor Basil II makes triumphal tour of Greece and visits Athens.
1054	Schism between Roman and Eastern Churches.
1081–4	Normans under Robert Guiscard invade Greece.
1204	Fourth Crusade. Capture and sack of Constantinople by Crusaders. Establishment of Latin Empire. Geoffrey de Villehardouin lands at Methone.
1205	Othon de la Roche first Latin Duke of Athens. Conquest of the Morea by Geoffrey I de Villehardouin and William de Champlitte.

428

1248	Siege of Monemvasia by William de Villehardouin.
1259	Battle of Pelagonia. Decisive defeat of Franks by Byzantine army.
1261	Greeks recapture Constantinople. End of Latin Empire of Constantinople.

Late Byzantine Period (1261–1453)

1311	Battle of the Cephisus. Franks routed by Grand Company of Catalans.
1311–87	Catalan rule in Athens.
1348	Manuel Cantacuzenus first Despot of Mistra.
1393–1414	Turkish conquest of Central Greece.
1402–56	Florentine Acciajuoli Dukes of Athens.
1427–32	Byzantine campaign against Latins in the Morea.
1439	Emperor John VIII Palaeologus and Patriarch of Constantinople attend Council of Florence.
1453	Fall of Constantinople.

Turkish Period (1453–1832)

1459	Fall of Mistra. End of Despotate of Mistra.
1499–1500	Venetians surrender maritime stations on Greek mainland to Turks.
1686–1715	Morosini expedition.
1687	Destruction of Parthenon during Venetian siege of Athens.
1801	Lord Elgin obtains firman to remove sculptures from the Acropolis.
1809–11	Byron in Athens.
1821	Standard of revolt against Turks raised by Bishop Germanos at Kalavryta.
1824	Arrival of Byron at Misolonghi. Death of Byron.
1825	Ibrahim Pasha devastates the Morea.
1827	Battle of Navarino. Destruction of Turkish fleet.
1828	French army under General Maison liberates the Morea.
1832	Protocol of London. Greece declared an independent kingdom. National Assembly at Nauplia ratifies election of Prince Otho of Bavaria as King of Greece.

Modern Kingdom of Greece (1833–)

1833	Arrival of King Otho at Nauplia, capital of new kingdom.

1834	Capital transferred to Athens.
1875–81	German archaeologists excavate Olympia.
1876	Schliemann excavates Mycenae.
1892–1903	Site of Delphi excavated by French School of Archaeology.
1896	First revived Olympic Games held at Athens.
1912–13	First and Second Balkan Wars.
1916	Venizelos proclaims provisional government at Salonica. Greece enters the war against the Central Powers.
1919–22	Graeco-Turkish campaign in Asia Minor. Expulsion of Greek population from Asia Minor.
1924	Establishment of Greek republic.
1935	Restoration of monarchy.
1940	Italian invasion of Greece.
1941	Landing and evacuation of British Expeditionary Force.
1941–4	German-Italian-Bulgar occupation of Greece.
1944–5	First Communist rebellion.
1947–9	Second Communist rebellion.
1967	Establishment of military dictatorship. King Constantine II leaves Greece.
1973	Re-establishment of Greek republic.
1974	Parliamentary democracy replaces military dictatorship.

8. Table of Byzantine Emperors

Dynasty of Constantine (East Roman)
Constantine the Great, 324–37.
Constantius II, 337–61.
Julian the Apostate, 361–3.
Jovian, 363–4.
Valens, 364–78.

Theodosian Dynasty
Theodosius I the Great, 379–95.
Arcadius, 395–408.

Theodosius II, 408–50.
Marcian, 450–7.
Leo I the Great, 457–74.
Leo II, 474.
Zeno, 474–91.
Anastasius I, 491–518.

Dynasty of Justinian
Justin I, 518–27.
Justinian I the Great, 527–65.
Justin II, 565–78.
Tiberius II, 578–82.
Maurice, 582–602.
Phocas, 602–10.

Heraclian Dynasty
Heraclius, 610–41.
Constans II, 641.
Heraclonas (overthrown), 641.
Constans II (Constantine III), 641–68.
Constantine IV, 668–85.
Justinian II, 685–95.
Leontius, 695–8.
Tiberius III Apsimarus, 698–705.
Justinian II (restored), 705–11.
Philippicus (Bardanes), 711–13.
Anastasius II, 713–16.
Theodosius III, 716–17.

Isaurian Dynasty (*Iconoclast Emperors*)
Leo III the Isaurian, 717–41.
Constantine V Copronymus, 741–75.
Leo IV the Khazar, 775–80.
Constantine VI, 780–97.
Irene, 797–802.
Nicephorus I, 802–11.
Stauracius, 811.
Michael I Rhangabes, 811–13.
Leo V the Armenian, 813–20.
Michael II the Stammerer, 820–9.
Theophilus, 829–42.
Michael III, 842–67.

Macedonian Dynasty
Basil I, 867–86.
Leo VI the Wise, 886–912.
Alexander, 912–13.
Constantine VII Porphyrogenitus, 913–59.
Romanus I Lecapenus (usurper, co-emperor
with Constantine VII), 919–44.
Romanus II, 959–63.
Nicephorus II Phocas, 963–9.
John I Tzimisces, 969–76.
Basil II the Bulgar-Slayer, 976–1025.
Constantine VIII, 1025–8.
Zoe (associated with her three husbands
and adopted son as below), 1028–50.
Romanus III Argyrus, 1028–34.
Michael IV the Paphlogonian, 1034–41.
Michael V Calaphates (adopted son of Zoe), 1041–2.
Constantine IX Monomachus, 1042–55.
Theodora, 1055–6.
Michael VIII Stratioticus, 1056–7.

Ducas and Comnene Dynasties
Isaac I Comnenus, 1057–9.
Constantine X Ducas, 1059–67.
Romanus IV Diogenes, 1067–71.
Michael VII Ducas, 1071–8.
Nicephorus III the Botaniates, 1078–81.
Alexius I Comnenus, 1081–1118.
John II Comnenus, 1118–43.
Manuel I Comnenus, 1143–80.
Alexius II Comnenus, 1180–3.
Andronicos I Comnenus, 1183–5.

Dynasty of the Angeli
Isaac II Angelus, 1185–95.
Alexius III Angelus, 1195–1203.
Isaac II (restored) and Alexius IV Angelus, 1203–4.
Alexius V (Ducas) Murtzuphlus, 1204.

Latin Emperors of Constantinople
Baldwin I of Flanders, 1204–5.
Henry of Flanders, 1205–16.

Peter de Courtenay, 1217.
Yolanda (widow of Peter de Courtenay), 1217–19.
Robert de Courtenay, 1219–28.
Baldwin II (assisted by John of Brienne
as regent 1229–37), 1228–61.

Lascarid Dynasty (Greek emperors in exile at Nicaea)
Theodore I Lascaris, 1204–22.
John III Vatatzes, 1222–54.
Theodore II Lascaris, 1254–8.
John IV Lascaris, 1258–9.
Michael VIII Palaeologus (usurper), 1259–82.

Palaeologue Dynasty (the Greek Empire restored)
Michael VIII Palaeologus (crowned in
Constantinople), 1261–82.
Andronicus II Palaeologus (with his son
Michael IX 1295–1320), 1282–1328.
Andronicus III Palaeologus, 1328–41.
John V Palaeologus, 1341–91.
John VI Cantacuzenus (usurper), 1341–54.
Andronicus IV Palaeologus (son of John V), 1376–9.
John V Palaeologus (1379–91).
John VII Palaeologus (usurper), 1390.
Manuel Palaeologus, 1391–1425.
John VIII Palaeologus, 1425–48.
Constantine XI Palaeologus (Dragases), 1448–53.

9. Table of Latin Dukes of Athens and Greek Despots (Epirus)

DUKES OF ATHENS (alternatively known as *Megaskyr*,
i.e. 'the great gentlemen', Lords of Athens, Dukes
of Athens and Thebes)

House of de la Roche
Othon de la Roche, founder of French
house, 1205–25.
Guy I, 1225–63.

John I, 1263–80.
William, 1280–7.
Guy II, 1287–1309.

House of Brienne
Walter of Brienne, 1309–11.

Catalan Grand Company and House of Aragon
Roger Deslaur, founder of the Spanish house,
   1311–12.
Manfred, 1312–17.
William, 1317–38.
John of Randazzo, 1338–48.
Frederick of Randazzo, 1348–55.
Frederick III of Sicily, 1355–77.
Pedro IV of Aragon, 1377–87.
John I of Aragon, 1387–8.

House of Acciajuoli
Nerio Acciajuoli, founder of Florentine house,
   1388–94.
Period of government by Venetian *podestà*,
   1394–1402.
Antonio I (restoration of Acciajuoli), 1402–35.
Nerio II, 1435–9.
Antonio II, 1439–41.
Nerio II (restored), 1441–51.
Francesco, 1451–5.
Franco, 1455–6 (Lord of Thebes only, 1456–60).

DESPOTS OF EPIRUS AND EMPERORS OF THESSALONIKI
Michael I, 1204–15 Despot.
Theodore, 1215–30 Despot and Emperor.
Manuel, 1230–7 Despot and Emperor.
Michael II, 1237–71 Despot, Emperor until 1243.
Nicephorus I, 1271–96 Despot.
Thomas, 1296–1318.

10. Some Books on Greece

This selective list is not a bibliography; it may, however, be of some use to travellers who want to learn more of the people, motives, political forces and artistic achievements that make up the four-thousand-year-old story of Greek ascendancy, decline and regeneration.

HISTORY

Ancient

A. R. Burn, *The Pelican History of Greece*, Penguin Books, 1966. Covers the ground from earliest to Roman times.

J. B. Bury, *A History of Greece* (to the death of Alexander the Great), Macmillan, London, 1951 edition. Standard work. Handy.

George Grote, *A History of Greece* (to the wars of the successors of Alexander the Great), 8 vols., John Murray, 1862. Standard work. A major piece of historical writing.

N. G. L. Hammond, *A History of Macedonia. Vol. 1, History, Geography and Prehistory*, Clarendon Press, Oxford, 1973.

W. W. Tarn and G. T. Griffith, *Hellenistic Civilization*, Edward Arnold, London, 1952.

E. Vermeule, *Greece in the Bronze Age*, University of Chicago, Chicago, 1964. A general account.

Medieval

Charles Diehl, *Figures Byzantines*, 2 vols., Librairie Armand Colin, Paris, 1930. Fascinating account of outstanding Byzantine personalities.

George Finlay, *A History of Greece* (146 BC to AD 1864), 7 vols. Oxford University Press, 1878. A historical and literary *tour de force*.

Edward Gibbon, *History of the Decline and Fall of the Roman Empire*, John Murray, London, 1855.

André Grabar, *Byzantium from the Death of Theodosias to the Rise of Islam*, Thames and Hudson, London, 1966.

R. J. H. Jenkins, *Byzantium: the Imperial Centuries 610–1071*, Weidenfeld and Nicolson, London, 1966.

William Miller, *The Latins in the Levant*, John Murray, London,

1908. The standard, if not only, work in English on Frankish and Venetian Greece.

Dimitri Obolensky, *The Byzantine Commonwealth: Eastern Europe 500–1453*, Weidenfeld and Nicolson, London, 1971.

Sir Steven Runciman, *Byzantine Civilization*, Edward Arnold, London, 1933. A scholarly general account.

David Talbot Rice, *The Byzantines*, Ancient Peoples and Places Series, Thames and Hudson, London, 1962. Useful introduction for the beginner.

A. A. Vasiliev, *History of the Byzantine Empire*, Basil Blackwell, Oxford, 1952. A definitive general history.

Modern

John Campbell and Philip Sherrard, *Modern Greece*, Ernest Benn, London, 1968. A succinct objective account, covering every aspect of the Greek character.

ART AND ARCHITECTURE

Ancient

John Boardman, *Greek Art*, revised ed., Thames and Hudson, London, 1973.

J. J. Coulton, *Greek Architects at Work: problems of structure and design*, Paul Elek, London, 1977.

Devambez, P., *Greek Painting*, Contact Books, Weidenfeld and Nicolson, London, 1962. A useful introduction.

A. W. Lawrence, *Greek Architecture*, The Pelican History of Art, Penguin Books, 1957. An invaluable work of reference.

R. Lullies and H. Hirmer, *Greek Sculpture*, Thames and Hudson, London, 1960. Introductory but useful, and magnificently illustrated.

G. M. A. Richter, *A Handbook of Greek Art*, Phaidon Press, London, 1959. Comprehensive and well arranged.

C. M. Robertson, *A History of Greek Art*, 2 vols., Cambridge University Press, 1975. The definitive work on Greek art.

Medieval

O. M. Dalton, *Byzantine Art and Archaeology*, Clarendon Press, Oxford, 1911. The standard work in English.

André Grabar, *Byzantine Painting*, Skira, Geneva, 1953.

André Grabar, *Byzantium, Byzantine Art in the Middle Ages*, Art of the World Series, Methuen, 1963.

Gervase Mathew, *Byzantine Aesthetics*, John Murray, London, 1963. A theoretical interpretation.

David Talbot Rice, *Art of the Byzantine Era*, The World of Art Library, Thames and Hudson, London, 1963. Useful for the beginner.

MYTHOLOGY

Robert Graves, *The Greek Gods*, 2 vols., Penguin Books, 1967. Exhaustive, discursive, imaginative.

J. C. Lawson, *Modern Greek Folklore and Ancient Greek Religion*, University Books, New York, 1964 (first published by the Cambridge University Press, 1909). Standard work.

H. J. Rose, *A Handbook of Greek Mythology*, Methuen, London, 1928. The most useful work on the subject.

TRAVEL AND TOPOGRAPHY

W. M. Leake, *Travels in Northern Greece*, 4 vols., J. Rodwell, London, 1835.

Edward Lear, *Journals of a Landscape Painter in Albania, Illyria, etc.*, reprinted under the title of *Edward Lear in Greece*, William Kimber, London, 1965. Witty, astute and brilliantly written.

Patrick Leigh-Fermor, *Roumeli*, John Murray, London, 1966.

Robert Liddell, *Mainland Greece*, Longman, London, 1965. Equally indispensable to the traveller in central Greece and Epirus.

GENERAL[4]

Sir Maurice Bowra, *The Greek Experience*, Weidenfeld and Nicolson, London, 1957. An appreciation of the ancient Greek achievement.

H. D. F. Kitto, *The Greeks*, Penguin Books, 1951. Useful account of the Hellenic achievement in the social and artistic spheres.

[4] With the exception of Leake and Lear, all the great travel writers (who were also scholars) of the nineteenth century, Mure, Curzon, W. J. Woodhouse, etc., are out of print.

MISCELLANEOUS (special aspects)

Brouskari, M. S., *The Acropolis Museum: a descriptive catalogue*, Commercial Bank of Greece, Athens, 1970.

R. M. Dawkins, *The Monks of Athos*, George Allen and Unwin Ltd, London, 1936.

Anthony Huxley and W. Taylor, *Flowers of Greece and the Aegean*, Chatto and Windus, London, 1977.

S. Karouzou, *The National Museum: illustrated guide to the museum*, Ekdotike Athenon, Athens, 1977.

Philip Sherrard, *The Marble Threshing Floor*, Valentine Mitchell, London, 1956. The post-War of Independence literary scene.

William St Clair, *That Greece might still be free*, Oxford University Press, 1972. An elegant account of the War of Independence.

John Travlos, *Pictorial Dictionary of Ancient Athens*, Thames and Hudson, London, 1970.

Timothy Ware, *The Orthodox Church*, Penguin Books, 1963. Useful to the Byzantinist.

C. M. Woodhouse, *Capodistria: The Founder of Greek Independence*, Oxford University Press, 1973. The political background to the War of Independence.

LIGHT LITERATURE

Edmond About, *Le Roi des Montagnes*, Amis du Livre, Paris, 1961 edition. Shrewd novel about Greek brigandage and party politics in the nineteenth century.

Mary Renault, *The Last of the Wine*, Longmans Green, London, 1956. Romantic but authentic novel about life in ancient Athens during the Peloponnesian Wars.

GUIDE BOOKS

The 1909 Baedeker is still the best of all factual guide books: erudite, precise and handy. But information regarding communications is hopelessly out-of-date; furthermore, it is out of print (second-hand copies sometimes obtainable). The French *Guide Bleu* (Librairie Hachette, Paris, English translation, 1977) is good on ancient sites, but sketchy on Byzantine and medieval ruins. The *Blue Guide*

(Benn, London, 3rd edition, 1977) is reliable, up-to-date, even indispensable. Less detailed but also good and reliable is Nagel's *Greece* (Geneva, English translation, 1976).

Small guides to major sites (Greek Archaeological Service) and museums (Apollo editions) are in course of preparation. As available they can be obtained at the sites and in the museums.

There are also:

The Athenian Agora Guide, American School of Classical Studies. 1976.

Good Food Guide to Greece (Esso-Pappas, 1977).

Index

Abdera, 320
Abderus, favourite of Heracles, 320
Abdul Hamid, Sultan ('The Damned'), 140, 205, 239
Acanthus, 248
Acarnania, 346–51, 356
Acharnae, 74
Acheloos, river, 343, 344, 346, 351
Acheron, river, 381; gorge, 381, 382; mouth of ('forest of Persephone'), 384
Acherousian lakes, 381; plain, 381, 401
Achilles, 128, 133, 155, 156, 238
Achilles, St, isthmus of, 236
Acontium, Mount, 95, 96
Acraephnion, 92
Actia, quinquennial festival at Nicopolis, 370
Actium, battle of, 141, 311, 354, 369, *373–4*
Adam, Sir Frederick, Lord High Commissioner of the Ionian Islands, 340
Admetus, King of Pherae, 159, 160
Aegae, 213; temple tombs, 213–14
Aegaleos, Mount, 79
Aegosthena, 81
Aeropotamos (The Windy River), 283
Aeschylus, 22, 79
Aetolian League, 336, 348
Aetolikon, 342
Aetolus, founder of Aetolikon, 336
Agamemnon, 84, 114
Agathon, Athenian tragic poet, 207
Agesipolis, King, 245
Agrapha (Unwritten) Mountains, 137
Agrinion, 346
Aiacus, Lord of the Elysian Fields, 213
Akakios, St, 282
Alamanna bridge, 129
Alaric and the Goths, 79, 179, 370
Albania and the Albanians, 68, 74, 135, 229, 236, 382, 391, 400; *see also* dialect
Alcestis, wife of King Admetus, 160
Alcibiades, 243
Alcmaeon, legendary founder of Acarnanian race, 343, 346
Aleudae, ancient family, 142

Alexander the Great, 85, 87, 96, 98, 114, 178, 179, 180, 207, 208, 209, 210, 211, 213, *215*, 226, 234, 236, 248
Alexander of Pherae, tyrant, 159
Alexandroupolis (Turkish Dedeagatch), 317, 321
Alexarchus, brother of Cassander, 249
Alexius, Tsar, 275
Alexius III of Trebizond, Emperor, 283, 285; chrysobull of, 285
Alimos (ancient Halimus), 65
Ali Pasha, Turkish Viceroy of Epirus and Albania, 354, 359, 372, 382, 386, 389, 390, 391, 392, *395*; house of, 395
Althea, mother of Meleager, 338
Ambelakia, 175–7; Schwarz house, 176–7
Ambelon, companion of Dionysus, 175
Ambracia, (ancient) citadel of, 357
Ambracian Gulf, 353–74
American School of Classical Studies, 44, 245
Ammon Zeus, temple of, 243
Amoudia (ancient Glycis Limen, the Freshwater Harbour), 384
Amphiaraion, Sanctuary of Amphiaraus, 73; oracle and theatre at, 73
Amphiaraus the Seer, 153, 346; sanctuary and oracle of at Amphiaraion, 73
Amphicleia, 103
Amphictyonic League, 115; temple, 117
Amphilochia (19th century Karavassaras), 352, 353–4
Amphipolis, Ennea Odoi (The Nine Ways), 301–3; battle of, 302; lion of, 303–4; sepulchre of Macedonian prince, 303; *see also* Kavalla Museum
Amphissa (Salona, La Sol), 104–5; castle, 104; Church of Ayios Sotiros (The Holy Saviour), 105
Amvrakia, lake, 351
Anauros, river, 151
Anavyssos, 66; kouros from, 56
Anaxarchus, philosopher, 320

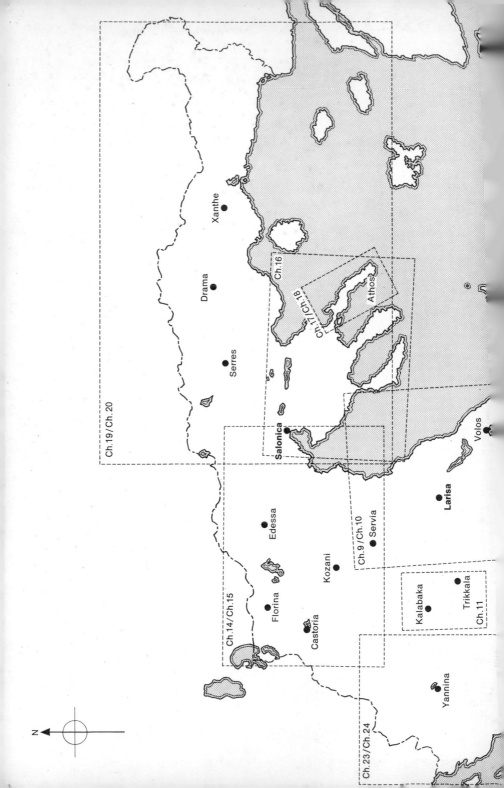

N

Xanthe

Drama

Serres

Ch.16

Ch.17/Ch.18

Athos

Salonica

Volos

Larisa

Edessa

Ch.9/Ch.10

Servia

Kozani

Kalabaka

Trikkala

Ch.11

Florina

Ch.14/Ch.15

Castoria

Yannina

Ch.19/Ch.20

Ch.23/Ch.24